Recognition and the Media

Recognition and the Media

Rousiley C.M. Maia
Associate Professor, Department of Social Communication,
Federal University of Minas Gerais, Brazil

First published 2014 by
PALGRAVE MACMILLAN

Palgrave Macmillan in the UK is an imprint of Macmillan Publishers Limited,
registered in England, company number 785998, of Houndmills, Basingstoke,
Hampshire RG21 6XS.

Palgrave Macmillan in the US is a division of St Martin's Press LLC,
175 Fifth Avenue, New York, NY 10010.

Palgrave Macmillan is the global academic imprint of the above companies
and has companies and representatives throughout the world.

Palgrave® and Macmillan® are registered trademarks in the United States,
the United Kingdom, Europe and other countries.

ISBN: 978–1–137–31042–2

This book is printed on paper suitable for recycling and made from fully
managed and sustained forest sources. Logging, pulping and manufacturing
processes are expected to conform to the environmental regulations of the
country of origin.

A catalogue record for this book is available from the British Library.

Library of Congress Cataloging-in-Publication Data
Maia, Rousiley.
    Recognition and the media / Rousiley Maia.
       pages cm
    ISBN 978–1–137–31042–2 (hardback)
    1. Mass media – Political aspects. 2. Mass media – Social aspects.
  3. Recognition (Philosophy) – Political aspects. 4. Honneth, Axel, 1949–
  I. Title.

P95.8.M35 2014
302.23—dc23   2014026129

This book is dedicated to my son and daughter, Rafael and Gabriela, and my students who pressure me in an everyday basis to see the world and the future in new ways.

Contents

List of Figures and Tables

Figures

Tables

Preface and Acknowledgments

Since my first contact with Axel Honneth's work in 1998, *The Fragmented World of the Social* and *The Struggle for Recognition* have struck me as an intriguing social-theoretical project. The specific aim of Critical Theory to not only provide sophisticated conceptual tools to explain social phenomena, but also supply a critical impetus for identifying social resources for practical transformation of current forms of domination, has always appealed to my political and moral concerns in both my academic and personal life. Meanwhile, the experience of teaching political communication, democratic theory and public sphere issues in combination with daily communicative practices – via traditional mass communication, fictional and non-fictional programs, the Internet, social networking sites – pressured me to look through the lenses of Critical Theory upon everyday interactions as a "pre-scientific realm of moral critique."

Today an interconnected and hybrid media environment shapes people's interactions in different spheres of everyday life – intimate, social, and political. Identity-building and conflicts regarding social recognition; disputes in the public sphere for the negotiation of individuals and groups' claims, rights and achievements; mobilization and social learning in the broadest sense, and finally institutionalization and governance processes, cannot be fully explained without seriously taking into consideration the role of the media in these dynamics. For some, the media undermine democratic processes and the achievement of justice; for others – and I align myself with this group – the media play an ambivalent role that can at times enhance these prospects. Thus, I contend that media structures, formats or genres, practices, operations of power and influences in each particular situation should be surveyed, and not presumed. In this book, my collaborators and I explore this complex landscape, focusing on some interfaces between particular types of media and struggles for recognition.

The project of this book started several years ago. In 2008, I published the book *Deliberação e Media* [Deliberation and the Media], which examined different cases of mediated deliberation. The subsequent *Deliberation, the Media and Political Talk*, published in 2012, situated the media within the deliberative system and moved towards the investigation of ordinary people's discussions on conflicting discourses displayed in the media arena. While keeping Habermas's discourse ethics and a number of normative controversies among deliberative theorists in the forefront of my research concerns, these previous works also included case studies of conflicts among group identity differences, and the contestation in the public sphere for democratic inclusion and greater social and political justice. The intention to undertake the project of *Recognition and the Media* arose in connection with the conclusions that I arrived at in these investigations.

In particular, several research projects carried out by my graduate students and postdoctoral researchers on minorities and disadvantaged groups – most of them organized within the framework of deliberative theory – greatly influenced me to delve into Honneth's program to reframe research questions. The effort to understand the three forms of recognition postulated by this philosopher, each of which contains potential motivation for social conflict, led me to further this approach within empirical research. While Honneth's theory has become increasingly influential in the last decade, it has been explored primarily in articles and books on social and political philosophy and political theory. My aim in *Recognition and the Media* is to explore Honneth's program about recognition by marking key elements of this approach, in conjunction with empirical experiences of a number of different disadvantaged groups. This book also attempts to situate the role of the media in struggles for recognition, in dialogue with political communication, and in media literature.

A sabbatical leave at Boston College in 2011 allowed me to sketch, from the recognition-theoretical approach, the direction of the research presented in this book, the way to look at problems regarding empirical material in each chapter, and debates focusing on certain controversial issues in Honneth's work. This book presents both my own scholarly work and that of my former and current graduate students – Ana Carolina Vimieiro, Danila Cal, Regiane Garcêz, Ricardo Mendonça, Thaiane Rezende – as well as a postdoctoral scholar, now my colleague, Simone Rocha. I am most indebted to them for their collaboration and enthusiastic discussions.

My thinking on the matters presented in *Recognition and the Media* has evolved in the last three years through debates with my students and other participants in the Research Group on Media and the Public Sphere – EME/UFMG – and my deepest thanks go to these individuals. It is impossible to list the vast number of people I am indebted to, but I would like to mention those who worked on the theory of recognition – Ângela C. S. Marques and Márcia Cruz. A special thanks is due to my current graduate students for their tireless help and commentary on drafts of this book, Danila Cal, Regiane Garcêz, Vanessa Veiga, Diógenes Lycarião, Alicianne Oliveira, Patrícia Rossini, Gabriella Hauber and a postdoctoral researcher, Bráulio Neves. I am profoundly grateful to my undergraduate students Rodrigo Miranda, Diego Bemquerer, Aline Cabral, Ana França, Anne Júlia Rocha, Camila Marques, Isabela Guimarães, Laís Oliveira, Raíssa Fernandes, Letícia Garcia and Cynthia Oliveira, who assisted with the review of the literature and preparation of this book. A special word of thanks is due to Diego Bemquerer for choosing the cover image. I owe thanks to Geesje Henry, Adriane Reams, Deborah Murray and Ricardo Bibiano, who provided invaluable revision and editorial assistance. I am grateful to Andrew Baird and Sara Crowley-Vigneau, my editors at Palgrave Macmillan, for their good work.

Several talks and participating in conferences have helped me improve my ideas, by providing me with the opportunity to share them with others. The first prospect of this book was presented during the MRAP seminars held at Boston College in February 2011, and I thank Bill Gamson and Charlotte Ryan and all "MRAPers" for their suggestions. Chapter 5 is partially based on a conference delivered at the ICA Conference, in Roubaix, France, in March 2012, and I'm grateful to François Cooren and Bernard Miège. I was also able present this topic at the XIV Jornada Multidisciplinar Mídia e Cidadania [Multidisciplinary Meeting on Media and Citizenship] at the Universidade Estadual Paulista (UNESP), Bauru-SP in May 2012, and I would like to thank Murilo Soares for this platform. I am grateful to Marcus Lima for organizing the I Colóquio em Mídia, Reconhecimento e Participação [First Coloquium on Media, Recognition and Participation] at the Universidade Estadual do Sudoeste da Bahia (UESB), Vitória da Conquista-BA in June 2012. While participating in a working mission at the Seminar für Medien-und Kommunikationswissenschaft at Mannheim University in Germany during the summer of 2013, I had the opportunity to discuss Chapter 6 and Chapter 10 with Hartmut Wessler, Eike Rinke and many students and professors who encouraged new insights and comments. Jürg Steiner has been a stimulating conversation partner on issues of conflict, everyday talk and deliberation and he has made generous comments regarding some of the book's chapters. Several chapters have already been presented in scientific forums: Compós (Juíz de Fora, Brazil); ICA (London, UK; Seattle, US); and ABCP (Gramado, Brazil).

This book is the result of a series of research projects, under my coordination, that have received funding from different Brazilian research agencies (CNPq, CAPES, and FAPEMIG). Three chapters draw on previously published work, and I am grateful to my publishers for permission to include reprints from the following:

Maia, R. C. M. & Cal, D. (2014). Recognition and ideology: assessing justice and injustice in the case of child domestic labor. *Journal of Political Power, 7*, 63–85.

Maia, R. C. M. & Garcêz, R. L. O. (2013). Recognition, feelings of injustice and claim justification: a case study of deaf people's storytelling on the internet. *European Political Science Review*, 1–24. doi: http://dx.doi.org/10.1017/S1755773913000143

Maia, R. C. M. & Vimieiro, A. C. (2013). Recognition and moral progress: a case study about discourses on disability in the media. *Political Studies*. doi: http://dx.doi.org/10.1111/1467–9248.12083

Notes on Author and Contributors

Rousiley C. M. Maia is an Associate Professor in the Department of Social Communication at the Federal University of Minas Gerais (UFMG), Brazil. She has a Ph.D. in political science (Nottingham University, UK) and coordinates the Research Group on Media and the Public Sphere (EME-UFMG). Her other books include *Deliberation, the Media and Political Talk* (2012), *Media e Deliberação* (2008) and *Comunicação e Democracia* (with Wilson Gomes, 2008). She has co-edited titles addressing the public sphere and civic engagement, the Internet and political participation in Brazil. Some of her recent work has been published in *Journal of Communication, International Press Politics, Journal of Community Informatics, Critical Studies in Mass Communication, Political Studies, Revista Brasileira de Ciências Sociais, Lua Nova, E-Compos, Famecos, European Political Science Review* and *Journal of Political Power*. She is an associate editor of *The International Encyclopedia of Political Communication* (ICA Wiley-Blackwell).

Danila Cal is an assistant professor at the University of Amazonia. She obtained her PhD in the Graduate Program in Communication at the Federal University of Minas Gerais, Brazil, and received a scholarship from the Foundation Institute for the Development of Amazonia (Fidesa). Her master's thesis was developed within the Department of Social Communication at the Federal University of Minas Gerais. The empirical data from this project are partially exploited in Chapter 4 of this book and were awarded first place as the best master's thesis about media, children, and adolescents between 1990 and 2007 in the national competition sponsored by the Information Program of the News Agency for Children's Rights (ANDI).

Regiane Garcêz is PhD student in the Department of Social Communication at the Federal University of Minas Gerais, Brazil. She holds a master's degree from this institution and is a journalist and activist for the deaf movement. Her writings have appeared in *Communication; Politics & Culture; European Political Science Review;* and several Brazilian journals.

Ricardo Fabrino Mendonça is an assistant professor in the Department of Political Science at the Federal University of Minas Gerais, Brazil, and one of the coordinators of the Research Group on Digital Democracy. He works with democratic theory, critical theory, politics of recognition, social movements and political communication. Some of his recent publications have appeared in *Constellations; Political Studies; Critical Policy Studies; Policy & Society; Brazilian Political Science Review; Opinião Pública; Dados; Revista Brasileira de Ciências Sociais* and *Lua Nova*.

Thaiane A. S. Rezende is master's student in the Department of Political Science at the Federal University of Minas Gerais, Brazil. She also has a bachelor's degree in social communication from this institution. She participates in the Research Group on Media and the Public Sphere (EME), as well as the Research Group on Methodology in Social Science, both at UFMG.

Simone Maria Rocha is an associate professor in the Department of Social Communication at the Federal University of Minas Gerais, Brazil. She is the coordinator of the Research Group in Communication, Media and Culture. She holds a master's degree in sociology from the Federal University of Minas Gerais and a PhD in communication studies from the Federal University of Rio de Janeiro. She has numerous publications focusing on mass media reception and television studies.

Ana Carolina Vimieiro is a PhD candidate in media and communication at the ARC Centre of Excellence for Creative Industries and Innovation (CCI) at the Queensland University of Technology (QUT), Australia. She has been researching everyday forms of political engagement and innovative methodologies and holds a master's degree from the Federal University of Minas Gerais (UFMG), Brazil. The empirical data explored in Chapter 10 of this book were collected during her research at UFMG. This work received an honourable mention in the 2011 Award for the Best Thesis and Dissertation of the Brazilian Journalism Researchers Association (SBPJor).

List of Abbreviations

ABGLT	Association of Lesbians, Gays, Bisexuals, Transvestites, and Transsexuals
APAE	Association of Parents and Friends of the Exceptional
CDA	Critical Discourse Analysis
CDL	Child Domestic Labor
CUF	Central Única das Favelas
DQI	Discourse Quality Index
ECA	Child and Adolescent Statute
FENEIS	National Federation for the Education and Integration of Deaf People
ILO	International Labor Organization
LGBTQ	Lesbian, Gay, Bisexual, Transgender, Queer
MORHAN	Movimento pela Reintegração das Pessoas Atingidas pela Hanseníase
PETI	Program for Eradicating Child Labor (Programa de Erradicação do Trabalho Infantil)
PETID	Program for Eradicating Child Domestic Labor (Programa de Erradicação do Trabalho Infantil Doméstico)
SNSs	Social Network Sites
WFD	World Federation of the Deaf

Introduction

In recent years, the notion of recognition has gained a central position in debates about multiculturalism, identity politics, problems of rights and justice, and the struggles of groups facing poor income distribution and cultural undervaluation. Axel Honneth's book, *The Struggle for Recognition*, which was published in Germany in 1992 and translated into English in 1995, generated a wide range of inquiries and investigations in diverse domains in the philosophical, social and political fields.[1] Several scholars have argued that Honneth's theory could revitalize the Frankfurt School tradition by bringing new insights into the assessment and analysis of contemporary society. While Honneth endorses Habermas's linguistic turn and the substitution of the subject–object model of cognition and action for an intersubjective model, he attempts to ground his critique in experiences of misrecognition as the normative and motivational force behind struggles against injustice. Honneth seeks to broaden the scope of social criticism by evincing social conditions that are necessary for humans to flourish and reach the social recognition of individual needs, rights, and contributions for a society.

This book aims to investigate some of the interfaces that the theory of recognition establishes with political communication and media studies. Although the theory of recognition has fostered a strong debate in philosophy, social theory, and political theory throughout the past decade, most of these discussions have been associated with the notion of face-to-face interactions. In contemporary, complex, multicultural societies, struggles for recognition to a large degree are – and need to be – mediated. The process of mediation that is employed by the media is unavoidable for the expansion of relationships of recognition or misrecognition.

This raises concrete questions not only about forms of representation and discourses in the media, but also about broader social and cultural interactions through which people interpret media materials in their daily conversations and cultural and political practices. Intersubjectivity and identity processes that emerge from these interactions cannot be satisfactorily explained without taking into account the role of the media. Likewise, no sufficient explanation can be given about how the public sphere and public debates are shaped as socially-wide processes. The same is true for how public interest is mobilized or collective learning processes arise in current conditions, without taking into account the interfaces that the media establish with these dynamics. Nonetheless, few studies[2] have sought to align the literature on recognition with that focusing on communication and media studies. This book, which is a result of seven years of research, aims to fill this gap and show how Honneth's theory brings a new perspective to dealing with traditional concerns of critical theory. This includes delving into the industrialized dissemination of images and discourses and changes in people's identity, the relationships that mass communication establishes with reification and ideology, and the role of the media in the social struggles of marginalized and exploited groups.

This book presents theoretical and empirical research. Honneth's theory has provided the most basic concepts that frame our perspective and empirical analysis. While this German philosopher's work has inspired much of the interest in and debate about recognition, there are different understandings of this concept that are based on distinct traditions of thought that are not necessarily compatible (Connolly, Leach, & Walsh, 2007; Fraser, 2001, 2003a, 2004, 2005; Hobson, 2003; Markell, 2003; Seymour, 2010; Taylor, 1994). Thus, we utilize Honneth's program in order to ensure a coherent theoretical grounding to our research and internal consistency across the set of empirical cases.

Besides my own scholarly work, this book involves the research of five of my current or former graduate students and one post-doctoral researcher. As empirical researchers, our intention is not to engage in the current debate with scholars working on the theory of recognition in purely theoretical terms, but we seek to examine some normative controversies in order to craft our inquiry using specific empirical case studies. Our first effort with this book is to promote an interplay between theoretical insight and empirical investigation. We focus on six controversial issues related to the theory of recognition: (a) the morality of recognition and disputes regarding the notion of identity in Honneth's program; (b) the concept of "ideological form of recognition"; (c) the role of emotions in social conflicts; feelings of injustice and claim justification, exemplified by the actions and words of the oppressed; (d) moral disagreement and the multiplicity of "others" in struggle for recognition; (e) the concept of non-recognition and misrecognition; and (f) the notion of moral progress. We bring these key issues into the current debate on the theory of recognition through a rich set of struggles experienced by disadvantaged individuals in the real world. These examples include slum-dwelling adolescents, leprosy patients, people with disabilities, women exposed to child labor exploitation, deaf individuals, lesbian, gay, bi, trans, queer (LGBTQ) and black women.

A secondary aim of this book is to align the literature on the theory of recognition with the literature on political communication and media studies by focusing on some interfaces between struggles for recognition and processes of technological mediation. The term "interfaces" is meant to convey the idea that any analysis in the communication field must begin by breaking down the generic term "the media," which is commonly used by commentators and many sociological and political scholars. It should be acknowledged that "the media" is a highly differentiated field with several types of media organizations, cultural norms, modes of address, and legal and technological features.

Theory focusing on communication, as well as research on media practices, has grown tremendously over the past eight decades and internal sub-fields have become internally more diversified. Founders of the Frankfurt School of thought – particularly Theodor Adorno, Max Horkheimer, Herbert Marcuse, and Walther Benjamin – were particularly concerned with the rise of the mass media, the massification of culture, the fetishization of commodities, and their consequences for shaping individuals' beliefs and behavior and social change alike. While first generation thinkers have produced a lasting influence on the media field, and renewed readings of their writings often underpin contemporary concerns, theoretical traditions have evolved as a result of advancing theories, models, and evidences. This has also generated ongoing debates among research communities and the development of a constellation of events.

Different from the mass communication era – whose communication models were characterized by the traditional mass media being organized in a centralized way with the elite operating as gatekeepers and holding a communication monopoly – my collaborators and I support the view of an interconnected and hybrid media environment in this book. The issue at stake is not solely the growing technological complexity of the Internet and social networking sites that has produced an interconnected media system that encompasses different types of media with multiple logics. Since media technologies co-evolve through users' practices and become part of the institutional organization of society, advancements in digital technology have produced several changes in the mass media environment itself, as well as in everyday life.

This book is organized into three parts. Each part begins with a theoretical chapter that surveys different sub-fields of political communication research, along with their contributions addressing recognition matters. This is followed by two empirical case studies built from a recognition-theoretical perspective. In the first part of the book, I deal with the literature on mass media representation and its impacts both on an individual's self-perception and cultural milieu. Fictional and non-fictional media material produce images, texts, and discourses that stereotype, exclude, and disrespect members of disadvantaged groups. Throughout the book, I retain the basic intuition of the Frankfurt School's first generation of thinkers to defend the view that mass media organizations relate to the larger cultural environment as both a reflection and producer of cultural and political meanings. However, following the linguistic turn and the pragmatic paradigm of social interaction, I explore key contributions of contemporary political media literature to explain how people use and experience mass media content. Through empirically-based studies, my collaborators and I delve into how oppressed individuals perceive mass-mediated content when viewing themselves and others. We focus on opportunities that allow for conflictive engagement with public concerns, social patterns of representation, and hierarchical evaluation.

In the second part of the book, I draw on the literature of the interconnected media environment and interactions through the Internet and social networking sites (SNSs). In the networked media environment, people combine various types of media into their routines; online conversations that share information with potential for global networking (Facebook, Twitter, LinkedIn); checking information through Google, blogs, and collaborative forms of peer-generated information; and divulging videos and creative products on YouTube and Flickr. I survey online media from three perspectives: (a) as sites for self-expression and identity-building; (b) as sites for everyday political discussion; and (c) as sites for online political activism and mobilization. The empirical case studies explore the use of online platforms by traditional social movements and ordinary individuals to divulge issues of concern and engage in discussions regarding emotional commitments, needs, rights and achievements. These studies also explore digitally-enabled activism.

The third part of this book involves an inquiry into the possibility of observing progressive change in the mass media environment as a reflexivity process of struggles for recognition structured within the fabric of everyday life. Instead of asking how the mass media affects social change, we asked how people struggling for recognition, including mobilized publics, change media organizations and media performances. I survey the literature on the activism of mobilized publics that seeks to hold the media accountable through mechanisms of public and social responsibility. The empirical cases investigate changes in patterns of the representation of disadvantaged groups, as well as alterations in "public concerns" embodied by norms and public policies that are expressed in news media coverage at the time.

In our research group, we used several methods. A detailed explanation of the research design in each case will be presented in respective chapters. To investigate news media material, my collaborators and I applied content and frame analysis to identify and measure discourses on recognition issues. We also engaged in in-depth qualitative reading of the media material.[3] In cases involving face-to-face conversations, we employed a "focus group" technique in order to create interactive contexts. The main aim was to capture how meaning is collectively constructed, contested, and rebuilt from the perspective of study participants in a given group.[4] When assessing people's expressions in an online environment, we used techniques designed to investigate computer-mediated communication, particularly everyday talk and discursive exchange.[5]

My goal for this book is that it helps to further research in three main aspects. My first aim is that it contributes to advance empirical research on dynamics of recognition. Some problems of moral and social philosophy are not easily (or directly) connected to sociological and political empirical investigation. While there is extensive literature dealing with conceptual and normative questions of recognition, not until recently have studies started exploiting these topics for understanding these phenomena in the social sciences.[6] This book attempts to promote a mutual dialogue between thinkers who work with the philosophical literature on recognition and empirical social and political researchers who study the media, democracy, public sphere, identity, minorities, civic engagement, and social movement.

A secondary hope for this book is that it helps to increase awareness among researchers about the interfaces between struggles for recognition and the media system. By using various media material – such as news media texts, fictional TV programs, TV shows – as well as digital-mediated communication on web sites and SNS platforms – this book attempts to give a systematic assessment of the opportunities and constraints of media practices in the real-life conflicts experienced by people. Thus, this research can shed some light on an important but neglected issue.

Thirdly, this book has the potential to promote a combined diagnosis of a set of different cases of struggles for recognition. In contrast to most anthologies that present stand-alone case studies, this book assumes an integrated perspective. The authors, who share a common theoretical framework and belong to the same research group, examine specific problems in the theory of recognition, as well as particular interfaces between the struggle for recognition and media practices. In composing this book, I re-interpreted data provided by my graduate students' research, in order to relate empirical data to philosophical problems or controversies. We believe that this type of procedure allows the reader to move beyond individual cases towards theoretical and empirical evidence accumulation.

The overall objective of this book is to shed light on possible connections between Honneth's theory of recognition and political communication theory and research. Since the context of this work addresses Brazilian society, our research reveals the workings of particular institutions and conflicts of shared forms of life. Brazil has become well known for innovations in participatory institutions with an effective capacity to attract the participation of poor citizens and distribute public goods. Therefore, this book utilizes a setting other than the well-studied cases of the US and Western Europe and has the potential to highlight some of the dilemmas associated with the media in struggles for recognition. Although we do not make a comparative study, we believe this analysis could raise new relevant questions for a recognition-theoretical research agenda.

The structure of this book

Chapter 1 aims to present Honneth's theory of recognition as a research agenda. This chapter contextualizes Honneth's work within the tradition of the Frankfurt School and presents a schematic reconstruction of the major lines of his research program. The purpose of Chapter 1 is not to engage in the current controversial debate, but to give an overview of Honneth's concepts in order to pave the way for establishing what should be regarded and investigated as a struggle for recognition. In anticipation of the analyses in subsequent chapters, I also outline some theoretical disputes among recognition thinkers and show some connections that can be drawn between these controversies and media practices. I contend that the controversial nature of Honneth's theory of recognition makes it a more interesting concept to study empirically.

The first part of this book investigates how individuals make sense of mass media-based representation under specific conditions. Chapter 2 explores the mass media as a site of struggle and discusses why fictional and non-fictional representations matter for a recognition-theoretical approach, as well as a social research agenda. Following this, I survey the main theoretical contributions to conceptualize a set of social, cultural, and structural conditions, along with psychological and cognitive mechanisms that help to explain how people use and experience mass media contents.

Chapter 3, which is co-authored with Simone M. Rocha, deals with the morality of recognition and investigates how adolescent slum dwellers make sense of their representation in a TV Series, *Cidade dos Homens* (City of Men). This series was developed by a non-governmental organization (NGO), Nós do Cinema, in partnership with Rede Globo (Globo TV), Brazil's largest television network. Its declared purpose was to promote a more positive symbolic representation of slum dwellers and a more complex understanding of their daily lives in order to challenge prejudices in Brazilian society against low-income populations. To assure greater proximity with everyday life in the slums, the cast consisted mostly of slum dwellers. The following questions guided our study: What is the personal identity that adolescent slum dwellers develop when facing the meanings conveyed in the television series? What judgment did the producers of this series have about the community that was relevant to these adolescents? What counts as recognition? Is there a difference between the self-understanding of adolescents from different slums? To develop our study we organized focus groups with adolescents in slums of Rio de Janeiro (Morro Santa Marta, the location where the series was filmed) and Belo Horizonte (Barragem Santa Lúcia). Findings show that the attitude of "recognizing" or "being recognized" does not reach a stable end point. The adolescents were able to detect distorted recognition and vocalize which of their moral expectations were violated, but they found it hard to agree about what recognition demands in a positive manner.

Chapter 4 focuses on the "ideological form of recognition" and examines child domestic labor (CDL) in Belem, a city in the north of Brazil. The chapter, co-authored with Danila Cal, investigates what oppressed individuals identify as harm and injustice in the light of public discourses, as well as their personal experience. This study draws on data from (i) local news articles on CDL from 2000 to 2004 and (ii) focus groups with women who were housemaids in their childhood. Findings show that local media professionals acted as agents of advocacy to defend the needs and rights of children and adolescents. For their part, on reflecting about the discourses in the newspapers, the women challenged these discourses and qualified CDL as a good or useful opportunity to gain autonomy and to integrate more positively with society. This chapter argues that Honneth's concept of the "ideological form of recognition" has great theoretical strength in explaining oppression in a way that avoids adding subjugation to disadvantaged individuals. However, his account still needs clarification in order to explain how oppressed individuals can overcome ideological forms of recognition. This work contributes to showing contradictory logics in the spheres of love and work in CDL and an advanced understanding of the role played by justice advocates for ideological critique.

The second part of this book analyses online interactions on the Internet and SNSs. Chapter 5 revisits approaches used for understanding how the Internet and related digital technologies have penetrated everyday life and focuses on how online interaction involves practices across different spheres of a relationship – intimate, social, and political. In order to construct a perspective capable of encompassing different dimensions of struggles for recognition in a networked media environment, I survey sites for: (i) self-expression and identity-building; (ii) everyday political discussion and deliberation; (iii) political activism and mobilization.

Chapter 6, co-authored with Regiane L. Garcêz, deals with the role of emotion in politics. The storytelling of deaf people is gathered from two virtual environments: (a) the website of the main Brazilian organization for deaf persons (FENEIS) and (b) Orkut, an online social network. This chapter evinces that subjects not only articulate feelings of injustice or claims for recognition in everyday experience, but also that they usually engage in interpretation, judgment, and justification of such claims. We endorse Honneth's view that "feelings of injustice" are an important source for the intelligibility of injustice and that disadvantaged individuals need to build a "shared interpretative framework" in struggles for recognition. However, we argue that Honneth's approach needs a more nuanced account of discursive justification in order to deal with dissent and moral disagreement. We suggest that Honneth's approach of subjective reaction to injury as a violation of conditions to practical identity can be brought together with notions of discursive justification in the

Habermasian fashion. This type of articulation can better equip scholars concerned with practices that aim to overcome injustice.

Chapter 7 focuses on how individuals and groups engage in episodic struggles for recognition not only with the "other," but with "multiple others," in a complex web of relations in society. The chapter's co-author, Thaiane A. S. Rezende, and I investigate how an expression of racism and homophobia made by a Brazilian deputy on a TV program aroused collective emotion and prompted digitally-enabled activism in Brazil. The chapter concentrates on how demands for recognition were expressed and how dialogue and conflict were shaped on: (i) a generic online domain that can focus on any topic or theme – the *Youtube* webpage providing access to the video of the TV Program; (ii) a feminist blog, *Escreva Lola Escreva* ("Write Lola Write"), and a male-aimed blog, *Papo de Homen* ("Talk of Men"); (iii) Facebook, an environment related to a circle of relatives and friends. Findings show that platforms with distinct affordances provide different opportunities and constraints for people to frame personal expressions, engage in debates, and deploy protest mechanisms. Evidence suggests that people who seek recognition engage in moral conflicts, in a conflictive field of respect as well as disrespect, in which they are not completely free to decide what order of justification they will use in order to attempt to solve a certain problem, or challenge a particular judgment.

The third part of this book investigates the dynamics through which the mass media environment may incorporate the moral perspective that results from struggles for recognition in the long run. Chapter 8 looks at factors that help to explain progressive changes in the mass media environment from three perspectives: activism of media professionals; civil society mobilization to advance media professionals' learning processes, media monitoring, and criticism; and alternative media. The chapter seeks to explain the conditions under which mass media organizations and performances are linked to mechanisms of public and social accountability. It contends that claims for recognition can be accommodated and balanced in different ways among operations of power in media organizations.

Chapter 9, co-authored with Ricardo F. Mendonça, addresses an often neglected and dangerous form of misrecognition – the effacement of the struggle in itself. Drawing on news articles about the leprosy issue in two national Brazilian newspapers from 1998 to 2007, the chapter investigates how political conflicts involving leprosy patients emerge in journalistic coverage. The analyses focus on two central struggles: (a) the future of leprosy colonies and (b) access to financial support. Results show that voices from the Movement for Reintegrating People Afflicted with Leprosy (Movimento pela Reintegração das Pessoas Atingidas pela Hanseníase or MORHAN) and other critical civic actors linked to this movement are neglected. The social movement's agency to define injustice and to propose remedies is overlooked and solutions for people with leprosy appear merely as government measures. The chapter argues that the media depoliticizes the issue and may hinder the progression of struggles by presenting problems and achievements without articulating them as conflicts. By obfuscating tensions and controversies, journalistic reports suggest the existence of an end, after which other forms of oppression become harder to unveil. Thus, non-recognition may emerge from a type of apparent recognition.

Chapter 10 discusses the notion of moral progress in the theory of recognition. The chapter, co-authored with Ana Carolina Vimieiro, uses frame analysis to investigate transformations in the portrayal of people with impairment, as well as in public discourses on the issue of disability in the major Brazilian news media from 1960 to 2008. Chapter 10 addresses three controversies: the notion of progress as a directional process; the problem of moral disagreement and conflict of interest in struggles for recognition; and the processes of social learning. The chapter argues that Honneth's program offers sophisticated theoretical guidance to observe and critically interpret emancipatory projects in contemporary politics based on ideas of individuality and social inclusiveness. By articulating empirically-based arguments and Honneth's normative discussions, this study concludes that one can talk on moral progress, without losing sight of value pluralism and conflict of interest.

The conclusion summarizes the book's findings and shows the differing roles played by the media in struggles for recognition. This chapter synthetizes empirical results by taking into account themes of the theory of recognition, thus regarding the dynamics of social conflict in the media environment, and real-world constraints as well as opportunities. The conclusion also assesses the implications of our findings for further studies on the media and recognition.

Notes

1. See for example, Busch & Zurn, 2010; Cooke, 2006, 2009; Deranty, 2009, 2010; Deranty & Renault, 2007; Forst, 2007a, 2007b; Fraser, 2010; Fraser & Honneth, 2003; Ikäheimo, 2009, 2010; Kompridis, 2004, 2007; Laitinen, 2002, 2009, 2010; Markell, 2003; McBride, 2009; O'Neill & Smith, 2012; Owen, 2007, 2008; Petherbridge, 2011a; Roberts, 2009; Rogers, 2009; Seglow, 2009; Thompson, 2006; Thompson & Hoggett, 2011; Thompson & Yar, 2011; Tully 2000, 2004;

van den Brink & Owen, 2007; Yar, 2003, 2011; Young, 2007; Zurn, 2000, 2003, 2005, 2010.
2. Garcêz & Maia, 2009; Kulick & Klein, 2003; Mendonça, 2011.
3. The authors have profited from many insights derived from Critical Discourse Analysis – especially in regards to a critical assessment of power and social inequality, as well as social and political contextual stances (Chouliaraki & Fairclough, 1999; Fairclough, 1995a, 1995b, 1998; Maia, 2012e; van Dijk, 1991, 1993; Weiss & Wodak, 2003).
4. Barbour & Kitzinger, 2001; Bryman, 2001; Gamson, 1992; Maia, 2012a; Walsh, 2004; Warr, 2005.
5. Black, 2008; Graham, 2008; Kies, 2010; Polletta & Lee, 2006; Steiner, 2012a; Steiner, Bächtiger, Spörndli, & Steenbergen, 2004.
6. Aranda & Jones, 2010; Calder, 2011; Couch, Pitts, Croy, Mulcare, & Mitchell, 2008; Cox, 2012; Kleist, 2008; Noble, 2009; Norris, 2012; O'Neill, 2012; Seglow, 2012; Yar, 2012; Zurn, 2012.

1
Axel Honneth's Theory of Recognition as a Research Program

This chapter contextualizes Axel Honneth's work within the tradition of Critical Theory. I begin by briefly discussing the placement of Honneth's project within the Frankfurt School of thought. Secondly, I present a schematic reconstruction of the major lines of Honneth's program from his earlier writings. Finally, I show some of the major implications of Honneth's theory on critical social research. This chapter has a survey-like nature in order to pave the way for conceptualizing what should be regarded and investigated as a struggle for recognition. Chapter 1 also outlines some controversial issues in Honneth's program that have served as a background for my collaborators and I to craft our inquiry in connection with political communication and media studies. The final component of this chapter presents how we have organized our empirical research.

Placing Honneth within the Frankfurt School tradition

The location of Honneth within the Frankfurt School tradition is still debated. Internal currents of thought in Critical Theory have developed in different directions; there are a number of disagreements within each generation, and theories intertwine and constantly change throughout various periods of time. However, the dialogues also share some common features and maintain a certain sense of continuity (Anderson, 2011; Deranty, 2009, 2011; Petherbridge, 2011b; Renault, 2010). The attempt to locate Honneth within the Frankfurt School tradition provides a useful point of entry into the thinker's research program, despite the unavoidable oversimplification of unifying themes and differences, along with the difficulty in addressing generational perspectives.

Although Honneth perceives himself within a broader tradition than that of Critical Theory alone, there is an agreement among scholars that his work has the features of a third generation (Anderson, 2011, p. 32; Deranty, 2009, 2011; Petherbridge, 2011b; Schmidt am Busch, 2010, p. 277). A central feature in Honneth's program is the attempt to place the notion of conflict between social groups and social struggle at the center of social philosophy, and thus, to advance the analysis and critique of domination. His program has been seen as oriented to give greater texture to social theory – to "re-socialize" the normative theories of political justice and democracy (Kalyvas, 1999, p. 103; Zurn, 2010, p. 9). Scholars have also read Honneth's work as an attempt to articulate domains that typically tend to be treated separately, such as critical sociology and political theory (Renault, 2010, p. 247), as well as the historical and normative branches of political theory (Deranty, 2009).

In developing his theory of recognition, Honneth takes a path that in some points is close, and in others moves away from the program set forth by the first generation of the Frankfurt School, particularly in the work of Adorno and Horkheimer, as well as Habermas during the second generation. An evocative suggestion for understanding Honneth's program is provided by Jean-Philippe Deranty (2009, p. 350, 2011, p. 84) and Emmanuel Renault (2010, p. 241). These scholars argue that, on the one hand Honneth uses Habermas's theory of communicative action and the view of intersubjective social integration to go against the dialectical materialism and functionalist premises of the founders of Critical Theory. Honneth, on the other hand, uses the Marxist perspective of class struggle and the experience of being subjected to domination, in order to criticize Habermas.

Early writings

Honneth attempts to develop a sociologically-oriented critique of social domination by returning to the first generation scholars of the Frankfurt School in his *Critique of Power* (1991). He rejects the negative understanding of modernity and the reductionist conception of reason interpreted only in terms of instrumental rationality. Honneth challenges the explanation of the cultural industry and the more general thesis of a fully administrated society that gives rise to obedient subjects passively integrated into the social order. Instead of this, he retains a basic view of the centrality of class struggle by giving it a culturalist appraisal. To the German philosopher, the reproduction and integration of society are intrinsically tied to an "ongoing cultural conflict" interpreted in terms of permanent struggle for recognition – an inspiration that is also extracted from Pierre Bourdieu's social theory. In Joel Anderson's words, Honneth provides an account "that emphasizes that society reproduces itself through the often-conflictive interaction of real social groups, which are themselves the products of ongoing activities of interpretation and struggle on the part of participants" (Anderson, 2011, p. 48).

The rejection of pessimistic interpretations of modernity can be seen as one important pillar in Honneth's overall project from the outset (Deranty, 2009, pp. 378–404, 2011, pp. 60–62; Zurn, 2010, p. 7). He regards modernity as a historical evolution that also gave rise to fundamental norms of value pluralism, individual freedom, and rights. In this sense, he fully embraces Habermas's major contributions – the intersubjective linguistic turn and a communicative theory of society. He uses these concepts to defend the argument that post-traditional society is integrated through conflicts between plural ethical values and growing demands for recognizing valid claims for individualization and different forms of life. Honneth follows Habermas's thesis that conditions for social emancipation are not to be observable through social labor, as in the Marxist paradigm, but rather through social interaction, as in the Communicative Action paradigm. As a result, he focuses on the constraints and inequalities inherent to institutionalized social life. By broadening the view of the exploration of labor to "permanent struggles" among culturally integrated groups, Honneth seeks to develop a theoretical approach capable of apprehending a full range of social suffering.

In *Critique of Power*, Honneth draws on Foucault to give greater attention to the role of power at the micro level of everyday interactions and to elucidate the relational structure of social domination in the lifeworld. Once again, Honneth takes an action-theoretic account of struggle and does not see social institutions as totalizing forms of power solely with disciplinary functions. He also recognizes institutions as results of social conflict and public debates that configure, maintain, and transform these institutions. To develop a reflexive critique of power, Honneth assumes that subjectivation is structurally conditioned by socialization; and, while understanding the interactions in everyday life as a realm of moral criticism, he attempts to further reconstruct the approach to practical reason based on a comprehensible theory of intersubjectivity.[1] This move allows him to conceive the social as a domain of strategic *and* communicative action, as well as to develop an antagonistic *and* normative explanation of social integration.

The theory of recognition

The Struggle for Recognition, which is considered Honneth's mature project, develops an intersubjective and normative account of both social interaction and institutional practice. Honneth draws on Hegel's Jena philosophy of recognition and combines it with anthropological features extracted from the work of G. H. Mead and Donald Winnicott. Beginning with the premise of radical intersubjectivity, Honneth, like Habermas (1993, p. 109, 1995, p. 199), posits that the formation process of subjectivity and socialization is deeply intersubjective and marked by vulnerability (Anderson & Honneth, 2005; Honneth, 1995, p. 262, 1996). He attempts to show that fundamental preconditions for successful subject-formation are related to three spheres of intersubjective relations of recognition – love, law, and achievement, which is a reference to Hegel's divisions between family, state, and civil society. Honneth elucidates that individual's subjectivity, autonomy, and agency are built *in* and *through* relations of reciprocal recognition with others in these spheres of interaction. The core idea is that specific patterns of recognition enable individuals to acquire, or obstruct individuals from acquiring, self-confidence, self-respect, and self-esteem; these forms of practical self-relation are interconnected and necessary for full self-realization.

The first sphere of recognition consists of primary relationships constituted by strong emotional attachments among parent–child, lovers, and friends (Honneth, 1996, p. 95). Successful affirmation of autonomy and affective bonds in this relationship of mutual recognition, while marked by permanent tension between the poles of dependency and independence, establishes the most basic conditions for subjects to develop the necessary self-confidence for engaging in social life. In *The Struggle for Recognition*, Honneth seems to treat the first sphere of affective relations with trans-historical anthropologic features. He makes it clear in his latter writings nevertheless that parents' expectations of their offspring, as well as lovers' expectations with their partners, are the result of historical development. "The recognition that what individuals reciprocally bring to this kind of relationship is loving care for the other's well-being in light of his or her individual needs" (Honneth, 2003a, p. 139). In his recent works, Honneth further develops his explanation of the tensions and anxieties present in reciprocal affirmation of autonomy (Deranty, 2011, p. 83; Honneth, 2011, p. 394; Petherbridge, 2011b, p. 26).

The second sphere of recognition is based on the principle of universal equal rights among individuals. In Honneth's account, legal equality, one of the most important achievements of modernity, takes the form of reciprocal recognition; it implies a cognitive attitude in which subjects reciprocally recognize each other in terms of moral accountability.[2] Such an attribution of moral responsibility does not designate any fixed right;

rather, it is seen, following Kant and Habermas's fundamental ideas on the centrality of moral equality, as an enabling condition for subjects to participate in the ongoing process of rational will formation in any democratic political community. For Honneth, adjudication of rights enables individuals to establish a positive self-relation and develop self-respect; in his words, "an adult subject gains the possibility of conceiving his action as a manifestation of one's own autonomy, respected by all others, by means of legal recognition" (Honneth, 2003a, p. 194). According to this reading, the expansion of rights in modern societies means not only a political institutionalization of certain attainments or a moral victory, but also an increase in recognition of the necessary means for more complete participation of citizens in collective life. Legal recognition, therefore, is related to individuals' self-perception as a subject with the ability of making their own decisions and responsibly expressing demands, in order to exercise rights and participate in struggles for expanding or deepening universal as well as special rights.

The third sphere of recognition is based on the principle of "achievement" and is related to social esteem. According to Honneth, to have esteem for one another symmetrically means to attribute value to the individuals' specific properties, abilities, and unique contributions to society. In Honneth's reading of modernity, the redefinition of the notion of honor gave rise to two opposing processes: while the legal standing and equal dignity of individuals becomes universalized, social standing, that is, individuals' contributions to shared praxis, becomes "meritocratized."[3] Since in post-traditional societies social esteem becomes detached from a group's status and the ultimate goals of a society are no longer linked to any substantial normative grounding, but become rather "abstractly defined" (Honneth, 2003c, p. 206) and "always open and porous" (Honneth, 2003c, p. 207), the capitalist division of labor gave rise to further horizontal competition to generate more symmetrical relationships. Symmetrical solidarity in this context does not mean "equal" solidarity, but valorization of the other's singular abilities and traits seen as significant for the realization of shared goals, within the system of social division of labor (Honneth, 2003a, p. 142, 2011, p. 409).[4]

Although one may assume, by reading *The Struggle for Recognition*, that the moral grammar of the third sphere would encompass claims for recognition of cultural identities,[5] Honneth clarifies in his later works that he speaks of "contributions" within the system of economic exchange (Honneth, 2003a, p. 141, 2011, p. 406). Individuals develop self-esteem according to his or her achievement as a "productive citizen." Thus, struggles for social esteem are better understood as conflicts to challenge and renegotiate symbolic cultural worlds that define representations and valuation of working spaces, status, professions, and activities necessary for society's material reproduction. Since what counts as relevant contributions to societal ends depends on dominant interpretations within the standards of social hierarchy, individuals who seek to expand opportunities to be estimated for their particular abilities engage in a struggle to change "how to interpret and evaluate" their own accomplishments. They seek to amplify public conceptions of what is seen as necessary for societal cooperation and material reproduction.

To summarize, in Honneth's program, subjects are perceived from three perspectives: as beings with particular needs, as beings with equal respect and autonomy comparable to all others in a political community, and as beings with unique contributions to society. The sphere of legal recognition, based on abstract universality, grants each subject the degree of autonomy and self-respect required to articulate individual aims. However, the spheres of primary relations and social relations, involve a practical self-relation regarding the concrete particularities of a person, and are necessary for developing and sustaining self-confidence and self-esteem. All these dimensions are seen as important for positive self-development.

Implications of Honneth's program on critical social and political theory

As has been constantly noted, Honneth's overall project has evolved with great consistency from the outset towards realizing major purposes of critical theory (Anderson, 2011; Deranty, 2009, 2011; Petherbridge, 2011b). In such a program, the recognition ideals are not to be seen as an abstract theoretical construct. Contrary to this perspective, they should be seen as "counterfactual ideals," potentially present in everyday interactions. The principles of recognition provide a normative horizon for identifying and challenging distinct forms of power and social injustices in the pre-scientific realm in order to enable emancipatory practices.

Honneth seeks to anchor his normative model of recognition through anthropological arguments (formulated as intersubjective recognition in terms of "practical self-relations"), as well as through historical arguments (formulated in terms of a "formal concept of ethical life"). Honneth stresses that the principles of recognition, while empirically confirmed along the course of history by real struggles that were aimed at securing basic conditions for individual self-realization and self-determination, are to be understood in the formal sense only.[6] These principles are not related to any particular substantive notion of the "good life." He explains that his "formal conception of ethical life," once seen as a "weak, formal anthropology" (Honneth, 2007d, p. 42) indicates only "general behavior" related to "autonomy" and "self-realization" "in the most neutral sense possible" (Honneth, 2002, p. 515). Importantly, he remarks that content should be provided by a plurality of groups aspiring for recognition; and outcomes should be left open to specific struggles seeking to attain the fundamental conditions for individual self-realization and self-determination in particular socio-cultural contexts.

For our purposes, it should be stressed that Honneth preserves the central goal of Critical Theory – which is to identify and advance the emancipatory impulses that are explicitly and implicitly present in social reality (the principle of "transcendence within immanence"). The principles of recognition are meant to provide a critical yardstick (as expectations for recognition) for individuals in the realm of everyday interactions to identify and challenge "actually existing" social pathologies, along with interlocking oppressive institutional arrangements and cultural social meanings. In this case, a brief reference to Habermas's program helps to further clarify the specificities of Honneth's program for critical social research. Habermas aims at explaining the general and formal conditions for reaching an understanding through language.[7] The goal is not only to provide a comprehensive theory of rationality embedded in the intersubjective structure of communicative action, but also to establish a set of normative criteria of the "ideal speech situation." As a regulative ideal,[8] these requirements are not to be literally achieved, but they offer a critical standard as the means for analyzing when these conditions are or are not met in speaking and acting in practical situations. Habermas's paradigm has provided the most basic concepts for the theory of deliberative democracy and his ideas have served as the starting point for many debates on normative controversies designed to identify standards and conditions for deliberation. His work has helped define goals to promote or achieve in democratic societies, as well as improve existing institutions and practices.

Honneth moves to construct a theory of recognition that can link normative reflection and the concept of intersubjective conditions, both of which are necessary for autonomy and successful individual self-realization. The three principles for recognition constitute normative standards for "healthy" forms of social relations against which it is possible to identify a wide range of social suffering and social obstacles that inhibit the full ability of subjects to flourish. Like Habermas, Honneth identifies a pre-theoretical basis to critique everyday life, but starts with the practical relationships of disrespected subjects. Within the recognition-theoretical program, critical perceptions of injustice are located within individuals' negative experiences that violate their expectations of recognition. The feelings that oppressed individuals of being inadequately or unjustly recognized in real life experiences of disrespect, legal exclusion, and denigration cannot be deduced from outside (Anderson, 2011, p. 53; O'Neill & Smith, 2012, p. 7; Petherbridge, 2011b, p. 26). Under favorable conditions, "feelings of injustice" can disclose expectations not met in social relations and can set in motion morally motivated struggles for expanded forms of recognition (Honneth, 2003a, p. 147, 2011, p. 403). From this perspective, critical theory extracts its critical drives from deficient social conditions related to marginalization, exclusion, and domination that hinder a subject's self-realization.

Recognition as a research program

Honneth's theory of recognition and the proposed normative requirements for justice have been criticized from several standpoints, either by critics who express deep disagreement or by those who adhere to his thinking. This section points out some theoretical controversies in regards to the theory of recognition and outlines how my collaborators and I have crafted our research inquiry.

Scholars have varying understandings about the notion of recognition, and have unleashed an extensive discussion about the precise concept of identity (individual and collective) within recognition studies (Fraser, 2000, 2003a, 2003b; Hobson, 2003; Markell, 2003; Seymour, 2010). Theorists disagree on how Honneth's theory addresses the issue of power in different spheres. Some doubt if his account can adequately capture certain forms of oppression that function without producing any struggle (Allen, 2010; Ferrarese, 2011), and others claim that particular expressions of recognition, by evoking a self-understanding that molds subjects to their expected social roles in society, can turn into an ideological mechanism of domination (Bader, 2007; Rogers, 2009; Rössler, 2007; van den Brink & Owen, 2007; Young, 2007). Others find that the notion of recognition itself is intrinsically related to power dynamics insofar as it invites individuals to search for a definite identity. From this standpoint, critics argue that struggles for recognition run the risk of leading to sectarianism and attempts to control, or even subjugate others (Alexander & Lara, 1996; Fraser, 2001; Markell, 2003).

Furthermore, a number of scholars are skeptical about the recognition-theoretical program's attempt to link moral norms to subjective experiences. Some are reluctant to tie moral norms to the psychological state of individuals because feelings of injustice are not seen as reliable sources for deciding about issues of justice (Fraser, 2001, 2003a, 2003b; Thompson, 2006). Others argue that individual claims for recognition as a matter of self-realization do not provide a consistent basis for criticism; and subjective experiences cannot secure a critical yardstick for the social conditions of the good life. In debates where theoretical divergences do not run deep, theorists dispute how broadly applicable the recognition principles should be and whether these criteria are fully adequate instruments to allow for social researchers to perceive injustice in contemporary society (Cooke, 2006; Thompson, 2006; Zurn, 2000, 2012). In disputes when theoretical cleavages are sharp, critics argue that Honneth's program is not capable of offering the normative prerequisites for a critical theory of society. Scholars advance objections that Honneth's program does not take contemporary cultural relativism and value pluralism seriously, and his account of recognition cannot respond appropriately to capitalist crises and global politics (Düttmann, 2000; Fraser, 2000, 2003b; Markell, 2003; van den Brink, 2011).

In our research, my collaborators and I align ourselves with scholars who argue that Honneth's program offers fairly extensive concepts for a substantial diagnosis and analysis of a number of issues (Deranty, 2009, 2011; O'Neill & Smith, 2012; Petherbridge, 2011b). To develop the empirical studies presented in this book, my collaborators and I have adopted two strategies. Firstly, each chapter deals with a specific dispute related to the theory of recognition and presents key controversial topics under discussion in a condensed manner. Since philosophical debates go far beyond what my collaborators and I can deal with, we survey the arguments from the perspective of empirical researchers. Our attempt is to examine theoretical controversies in order to think critically about particular problems stemming from our empirical study cases.

Indeed, interdisciplinary research on recognition has grown remarkably over the last decade, and there has been a recent surge in empirical work in this field. Through the lens of Honneth's contributions, scholars have investigated a number of social conflicts. Examples of these issues include injuries to the intimate relations in marriage and domestic work (Zurn, 2012; Maia & Cal, 2014); conflicts among cultural groups, as well as religious groups (Cox, 2012; Garcêz & Maia, 2009; O'Neill, 2012; Seglow, 2012) and those involved in immigration, crime, and disability (Calder, 2011; Yar, 2012; Maia & Vimieiro, 2013); problems of social esteem and conflicts in the sphere of work (Mendonça, 2011); and reform to governmental institutions, including healthcare and state-membership regimes, as well as global politics (Cox, 2012; Owen, 2012; Skillington, 2009).

The second research strategy adopted by my collaborators and I was to examine issues in reference to the theory of recognition in connection with media and political communication literature. Insofar as Honneth's theory produces insights into various levels of social life and social conflicts, we organized our empirical studies into three sub-fields of media research: (i) mass media representations, focusing on disadvantaged individuals' interpretations of media-related material, as well as their perception of injustice; (ii) interactions of disadvantaged individuals through the networked media environment, focusing on conflicts emerging as responses to feelings of disrespect and denigration; discursive engagement across moral disagreements, as well as activism through different online platforms; and (iii) long-term progressive changes in patterns of recognition in the media arena.

To promote interplay between theoretical insight and empirical investigation, we surveyed the following controversial issues that address the political philosophical literature of recognition:

(a) the morality of recognition and controversies regarding the notion of this concept. We deal with the criticism that Honneth's ideal of recognition leads to the essentialization of identities, which can project a vision of a sovereign agency that seeks to eliminate contradiction and misunderstanding from social interactions.

(b) the problem of the ideological form of recognition and the engagement of contradictory logics in distinct spheres of recognition that can feed subjugation. We focus on the debate related to the ideology-critique and difficulties in re-conciliating the validity of oppressed subjects' senses of harm and advocacy agents' definitions of injustice.

(c) the role of emotion in politics, particularly when issues of injustice are at stake. We inquire into the concept of "feelings of injustice" and deal with the inevitability of the moral disagreement that arises in the construction of an individual's "shared interpretative framework of injustice," as well as the problem of the justification of claims for recognition.

(d) the various forms of interaction carried out by those struggling for recognition and concomitant possibilities for action, in a conflictive field of respect and disrespect in the everyday life of a pluralist society.

(e) the concepts of non-recognition and misrecognition, and the complexity of disrespect in each and every practical situation. We pay attention to dynamics that omit the existence of conflict in the public domain and the subsequent production of invisibility or non-recognition of collective actors who make claims for recognition.
(f) the notion of moral progress and the recognition criteria for observing and examining emancipatory projects. We address controversies about the notion of progress as a directional process; and we tap into the problem of value pluralism or conflict of interest, along with the process of social learning.

Although Honneth's theory has provided the most basic concepts that frame our perspective, the debate about the above-mentioned issues among his critics helped my collaborators and I to craft our inquiry in each empirical case study. The level of sophistication and erudition shown by Honneth and his detractors clearly goes beyond our ability to translate abstract concepts into operational forms for the purpose of empirical analysis. Still, insofar as the recognition-theoretical approach provides sound social and political guidelines and a normative standard for making sense of observation, it also paves the way for conceptual and empirical advances in specific fields of social research. In this sense, I hope the studies presented in this book can shed some light on the dynamics of social conflicts and specific interfaces with the media system, seen through the lens of the theory of recognition.

Notes

1. Some critics examine how in *The Struggle for Recognition*, Honneth replaces Foucault's analysis with a morally motivated concept of social struggle extracted from Hegel's earlier writings on intersubjective recognition (Allen, 2010, p. 23; Petherbridge, 2011b, p. 12; Sinnerbrink, 2011, p. 184).
2. According to Honneth (1996, p. 110), "Legal subjects recognize each other as persons capable of autonomously making reasonable decisions about moral norms." In another passage he states, "The more demanding this procedure is seen to be, the more extensive the features will have to be that, taken together, constitute a subject's status as morally responsible" (Honneth, 1996, p. 114).
3. Since honor, in Honneth's view, becomes detached from group status and separated from traditional forms of social hierarchy, the *individualization* of social esteem created the possibility to attribute "social value" to "particular qualities that characterize people in their personal difference" (Honneth, 1996, p. 122). In Honneth's words, "The more conceptions of ethical goals are open to different values and the more their hierarchical arrangement gives way to horizontal competition, the more clearly social esteem will be able to take on an individualizing character and generate symmetrical relationships" (Honneth, 1996, p. 122).

4. In Honneth's account, symmetry is not to be seen in terms of "an exact comparison of the value of individual contributions" (Honneth, 1996, p. 130), but rather in the sense of a "cooperative contribution." In his words, "'symmetrical' must mean instead that every subject is free from being collectively denigrated, so that one is given the chance to experience oneself to be recognized, in light of one's own accomplishments and abilities, as valuable for society" (Honneth, 1996, pp. 129–130, 2003c, p. 206).

5. Since Honneth (1996, pp. 126–127) explicitly refers to "life-styles" and "forms of life" when explaining the third sphere in *The Struggle for Recognition*, it is plausible to understand demands for the recognition of cultural identities as included in this realm. In latter works, Honneth clearly admits the mistake of confounding social esteem based on individual achievement in economic exchange with groups' different life aims. He contends that, "this gives the false impression that solidarity in our highly ethically pluralised societies requires a comprehensive normative consensus on the basis of which all individual life aims (that are in conformity with that society's constitution) can be not only tolerated, but esteemed" (Honneth, 2011, p. 407).

6. Conceiving that Honneth's program aims at unifying the historical and normative branches of political theory, which typically tend to be treated separately, Zurn (2010, p. 7) argues "the type of autonomous individuality that liberalism seeks to protect and foster is understood as a result of those historically specific forms of intersubjective, ethical life that enable it to flourish in the first place." For a comprehensible discussion on this issue see also Deranty (2009, pp. 378–394).

7. According to Habermas, "rational discourse" should include any attempt to reach an understanding involving problematic validity claims, and more demanding forms of argumentation, such as deliberation, are to be seen as growing out of "inconspicuous *daily routines* of asking for and giving reasons" (Habermas, 2006, p. 413). Habermas defines the notion of rational discourse as follows: "The conception of rational discourse results from the *reconstruction* of an actual practice and captures just those pragmatic features of a communicative setting that anybody tacitly presupposes once he seriously enters an argumentation in order to check a problematic validity claim by either supporting or denying the truth or rightness of some statement with reasons pro and con" (Habermas, 2005, p. 385).

8. As a regulative ideal, deliberation should meet several criteria: (a) an expectation that participants will rationally question and transcend whatever their initial preference has been (mainly because of the impact of arguments); to this end, participants should present each other with reasons that they think others can comprehend and accept; (b) full inclusion of all people who might be affected by a decision; (c) equality among participants, considered as free and equal persons; (d) free and unforced interaction; therefore, participants should speak truthfully and treat one another with mutual respect during the process of mutual justification; (e) no restrictions regarding topics and topical contributions; (f) the possibility of reversing outcomes (Habermas, 1992, p. 449, 1996, pp. 305–306, 2006, p. 413).

Part I
Mass Media: A Site of Struggle

2
Mass Media Representation, Identity-Building and Social Conflicts: Towards a Recognition-Theoretical Approach

Since its inception, mass media has become a crucial site of struggle. By surveying television dramas, films, journalism, commercial and non-commercial advertisements, etc., a number of scholars have attempted to understand social conflict through approaches such as the "struggle around the image" (Hall, 1997b, p. 257), "struggle over representation" (Shohat & Stam, 1994, p. 178), "struggles for and over social and cultural life" (Gray, 1995, p. 55; see also, Larson, 2006, p. 14). The mass media is also seen as a "site of ideological-democratic struggle" (Carpentier, 2011) and an "arena" for civic debate (Butsch, 2007; Dahlgren & Sparks, 1993; Ferree, Gamson, Gerhards, & Rucht, 2002; Gomes & Maia, 2008; Maia, 2008, 2012a; Norris, 2000; Page, 1996; Peters, 2008; Wessler & Schultz, 2007; Wessler, Peters, Brüggemann, Königslöw & Sifft, 2008).

Despite adopting different approaches, these scholars share the concern that mass media imagery and discourses constitute cultural and political interpretations – a background against which members of groups define the significance of their identity status and the value of their demands. The mass media is also a locus for public articulation, negotiation and dispute over a wide range of issues; it is crucial for bringing issues before the public, for expressing opinions and exchanging arguments for positions – and thus building issue agendas and debates that extend through time and space. Audiences draw on media material for their own reflections and discussions whenever they occur. In this part of "Recognition and the Media," my collaborators and I investigate how mass media material establishes important interfaces with struggles for

27

recognition and how members of disadvantaged groups[1] make sense of media content.

In this chapter, instead of going through dominant theories and findings in media studies, I explore connections between the theory of recognition and the slippery realm of mass media representations and discourses and their impacts on one's self-perception and cultural milieu. First, I point out why fictional and non-fictional representations matter for a recognition-theoretical approach as a social research agenda. I particularly consider media scholars' critiques of different strategies at play in the mass media environment that exclude, stereotype and misrepresent disadvantaged groups. Then, I explore theorists' recent moves to go beyond the debate on "positive" or "negative" depictions, which attempt to overcome a simplistic model of symbolic representation that assumes people's traits, interests and expectations are fixed, clear and visible. Third, I explore some key contributions to understand how people use and experience mass media content. Retaining and reworking these concepts, I argue that Honneth's account should not be conflated with identity politics and point out that his theory offers a distinct approach to re-thinking a range of existing controversies about media interfaces with identity-building and social conflicts. In the subsequent two chapters, my collaborators and I expand on this argument through empirically-based analysis.

I use the term "mass media" to refer to national newspapers, magazines, TV and radio, whose content usually addresses widespread audiences. However, I fully acknowledge the diversity of mainstream media organizations and their complexity of forms, genres, content, logic, styles, modes of addressing the audience, etc. It is quite misleading to attempt to explain mass media content and possible impacts on the individual without seriously taking into consideration technological features, the media format under discussion and the expectations of the public at stake. Meaning is constructed in different ways in fictional, non-fictional and hybrid forms – news reporting, TV dramas, profit and nonprofit advertising, "reality shows," etc. Particular strategies are at work in these different genres to build narratives and characters that produce certain discourses, judgments or draw lessons regarding fundamental cultural, political and historical conflicts in society.

In the term "media professionals," I include experts such as TV producers, writers, directors, editors, journalists and so forth. Because these media professionals perform specific tasks under conditions that are socially and historically informed, it would be inaccurate to describe media professionals as unified and self-conscious agents, as some scholars and observers seem to suggest.

Why does media representation matter for research on recognition?

Media representation studies are supported by theories ranging from psychological and linguistic theories to the sociological which have generated numerous models and methodologies. Representation[2] is a complex phenomenon that has been investigated in a number of different ways.

Four traditions illustrate different approaches one could take in the study of "media representation." First, from the perspective of linguistic and semiotic theories, as per Ferdinand de Saussure and Charles Pierce, media scholars attempt to explain how media materiality – inscriptions, images and texts – "present" individuals and groups in certain ways and thus "say something" about what subjects look like in terms of traits, values, activities, style of living and so forth. This perspective, while paying attention to the complex interplay of written text, images and other graphic elements in signifying practices, tends to see language as an objective system; cultural variables and other effects are usually not raised.

Second, from the perspective of social-psychology and interactionism, as put forth by the Chicago School,[3] media scholars are particularly concerned with the constitutive dimension of representation and how interpretation arises out of social interaction. Within this tradition, scholars inquire into how media content interpellates individuals in contextually specific ways; that is, how they produce interpretation in dialogue with others under specific situations of interaction. Thus, media representation is seen as a practice, one that helps to constitute socially shared meanings and sustain cultural knowledge in society.

Third, from the perspective of anthropological and cultural studies, particularly in the British tradition,[4] scholars highlight that media representation gives meaning to people and groups within a classification. While partially derived from the same social-psychoanalytical and cognitive intellectual tradition as well as being context-sensitive, this perspective differs from the former by drawing on various streams of Marxism and adjacent social theories to bring problems of individual differences and social conflicts to the forefront.[5] Within this tradition, scholars mainly investigate how media imagery and discourses provide instructions for assigning different roles and positions to individuals within social hierarchies and how this process shapes expectations about one's place in relation to in-group and out-group positions.

Fourth and finally, studies based on Critical Discourse Analysis (CDA), an approach founded on linguistics, pragmatics and sociology, pay particular attention to structures and functions of media discourses.[6] The CDA seeks to develop an integrated theoretical framework to investigate the connections between texts and discourses through practices within wider frames of reference and contexts, such as in social systems. Thus, media scholars following this broadly conceived discourse analysis are concerned with the socio-political approach to the structures of media discourses – encompassing the cognitive, social and political structures or processes that define their context. This investigation takes a specific interest in the relationship between language and power; and it pays attention to the multiple relations between text and context to examine the production and reproduction of systems of beliefs, ideologies and attitudes as well as social conflicts in several domains.

The perspectives sketched above offer a glimpse of the different ways that media representation can be investigated including their linguistic; psychic; socio-cultural and political levels of analysis. Different strands in these approaches are often revised and combined for theory-building and empirical analysis.

The question that interests me here is the interface between the theory of recognition and media representation studies. Broadly speaking, media scholars usually present a two-fold concern regarding issues of self-identification and social recognition. On the one hand, media scholars are frequently concerned that media material may have an impact on one's sense of self insofar as individuals use media materials to "see" and "measure" themselves against the attitudes and points of view of others.[7] On the other hand, researchers are concerned that mass media representation may become a major resource for people imagining other individuals and groups since it provides "mental models" or may "shape" cultural perspectives.[8] While most scholars do not use recognition as an analytical framework, they constantly pose questions that can be interpreted in terms of struggles for recognition.

Indeed, the link between mass media material and the stock of cultural interpretations has long been the cornerstone of studies on representation. To align the theory of recognition and communication studies, I follow scholars who view media representation as part of cultural and political discourse in the vast realm of social struggle.[9] I endorse the argument that negative media representations and discourse are socially and culturally rooted and thus historically constituted. As stated by Jason Mittell: "While the identity of creators can help shape representations, they can never be seen as simply the defining factor in determining the meanings of a television text" (Mittell, 2010, p. 308). In a similar vein, Stephanie Larson in her study on race/ethnicity issues states: "The particular negative images used in television and films were not created there; they are historically constituted…from a long legacy of social inequality and oppression, and their retelling strengthens these beliefs in white supremacy" (Larson, 2006, p. 15). In Nico Carpentier's words, "media discourses…(re) produce discourses on the power relations that lie behind the participatory process, and on conditions of possibility and limits of the participatory process" (Carpentier, 2011, p. 179).

I advocate that viewing media representations, as part of cultural and political discourses within a broader social milieu, is important for a recognition-theoretical approach for several reasons. First, this perspective shifts the research effort from pinning down meaning in unique, isolated, media material to enquiring how meaning is generated and constructed more broadly through social dynamics. Within critical cultural perspectives, many scholars focus their attention on the repertoire of images and representations across various media and platforms to identify "patterns of representation" in a particular historical moment. Stuart Hall, for instance, speaks in terms of a "regime of representation" to convey that "similar representational practices and figures [are] repeated, with variations, from one text or site of representation to another" (Hall, 1997b, p. 232). Similarly, Elfriede Fürsich (2010, p. 116) argues that a "stockpile of mediated representation types…[is] constantly recycled in a variety of media outlets." Thus, such a broad cultural approach is theoretically and politically important because it raises questions about patterns of value and treatment that are intersubjectively accorded to individuals and groups in a given society.

A second reason for regarding media representation as part of cultural and political discourse is that such an approach compels us to understand media professionals not only as "makers" but also as "addressees" of representation in society. Media professionals are often the target of campaigns of disadvantaged groups who seek to change their representational image and/or to promote popular awareness of their demands. A wide range of actions and strategies, including active media monitoring, are established by women, racial minorities, people with disabilities, gays and lesbians, human rights' movements, etc., to exert pressure on media professionals to adjust their performances, story lines and the quality of news coverage on certain issues.[10]

In Chapter 8, I discuss different mechanisms of accountability in the media environment – legal, market, professional and public accountability, which have different power wielders, mechanisms of responsiveness and strength of constraints.[11] Therefore, I understand that the attitude of recognition is something that is worked out not only between media professionals and those affected, but by many other social groups. I contend that media professionals, as socialized subjects, are positioned in the social field and participate actively in, and also stand as observers of, different types of struggle in society.

Third, seeing mass media representation as part of cultural and political discourses makes us more sensitive to understanding patterns of representation as an ongoing and unfinished process, rather than a fixed one. As I have been emphasizing, media-based representation and discourses are not simply a selective meaning-making practice in one direction but they are also made up of and transformed by agents of contending groups. The characteristics of symbolic representation are constituted through a political process, within conflicts and collective action.

To understand the "mutual constitution" of attitudes of recognition from a recognition analytical framework, it becomes particularly important to keep in mind that mass communication does not only provide much of the information that circulates in the background of discursive contexts but it is also a locus where political issues are debated. In studies of political communication and the public sphere, the view of the news media as an "arena" or a "forum" is well known.[12] Media debates comprise a large quantity of factual information as well as opinions and arguments regarding controversial issues on administrative routine, on implementation of new rules and political policies, on claims of groups, on demands for accountability and so forth. Studies in this field seek to unravel how media professionals operate both as active reason-giving agents and as mediators of the debate forum; the structure of opportunities for accessing the media (who participates and when); the content and style of expression (how voices are processed and frames are constructed); and whether alternative interpretations and discourse contestation appear in the media arena.[13]

My argument is not meant to minimize criticisms of *power operations* that exist in the traditional mass media environment. Even though power relations penetrate institutional structures of mass media organizations and give support to political and economic elites, these arrangements should not be conceived as uncontested, all-encompassing status hierarchies. I agree that mass media content often follows norms favoring hegemonic patterns that support privilege and subordination in contemporary societies. Since power asymmetries, related to sexuality, gender, race/ethnicity, class, religion, nationality and so forth, cannot be easily changed throughout society, the same holds true for the mass media environment.

I understand that disadvantaged groups face many hindrances accessing mainstream media to make their perspectives heard – to express their own values, interests, and concerns. Indeed, many minority groups lack the means – resources, opportunity and mobilization – to resist exploitation, humiliation, and disrespect in society, let alone do something about misrepresentation in the media arena. Yet, it is important to investigate whether pluralistic and transcultural flows pervade the mass media environment, or not. The literature shows that social movements and activists are quite aware of these problems and reflectively develop a series of tactics to interact with media professionals.[14] Sometimes advocacy organizations – NGOs, intellectuals and moral entrepreneurs – that speak and act on behalf of vulnerable subjects, are seeking to promote certain values and policies, and face collective action problems. In viewing mass media as sites of struggle, we should be sensitive to the complex and often contradictory processes that take place there. My collaborators and I will return to some of these issues in our empirical study cases.

How is misrecognition built into the mass media environment?

To understand the mass media environment as a site of social conflict, it is crucial to pay attention to the conditions under which representation-makers construct meaningful representations and media discourses. It is important to be aware of the connection between media producers' construction of symbolic meanings with ideas circulating in a given society concerning disadvantaged groups' marginalization, exploitation and domination, on the one hand, and the interplay of these meanings, on the other. Furthermore, if we are to be more cautious about what is good or bad in representation, then it is fundamental to inquire into how affected individuals make sense of and judge the way they are represented.

A great body of scholarship on gays, lesbians, immigrants, women, race and ethnicity has shown that fictional films, TV programs and news tend to homogenize, marginalize and ridicule minority groups.[15] Concerned with unequal power relations affecting minorities, most media scholars seem to agree that diversity of representation contributes to broaden and introduce complexity in the manner through which a given group is perceived. While endorsing this view, I contend that a fuller and more nuanced understanding of misrecognition requires us to go beyond the idea of a multiplicity of representations.

My initial claim is that the search for one best meaning of representation is fruitless. Although it is common to discuss groups as if they were *units* or *homogeneous aggregates,* groups are always made up of individuals who always have multiple identifications and affiliations; their collective interests cannot be taken as a given (Benhabib, 2002; Fraser, 2003a; Gutmann, 2003; Weldon, 2011; Young, 2000). Critical analysis of the representation of minorities should be informed by several axes of difference; one cannot expect that a single character can stand for an entire group.[16] Furthermore, character-based analyses that exclusively focus on "good" or "bad" characters can easily evoke an abstract or generic debate on vices and virtues of fictional actions, and fail to capture the complex link between representation and cultural meanings (Gray, 1995; Shohat & Stam, 1994). I endorse the argument that to understand media representation and discourses, one cannot overlook the importance of the cultural horizon across given programs – institutional settings, language, casting, and cultural variations – and the practices of marginalization, exclusion, domination, and subordination in society (Mittell, 2010, pp. 310–311; Shohat & Stam, 1994, p. 9; van Dijk, 1991, 2012).

A question I wish to ask is how should we conceptualize misrepresentation (or misrecognition) in the mass media environment? Discussing media images and discourses in the abstract as positive or negative makes no sense. Still, it is useful to briefly point out some strategies present in the mass media environment that produce distorted representation or misrecognition, such as invisibility, stereotyping and exclusion. Invisibility implies a non-presence of groups or certain issues in media imagery, texts or discourses; it involves a literal absence in the media scenario and a figurative non-existence in social terms (Barnhurst, 2007). The act of non-perception or the act of making someone or something disappear is understood as highly humiliating because it indicates the insignificance, or the social meaninglessness, of the person or issue at stake (Honneth, 2001). Disadvantaged groups in this sense usually struggle against invisibility to affirm their existence, to be noticed, or to have their expressions somehow publicly considered.

Stereotyping is a much-debated issue in media studies. Stereotyping practices reduce people and groups to a few, oversimplified and fixed characteristics. Hall (1997b) summarizes three aspects of this practice: (i) it "reduces, essentializes, naturalizes and fixes [people's or groups'] 'difference'" (Hall, 1997b, p. 258); (ii) it helps to establish group boundaries and to promote exclusion by grouping people on the basis of clear-cut binary categories such as normal/abnormal, acceptable/unacceptable, insiders/outsiders; (iii) it applies hegemonic groups' own evaluative patterns to classify norms to subordinate or exclude others (Hall, 1997b, p. 258).

Many critics decry stereotyping's focus on distinct forms of exclusion and marginalization through media representation and discourses and argue that minorities are often depicted as those who cause trouble or need help. Larson claims that racial minorities are usually included in films and TV entertainment programs through "selective exclusion" (Larson, 2006, p. 16) insofar as national or ethnic variations are ignored and differences in culture, language, history, and physical attributes among group members are omitted. In such circumstances, symbolic representation effaces distinctiveness, either by using one group to represent all others or by homogenizing subgroups – which are then seen as a "generic" Indian, Hispanic, Asian American, etc. There is a vast literature on debates over the ideological function of mass media,[17] and various in-depth case studies of films and media programs that show how media producers disregard historical and material conditions, and blame those in subordinate positions for problems whose real causes lie elsewhere. Also familiar are programs in which members of minority groups are depicted as fully included in society and not threatened in their self-conception or in their most cherished ideals. Not only do these programs fail to take full measure of problems of social structures and cultural meanings, they too easily gloss over the social obstacles to autonomy and agency of marginalized individuals. The picture emerging from films, fictional programs and TV shows in such cases is that oppression does not exist or it is something that existed in the past but has been overcome.

Misrecognition also abounds in news and non-fictional programs. There is a vast literature showing that news reporting, while having the weight of factuality, can also promote exclusion and negative stereotypes, tell particular stories in ways that privilege some people or groups and present points of view over others. Research in this field has shown that journalists and reporters tend to corroborate social hierarchies.[18] While adopting newsworthy criteria and operating as gatekeepers, they choose what is included in news, what significance is attributed to events and how prominently coverage is displayed among other issues. Media professionals need to select certain aspects of perceived reality, which is always in flux, since it is impossible tell an "unframed" story. Yet, they have considerable autonomy to define frame stories and interpret what is going on.

"Stereotyping," "selective exclusion" and "de-contextualization" are strategies also largely seen in news narratives. Some scholars show that issues of gender and minority are rarely converted into hard news stories and individuals of disadvantaged groups rarely appear as news sources (Barnhurst, 2003; Campbell, 1995; Entman & Rojecki, 2000; Miguel & Biroli, 2009; Ross, 2010). Other scholars, surveying journalistic coverage of social conflicts, show that news media narratives focus mainly on clashes with violent demonstrators and ignore political motivations underpinning the upheavals (Liebes, 1997; McCurdy, 2013). News media frames may sanitize the screen from people's outrage and suffering, and ridicule or demonize protesters, labeling them as mobs and rioters. In addition, coverage decontextualizes specific conflicts by showing them as separate occurrences.

Increasingly sophisticated studies have shown that we should also be sensitive to indirect, subtle and complex forms of exclusion and marginalization – not only to radical, violent or blatant forms – in entertainment and news stories alike.[19] Dealing with the growing visibility of queer identities in the media in the US since the 1960s, Kevin G. Barnhurst (2007) explores several paradoxes of visibility such as stimulating tolerance through stereotyping; exchanging assimilation for inclusion in public discourse, and transforming radicalism into a market niche. Guillermo Avila-Saavedra (2009) argues that the sudden increase of gay male characters in American TV shows and the perceived advancement in gay representation do not challenge hetero-normative notions of masculinity. He explains that there remains an overwhelming presence of gay white males in TV programs whose narratives focus on interpersonal issues of homosexuality and ignore concerns of other gender and sexual minorities. His conclusion is that such TV programs, by avoiding conflictive political issues, underscore hegemonic models of social relations. Bruno S. Leal and Carlos A. Carvalho (2012, p. 38) surveyed mainstream news media coverage of homophobia issues related to denunciation of physical and symbolic aggression against lesbian, gay, bi, trans, queer (LGBTQ) communities during 2008–2010 in Brazil. These scholars reached the conclusion that increased visibility of such themes was not broad enough to include all identities and social classes within this universe.

By investigating the representation of black characters in 53 Brazilian telenovelas in the 2000s, Wesley Grijó and Adam Sousa (2012) noticed some major innovations in this TV genre such as blacks as protagonists and a nucleus of black people playing central roles, as well as explicit discourses against racism in the narratives. Still, they acknowledge that in the majority of telenovelas, black people remained attached to subaltern roles such as employees and bandits; the imagery of black sensuality and overstated eroticism prevailed in these representations. Evelyn

Alsultany's (2012) study on the proliferation of sympathetic representations of Arabs and Muslims in the US commercial media, particularly in prime-time TV dramas after 9/11, is another evocative illustration. Alsultany notes that media producers of such TV series, seeking to avoid obvious stereotypes, use a series of new strategies such as: picturing patriotic Arab or Muslim Americans in plots; sympathizing with their plight; challenging the Arab/Muslim conflation with diverse Muslim identities; flipping the enemy and humanizing the terrorist. Because the majority of Arab and Muslim representations still occur in contexts related to terrorism, Alsultany argues there remains the submerged message that they pose a terrorist threat to American life and freedom. The key argument of this study is that such "simplified complex representations" create a post-race illusion that absolves viewers from confronting the persistence of institutionalized racism.

While social conflicts undergo changes, new contradictions and forms of domination can be created. My argument is that neither the move from "negative" to "positive" images in the mass media environment nor the progress from oversimplified images to plural ones necessarily eliminates denigration and subjugation. For the time being, it suffices to stress the complex link between media-based discourses and representations and cultural meanings underpinning social and political conflicts. The theory of recognition regards the social order as always conflict-driven and sustains the idea that crushing experiences of disrespect and misrecognition promotes motivation for disadvantaged groups to struggle for recognition. In Chapter 8, I return to the development of patterns of representation and discourses in the media arena in the historical process of cultural transformation. I discuss the significance of mechanisms of media accountability for changing these standards in terms of a recognition-theoretical approach. In the next section, I build on media reception studies that aim to explain how individuals make sense of media fictional and non-fictional representations and discourses.

Reception practices: making sense of media content

Reception studies can be regarded as complementary to representation studies, since the key question here is how people make sense of media content and what they do in relation to media in their contexts of action. To understand the interfaces between media representation and problems of recognition, I shall briefly outline reception studies. Again, I do not intend to offer an assessment of many contributions in this field of research, since this task would take a lengthy book in itself. Instead, my aim is to present some suggestions stemming from interactionism and critical cultural traditions that provide theoretical guidance to my collaborators and me to craft our research inquiry.

Since researchers have theorized media-related practices and people's interpretation of mass media content from distinct schools of thought, it comes as no surprise that a number of controversies produce recurring debates over: how individuals and groups of people interpret and experience media content; what effects these encounters have in maintaining, reinforcing or challenging social order; and, what levels of power, control and agency readers or spectators have. Insofar as different theoretical perspectives have shaped reception studies, empirical findings remain unresolved.

Understanding people's processes of interpretation of media material has long been a cornerstone of media studies. Psychosocial and interactionist approaches are particularly sensitive to different factors of mediation and to contextual variables alike. Reacting against functionalist studies, Chicago School-based media scholars allow for greater diversity of cognitive and affective responses. Following G. H. Mead's legacy, particularly re-worked by Herbert G. Blumer and Erving Goffman, media scholars are committed to understanding the individual's process of interpretation in the course of interpersonal interactions and the complex operation of individual roles and sets of expectations. Although such an approach offers valuable mediation models, it gives a limited account to structural issues and power asymmetries. Standing alone, interactionist approaches provide categories that are too limited to develop the nuanced account of social conflicts that provide the basis we now require for understanding struggles of recognition.

Critical cultural studies, particularly in the British tradition, reappraise the link between emotional-cognitive schemes and social power asymmetries to explain the audiences' repertoire for media response. Against the rigid interpellation thesis and the empiricism of behavioral psychology, theorists such as Stuart Hall and David Morley seek to further conceptualize the social context as a site of struggle. By combining L. Althusser's materialist theory of ideology, A. Gramsci's thesis of hegemony and E. P. Thompson and R. Hoggart's attempt to historicize culture, earlier critical study theorists have sought to show that media interpretations are related to pre-existing conditions that organize such practice.

Instead of viewing people as atomized individuals who randomly produce meaning in different sites of experience, Morley's (1980,

1986) ongoing research on television in the eighties advanced the key argument that members of different groups actively interpret and use media material in distinct ways that are related to their socio-economic positions. In the same vein, Stuart Hall (1991, 1997b) conceives the audience's differential interpretations not merely on the basis of individual psychology at a personal level, but emphasizes the importance of their shared horizon of expectations or "framework of knowledge," which are linked back to the socio-economic structure of society.

This approach is particularly important for a recognition-theoretical approach because it places social conflicts, interpreted from a cultural and historical perspective, at the forefront of its concern. Still, we should consider some of its difficulties to take full notice of multiple, shifting and contradictory ways through which people engage with mass media content to make sense of their experiences. Considering Hall's long-term influential model of encoding/decoding (Hall, 1980)[20] and the typology of the audience either as "passive," "active" or "resistant," Janet Staiger (2005, p. 83) critically summarizes these difficulties:

> (1) television and other texts do not necessarily reproduce dominant ideology in any coherent sense, so determining a preferred meaning is difficult; (2) a tendency exists to assume classes are unitary and unaffected by other identities and pleasures, making difficult the slotting of actual readings into one of the three categories; (3) to read in a resistant manner assumes knowing the preferred interpretation; (4) no evidence exists that an oppositional reading gives an individual any real social agency or produces any social change; (5) as Hall himself notes, the model does not consider the decentered subject and pleasure; (6) oppositional could be defined anywhere from reading differently than expected to not reading at all; and (7) ultimately, then, most readings are 'negotiations'. Thus, the system provides little felicity in describing what is occurring in any viewing event.

In response to these difficulties, several scholars have attempted to relate individuals' use of media material and their broader social interactions for theorizing about: group identity; multiple affiliations and affinities; issues of place, territory and identity; and, the building of collective commitments and collective action. Along with growing interest on identity politics and multiculturalism in the nineties, media scholars opened new paths to explore how different forms of social confrontation occur in talk shows (Gamson, 1999; Livingstone & Lund, 1994;

Wessler & Schultz, 2007; how diasporic groups, by viewing films and television programs, are able to construct identity and create civil society alike (Dayan, 1998); how narration of crisis may facilitate the construction and reconstruction of collective identities and solidarities (Alexander & Jacobs, 1998); and, articulation of resistance in youth and minority groups' subcultures, related to gender and generational differences (McRobbie & Garber, 1976). Several Latin-American scholars have also developed a number of models to approach multi-mediations in people's experiences of media content, referring to both individual as well as group-based mediations, encompassing aspects related to cognitive perception, acquisition of information and knowledge along with socio-cultural aspects and group-affiliations (Canclini, 2009; Martín-Barbero, 2009; Orozco, 2002, Sodré, 1999).

Recently, studies on media reception have increasingly been moving towards the view of media "practice" – an approach that seeks to grasp people's engagement with the media by taking into account when and where it occurs and takes form. Nick Couldry, one of the advocators of such an approach, argues, "It asks quite simply: what are people (individuals, groups, institutions) doing in relation to media across a whole range of situations and contexts? How is people's media-related practice related, in turn, to their wider agency?" (Couldry, 2013, p. 37).

For a long time, scholars, who have developed reception and ethnographic studies, have shown the looseness and openness of peoples' activities linked to media. They have cautioned that the influence of mass media cannot be taken for granted since people may give little attention to its content; media experience may be fragmented and ephemeral among other mundane engagements (Couldry, 2000; Dahlgren, 1988; Duits, 2010; Silverstone, 1994). Scholars in this field have avoided developing general conceptualizations about the nature of mass media effects and have highlighted the complexity of the phenomena.

Reviewers of media effects literature have mapped different sources for this complexity regarding issues such as: type of effects (cognitive, attitudinal, belief, affective, physiological, behavioral, or some combination); level of effect (at the micro-level, the macro-level, or both); influence and change issues (indirect or direct influence; change as alteration and stabilization, gradual long-term change and short-term fluctuation); type of media stimulus and pervasiveness issues (diffuse-general influence on the culture or content-specific factors in their messages; influence on everyone or on members of a specific group); and difficulties of tracing mass media influences due to timing of effect as well as measurability of the phenomena (Neuman & Guggenheim, 2011; Potter, 2011).

To complicate this picture, ever more scholars have been investigating how people engage with different mass media genres and how this practice is combined with other influences within a hybrid media system, encompassing the Internet and SNSs (Cammaerts, Mattoni, & McCurdy, 2013; Chadwick, 2013; Dahlgren, 2009, 2013). I return to this topic in Chapter 5.

To develop a recognition-theoretical approach, I follow such a practice-based model to inspect closely "what people are doing, saying and thinking in relation to the media" (Couldry, 2013, p. 40). Still, from a recognition-theoretical driven reflection, I contend that it is crucial to investigate the interplay between one's subjectivity and the nature of others' responses in everyday interactions, within a broader horizon of ethical life. While the theory of recognition is centrally concerned with social conflicts and a full range of experiences of suffering related to individuation, socialization and social inclusion, media studies offer an array of evidence of these real processes in everyday life. Empirical research provides many routes for grasping diverse forms of social power entangled in media's everyday representations and individuals' media uses that enact social oppression as well as emancipation. My collaborators and I support the argument that media-related practices must be analyzed to: answer questions about how and under which circumstances media practices facilitate operations of power or contribute to raising awareness of domination; allow self-identification to groups or contestation of belonging; enable the construction or deconstruction of common interests; and, promote accommodation into social roles or mobilization for social change, etc.

To illustrate this point, let me give a few examples of how media scholars have been focusing on open-ended processes of power-relations and highly varied, plural, media practices. In his study on London-based Filipino migrants' practice of reception of both hard news, named by the author as a "public knowledge project," and entertainment media on karaoke, regarded as a "popular culture project," Jonathan C. Ong (2009, p. 176) argues that "different media – 'soft' and 'serious,' national and transnational, mass and particularistic – are all implicated in issues of identity-formation and belonging, inclusion and exclusion." Ong's key argument is that rather than determining affiliation to a national community, such practices provide resources for migrants to "weave in and out" of their desire as well as their anxiety to take part in British society, to associate and dissociate with their homeland's marks and imagery, and to combine their loyalties to British and Filipino publics (Ong, 2009, p. 162). In his study on practices of viewing Flemish domestic soaps by young adults of Flemish and ethnic minorities with Moroccan or Turkish backgrounds, Alexander Dhoest (2009) questions if such practices produce a national "imagined community" of viewers. While confirming the importance of ethnic identity in television viewing, this study shows that there are many internal varieties in each community; ethnicity is not always a relevant factor for individuals to make sense of their experiences. Dhoest (2009, p. 305), in conclusion, remarks that "similarities found caution against a binary opposition between native Flemish and ethnic minority viewpoints."

In light of the points already made in Chapter 1, I should reiterate that Honneth's theory of recognition should not be conflated with identity politics or with "politics of recognition" as developed by Charles Taylor. In Honneth's project, self-realization has less to do with the conventional concept of identity, in terms of a complex set of affiliations and mutual identifications, and more with the idea of a full sense of self which entails the view that individuals' autonomy as well as agency is achieved in interaction with others. Honneth's account links individual's self-realization with social conditions, that is, with current cultural meanings, social practices, institutions and structures. The recognition theoretical approach thus allows us to articulate how power embedded in media material is effectively enacted in real people's negative experiences in different spheres such as personal oppression, legal exclusion and cultural denigration. Media researchers can develop multidimensional criteria to analyze social conflict and social pathologies while also searching for a source of emancipation within individuals' negative experiences.

Conclusion

In this chapter I have argued that the mass media environment is highly diversified and the complexity of the media as a site of social struggles cannot be overlooked. Understanding diverse forms of power that operate through media material, regarding issues of invisibility, stereotyping, denigration, exclusion and so forth, requires the examination of each specific case of conflict within broader societal dynamics. The role played by media professionals as 'representation-makers' in a given social conflict should be surveyed, not presumed.

In the two subsequent chapters, my collaborators and I inquire into how the recognition-theoretical approach can infuse, with new insights, empirical analysis of mass media as a site for social struggles. We focus on how members of disadvantaged groups interpret mass media content related to given social conflict and we investigate these individuals' self-perceptions of their lived experiences in society.

Our first case study illustrates situations in which mass media professionals are aware of their dominant positions and try to counteract prevalent stereotyping practices. It focuses on a TV Series, *Cidade dos Homens*, in which the production team of the largest TV broadcasting company in Brazil, *Rede Globo*, joined efforts with an NGO, *Nós do Cinema*. The directors of this TV Series claimed their aim was to offer unconventional roles and flexibility of character for slum-dwellers and to picture everyday life situations in the slums that are not related to crime, drugs and violence, to challenge crude, blatant, stereotyping against slum-dwellers in Brazilian society.

Our second study also illustrates a situation in which media professionals arguably operate in favor of disadvantaged groups, in this case, as agents advocating for the rights of children and adolescents. Our study was conducted in Belém, a city in the north of Brazil where child domestic labor (CDL) is a deeply rooted cultural practice. Our analysis of local news stories shows that journalists, when writing reports on CDL, systematically choose sources from civil society associations that combat this type of labor. They use advocacy organizations' preferential frames to express that CDL is invisible and socially neglected, and involves exploitation, domination and marginalization. Even if such cases are seen as rare within the mainstream media environment, they shed some light on the complex way media agents can participate in broader struggles to politicize issues and make injuries into an object of public reflection.

In the chapters that follow, my collaborators and I are particularly interested in investigating how affected individuals make sense of media content and understand their lived experiences of disrespect. In both studies, we use a focus group technique to obtain study participants' interpretations.

In Chapter 3, we examine how slum-dweller adolescents appreciate their symbolic representation in the TV Series *Cidade dos Homens*. Since the producers of this program intended to challenge the slum-dweller stereotypes, this case is an interesting one for examining the morality of recognition and the tensions between media representation-makers and those represented when it comes to the question of what is to be considered valuable and relevant in slum dwellers' identities and achievements. Findings show that the adolescents have a critical perception of this TV series. By contesting misrecognition, they also disclose what they see as a violation of their moral expectations.

In Chapter 4, my collaborator and I examine how women, who were housemaids in their childhood, engage, in light of their experiences, with media discourses that define CDL as an injustice. Results show that study participants contest advocacy media discourses and defend CDL as a useful opportunity through which to seek emancipation. Hence, this study investigates problems related to ideological and justified forms of recognition.

Notes

1. I use the term "disadvantaged groups" in a broad sense to convey minorities, who do not fit into the dominant roles, according to sociology's functional explanation, as well as oppressed people, according to the conflict theory perspective. The term "disadvantaged groups" is also meant to encompass what some scholars have conceptualized as "Others," that is, people that "are in any way significantly different from the majority – 'them' rather than 'us'" (Hall, 1997b, p. 229). Within such a perspective, one can distinguish between "Others in a nation (i.e., ethnic, linguistic, racial, religious or sexual minorities) and "Others outside the borders" (Fürsich, 2010, p. 116; see also Staiger, 2005, p. 140). Although these terms hold specific connotations, I use them interchangeably in a more neutral sense as "disadvantaged groups."

2. Representation is an elusive and multi-sided concept. Broadly speaking, representation means making something present that is absent (Couldry, 2013; Hall, 1997a, p. 17; Pitkin, 1967, p. 69). It involves production of meaning through which human beings constitute and make "present" or "render visible" the social world – objects, people, events, norms, etc.

3. While being one of the major alternative approaches to functionalism and to media effect studies, symbolic interactionism deriving from the Chicago School theorists – such as George H. Mead, Herbert G. Blumer and Erving Goffman – has inspired a number of theoretical models and empirical media research.

4. The Birmingham Centre for Contemporary Cultural Studies (CCCS), founded in 1964 by Richard Hoggart and then directed by Stuart Hall from 1969, is a key reference in this field.

5. See for example, Hall, 1991, 1997b; Morley, 1980, 1986; Staiger, 2005.

6. See for example, Chouliaraki, & Fairclough, 1999; Fairclough, 1995a, 1995b, 1998; van Dijk, 1991, 1993, 2012; Weiss & Wodak, 2003.

7. See for example, Barnhurst, 2003, 2007; Carpentier, 2011; Gaines, 2001, pp. 12–13; Hall, 1997a, 1997b; Larson, 2006; Mittell, 2010; van Dijk, 1993, 2012.

8. Several scholars have pointed out that mass media contributes to shaping widespread, cultural ideas in society. In Mittell's words, "representations of identity help define what a culture thinks is normal for a particular group, how behaviors and traits fit into a society's shared common sense" (Mittell, 2010, p. 306). In a similar vein, Larson contends that "due to continued racial segregation, the media are the primary forum through which whites 'come to know' non-whites; therefore, individual minorities in the media come to

symbolize these groups for white audiences" (Larson, 2006, p. 3). Also van Dijk remarks that "as long as people have no direct personal experiences with minorities or immigrants...they have no concrete mental models as a basis for the formation of general attitudes. In that case, such mental models are taken from the mass media" (van Dijk, 2012, p. 27). In Fairclough's words, "media discourse should be regarded as a site of complex and often contradictory processes, including ideological processes" (Fairclough, 1995a, p. 47).

9. For more extensive discussions see, Barker, 1999; Couldry, 2000, 2013; França & Guimarães, 2006; França & Corrêa, 2012; Gamson, 1992; Gomes, 2004; Gomes & Maia, 2008; Maia, 2008, 2012a; Hall, 1997a, 1997b; Miège, 2010; Mittell, 2010; Peters, 2008; Wessler, 2008; Wessler, Peters, Brüggemann, Königslöw, & Sifft, 2008.

10. For more extensive discussions see specially Barnhurst, 2003; Carpentier, 2011; Couldry, 2000; della Porta, 2013; McCurdy, 2013; Porto, 2012; Ross, 2010; Waisbord, 2009.

11. To consider the problem of media accountability within a "system of social response," José Luis Braga (2006) points out a variety of practices such as debates about media programs carried out both within and outside media industries, press councils, journalism reviews, newspaper film critics and academic books about the media and market mechanisms. By distinguishing diverse types of accountability in the media environment, Dennis McQuail (2003) and Mauro Porto (2012, pp. 146–147) discuss legal/regulatory accountability, financial/market accountability, public or social accountability and professional accountability.

12. Bennett, Pickard, Iozzi, Schroeder, & Caswell, 2004; Butsch, 2007; Correia, 2002; Dahlgren, 1995; Dahlgren & Sparks, 1993; Ettema, 2007; Ferree, Gamson, Gerhards, & Rucht, 2002; Gamson & Modigliani, 1989; Gastil, 2008; Gomes, 2004; Gomes & Maia, 2008; Habermas, 1991, 1996, 2006, 2009; Miège, 2010; Norris, 2000; Page, 1996; Peters, 2008; Simon & Xenos, 2000; Wessler, 2008; Wessler & Schultz, 2007; Wessler, Peters, Brüggemann, Königslöw, & Sifft, 2008.

13. In previous works, I have explored several situations of public debate in the media arena (Cal & Maia, 2012; Maia, 2006, 2008, 2012a; Maia e Cal, 2014; Marques & Maia 2010; Mendonça & Maia 2012). Several studies focused on the structure of positions and counter-positions with respect to a specific controversy in the media forum: the institutionally defined roles of speakers; participants' provision of explanatory reasoning; the openness to dialogue among the categories of participants who hold divergent views, and the attempts to redeem claims that have been criticized in the public arena over time. The point to be stressed here is that the mass media comprise differential structures and opportunities for public articulation and contestation of discourses.

14. See for example, Couldry, 2000; della Porta, 2013; Mattoni, 2013; McCurdy, 2013; Porto, 2012; Ryan, 1991; Ryan, Jeffreys, Ellowitz, & Ryczek, 2013.

15. See for example, Gray, 1995; Grijó & Sousa, 2012; Hall, 1997a, 1997b; Larson, 2006; Shohat & Stam, 1994; Sodré, 1999.

16. Concerned with racial representation, Mittell has lucidly observed, "there is no ideal way of representing a racial group; no single character or program can represent an entire race" (Mittell, 2010, p. 327). To capture forms of

oppressions intersecting internal axes of difference of gay groups, Guillermo Avila-Saavedra has argued that critical studies "need[s] to be informed equally by notions of gender, sex, class and race" (Avila-Saavedra, 2009, p. 7).

17. See for example, Fairclough, 1995a, 1998; Grijó & Sousa, 2012; Gray, 1995; Larson, 2006; Shohat & Stam, 1994; van Dijk, 1991, 2012.

18. For a more extensive discussion see specially Blumler & Gurevitch, 2000; Cottle, 2008; Entman, 1993, 2004; Fairclough, 1995a; Gitlin, 1980; Gomes, 2004; Gomes & Maia, 2008; Reese, 2007; Schudson, 2003; Shoemaker & Vos, 2009; van Dijk, 1991, 2012.

19. Alsultany, 2012; Avila-Saavedra, 2009; Barnhurst, 2007; Liebes & Kampf, 2009; van Dijk, 2012.

20. Hall's model of encoding/decoding (Hall, 1980) proposes three general ways that people respond to media material: (i) "preferred reading," when individuals interpret the text in the manner that the makers would expect to; (ii) "negotiated reading," when individuals work out a part of the text in a particular fashion to find their own meaning; and (iii) "oppositional reading," when individuals contest, reject or reframe the meanings that makers had hoped they would make. In critical dialogue with Hall's work, contemporary scholars have sought to expand "forms" or "types" of reception, and thus promote continuities and breaks in the aforementioned typology (Edgerly, Toft, & Veden, 2011; Morley & Chen, 1996).

3
The Morality of Recognition: Adolescent Slum-Dwellers Discuss a TV Series Representation of Their Lives

Rousiley C. M. Maia and Simone Maria Rocha

This chapter investigates the morality of recognition. A number of critics are distressed by Honneth's proposition that anchors critical political claims in a theory of subjective identity and self-realization. Many of these critiques are based around the understanding that the notion of recognition – as proposed by Honneth – results in the essentialization and objectification of identities (Düttmann, 2000; Fraser, 2000, 2001, 2003a; Markell, 2003). My collaborator and I argue that several of these analyses are grounded in entirely different notions of identity and recognition, and we contend that Honneth's program provides fairly extensive theoretical insights into the vulnerability and contingency of subjective formation. These concepts help investigate the disagreement and open-endedness that characterize struggle for recognition in social interactions.

In this chapter, we explore how adolescent slum-dwellers make sense of the first four episodes of a Brazilian television series – *"Cidade dos Homens"* (City of Men). The program is explicitly aimed at producing a more positive representation of slum-dwellers and their daily lives. As was discussed in the previous chapter, the investigation of representations of ethnic, racial, gender or sexual minorities has produced broad evidence that media imagery in the news, movies, and entertainment programs tend to stereotype disadvantaged groups. Those who are victims of devaluation, marginalization, and oppression, are usually portrayed in problematic ways. Individuals are often expressed using limited or oversimplified images. For example, characters are shown as being exotic or essentialized through some fixed attribute, or they are depicted as abnormal or deviant. *Cidade dos Homens* is an intriguing case study because its producers explicitly sought to challenge prejudices against low-income populations in Brazil. This series was conceived and developed by an NGO "We From the Cinema" (*Nós do Cinema*) in partnership with Brazil's largest television network – Rede Globo. To gain first-hand experience of daily life, it was filmed in a slum in RJ (Morro de Santa Marta) and the cast, including the protagonists, consisted mostly of slum-dwellers.

As was also discussed in the previous chapter, media scholars are particularly concerned with oppressive connotations of stereotyped representations since they tend to confirm or reinforce hegemonic patterns of interpretation and evaluation across society. Media imagery and texts contribute to the production of shared cultural meanings, and add to the body of knowledge used by individuals when they construct their place in social hierarchies (Couldry, 2000; Hall, 1997b; Larson, 2006; Mittell, 2010; Morley, 1986). Our study inquires how adolescent slum-dwellers express their self-awareness when confronted with this TV series. We attempt to determine which features from *Cidade dos Homens* that adolescents identify with, and whether individuals living in different slums display a distinct understanding. To answer these questions, we conducted focus groups with adolescents living in slums in RJ (Morro Santa Marta), and in Belo Horizonte, also known as BH (Barragem de Santa Lúcia).

From a theoretical perspective, this study presents two major contributions. First, our general argument gives support to Honneth's thesis that the individuals' attempts to challenge non-recognition or misrecognition help them to uncover their valuable attributes. This is due to the treatment they think they deserve and their relevant achievements. Our findings show that upon watching the episodes of the series, the adolescents were able to detect and assess misrecognition, even if they could not agree about what recognition demands in positive terms. Study participants in both cities were generally dissatisfied with their representation, and expressed feelings of outrage and indignation because what they considered as being their "positive" attributes – "worthy properties" and relevant achievements in different spheres of life – were ignored or not even acknowledged by the series producers.

The second contribution of our study corroborates the view that the attitudes of "recognizing" and "being recognized" are better seen as a conflict-ridden process. Contrary to the critique that Honneth's theory leads to identity essentialization, our findings highlight the complicated and often contradictory attempts involved in expressing recognition.

Our study explores two levels of tension. A first level of conflict is seen between the attempt of representation-makers to build a positive representation and those on the receiving end of the recognition. Media professionals' attempts to clarify problems that require new social understandings obscured valued aspects of this socially-excluded population, along with relevant aspects of social conflicts. A second level of tension in attitudes of recognition is seen among adolescents living in different cities. They criticized distorted recognition in relation to their own community, but tended to use the same negative assumptions and stereotypes when referring to people living in other slums.

This chapter is structured in the following way. The first section clarifies the concept of identity within Honneth's theoretical framework and responds to criticisms that it considers identity as fixed and monolithic, and that this outlook fails to perceive the danger of reification and oppression. We explore Honneth's approach to identity and the morality of recognition. In the second section, we characterize the TV series *Cidade dos Homens* and present the methodology used in this study. The ensuing sections exploit excerpts of discussion groups and focus on different tensions pervading the dynamics of recognition. To conclude, we highlight some of the important interfaces that the mass media establish with the dynamics of recognition in contemporary society.

Recognition or identity politics?

The notion of identity is understood in several ways within recognition studies. Scholars who approach recognition from the perspective of identity politics – such as Nancy Fraser, Iris Young, and Judith Butler – tend to conceive identities of individuals as complex sets of affiliations, mutual identification, and differences in relation to others, along axes such as language, nationality, gender, sexual orientation, race, etc. Other scholars, including Axel Honneth and Charles Taylor, approach recognition through the perspective of Hegel. This point of view tends to consider identity in terms of a broader philosophical treatment of a person based on a set of qualities worthy of value. These values define how subjects come to deserve the respect of others, as a part of various processes of socialization in a given society.

Several scholars are reluctant to tie demands for justice to individual identity; and claim that Honneth's theory is based on an essentialized view of identity that can lead to sectarianisms and domination. In this chapter, we contend that many of these critiques are grounded in an entirely different notion of recognition and do not accurately apply Honneth's assumptions.

Alexander García Düttmann argues that in proposing an "idealized anticipation of the conditions for successful and non-distorted recognition" (Honneth was quoted in Düttmann, 2000, p. 146), Honneth assumes the ideal of a "complete," "intact" and "true" identity. As a result of Honneth describing the contrast between unilateral, myopic, and heterogeneous recognition *and* reciprocal, symmetrical, and homogeneous recognition, Düttmann interprets that recognition struggles would attain a point of stability. According to Düttmann (2000, p. 151), at this stage, recognition "finally exhibits its true, repeatedly re-cognizable, 'undistorted' form or figure." He defends the idea that acts of recognition are based on an inherent conflict that is never free from contradictions and tensions, and therefore never become stable. Any attempt to obtain a non-distorted recognition would paradoxically show that this achievement is always further along the way.

Patchen Markell presents a similar concern. He contends that Honneth invokes an identity image given beforehand as a *fait accompli* – "who the person truly is" – as a criterion for distinguishing recognition from misrecognition (Markell, 2003, p. 23). Operating within an Arendtian paradigm, Markell argues that the ideal of recognition seeks "a clear understanding of who you are and of the nature of the larger groups and communities to which you belong" (2003, p. 12); and this search for self-knowledge may nourish a desire for self-sufficiency, safety, control, and finally, a "sovereign agency." In Markell's words, "the politics of recognition is animated by a vision of sovereign agency, in which people are empowered by self-knowledge and by the confirming of recognition of others to act in accordance with who they really are" (Markell, 2003, p. 63). Drawing on Greek tragedy and Hannah Arendt's view of freedom as non-sovereignty in his *Bound by Recognition*, Markell proposes replacing the notion of "recognition" with "acknowledgement" in order to adequately take into account our own condition of contingency, finitude, and vulnerability. According to Markell (2003, p. 38), "acknowledgment involves coming to terms with, rather than vainly attempting to overcome, the risk of conflict, hostility, misunderstanding, opacity, and alienation that characterizes life among others."

Fraser (2001, p. 24, 2003a) is also particularly dissatisfied with Honneth's theory because, in her view, group identity as an object of recognition projects an image of an "authentic" collective identity which covers up the complexity of people's experiences, multiple belongings, and affiliations. Among several criticisms focusing on Honneth's theory, Fraser argues that when a specific group wishes to defend the validity of their own identity, this intent may give rise to hostility towards other communities and result in either sectarianism or domination over minority sub-groups.

These are important critiques that highlight the dangers of identity reification. While objections that identity politics can lead to sectarianism, animosity among groups, and domination are correct, we do not see Honneth's concept of recognition as conducive to these problems. As was already discussed in Chapter 1, it is misleading to consider Honneth's theory as a version of the "politics of identity"[1] or as similar to Charles Taylor's model of "politics of recognition." Taylor's project revolves around the idea of new social movements seeking acceptance within the specificities of groups and differing forms of life. Unlike Taylor, who focuses on Hegel's *Phenomenology*, Honneth surveys Jena manuscripts in order to explain social integration in both antagonist and normative ways by reflecting the influence of Habermas. Honneth also draws on Mead as a means to explain identity as socially constituted and yet open to continuous innovation. Thus, his program is based on the idea that human beings, as they are intersubjectively constituted, are vulnerable and dependent on the nature of others' responses within social and historical conditions in order to develop.

Before presenting our empirical study, it is important to clarify certain key aspects of Honneth's account of the relationship between recognition and identity, in order to evince the tensions within the dynamics of recognition. To begin with, Honneth usually uses terms such as "self-realization," "integral development," and "positive self-relation," instead of "identity" to refer to his model of subjectivity (Deranty, 2009, p. 431). He does not assume that identity should be taken as a positive – or set of "already formed," "pre-established," attributes that a particular group claim should be recognized and valued (in the sense of posterior confirmation), when facing distorted recognition or non-recognition in a given social context. Rather, Honneth presents a radical inter-subjectivist theory of subjective formation. By updating the insights of Hegel's original writings with Mead's social psychology,[2] the German philosopher assumes that the self can only develop in a constant interactive and intersubjective process. In other words, subjects learn to relate to themselves by integrating attitudes that others address towards them. Thus, recognition as described by Honneth may be better understood as a *condition* for constructing the self and identity (Deranty, 2009, pp. 433–434; Ferrarese, 2009, p. 604).

Secondly, because subjects depend on recognition from others, Honneth, like Habermas,[3] assumes that vulnerability is a central condition for subjective formation: "they [the individuals] owe their identity to the construction of a practical self-relation that is dependent upon the help and affirmation of other human beings" (Honneth, 2007a, p. 136). The basic premise operating here is that a person becomes able to develop his or her true autonomy – bodily and psychological security; ability to take part in responsible action; chance to make socially estimated contributions – with a dependence on other subjects. Subject formation is therefore seen as intrinsically related with social and historical conditions that enable or obstruct integral self-development. Honneth's account of different kinds of self-relations and their social conditions[4] has a much broader consequence on democratic politics than the notion of identity politics, defined in terms of group valorization.

Thirdly, "recognition" according to Honneth's theoretical framework, should be seen as a moral act, besides its social and political dimensions. Honneth states, "acts of recognition are oriented not towards one's own aims but rather towards the evaluative qualities of others" (Honneth, 2002, p. 513).[5] He defends the view that the recognition act is intrinsically connected to the aim of protecting human beings from injury: "morality is the quintessence of the attitudes that we are mutually obliged to adopt in order to secure jointly the conditions of our personal integrity" (Honneth, 2007a, p. 137). He argues that "to recognize someone is to perceive in his or her person a value quality that motivates us intrinsically to no longer behave egocentrically, but rather in accordance with the intentions, desires, and needs of that person" (Honneth, 2007b, p. 337). Although the desire for domination and sovereign agency – which Markell fears – is an ever present risk in human relationships, according to Honneth these factors should not be seen as a result of struggles for recognition.

As a fourth and final point, identity in Honneth's program is never finished or fixed, but rather it is open to permanent innovation within conflict-ridden interactions in society. The specific values of groups are fragmented and pluralized, and because some groups have more power than others, compromises for social integration are never symmetrical or perfectly equitable. Individuals can still experience harm even when rules are institutionalized and policies are implemented to overcome unfair situations. Thus, social arrangements are constantly open to debate as they still fail to provide an appropriate remedy or meet more demanding normative expectations. Struggles for recognition do not assume a fixed *telos*, as some authors have suggested (Düttmann, 2000; Tully, 2000), but are subject to indeterminacy and contingency.

From this theoretical background, my collaborator and I have extracted some important implications for crafting our empirical study. To begin with, we assume that the TV series *Cidade dos Homens* can be understood as an expression of recognition granted by the NGO *Nós do Cinema* and the TV Globo media producers to the low-income population living in slums. We assume that this attitude of recognition is an intentional act of will. It involves a cognitive dimension – a practical and affective response – that takes note of "valuable qualities" in others. This does not mean that these agents adequately or correctly interpret and express these qualities.

The scope of this study is not to analyze the images and narratives in *Cidade dos Homens*. We are concerned with examining the adolescents' perceptions of the meanings conveyed in this TV series. Since the reciprocal dynamics of recognition cannot be externally deduced, we understand that it is essential to investigate how adolescents living in slums describe and assess the alleged expression of recognition in this program

Following the recognition-theoretical approach, our work accepts that recognition is important for individuals to establish positive practical self-relations. Therefore, we assume that the adolescent slum-dwellers in our case study are likely to, in some way, take note, reject, accept, or interact with the symbolic television representation and alleged expression of recognition. Our hypothesis is that once study participants identify negative experiences of denigration and disrespect in the TV series, they will vocalize expectations that were violated, by contesting and trying to correct misrecognition. By doing so, they may reveal shortcomings, problems, or even further forms of oppression in the alleged attitudes of recognition.

Surely, less powerful agents – such as the slum-dwellers in our case study – are unable to directly sanction the understanding of more powerful agents, like mass media professionals. Even when disadvantaged groups – including poor people themselves – seek to provide knowledge for the purpose of revising their treatment by other groups of society, they face huge difficulties due to poverty, illiteracy, and social and political exclusion. Nevertheless, we still comprehend that such a critical stance is not necessarily absent. Based on these considerations, our study attempts to answer the following questions: What is the self-identity that the adolescent slum-dwellers express when confronted with the imagery and narratives in *Cidade dos Homens*? Which judgments that the producers of this TV series made about the community were relevant to these adolescents? What counts as recognition? Do adolescents living in slums in different cities assess the TV series in significantly different ways?

The TV Series *Cidade dos Homens*

In this section, we draw attention to the complicated and often contradictory attempts by media producers to build "positive" representations of disadvantaged groups, when seeking to offer an attitude of recognition. Whereas outright stereotypical portrayals and group defamation can be easily identified, it is far more difficult to define "accurate" forms of representation. As was already discussed in Chapter 2, groups are made up of individuals with plural values that have distinct sets of affiliation and complex experiences. As a result, there is no ideal way of representing ethnic-racial, religious, linguistic collectivities because there is no single character that can stand for the entire group (Mittell, 2010, p. 329). Furthermore, collective interests are not given, but rather created and transformed dynamically throughout political processes. Thus, there is always a great deal of indeterminacy regarding collective preferences; and members of a given group often disagree on values, interests, or beliefs that are claimed as being relevant to them. The population living in both slums in our case study is diversified and features heterogeneous groups and pluralistic ethical values.

A number of studies, as was discussed in Chapter 2, show that media programs aimed at challenging prevalent stereotyping of disadvantaged groups – by offering new unconventional roles and flexibility of identity, or by providing space for marginalized self-expression of subjects – are often seen as problematic since they are linked to elite perspectives or customary modes of commercial production. These types of representations can become didactic, inauthentic, or fall back to hegemonic patterns, through humor and exaggeration (Dennis, 2009, p. 191; Fürsich, 2010; Hamburger, 2007; Larson, 2006). Attempts to develop positive representation can create contradictions and new forms of domination with consequences that cannot be foreseen and controlled (Alsultany, 2012; Avila-Saavedra, 2009; Grijó & Sousa, 2012).

In our case study, we deal with a situation in which media professionals are aware of their dominant position and the stereotypes used in regular news reporting. While it is not entirely clear why media agents attempt to overcome prejudice and undervaluation of the population living in slums – a specific research project would be needed to address this question – it is important to explain that this TV series is not an isolated initiative in the Brazilian context. In the last decade, a growing number of films and TV programs in Brazil – including fictional dramas, documentaries, soap operas, and TV series – have brought the universe of impoverished living to the center of the public's visibility, where poor people and blacks are the protagonists[6] (Bentes, 2007; Hamburger, 2007, 2011; Rocha, 2005, 2006). These productions depict life in slums utilizing various perspectives, genres, and narrative styles.[7] Some representations build the storyline from the perspective of people living in slums themselves,[8] while others use professional artists in studio scenography.[9]

Following Honneth's framework, we can assume that the media producers' act of recognition in *Cidade dos Homens* is not "ahistorically" given, but signals towards changes in the configuration of social interactions. Most importantly, Honneth's program instructs us to see this act of recognition as constituted by "revisable grounds for the value or worth of other persons" (Honneth, 2002, p. 508).

In order to understand the issue at stake, a brief discussion focusing on the contours of the prejudices against slum-dwellers in Brazil and the most common stereotypes related to them is necessary. Studies have shown that slum-dwellers are often perceived as being poor – a perspective that carries several negative connotations throughout time (Demo, 2002; Oliveira, 1997; Rocha, 2005, 2006; Zaluar, 1997, 2004). The term "favelado" (those who live in slums) was originally given to a population of ex-slaves who lived in shanty settlements on hills around the center of RJ (Zaluar & Alvito, 2003, p. 8; Burgos, 2005).

Scholars argue that during the first decades of the 20th century, slums were perceived as being places of promiscuity and idleness that harbored vagabonds, criminals, crooks, robbers, and prostitutes. Slum-dwellers were seen living an existence considered as deviant or even sub-human. The sociologist Luciano Oliveira (1997, p. 51) stresses that people living in slums were "expelled…from the *orbit of humankind* itself."

During the period of Brazilian modernization and industrialization, the slums came to be seen as "the opposite of a city" and their inhabitants were considered "social outcasts" without "urbanity, hygiene, work ethics, betterment, and civility" (Burgos, 2005, p. 190). A number of scholars point out that poor people living in these informal and unauthorized settlements came to be seen as groups that could not adapt to the logic of the market; they had none of the required competencies for work, and thus, were "economically unnecessary" or "dispensed labor" (Oliveira, 1997). Furthermore, slum-dwellers, who usually lacked formal education and did not fulfill the requirements necessary for political participation, were also viewed as "disorganized popular sectors," "sub-citizens," or "structural rabble" (Souza, 2004, p. 109; see also Souza, 2009, 2011).

In the 1970s and 1980s, the slums started to face new problems due to the expansion of drug dealing and organized crime. Terror was imposed both by factions seeking to control the commerce of drugs and weapons, as well as the police, who attempted to repress illegal activities. In this context, slum-dwellers were perceived as being a dangerous threat to social order, and therefore were to be eliminated (Oliveira, 1997, p. 51; Souza, 2006, 2009). Everyone, children included, came to be considered suspects and potential criminals.

In such a context, the production team of *Cidade dos Homens* used several strategies to challenge most crude and blatant stereotyping towards people living in poor neighborhoods. To begin with, this TV series was not produced according to the conventional logic of large broadcasting companies, as Rede Globo professionals joined efforts with an NGO that states its mission is to "promote the inclusion of low-income communities by using films and video-technology."[10] *Nós do Cinema* offers film-making and acting courses to young people living in poor communities. This NGO created and developed the script for *Cidade dos Homens* within a larger set of actions meant to empower poor people to produce their own videos and express their own identity and narratives. As a way of decreasing the control of the production's crew over the representation and scenario, the series was filmed in the slum Morro Santa Marta in RJ. As mentioned earlier, the cast – including the protagonists – consisted mostly of slum-dwellers rather than professional actors. Notwithstanding the unequal distribution of power between TV Globo filmmakers and the people it portrayed, the production of *Cidade dos Homens* can be perceived as a conscious effort to creatively integrate the images and voices of slum-dwellers into the mainstream media sphere.

Thus, there are valid grounds for assuming that media producers sought to somewhat avoid problematic representations. One of the directors of *Cidade dos Homens* clearly expressed his intention to alleviate stereotypes and prejudices against the low-income population by providing space for different roles. Characters were portrayed as more than just victims, threatening people, or exotic individuals:

> JORGE FURTADO: "...the TV series talks about the daily life of these communities, the hardship and difficulties of life, the grandmother

that makes snacks to sell, or the mother who works as a domestic servant. This is why it's cool, for it helps to revert and end prejudice" (DVD of the first year that the Television series was aired, in 2002).[11]

Another director of the TV series expressed his attempt to raise public awareness about the fact that there are common issues regarding people, humanity, problems in everyday life, and community engagement in poorer suburbs:

> GEORGE MOURA: "When *Cidade dos Homens* was aired, the idea was … to show that daily dramas were present in slums, that it was not only the matter of violence because of drug dealing. *Cidade dos Homens* has shown this throughout these years by *chronicling the private lives* of its main characters."[12]

It should be noted that the TV producers consciously attempted to publicly express what they considered relevant qualities of slum-dwellers. To reiterate, this does not mean that they have effectively moved away from conventional TV narratives, or that even such an alleged expression of recognition is an "appropriate" or "correct" one. Indeed, this TV series received several criticisms in Brazil. In a study analyzing news articles from when *Cidade dos Homens* was aired, Simone Rocha (2006) shows that several speakers argued that the series did not break down dominant regimes of symbolic representation of "the poorer suburbs on TV." These critics contested that the series represents an aestheticization of the slums, a spectacularization of poverty, and the infantilism of the narrative focus (Rocha, 2006, pp. 13–14).

Methodology

We adopted unique methodological strategies in order to develop our study. First, we decided to form focus groups with adolescents because the TV series narrative was built from the perspective of two adolescent protagonists – Acerola and Laranjinha. A secondary step was to investigate how this TV series – which clearly refers to Morro Santa Marta in RJ – would be interpreted by adolescents living in this location, along with adolescents living in slums in other cities, namely BH. The third component of our study was to utilize the perspective of adolescents who participated in civic groups in their community. These individuals were targeted because our intention was to discuss recognition relationships with subjects who were already engaged in some kind of civic association.

Based on this research design, we contacted adolescents from the following groups:[13]

1. The ECO group, in the *Morro Santa Marta* in RJ.[14] This is a voluntary association created in 1977. Their members met weekly to debate topics related to politics in general, the importance of collective actions, life in their neighborhood, as well as particular issues including drugs, health, sexuality, and so forth. The participants produce a newspaper (*Journal ECO* – four issues per year), organize dramatic arts, poetry, and musical performances, as well as sports and leisure activities.
2. The Agente Jovem group, from the *Barragem Santa Lúcia favela* in BH. This group was created by an NGO in partnership with the local government with the purpose of providing alternative activities for young people when they were not attending school. Members of this group met three times a week to debate topics similar to those addressed by the group in RJ. They also meet to participate in workshops and take part in sports activities.

In both groups, the adolescents were aged from 15 to 18 years. Our initial contact with these groups occurred in August and September 2005. Communication with the study participants was facilitated by the fact that the adolescents already had regular meetings. The researcher Simone Rocha engaged in their meetings, participated in their cultural events, and visited a few households before explaining her presence for the purpose of developing this study. Following these contacts, she carried out the focus group meetings in October, November, and December 2005. Two focus groups were conducted in each city; in BH each group had 10 participants, and in RJ each group had between four to six participants.

We used the focus group technique because it aims at building meaning through collective discussion, rather than individual reflection (Barbour & Kitzinger, 2001; Bryman, 2001; Marques & Rocha, 2006; Morgan, 1997; Warr, 2005). The focus group dynamics started with the moderator showing the four first episodes of *Cidade dos Homens* to motivate collective debate. Discussion followed a semi-structured script organized into three axes: (i) the relationship between the slum where the adolescents lived and the TV series representation; (ii) the perception of the representation of slum-dwellers on TV programs in general (i.e. in films, news, advertisements, and so on); (iii) the relationship between slum-dwellers and people living in the city – an opposition usually referred to in Brazilian society as "the hill and the asphalt." We used three methods for registering the adolescents' opinions and dialogues: (i) recording the debates of the focus groups; (ii) recording individual oral statements that some adolescents spontaneously wished to provide; and (iii) written statements that the majority of participants chose to produce in the first group in BH.

What is the self-identity that adolescent slum-dwellers express when watching the television series?

It is clear that every interpretation of media content takes place in a specific social and historical context, over a cultural background with a set of expectations, in which participants make sense of themselves, others, and the social order. After the exhibition of episodes from the TV series, the adolescents showed that they were uncomfortable with the series' representation of everyday life in slums. Rio de Janeiro (RJ) adolescents agreed that what was shown in the TV series was in fact what happened in the slums. Nevertheless, they argued that violence should not be perceived as being a synonym for daily life in slums, because their experiences are multiple and much richer than what was shown in *Cidade dos Homens*:

(Morro Santa Marta) Monique: "I think that on the hills [slums] there are a million things happening that are not criminal. But the goal of the film is to focus on criminality.

Vanessa: Well, in the film [TV series] I think it showed only the negative side of daily life; there is more than bullets in the neighborhood, there are activities. I think they wanted so much to show the reality, that they went too deep into the negative side only, like children thinking about crime, teenagers selling drugs, people shooting each other here and there..."

Fátima: "In the episodes I watched, I think they were accurate, I think they did not exaggerate. Of course the hill is not always like they showed, of course not....But it is true that it happens, it is really true....I think they were very fortunate in what they showed. I think they did good research, because I thought it was very real. Of course it is not like that all the time."

BH adolescents also expressed concern that the TV series showed only violence, the power of drug dealing, and lack of security. They claimed that what was shown "was not true" for their own reality:

> (BARRAGEM SANTALÚCIA– BH) MODERATOR: "How do you think slums were shown in this TV series?"
> ELISANDRA: "Through the eyes of higher-class guys... [who] think that just because there are blacks and slum-dwellers, they are street kids, criminals, who were about to rob them."
> DANILO: "It only showed the ugly side of slums, the dark side. It did not show the other things that slums have."
> RITA: "Even the time in which it was aired. Was it so violent to the point of being shown only late at night? Why?"

Adolescents in our focus groups bring up socially acquired background knowledge to express awareness of the demeaning evaluation of their lives. Like Honneth notes, they are reflecting "personal disappointment as something that affects not only the individual self, but also the circle of many other subjects" (Honneth, 2003b, p. 258). They repeatedly contest that they were portrayed only from a negative perspective and through stigmas such as being "street kids," "idlers," "blacks," "crooks," and "criminals." Participants exhibit awareness that they indeed live in an environment of violence and fear, but that "there are a million [other] things happening" and that "it is not like that all the time." Such a perception is coherent with sociological studies that contend that middle and upper classes in Brazil see slum-dwellers as a homogeneous, needy, or dangerous social type, and that slums are places that reflect multiple "lacks" and social chaos (Zaluar & Alvito, 2003; Rocha, 2005, 2006; Souza, 2006, 2011; Zaluar, 1997, 2004).

Moreover, the adolescents are also able to stress the "normalization" of such patterns of representation. They are aware of the undervaluation and the negative behavior they can expect to receive from the middle and upper class perspective:

> SÉRGIO HENRIQUE: "No, I'm not impressed. For me it is normal, it is routine. Not constantly, but unfortunately it only shows negative things...."
> ANGÉLICA: "I think that today, people who live in the districts, upon watching the film, it reaffirms what they think about slum-dwellers. And they think that there is only war, criminals, and drug dealing in the [slum] hills."

SÉRGIO HENRIQUE: "…Honestly, if the idea was to bring slums and districts closer, in my opinion, they did a lousy job. Because it is not good."

The adolescents clearly expressed feelings of humiliation because, in their eyes, the TV series represented them in an unfair way. They did not complain much about class inequality, spatial segregation, or marginalized housing conditions, but rather the stigma of failure and propensity towards crime and delinquency that was highlighted. The focus group participants responded to misrecognition in three major ways. To begin with, they criticize any real or imagined assumptions about common characteristics of slum-dwellers, except for their sense of being collectively undervalued – the only shared experience they have is that of being discriminated against. Such a conflict is clearly expressed in Rita's words: "Is there only violence in slums? If so, why are we here?" This concept also arises in Sérgio Henrique's words "you don't become a 'favelado' just because you live in a slum."

Secondly, the adolescents criticize any generalization of negative attributes, which in fact should be applied only to a minority of people living in slums.

(MORRO SANTA MARTA) FÁTIMA: "The problem is in the way that they showed it, the impression that we get is that most people in slums are like that; but it is not so, do you know? It is a minority, do you understand? Folks work, study, and have little time to play around in the middle of the streets."

(BARRAGEM SANTALÚCIA) DANILO: "Just like I have said already. Many people that live down there [in the districts], who have money, think that those who live here are crooks, those who live here steal things, are idle, bums, and have nothing to do. But it is not like that. There are people who work, who wish to raise their kids. There are many college students in our neighborhood. *Here there are more individuals than idle people. Bums, I can say, are not even 1% or 2%; 1.5%.*"

Thirdly, the adolescents protest against distinct forms of misrecognition in several spheres. They express that when they are not represented with dignity in the TV series in regards to their intimate relationships, that this hurts the integrity of those who take care of and attempt to fulfill the needs of their loved ones. Their expectations of being treated with respect in the political realm are violated when they are seen as being second-class citizens. As a result, their engagements in political and civic projects are neglected. Furthermore, they are frustrated by not being valued for their particular capacities and cooperation on collective projects, and this is detrimental to those who study, work, and contribute "to a million things happening in favelas":

> (Morro Santa Marta) Bruno: "It only showed the criminal side, violence, and racism. There are projects here, several NGOs... "
>
> Andriele: "They didn't show the social projects in the slum. The family union that may not be that much but there is some. No, that isn't shown."
>
> Fátima: "I think they got it wrong by not showing many of the good things in slums. But they said they did, for instance, when a boy is shown going to school; but it is so little. That is, *we ended up with the idea that there are only crooks in slums*, that children are introduced to crime very early on."

The adolescents call attention to the conflict between socially sanctioned misrecognition and a positive self-understanding that they, in some manner, are able to build. During the discussions, they appear to have frames and languages that allow them to distance themselves from the predominant views in society. As we will discuss in the next section, the adolescents clearly question misrecognition, even if they do not fully articulate or elaborate what recognition should mean in a positive way. They draw on abundant evidence from their everyday life in slums to critically express "what" needs to be recognized.

What judgment did the TV series producers make about the community that was relevant to the adolescents? What counts as recognition?

Given the adolescents' insistence that the TV series presented only the negative side of slums, we intervened in this debate to suggest that by being so used to seeing slums represented negatively, they might be predisposed to interpret any message in this light. We considered this observation was justified because of the oscillations and contradictions in the adolescents' opinions. If on the one hand they protested that the series focused on violence, they also confirmed, on the other hand, that their environment was in fact violent. It should be kept in mind that the TV series producers thought that one of the program's "advances," in contrast to conventional media programs, was to approach daily life in the slums in such a way as to show human dramas pertaining to the family, education, and work. After all, what would the adolescents consider an adequate representation of them and what would count as recognition?

> (Morro Santa Marta) Moderator: "But didn't the television series try to show other things, not only violence? For instance, kids going to school, being concerned with their grandmother, their sister, with friendships – isn't this another representation of slums and its inhabitants?"
>
> Marcos: "Yes, of course. If my mother is not feeling well, of course I will be concerned about her."
>
> Isabele: "I don't think that this type of concern shows the positive side of slums. I don't think so. *For if you take any criminal here, of course they worry about their mothers*, just like any normal person worries about his or her mother. No, I don't think there is a positive side that is specific to slums."

The adolescents complain that the TV series, in spite of depicting some characters' positive feelings, such as expressions of love and friendship, did not really show the personal value of slum-dwellers; for "any normal person" or even "criminals" display kindness towards their loved ones. In this sense, the adolescents share the perception that, although the TV series intended to offer an adequate representation, it only touched upon aspects that "merely" insert them within the circle of humankind. They make it clear that this type of recognition response – that is, to be seen as human beings with positive feelings – is indeed insulting. In a conversation sequence from the BH group, Rose states that the demonstration of friendship between the young protagonists was a positive point in the series – "It was good for people to see that those who live in slums also have feelings." To contest this view, Rita states that such an assumption is actually an insult to people living in poor neighborhoods: "But, do people really need this to go on TV for them to see it?"

Recognition requires that persons take notice of the value and needs of the other. According to Honneth (2007b, p. 337), "when we take up the stance of recognition, the evaluative qualities of the other, not one's own intentions, are what guide our behavior." Acts of recognition entail, as Deranty states, "to *see* in him or her, the needs and the interests that demand to be fulfilled" (Deranty, 2009, p. 367; see also Honneth, 2007b, p. 332; Ikäheimo & Laitinen, 2007, p. 44). In the same vein, Laitinen argues that "to say that 'to recognize'" in the relevant sense is not necessarily "to take as a person," but rather, "to regard as someone who counts as a possessor of some normatively relevant features" (Laitinen, 2010, p. 336). The adolescents showed indignation because the TV series does not show the properties and qualities they considered as potentially making a difference in how they are perceived and treated by others.

In a discussion with the Morro Santa Marta group, participants complain that the depiction of friendship between the protagonists was indeed based on a negative underground viewpoint. Monique complains that: "Friendship led Laranjinha to ask for money on the drug corner so that he could give money to his friend." Regarding classes at school, Sérgio Henrique says: "The kids at school were never shown sitting in a decent class…the class was always disorderly, kids throwing bits of paper, what the teacher said was incorrect; she didn't even answer their questions. She was a hysterical teacher that was always shouting."

Fighting for their dignity, the focus group participants affirm that they were not the "other," but rather "decent" college students, workers, and worthy people with multiple qualities and achievements. The adolescents thereby seek to disclose their truly relevant attributes and achievements that the TV series obscures: their concerns and abilities in regards to "a million things," their involvement in the "initiatives in the hills," and work on "NGO programs and projects." These unaddressed characteristics could potentially make a moral difference by showing that they are, in Honneth's terms, "equally entitled to autonomy and equally capable of achievement" (Honneth, 2007b, p. 337).

(Morro Santa Marta) Sérgio Henrique: "We have so many projects here. Producing events, with sound effects, NGOs; look, we spent a lot of time doing courses, but we don't see any news about this, about anything. This is what is amazing."

Angélica: "But this will not sell. Nobody wants to buy a newspaper because slum kids are graduating from some course. What do they want to see? They want to see gun shootings."

Fátima: "One thing is true: in TV news and printed press, they [the producers] find it very hard indeed to divulge good things about slums. It's incredible. If there is a gunshot at night here, then it fills up with reporters. Now, there are activities here in the slum, including our group [ECO]; my dear, you have to really sweat to bring a reporter up here. More are coming these days; why? Because the state government is here, to urbanize the slum."

The adolescents have good reason to be angry and resentful of their misrepresentation. Several studies have shown that in the past Brazilian slums were the communities of people who did not share the ethics of modern labor. However, this naïve image no longer applies to the current reality. Scholars have argued that people living in poor neighborhoods have long adopted attitudes of the *homo economicus*. In the economic sphere, inhabitants of slums think and act according to market rules, seek opportunities to raise their incomes, and engage in speculation of their homes and land, even if it is invaded land (Burgos, 2005; Taschner, 2003). There is an active market, albeit mostly informal, in the mid-sized and large slums of RJ, in which goods and services are traded to an ever more diversified and consuming population (Valladares, 2005). Furthermore, entrepreneurs, NGOs, community leaders, and public agents have undertaken several initiatives to urbanize, pacify, and change slums into tourist sites, within the logic of global capitalism; and guides and advertisements about "alternative tourism" circulate world-wide (Freire-Medeiros, 2007).

In the cultural sphere, a number of studies point out that slums have more than just traditional religious feasts, music, or soccer, but rather new expressions of art – hip hop, funk, and the so-called marginal literature (Cruz, 2007; Hamburger, 2007, 2011). Several initiatives led by the low-income population seek to value marginalized identities and contest exclusion and the narrowness of territorial stereotypes that separate the city from the hills. Many communication initiatives in slums autonomously produce and disseminate information of interest to these populations – including news agencies, independent video productions, internal TV channels, community radios, blogs, and specific websites (Cruz, 2007; Hamburger, 2007, 2011). These are multifarious expressions of different groups, with distinct identities, values, beliefs, and interests.

Furthermore, in the political field the slums have a tradition of organized political movements, such as the Central Única das Favelas (CUFa – Unified Center for Slums) and the Movimento Popular de Favelas (Popular Slum Movement). The literature reports the effervescence of civic engagement by slum-dwellers in RJ and in other major Brazilian cities (Burgos, 2005; Leite, 2003; Machado da Silva & Leite, 2004). Indeed, despite these associations facing several problems, people living in the slums find many routes for organizing resistance, including through demonstrations and protests against violence. They also act as subsidiaries supporting government programs and services, and cooperate with NGOs and other civic groups.

The adolescents in our focus groups, being aware of their value, want to confirm their self-perception by gaining recognition from others ("people down there," "those who live in districts," "people who have money"). Invisibility of the qualities considered relevant by the youths is humiliating because it implies, in Honneth's terms, "non-existence in a social sense" (Honneth, 2001, p. 111). Study participants have rather to fight against the maligned perception of slum-dwellers as being criminal and dangerous.

The exercise of describing their condition in terms of poverty involves several ambiguities. While it is clear that the adolescents disclose their expectation of recognition for their dignity, cultural deeds and civic engagement, they do not seem to emphasize unfair social conditions and economic inequalities. Issues such as economic marginalization, poorly paid work, restricted access to higher standard of living do not seem to have played a prominent role in constructing their identities during group conversation. We could notice in our visit to study participants' houses that they had access to diverse goods similar to middle class standards and many of them studied in private school, by means of grants. However, they faced, of course, problems of redistribution and inequalities of labor division in the social system.

The theory of recognition instructs us to see the sources of recognition as distinct in different spheres, even if they relate closely to each other. It is worth stressing that demands for recognition are essentially incomplete if issues of material fulfillment are not addressed. Our study provide good evidence for viewing that effects of poverty and inequality do not undermine individuals' self-development in other spheres. Economic deprivation does not damage the adolescents' understanding of themselves as reflective beings, with self-respect and agency. However, economic exclusion is different and cannot go unmarked.

The adolescents' self-descriptions contain their own contradictions. On the one hand, study participants somewhat acknowledge their worth not only as people, but also as citizens and individuals with relevant social projects. They are able to contest several predicaments of "the poor" in prevailing terms of those in need, in absolute deprivation and insecurity. Even when recognition is denied under existing social conditions, the adolescents seem able to imagine another situation in which inequalities and marginalization are reduced.[15] On the other hand, study-participants' statements appear to dilute elements of misrecognition due to unfair economic exchange (employment, housing, education, transportation) and thus convey the idea that these problems could be solved by their achievement of recognition in other spheres. They do not say in sufficient detail how socio-structural barriers in the realm of labor restrict their self-development and their inclusion in society. Keeping the three spheres of recognition in view is therefore important for identifying inherent obscurities in their demands for recognition.

Is there a difference between the self-awareness of adolescents in different slums?

Honneth (2003b, p. 259) speaks of "anticipated recognition" and Ikäheimo and Laitinen (2007, p. 47) use the term of "imagined" recognition to explain how disadvantaged subjects do not passively accept their reduced social status or their subordination. In the context of our research, we asked the adolescents how they think about inhabitants of other slums and their everyday situations. Could they project an "image of the community" and express "recognitional behavior" (Honneth, 2007c, p. 337; Ikäheimo & Laitinen, 2007, p. 44) in the sense of perceiving the qualities and values of those who live in other slums?

Our question focusing on whether events shown in the TV series could be generalized to represent other places motivated the adolescents to mark differences between "us" and "them," "here" and "there," and thus, revealed further dilemmas of "recognizing" and "being recognized" (Honneth, 2007c, p. 337). In BH, the adolescents reiterated that the TV series presented a "different" reality with which they could not identify.

(BARRAGEM SANTALÚCIA) WELLINGTON: "The TV series *Cidade dos Homens* shows a reality of slums in RJ, such as the authority of criminals, who decided what was best for the community. The drug-dealing chief prohibited the postman from climbing the hill and chose Acerola to be the new community postman. It also shows another reality, which is that of children walking around armed and doing drugs. They chose this life because, maybe, it is even the government's fault, because they may have forgotten the slums...I think that their problem is that there are many people wanting power and few willing to solve problems, and think about the future of everyone."

ELISANDRA: "The gangs there are far more dangerous. Here, there are also rival gangs...but not as bad. You can't even pass or cross the place; there are people living down there that cannot walk up there. We don't have the commands that they have there, in the drug corners...in Rocinha, RJ; there it is really just like that reality [of the TV series]. Because in the Rocinha, you need permission for everything, to enter [there], to leave; even the police need permission to enter. Whenever the police enter for shootouts with criminals, either a policeman or a crook dies."

The adolescents in BH mention the existence of "drug-dealing chiefs" and "crooks" that are traditionally perceived as being the "owners of the slums" in RJ. Even though they point out that "it is obvious that it has its good side, and there are other projects..." they stress the absence of the means for exercising the most basic civil rights, such as moving around freely and taking control over one's own life. The focus group participants accentuate the early entrance into criminal life of youths, and people's helplessness in a territory characterized by violence – they call it "Rocinha," a famous slum in RJ. They also note that local officials and authority figures lack the will to "solve the problems." These excerpts suggest that the adolescents in BH use the same negative commonsense assumptions that they reject when referring to themselves and their community. Thus, they seem unable to overcome the fear that is inspired by hegemonic representations. Elisandra summarizes it as: "My God! If I lived in a place like that [Morro the Santa Marta slum] I would move away!" Consequently, the demands of study participants for recognition seem as though they are not extended to inhabitants of other slums in RJ.

Interestingly enough, study participants, in a given moment in the context of the conversation in BH, situate their reflection and critique in a standpoint that could break their ordinary convictions. Questioning her peers' views about RJ slum-dwellers, Rita makes the significant remark: "what we are seeing is what the TV is showing, we did not go there to see; we did not live there one single day to perceive how things are." The adolescents agreed that they do not have enough (or consistent) knowledge to make generalizations about the social environment of others. They thus seem to display a concern similar to media theorists regarding the role of the media in shaping "mental models" (Larson, 2006, p. 3; Mittell, 2010, p. 306; van Dijk, 2012, p. 27). Study participants, in this circumstance, seem to have reached a diagnosis that their evaluative and perceptive dispositions about others – with whom they do not have direct personal experiences – could have been informed and shaped by the media.

It should be highlighted that the adolescents in both cities show a general understanding of the mass media as sites of complex, and frequently contradictory, processes. They obviously do not adopt the standpoint of social theorists aiming at articulating sophisticated explanations and adequate evidences. They were able to address different roles of the media, which have to be negotiated in concrete circumstances. They point out that the mass media are economic organizations concerned with profit and that these institutions establish connections with power-holders. The media is also committed to capturing the public's attention. Still, they also acknowledge that media professionals can be regarded as important allies "to produce programs to show our reality." Referring to the intentions of the producers of *Cidade dos Homens*, one study participant in BH summarizes: "at least they [media professionals] are trying [to improve their perceptions] even though we have a lot of resistance." While being able to resist to several flaws in the media producers' vision and expression, the adolescents slum-dwellers themselves, when talking about other social contexts, showed difficulty to publicly expose problems that require a new form of social understanding and appropriate treatment. These contrasts between "recognizing" and "being recognized" contribute to operate on and change each other.

Conclusion

This study examined the morality of recognition by drawing on discussions among adolescent slum-dwellers about a TV series explicitly aimed at producing a more positive representation of the inhabitants of slums and their everyday life. Our findings show that the adolescents, while acknowledging some novelty in the producers' intentions, take note of the shortsighted view of the series and its misunderstanding or negligence of relevant questions. Our study also shows different levels of conflict and opacity in the dynamics of recognizing and being recognized.

Firstly, in the face of the alleged "positive representation" expressed by the producers of the TV series, the adolescents expressed feelings of unfair treatment and vocalized different forms of disrespect, exclusion, and marginalization that were portrayed in the series. Study participants contested the homogenization of slum-dwellers, generalization of negative attributes, as well as the exclusion of important issues in *Cidade dos Homens*. The omission of issues that they considered as morally relevant about themselves and their communities – achievements in family life, education, work, community commitments, civic engagement, and cultural deeds – is outrageous, in the adolescents' eyes. Any of the qualities that could make a difference in the way they are seen and treated by others in society was not even acknowledged.

If one of the editors of *Cidade dos Homens* expressed a desire that this series could contribute to "reverting and ending prejudice," the adolescents showed a clear awareness that, under these circumstances, the series does not offer any help in ameliorating the recognition of the moral and social worth they find within themselves. Although being very critical of the TV series representation of their life, study participants do not raise discussion on the producers' disregard of the historical and social conditions of inequalities in the sphere of production and economic exchange. As a result, they do not spell out in sufficient detail how unjust consequences may affect their lives and threaten their valued ideals in this realm.

In this sense, our study suggests a more serious problem for recognition-theoretical approach. The struggle of disadvantaged groups to receive recognition in one sphere risks obliterating specificities of problems in others. The light that the adolescents shed on their valued qualities in order to show that there is good evidence for revising socially-shared knowledge about slum-dwellers as being dangerous second-class citizens (and the slum as places of chaos and deprivation) seems to obfuscate their disadvantaged place in an unfair social division of the labor system. Although conditions for positive self-development closely relate to one another, they are based on different sources of recognition and neither subsumes the other.

Another level of conflict and opacity in the dynamics of recognition is seen in the disadvantaged groups' description of others who are similarly discriminated against. When projecting an "anticipated" or "imagined" recognition, adolescents in BH seem to have detached themselves from hegemonic representations linked to disrespect and devaluation of slum-dwellers. They showed themselves quite able to contest misrecognition about their lives and environment. However, study participants in BH, when referring to slum-dwelling adolescents in RJ, showed a perception that apparently is in agreement with widespread, socially dominant convictions regarding this population. In this dimension, our study suggests that the attempts of oppressed subjects to clarify problems that emerge in the context of misrecognition may not be enough to disclose problems of others living under apparently similar conditions. Thus, efforts to articulate what needs to be recognized should be continually and mutually adjusted "in accordance with the intentions, desires, and needs" of those seeking recognition (Honneth, 2007b, p. 337). All in all, there is a good case for viewing struggles for recognition as open to permanent conflict, indeterminacy, and contingency.

Notes

1. By taking into consideration different contexts of Honneth's program reception, Jean-Philippe Deranty suggests that the "major factor explaining the widespread misreading of Honneth, probably relates...[to the fact that] in the English-speaking world, especially in North America, the reference to the concept of recognition is always predetermined by the debates in political theory around multiculturalism and Charles Taylor's decisive intervention in them" (Deranty, 2009, pp. 431–432). In the same vein, Chistopher Zurn argues that "such a gross misreading" of Honneth's program is an "overtly-hasty assimilation of Taylor's constricted conception of recognition struggles" (Zurn, 2003, p. 531).

2. To develop this psychological-anthropological argument, Honneth draws on Mead's insights of the inter-subjective nature of the construction of the self, as was discussed in Chapter 1. In Mead's words, self-awareness, "far from being a precondition of the social act, the social act is the precondition of it" (Mead, 1934, p. 18).

3. For Habermas, the "extreme vulnerability" of personal identity is central to the ethics of discourse. In his *Moral Consciousness and Communicative Action*, he says: "Unless the subject externalizes himself by participating in interpersonal relations through language, he is unable to form that inner center that is his personal identity. This explains the almost constitutional insecurity and chronic fragility of personal identity – an insecurity that is antecedent to cruder threats to the integrity of life and limb" (Habermas, 1995, p. 199). In *Justification and Application*, Habermas (1993, p. 109) states: "No one can preserve his integrity by himself alone. The integrity of individual persons requires the stabilization of a network of symmetrical relations of recognition in which non-replaceable individuals can secure their fragile identities in a 'reciprocal' fashion only as members of a community. Morality is aimed at the chronic susceptibility of personal integrity implicit in the structure of linguistically mediated interactions, which is more deep-seated than the tangible vulnerability of bodily integrity, though connected with it."

4. For Honneth, these conditions for integral self-development, as was discussed in Chapter 1, include the provision of an ambient free from physical injuries or degradation for the building of basic self-confidence; without denial of rights for the advancement of self-respect and, finally, free of denigration within a community of value for the promotion of self-esteem.

5. According to Jean-Philippe Deranty (2009, p. 367), "To recognize someone in a normative way is to 'see' in him or her, the needs and interests that demand to be fulfilled...A denial of recognition is the failure on the part of the others to acknowledge, to see, the needy nature of a human subject" (p. 367). Heikki Ikäheimo and Arto Laitinen (2007, p. 44) have proposed that attitudes of recognition involves "taking someone as a person, the content of which is understood and which is accepted by the other person."

6. Examples of films are: *Palace II* (2000); *Cidade de Deus* (2002); *O invasor* (2002); *Carandiru* (2003); *Cidade dos Homens* (2007); *Tropa de Elite I* (2007); *Era uma vez* (2008); *Maré – Nossa História de Amor* (2008); *Tropa de Elite II* (2010); *Cinco Vezes Favela – Agora por nós Mesmos* (2010); *Bróder* (2010); *400 contra 1* (2010); *Totalmente Inocentes* (2012); *Alemão* (2014). Documentaries:

Ônibus 174 (2002); *O Prisioneiro da Grade de Ferro* (2004); *Sou feia, Mas estou na Moda* (2005); *Falcão, Meninos do Tráfico* (2006); *Jardim Ângela* (2006); *Vidigal* (2008); *Favela Bolada* (2008); *Eu, Favela* (2012); *Complexo, Universo Paralelo* (2011); *À Margem do Concreto* (2013); *Pelada – Futebol na Favela* (2013); *Remoção* (2013).

7. Examples of telenovelas are: *Vidas Opostas* (Record, 2006); *Duas Caras* (Globo, 2007); *Salve Jorge* (Globo, 2012); *Lado a lado* (Globo, 2012). TV series: *Turma do Gueto* (Record, 2002); *Cidade dos Homens* (Globo, 2002); *Antonia* (Globo, 2006); *A Lei o e Crime* (Record, 2009); *Suburbia* (Globo, 2012); and TV programs: *Central da Periferia* (Globo, 2006); *Esquenta* (Globo, 2012); *Manos e Minas* (TV Cultura, 2008).

8. The documentary *Falcão, Meninos do Tráfico* (2006), produced by MV Bill and Celso Athayde, is a typical example of a film with its narrative built from the perspective of members from disadvantaged groups. The film aired on the television program *Fantástico*, which is one of the highest rated shows in Brazil.

9. The telenovela *Duas Caras* (2007), written by Aguinaldo Silva and broadcast by Globo TV, is a typical example.

10. The NGO *Nós do Cinema* was created in 2001. Available at http://www.nosdocinema.org.br/mambo.

11. These statements were taken from a DVD of the first four episodes of the television series, shown in 2002. DVD Cidade dos Homens. A production with 2 films – cultural production of the Central Globo de Produção, © 2002 TV Globo Ltda.

12. This statement was taken from a web interview with Simone Rocha on October 24, 2005.

13. Researcher Simone Maria Rocha carried out the entirety of the field research; she was the moderator of all of the focus groups.

14. The Eco Group webpage is available at http://www.ser-eco.org/grupoeco.htm.

15. Here I follow Jean-Philippe Deranty's (2009, p. 44) suggestion that "dominated groups have [in these circumstances] been able to project a different image of the community, one in which domination is reduced, equality better realized."

4
Recognition and Ideology: Assessing Justice and Injustice in the Case of Child Domestic Labor

Rousiley C. M. Maia and Danila Cal

Some cases of injustice are hardly perceived as such by individuals who experience them, even when there are established legal frameworks, public policies and social mobilization to combat a particular situation of injustice. This chapter examines one of these situations, namely child domestic labor (CDL), a deep-rooted socio-cultural practice found in many parts of the world. Our study focuses on CDL in Belém, the state capital of Pará, in Northern Brazil, where the International Labor Organization (ILO) has implanted a pilot program combating child work.

This chapter aims at adding a new layer to the current debate on work, recognition and ideology. While paradoxes of recognition in post-Fordist work have been the subject of several studies (Hartmann & Honneth, 2006; Honneth, 2004; Smith, 2012; Smith & Deranty, 2012), problems of recognition in domestic and informal work involving children remain poorly understood. To examine what disadvantaged subjects identify as injustice in the light of public discourses, as well as their personal experiences, we organized our study along two main lines: (i) an analysis of how the topic CDL is presented in mainstream newspapers in the state of Para from January 2000 to December 2004 – the first five years of the program against CDL in the state of Para (PETID); and (ii) an analysis of conversations about media discourses on CDL gathered in focus groups of women living in poor suburbs of Belém who themselves had been domestic workers in their childhood. The focus groups took place in July and August 2006. Findings show that media professionals acted as agents of advocacy, defending the needs and rights of children and adolescents, and clearly condemned CDL because it involves exploitation, domination and marginalization. For their part, women who had been domestic workers in their childhood contested media discourses and qualified CDL as a good or useful opportunity to gain autonomy and to integrate more positively with society.

Our study, by focusing on social agents' perception of justice and injustice in everyday life, can complement scholarship on recognition, work and the social bonds in two ways. First, we argue that Honneth's approach has great theoretical and critical strength for dealing with the problem of ideology, without falling prey to social relativism and subjectivism alike. The distinction he makes between "ideological" and "justified" forms of recognition enables us to explain why oppressed individuals may more or less fully accept the hierarchy of prestige linked to other power asymmetries, without adding incapacity to the incapacitated (Honneth, 2007b). We contend that Honneth's account, however, needs clarification and extension in cases in which oppressed individuals transit from expectations in different spheres of recognition that generate contradictory oppressive effects. Our study, by evincing the interweaving of logics across the spheres of love and work, can contribute to advance understanding of conditions that undermine critical reflection, when long-standing cultural framework underscores class-based oppression.

Second, insofar as Honneth's theory provided guidance to our study at various levels of analysis, we are left with no explanation of how subjugated individuals can overcome domination in cases of ideological recognition. His account fails to take full measure of the role played by justice advocators in struggles for recognition. Thus, our study, by reappraising the link between the perspective of subordinate groups as well as that of moral entrepreneurs in processes of emancipation, can help fill this gap. We outline an argument that explains how moral entrepreneurs' critique of ideology can exert an emancipatory function in struggles for recognition. We argue that this is necessary for building both socially effective critique and sociological models aiming at advancing social justice.

This chapter is divided into six sections. The first section presents critiques of the recognition theory with respect to issues of power and ideology. Next, we briefly contextualize our case study, describing regulations pertaining to CDL and pointing to some of the public policies and programs created by civic associations aimed at combating this type of work in Brazil, and specifically in Para state. In the third section, we describe the methodology used in this study. The fourth section presents the main discourses about CDL in the local media, within the selected time frame. Then, we examine the results of focus groups in the fifth and sixth sections and next we discuss the relation between vulnerability, ideology-critique and agency. We conclude with a summary of empirical results and possible normative implications for further studies on the issue of ideology and relations of recognition.

Recognition and ideology

Honneth's theory of recognition underlines the nexus between individuals' development and social practices of humiliation and disrespect that prevent individuals from establishing a positive practical self-relation (Honneth, 1996). As was already discussed, the central idea is that if denial of recognition or distorted recognition on the one hand undermines the essential condition for development of human autonomy, on the other hand it provides the moral motivation that sets in motion struggles for recognition. Although "recognition" is usually understood as the opposite of disrespect, denegation of rights and subjugation, it has recently also been seen an ideological form of consciousness with regulative power. Within different traditions – neo-Marxian, post-Hegelian and feminist studies, a number of scholars (Bader, 2007; Rogers, 2009; Rössler, 2007; Young, 2007) have pointed out that recognition in some cases may legitimate value hierarchies in the social order and justify the subordination of certain groups to others in daily-life routines; hence recognition would evoke a self-understanding that molds subjects to their expected social roles in society.

The notion of ideology is at the kernel of these criticisms. Although the concept of ideology has obviously a complex history, with varied debates in different traditions of sociological and political thought,[1] a number of scholars draw our attention to the fact that a form of social consciousness is ideological because of certain properties (Geuss, 1981; Rostbøll, 2008; Shelby, 2003). At an epistemic level, critics claim that an ideological system of beliefs (or a worldview widely shared by members of a given group and known to be so), through which individuals make sense of themselves and their own social situations, has some kind of cognitive defect, such as the lack of empirical support, consistency, logical validity and so forth. At a functional level, critics highlight that the wide acceptance of this network of beliefs helps to establish and sustain relations of power that are systematically asymmetrical, or further the interests of a hegemonic group. At a genetic level, scholars pay attention to the negative features of the history or the origin of such a worldview that obstruct or curtail it in some way.

Our concern here is with the relation of recognition and ideological forms of consciousness. Increasingly sophisticated studies have shown that recognition can operate as a form of social cognition that coordinates actions across relations of domination. In this context, recognition facilitates social integration because these beliefs go unrecognized and usual observations of everyday life seem often to confirm them. In the field of philosophy and sociology of work, Emmanuel Renault, Nicholas H. Smith and Jean-Philippe Deranty claim that the post-Fordist organizations and the new neoliberal management in complex and pluralist societies provide a typical example: the recognition of increased autonomy, creativity and flexibility for workers often results in more precarious working conditions and a lower negotiating scope (Deranty, 2012; Renault, 2010, p. 245; Smith, 2009, 2012; Schmidt am Busch, 2010, p. 258). Increased opportunity for individual self-realization is converted into a relentless pressure for re-invention of oneself in order to keep the job or maintain the career, which in turn brings anxiety, illness and oppression. Broader possibilities for individual self-expression impinge on employees' responsibilities for things beyond their control. On the expansion of the recent capitalist labor market, Honneth himself acknowledges that the alleged recognition may turn paradoxically into an agent of oppression (Honneth, 2004, 2010). Taking into account the practical conversion of normative intentions, Hartmann and Honneth (2006, p. 47) claim that "a contradiction is paradoxical when, precisely through the attempt to realize such an intention, the probability of realizing it is decreased."

Differently from post-Fordist work, forms of power imbedded in the informal economy of domestic labor, childcare and care work, flow across the spheres of social esteem and love. Both Beate Rössler (2007) and Iris Young (2007) lucidly argue that the theory of recognition, although attentive to the implications of the division of labor in families and the struggle of women for esteem, does not adequately address forms of power across spheres of love or of social esteem that contribute to reproducing predominant gender-based division of labor. By approaching different rationalities in family work (including childcare) and paid work, Rössler (2007) seeks to show that the principle of esteem based on economically remunerative labor may hide issues of well-being that may count as recognition in domestic work. Young (2007) claims that the theory of recognition neglects peculiar expectations about care for the physical and emotional needs of others, which cannot be equated with gainful employment. In Young's perspective, care work implies a distinct retribution compared to regulated work in the market; this retribution expresses itself as gratitude for meeting an individual's specific needs in an intimate or particular manner. The gain in recognition may thus operate against gender equality.

By observing nurses at work, Pascale Molinier (2012) surveys three important reasons for the invisibility of care work. First, care work involves not only technical know-how and highly sophisticated skills but also, and perhaps more importantly, the ability to conceal the technical-based aspects of such work. Since the affective and skill-based dimensions are profoundly linked in care work, the performance of tasks to be effective cannot appear "just as a job" – otherwise it would no longer count as "care." Second, because care is mostly considered as a woman's activity because of their alleged feminine abilities (or the feminine side in a man), the achieved capacity for effectively performing this work is regarded not as a competence, but rather as a sort of female quality or attribute. Third, since care workers deal with bodily needs, intimacy, vulnerabilities and many embarrassing aspects in everyone, the most difficult aspects of the job can hardly be publicly discussed and socially recognized.

Our study focus is on domestic child labor which, in addition to involving domestic labor and care tensions, also has specific vulnerabilities. This activity is carried out by children – who are under a peculiar condition of emotional, social and physical development, which adds more complexity to the problem. The ambiguity of belonging or not belonging to their employer's family is more deeply felt than in the case of adult domestic workers, inasmuch as whoever employs children often also raises them. In order to enter domestic labor, many children and adolescents lose family and community bonds in order to be employed in a third party's home in urban nuclei (Blagbrough, 2008; International Labor Organization, 2013). As we will discuss later, drawing attention to these complicated and sometimes contradictory logics in the sphere of love and work entrenched in CDL helps us to explain how domination can become obscure across differences of class and gender.

The difficulty of oppressed subjects to discern what counts as recognition under specific circumstances is brought to its clearest expression in Honneth's recent distinction between forms of "ideological recognition" and "justified recognition" (Honneth, 2007b). This distinction is meant to emphasize two things. First, to refute the idea that recognition would be a mere instrument of voluntary servitude or be intrinsically oppressive from the start, Honneth argues that there is no clear distinction between "correct" and "false" judgments if people do not experience practices as repressive, restrictive or based on stereotypes

(Honneth, 2007b, p. 327). Second, this distinction seeks to provide a normative ground for ideology critique, in addition to sociological and political ones.

While conventional analysis explains domination by focusing on concepts such as "false consciousness" or "false representations," or through "internalization" of societal value hierarchies or "identification with the oppressor," Honneth argues that people, who experience practices that do not employ methods of repression, cannot straightforwardly assess their experiences as oppressive (Honneth, 2007b, p. 327). Only from a morally advanced perspective or from a historical retrospective evaluation can such practices be reconstructed as domination. Honneth's intention is not to deny that some network of beliefs expressed as recognition can indeed sustain relations of domination, but rather to clarify the specific social conditions under which this occurs.

Honneth (2007b, pp. 337–340) sets down three criteria for a system of beliefs to be effective as an ideology. The system of beliefs should: (i) provide a positive expression of value to people or members of a group so as to establish a positive self-image; and thus not be perceived as discriminatory, diminishing or damaging; (ii) be "credible" for those to whom it is addressed – perceived as something that realistically reinforces one's own feelings of self-value and autonomy; and (iii) allow the creation of a new value for themselves or future achievements, compared to the past or to previous situations. Such conditions could motivate individuals to attain certain goals and to carry out social functions without resistance. In the ideological form of recognition, however, the promises of recognition, including material fulfillment, are not truly met. Indeed, it motivates a compliant behavior that contributes to establishing or stabilizing relations of domination.

In contrast, justified forms of recognition effectively expand the individuality and autonomy of subjects as well as their inclusion in society, as Honneth discusses in detail in his *The Struggle for Recognition* and subsequent essays. In such cases, the gains in recognition "allow a consistent realization of these new values" (Honneth, 2007b, p. 346). In other words, recognition in the form of love implies a coherent conduct based on the continuity of affective ties; legal recognition of citizens based on equal juridical treatment consists in effective opportunities to participate in a political community on equal terms with others; and recognition in terms of solidarity results in a perfected social appreciation of specific qualities or contributions of the individuals to society. In justified forms of recognition, the moral obligation to meet the other in an appreciative way is not only well founded and comprehensible, but also concretely applied in both institutional arrangements and the way subjects treat each other.

We find that Honneth's distinction has great theoretical and critical strength for dealing with the problem of ideology without victimizing the subjects more than they actually are. The aforementioned criteria enable him to contend that affected subjects have evidence with enough persuasive power for them to reasonably explain their own choices and actions as positive for them. Axel Honneth's distinction between "ideological recognition" and "justified recognition," which entails a normative perspective, seems to offer a concrete analytic way to investigate Steven Lukes's (2005) third dimension of power. This dimension contemplates power relations based on latent conflicts, which are hard to observe, especially by subjects under domination. According to Lukes, "What one may have here is a latent conflict, which consists in a contradiction between the interests of those exercising power and the real interests of those they exclude" (Lukes, 2005, p. 28). For an analysis of latent power relations, Lukes proposes confronting whatever happens to the dominated subjects and what their real interests would be. However, how to define the "real interests" meets theoretical and methodological challenges.

In the second edition of his influential *Power: a radical view*, Lukes (2005) acknowledges this difficulty, yet reaffirms the theory's explicative power to observe concrete phenomena.

> I conclude, then, that, in general, evidence can be adduced (though by nature of the case, such evidence will never be conclusive) which supports the relevant counterfactuals implicit in identifying exercises of power of the three-dimensional type. One can take steps to find out what it is that people would have done otherwise. (Lukes, 2005, p. 52)

Yet the difficulty still remains to analyze a potential phenomenon, something that did not occur but might have (Haugaard, 2010, p. 425).

In Honneth's theoretical framework, the principles of recognition (in the spheres of love, right and social esteem) represent the normative perspective from which social agents can imaginatively project how recognition should be given in certain specific ways. As he explicitly places "norms" in the centre of his social theory, he gives us good or "thick" reasons for being suspicious or skeptical about certain forms of consciousness that sustain relations of domination. Such a horizon of normative expectations is not to be seen as "an ahistorical *given*"

(Honneth, 2002, p. 511 emphasis in the original; see also Honneth, 2012, p. 115; Maia & Vimieiro, 2013), nor as a result of a hypothetical social contract nor even as an abstract cognitive rationality, but as the outcome of historical struggles for emancipation. This horizon of normative expectation – based on ethical knowledge that is acquired through socialization – opens ways of innovative interpretations and allows one to identify pathologies in social arrangements. In Honneth's words "it is a reference to which subjects can reasonably argue that existing forms of recognition are inadequate or insufficient and need to be expanded" (Honneth, 2003a, p. 143). Since this point of reference is never completely or finally determinate, it must constantly be actualized in public expressions of recognition or practical attempts to overcome de facto practices of injustice.

Our study, by analyzing public discourses on CDL displayed in the news media and using data from discussion groups with affected individuals, examines this problem from an empirical perspective. In Honneth's theoretical framework, critical perception of injustice is located within individuals' negative experiences of disrespect or humiliation that violate their moral expectations. We argue that in many cases of domination, moral entrepreneurs and justice advocates (academics, intellectuals, artists, voluntary associations and media agents) are those who name injustice, defend values, and represent and act on behalf of subjugated individuals. Disadvantaged subjects, such as poor children in our study case, may be exposed to extreme poverty, oppression and lack of freedom; and they may not be able to clearly perceive their own situation of injustice (Bohman, 2007; Celikates, 2012; Ikäheimo, 2009; Maia, 2012e; Sen, 1999; Souza, 2006, 2009). While this is an important issue, it has not been systematically taken up by Honneth himself.

We should make the caveat that moral entrepreneurs and advocacy agents, no matter how well-intentioned and informed, are always subject to a "democratically illegitimate paternalism" (Bader, 2007, p. 226; see also Rubenstein, 2007, p. 629), because demands made in the name of others are always partial and may be deceitful or become new sources of oppression (Alcoff, 1991; Kompridis, 2007; Maia, 2012e; Maia & Garcêz, 2013). In response to this caveat, we follow scholars who contend that in any democracy, defensible on an ethical basis, individuals should be regarded not as "recipients of justice," but, instead as "agents of justice" (Forst, 2007b, p. 300; see also Bader, 2007; Maia, 2012e; Rubenstein, 2007). In keeping with Jürgen Habermas (1996) and Honneth (1996), we argue that it is essential to preserve the autonomy and freedom of subjects to think for themselves, and to speak out about their own immediacies regarding their identities, aspirations and needs.

Thus, advocacy agents should take measures to empower oppressed subjects and trigger self-reflection processes; and should aid in structuring communication venues for them to speak with their own voices. However, it is up to these subjects to define what needs to be perceived and recognized in a given context; and this includes contesting and correcting the discourses of those who speak on their behalf. From this point of view, women's questioning of public discourses of institutional and legal recognition in our case study has far-reaching consequences for recognition theory as social research. The manner of reconciliating activist moral entrepreneurs' judgments and the validity of child workers' sense of harm requires nuanced examination.

Legislation, public policies and advocacy regarding CDL in Brazil

Following international conventions, there are in Brazil several laws and initiatives to combat child labor.[2] Brazil has signed Convention 138, which took effect in 1976, establishing a minimum employment age, with adequate to basic schooling time. In 1990, the Brazilian government signed the ILO Convention 182 and Recommendation 190, which respectively ban child labor and demand immediate action to eliminate the worst forms of child labor. Even stronger since 1990 is the Child and Adolescent Statute (ECA), which regards boys and girls as bearers of rights and duties; makes families, government and society share responsibility for their protection; and spells out the principle of absolute priority for childhood and adolescence in public policies. Child labor is forbidden for boys and girls aged under 16 years except in a context of learning activities from age 14 years. Since 2008, CDL has been seen by the Brazilian government as one of the worst forms of child labor, a type of work to be engaged in only after one reaches 18 years of age, following the ILO Convention 182. These moves in the legal sphere as well as growth in awareness over the state's protective duty towards children have motivated several governmental programs for combating child labor in the country. Some examples are the Program for Eradicating Child Labor (PETI) in 1996; and School-grant (Bolsa-escola), in 2001, which implement preventive welfare measures and transfer income to poor and extremely poor families. It should be stressed that several programs for combating CDL in Brazil result from the initiative of civic actors, and local, nationwide and transnational entities through various types of partnerships with the government.

In the state of Pará, a local civic organization (República de Emáus, by means of the Cedeca-Emaú) in partnership with UNICEF, Save the Children and other local entities focused specifically on CDL through PETID (Program for Eradicating Child Domestic Labor). This program, lasting from 2000 to 2010, developed several actions aiming at (i) developing the critical abilities of adolescents and parents sending their children into domestic labor, and training them so that they might find alternative sources of income; (ii) promoting conferences in different Brazilian cities and nationwide awareness campaigns against CDL; (iii) exerting influence on local media organizations, by means of debates and educational workshops to enhance journalists' abilities to deal more appropriately with the CDL topic in their reporting. We argue that this is a typical case of advocacy – in which individuals, groups and associations make demands in the name of interests and values that should be safeguarded, in order to protect "vulnerable subjects," to prevent harm, or in the form of a "special responsibility" (Goodin, 1985; see also Rubenstein, 2007).

Although the norms of childhood are based on the international human rights system, one cannot disregard that the conception of rights is inherently connected with cultural values, the political system and attitudes to law in any given society (Boyden, 1997, p. 199). Furthermore, childhood is a social construct, which appears in a variety of forms related to different understandings of competencies and incapacities (Earls, 2011; Prout & James, 1997). In the state of Pará, CDL work has deep historical and cultural roots, which goes back to the period of slavery. As will be discussed in this study, since the definition of "work" and "right" stems from such a local historical and cultural background, the means of protecting and nurturing childhood in practical terms can become highly controversial; assessment of policies aimed at operating in the best interests of the child may be contested among the affected subjects themselves.

Methodology

The dual aim of our study is to investigate publicly articulated discourses on CDL as well as perceptions of disadvantaged subjects who engaged in this type of work during their childhood or adolescence in Belém. Local news articles allow us to analyze opinions, discourses and definitions of problems and solutions regarding CDL that publicly circulated in this society (Ferree, Gamson, Gerhards, & Rucht, 2002; Maia, 2012a; Peters, 2008; Wessler & Schultz, 2007). In contrast, informal discussion among study participants allows us to tap into affected subjects' self-understanding, in light of interpretations of CDL expressed in the media as well as their own life experiences. Our investigation is structured along two lines:

(1) analysis of the coverage of the topic CDL in the major daily printed newspapers in the state of Pará – *O Liberal* and *Diário do Pará*, during the first five years of PETID, from January 1, 2000 to December 31, 2004. We did not include nationwide vehicles as this study had a local scope. A total of 55 news articles were analyzed (32 in *O Liberal* and 23 in the *Diário do Pará*). Each news piece was examined based on a codebook to identify: (a) the speakers (sources) in the articles; (b) the frames and discourses about CDL made by each speaker; and (c) stated references to PETID.

(2) analysis of informal conversation in focus groups carried out with women who had been domestic workers in their childhood – three groups were recruited from poor neighborhoods in Belém (Bengui, Tapanã and Telégrafo). Each group consisted of five participants, which may be considered an adequate number for exploring how participants' experiences, opinions and concerns are expressed, complemented or contested within the group (Barbour & Kitzinger, 2001; Morgan, 1997). As in Chapter 3, we chose the focus group technique because it allows participants to interact and talk about specific issues, with relative freedom to generate their own questions and frames, and to pursue understanding with others on their own terms and vocabularies (Cal & Maia, 2012; Duchesne & Haegel, 2010). The focus groups took place during July and August 2006 and neighborhood associations and/or community leaders indicated who were the women to be invited.

Altogether 15 women took part in the experiment and the groups had a heterogeneous age composition. Four participants were 20–30 years old; five were 31–40; four were 41–50 and two were over 51. As for their current occupation, they identified themselves as domestic workers (7), housewives (2), seamstresses (3), washerwomen (1), saleswomen (1) and school janitors (1). None of them is still working for the same domestic labor employer. However, most of the participants have not been able to change their occupations since 66.7 percent of them continue to work in domestic service. With regard to their monthly household income, most of these women (60 percent) said that it was under US$160.00 and others (40 percent) said it ranged between US$160.00 and US$320.00.

Each group meeting took two and a half hours. Participants were allowed to express divergent opinions and were stimulated to participate. Two of the meetings were organized at participants' homes (Tapanã and Telégrafo) and one in a neighborhood association (Bengui), where some of the women frequently work. To encourage discussion, we used the "funnel strategy" (Morgan, 1997). This method consists of starting the group meeting with a free discussion and, then, moving towards a more structured discussion on specific questions. Therefore, initially the women freely talked about topics such as gender, domestic work and roles in the household – issues which easily engaged participants in conversation. Next, the CDL issue was gradually introduced as well as discussion about previously mentioned selected news media articles. We followed Gamson's study and used a wide range of frames and voices available in the media material as "conversational resources" (Gamson, 1992; Maia, 2012a). The main goal was to encourage the participants to share their opinions and engage in dialogue.

Media and advocacy: public expression of new forms of recognition

In a previous study, we examined the news media coverage on CDL in Pará within the stipulated period (Cal & Maia, 2012). We found that the main speakers in the media were civic actors associated with the struggle against CDL, namely the Cedeca-Emaús/Movimento República de Emaús, and agents of PETID and its partners, which comprised 58 percent of all speeches in the selected period. There was little diversity of sources in this set of news articles; government agents rarely expressed themselves on this topic.

The significant presence of voices of civic speakers in our case study is particularly surprising, as journalism in Latin America is strongly connected with the State and the market, but connects poorly with civil society (Gomes, 2004; Waisbord, 2009; Weber, 2011). In general, news about social development issues, such as poverty, hunger, health and education are presented from an official perspective (Agência de Notícias dos Direitos da Infância, 2003). Still, mainstream media in Brazil frequently also play a politically active role, alongside unclear party lines (Albuquerque, 2012; Maia, 2012a; Porto, 2012).

The prevalence of voices of civic actors and moral entrepreneurs in our case study can be explained first by the social credibility that the Movimento República de Emaús and the Cedeca-Emaús enjoy in local society, given their traditional engagement in a variety of programs aiming at assuring the rights of children. Secondly, the Cedeca-Emaús had two journalists in its team to help formulate and carry out communication strategies for the Program, including its relationships with different types of media.

It should be stressed that traditional discourses in local society, which legitimatize CDL, did not gain visibility in the media within the study period. We noticed that public discourse on the topic was expressed through two main frames: the invisibility of CDL and the injustice of CDL.

Media commentators drew public attention to the fact that CDL is barely noticed and they explained this invisibility by three main reasons: (a) CDL is carried out mostly by girls, who "naturally" are in charge of domestic tasks and childcare; this practice follows hegemonic concepts of labor division based on gender and thus it raises no questions; (b) CDL has deep cultural roots, it is perceived as "proper" for poor women rather than a "problem" to be dealt with and solved; and (c) CDL occurs in the intimacy of households, a supposedly welcoming environment, it raises little public attention, as opposed to child labor in hostile environments such as plantations or coal mines (Table 4.1).

Our analysis shows that news stories disseminated ideas congruent with transnational entities' diagnosis that children involved in CDL are "the most hidden, invisible and inaccessible of all child workers" (Black,

Table 4.1 Media frame on CDL's invisibility. Examples of discourses presented in the media

---

"Unfortunately, it is considered something positive in Brazilian culture for a poor girl to work as a housemaid." (Armand Pereira, Director of the ILO Brazil). *IBGE wants more details about child work*. Diário do Pará, p. B4, January 5, 2000.

"We have reached the point where child labor is often considered natural; that is where things, in fact, become complicated. The cultural connotation of this tragedy needs to be eliminated." (Simão Jatene, Governor of the state of Pará). *Pará in the struggle against child work*. Diário do Pará, p. A4, January 10, 2004.

"The cultural determinism about the female gender is at the root of the problem of child domestic labor, but, in current society, other factors are determinant, such as social and economic exclusion." – *A 'disguised' crime robs children of their rights*. O Liberal, Social Responsibility page, February 12, 2004.

"ILO project coordinator, Renato Mendes, reminds us that the work of minors in households does not raise the same revulsion as child labor in rubbish dumps or coal mines, or news about sexual exploitation." – *Child labor also makes victims in Pará*. O Liberal, March 20, 2002.

Source: EME-UFMG Research Group.

2002, p. 2). The interpretation also followed feminist critiques that challenge genre naturalism and claim that domestic work is not valued as a "productive contribution" (Hoyos, 2000; Lamarão, Menezes, & Ferreira, 2000). Furthermore, news stories are based on criticism that cultural notions originating in the colonial past support CDL. Since domestic chores require a lot of effort but need little training they are often characterized as being "specific" to poor women (Carneiro & Rocha, 2009).

The second frame seen in Table 4.2 refers to injustices in CDL, which includes discourses that define this practice as exploitation, domination/oppression and exclusion. To begin with, speakers in the media argue that CDL is exploitation because children and adolescents are unpaid or poorly paid; and their families often administer the money. It is "unregulated" exploitation since the working terms and conditions – working hours, tasks and payment – are obviously not prescribed in contracts. Secondly, several news stories point out that CDL is domination or oppression because girls are exposed to the potential risks of work and abuse, and to punishment and violence, including sexual abuse from bosses. Right from the beginning, children and adolescents have no authority and no negotiating power, and are therefore at the mercy of the employing family. Thirdly, speakers in the media highlight that CDL is a form of exclusion or marginalization because child rights

Table 4.2   Media frame about different injustices in CDL. Examples of discourses presented in the media

"'To exploit child domestic labor is to *disrespect* the fundamental right of children to play and to study'; this is a statement by the communications advisor of Cedeca, Luciano Miranda." – *Cedeca launches a campaign for raising awareness and denouncing such situations.* O Liberal, Social Responsibility page, March 18, 2004.

"Child workers comprise boys and girls that are forced to work as slaves in domestic work, generally in private family households; they are subject to all sorts of humiliation and exploitation, provide free labor, and do not enjoy the right of health and education. In this setting, children and teenagers are subjected to long working hours, which robs them of the opportunity for going to school; they have no medical care and no leisure. Those receiving payment or benefits are few. Unfortunately, girls may be victims of sexual abuse, which causes lasting psychological and physical harm." – *A social stain, Editorial.* O Liberal, June 18, 2004.

"Experts state that the problem feeds a poverty cycle, because children doing domestic work will be employed as domestic maids when adults." – *A 'disguised' crime robs children of their rights.* O Liberal, Social Responsibility page, February 12, 2004.

Source: EME-UFMG Research Group.

are violated, including the right of enjoying childhood, education, citizenship and dignity. This type of work hinders any development of the abilities and competencies that children and adolescents require to find a place in the labor market in the future by means of qualified work, thereby reproducing the poverty cycle.

In the Pará newspapers, the general interpretation about CDL largely followed humanitarian rights discourse. Because of the types of injustice found in CDL, several speakers in the news articles – including an editorial – associated this practice with "slavery," an analogy frequently used in studies on CDL in different countries (Black, 2002). From the perspective of recognition, Ikäheimo refers to the status of 'slave' as being

> without freedom, without love, and without gratitude: Slavery instantiates all of these three harms: (1) the activities that fill the life of a slave are not free; (2) his well-being has ideally only instrumental value for the master; and (3) because his work is unfree, it does not count as genuine cooperation and does not produce the satisfaction and fulfilment that someone working freely and altruistically may receive in the form of gratitude from others. (Ikäheimo, 2009, p. 40)

To summarize, the local media in our case disseminated ideas invoke the principles of recognition, which, in Honneth's terms, subsequently "compel us to widen our perception value horizon and thus to intensify or amplify recognition" (Honneth, 2007b, p. 341). From a broad ethical horizon related to human and children's rights, feminist critique and post-colonialism, speakers in the media presented "thick" or "good" reasons for rejecting CDL. Journalists and critical speakers attempted to show that there were cognitive failings in understanding CDL as an oppressive practice, and sought to lead members of the local society to acknowledge that they were implicated in relations of domination and exploitation. However, this does not mean that these discourses are "shared" by the members of the public, in terms of being commonly accepted. As we will discuss in the next section, women who were housemaids in their childhood did not endorse media advocate arguments and some even contested them in our focus groups.

CDL: The intersecting logics of love and work

When exposed to media discourses in our focus group, many women who worked as domestic servants in the past, and who also send their daughters to work in family households, perceive CDL mainly through a positive perspective. However, they are also aware of several types of harm involved in this practice. They report that they were, and still continue to be, exploited ("we are exploited, especially if we [earn] a domestic salary"). They report emotional insecurity, mistreatment and disrespect ("I could never get used to the houses at 12 years of age, but then I slowly became used to it"). How can we explain the fact that these women, even though they name experiences of mistreatment and identify disrespect in their lives, do not articulate a clearer perception of injustice in this situation? Honneth's three requirements to define ideological recognition appear to be met in our study case.

Expectations and contradictions in the sphere of love

The women in the focus group seem convinced that the promise of a better life through CDL is an opportunity for personal development. Because of multiple and severe deprivation in their homes of origin, they perceive CDL as a way to escape poverty or avoid entrance into prostitution. Participants brought up several beliefs that cannot be merely considered as irrational, but are supported by reasons with "power to convince" (Honneth, 2007b). Since CDL is associated with the cultural idea of "taking the child to raise or taking care of the child for her mother" – including material needs and care (psychological care, rest and leisure), and resources for self-development (study and other opportunities) – the first requirement for an ideological form of recognition seems to be present here. Differently from ideologies that have an exclusionary character, such as racism, xenophobia and homophobia, CDL causes no harm to the self-image of girls and allows them to relate positively to themselves in a new "home." When referring to the people they work for, the women use terms such as "godmother" and "aunt," rather than employer, which ambiguously suggests that children would be protected by people who care for their personal well-being (Cal & Maia, 2012; Lamarão, 2008).

> AMANDA: "I think that it is better, because back there [in the hinterland] parents are unable to give, to do things for their children, to provide education for their kids; I think that this is better."
> JOANA: "As Vera said, I am thankful that my daughter moved over here with her godmother; she was thirteen, and did not want to study any more over there. To this day I am happy that my daughter is here...with her godmother, thank God." (Tapanã group)

The second requirement for ideological recognition seems also to be present in this situation: the advantages of CDL are at least partially perceived as positive and credible. The women value it mostly as an opportunity to gain education so as to become "somebody in life." Statements by these women show that, in their role as mothers, they expect more for the lives of their children and teenagers than merely domestic work. It should be noted that in Brazil, as opposed to Andean countries, Central America or Haiti, there is an expectation that employers will send these children and adolescents to school and many of them actually do (Black, 2002). As opposed to countries such as Bangladesh, India or Nepal, where girls serve their employers any time of the day or night and rarely leave the house (Black, 2002), the expectation in Brazil is that CDL should not be restrictive, but should open the door to opportunities for socialization in middle and higher classes.

> DEUSA: "I brought over my nieces, three nieces from Marajó, to work here; but thank God they worked, studied, right, they moved well forward at school, they really had good employers; but there were girls that came from the hinterland and their employers would not let them study; to this day they are adults that don't know even how to write their names, because their employers never put them in school, never let them study."
>
> CARLA: "I agree with her, *there are good employers, there are bad employers*, some that want to be cruel with teenagers, as we watch on television, the case of the girl." [Participants were referring to the case of 11-year-old Marielma who was murdered by her employers; the case became notorious in newspapers in 2005.] (Telégrafo group, our emphasis)

At this point it is important to acknowledge that class relations are reproduced, not only through economic relations but also by means of cultural and symbolic forms that sustain unequal distribution of distinction and privilege, as Edward P. Thompson (1989) and Pierre Bourdieu (1977, 1984) have made clear. In this sense, participants in our focus groups expect that CDL would provide opportunities for the girls to surpass their own "social class culture" and acquire what Bourdieu terms "cultural capital" – the possession of certain intellectual or educational goods – motivations, dispositions, tastes and preferences.

> VERA: "I think it is an opportunity. There are places we wish to go but for which we don't have the means; but [we do] when going with

our employer. She takes the girls. The girls develop, become interested by watching those people that say they are different and take part in better things. [This] gives us influence; for those that want it, there is a good future, I think it is very good."

AMANDA: "I also think it leads to a better future; it is very good... We want to go to a beach that we have never seen in life, and don't have the means to go there, and then they take us... it is the only opportunity I have."

Focus group participants show awareness that "girls can progress" under certain conditions – personal effort, and being lucky to "have a good employer." In a previous study, we noticed that these beliefs are widely shared by mothers, who are concerned to find "good" persons to entrust their child to, and also by employers, who conceive of themselves as alleviating the child's destitution (Cal, 2007; Cal & Maia, 2012). Indeed, most of the employers' showed indignation at "harsh" cases of maltreatment and abusive workloads. They claimed that what the girls do in their home was "just light work" or "just help," and never acknowledged that they were implicated in relation to oppression (Cal, 2007; Cal & Maia, 2012). Once CDL is regarded as providing conditions, resources and capacities for the girls to "prepare themselves for something better" they can nurture the "dream to become somebody in life," which would be unimaginable in a condition of extreme deprivation. The women shared the view that CDL provides a "good future" compared to life on the farm fields; and it is an alternative to idleness and prostitution as well as a source of income. Thus, Honneth's third requirement for ideological recognition to be effective – the contrast between a specific situation perceived as positive compared to the past or to a previous condition appears to operate in our case.

However, the promises of CDL are permeated by many contradictions, which have oppressive consequences. First, although CDL is often mistaken for the obligation to care for and meet the other's needs, there is a twisted expectation that working girls should meet the immediate needs of the family to which they are attached in exchange for food, medical care, housing, access to education, etc. This "exchange" does not entail duties in the normative sense of the principle of love, in which "godmothers" or "aunts" would perceive the girls' needs and thereby become more sensitive and able to care for their well-being (Rössler, 2007; Young, 2007).

For many employers, the labor of girls and adolescents often has only an "instrumental value," as Ikäheimo (2009) says; by carrying out routine domestic tasks, which have no social value, this labor force allows employers to take on more pleasurable and useful activities. Second, domestic workers – especially children and adolescents – rather than receiving retribution in the form of gratitude, as Young (2007) discusses, frequently become the target of aggression or humiliation. Working girls and adolescents are asked to care for children and babies, tasks for which they are not adequately trained or are unable to carry out. The women in our focus groups reported disrespectful experiences, aggression and cruelty, which were described as unbearable: "their children [of the employers] like to shout"; "a [boy] once hit me in the face"; "I had my face hit with a plate, then I left so that he would not mistreat me anymore."

Again, the ambiguous status mobilized by the care relation (Molinier, 2012), on the one hand, and their submission to the person benefiting from care, on the other, do not enable the girls to express and negotiate with their employers the disgust and hate that CDL sometimes causes. Third, poor children and young workers when treated as the property of employers are supposed not only to carry out domestic chores or assist the other in their needs, but also fulfill erotic and sexual desires. The girls thus become de-humanized; being regarded not as a subject but as a physical body, the men in the house can "do as they please" with them:

MARIA: "I once worked in a house of these folks, ... there was a birthday party I don't know whose it was, I sat there on the chair, and we could not go to bed until the party was over; then the son of my employers came over trying to touch my breast, then I protested and went to tell her, then she said: 'What's the problem? He is a man and is the son of your employer, and your boss can also do what he feels like doing with you.'"

MODERATOR: "The employer said that?"

MARIA: "Yes, then I took all my clothes and hid in the yard, and then when they were distracted, I went away, and lost my way home, and ended up at the house of a woman, and only the next morning did I find out where I was."

MODERATOR: "How old were you?"

MARIA: "About 16." (Telégrafo group)

In several situations, participants in our focus group were angry and resentful about "bad employers" and their "mistreatment" or "abuse." Nevertheless, they recurrently make a distinction between "good" and "bad" employers ("there are some that treat us well; there are some that do not"). These women identify the injury caused by CDL as occurring in contingent or specific cases, because of bad luck or lack of personal effort.

Expectations and contradictions in the sphere of work

To explore the expectations held by these women in the sphere of work, we need to return to a number of aspects introduced in our discussion about the symbolic universe of love. The distinction between these two spheres is hard to make because girls and adolescents in CDL are still in stages of emotional, social and physical development and thus work and caring flow together.

Concerning the first requirement for the ideological form of recognition, study participants project for girls in CDL an employment with meaningful content in the future. By going to school, the girls could acquire "socially useful skills," which could enable them to pursue prestigious careers; this would change their place in the social hierarchy and include them in the context of productive contributors to society (Rössler, 2007). Tied to the expectation of qualified work is the assumption that the employers would help them to acquire those abilities and talents.

> VERA: "What I think is, that for those without the means, we can't do much in this case...folks from the hinterland; they become farm workers, who don't have a future. In a family house, if the person knows it and wants to, in the future they may become doctors, graduate to be good lawyers..., in other words, something good. Because a domestic servant is paid a salary, the girls live a fairly good day-to-day life, take part in the same things as their employers; with all of this we are becoming prepared for something better."
>
> LETÍCIA: "I would rather work as a domestic servant than sit at home doing nothing and not earning my salary;...the salary helps us to buy clothes, to go out, and without this money we cannot do many things, right?"

Moreover, the prospect of social inclusion is seen as credible to the participants because many employers demonstrate commitment to education and are benevolent with their child workers; and thus set them on a path towards possible upward mobility. Personal attachments and bonds of gratitude to good employers further obscure the asymmetries in power in this relation and the subordinate place occupied by these girls in a class society.

AMANDA: "I enjoy life,...because my employer,...says like this, 'Oh Amanda, you work here'; they treat me as if I belonged to the family, 'ah, you work here, but I want you to become another person, I want you to study, to conclude your studies, to become somebody in life'; and, for her, I would have concluded my schooling, but I never managed, because sometimes I arrived tired from work and then had to go to school, and then I was tired; but for her I would be studying." (Tapanã group)

Although social interactions proceed as if "norms of recognition" were in place, children and adolescents in CDL do not enjoy the same status of other children in the family. The housework carried out by the girls is usually not regarded as "work" but just as "help"; and when these children and adolescents are sent to school, they usually go to public schools – mainly in evening classes. Because they do not have adequate time for resting and studying, they are prone to failure (Carneiro & Rocha, 2009; Lamarão, 2008; Lamarão et al., 2000). Like Amanda, many girls are encouraged to relate to themselves as autonomous and active agents, and thus they tend to assume personal responsibility for their own failure. Since lack of success is more easily explained at the individual level, study participants do not criticize CDL as conducive to personal underdevelopment in terms of systematic exclusion and exploitation. Thus, they seem not able to foster a common ethos to challenge the social order.

Our focus here is on the particular strain of responses that could uncover power relations in these women's experiences. As social scientists or observers, we could expect different outcomes and alternative reasons for these women to engage in CDL. First, study participants could have emphasized their agency in choosing to take up domestic labor as children, but at the same time acknowledge the institution's role in the oppression and subjugation of children. Second, critical opinions and judgments circulating in the media arena could have provided a language and counter-hegemonic framings about CDL for these women to move away from the predominant value hierarchy. Third, study participants do not have to defend the institution of CDL to shore up their sense of self-worth.

Furthermore, one could regard these women's statements as rationalizations. Although domestic workers in Brazil have achieved several rights in the past few decades, such as regulated working conditions and improved wages, they still cannot find a place in "good society" (Carneiro & Rocha, 2009) and suffer the moral pain of social devaluation (Souza, 2009). As we have emphasized, study participants are very aware that they are engaged in low-wage, low-status work and do not receive social recognition ("if we don't have advanced study we are nothing"; "there are people over there that ignore and do not speak to domestic servants").

In this context, we find that Honneth's account of ideological forms of recognition is valuable for explaining these women's self-conception and their network of beliefs as based on arguments with convincing power, and not as illusions irrationally held. Honneth's account allows us to see that there are other structures – such as the desire for emancipation, autonomy and social esteem – that can be mobilized to reinforce, paradoxically, relations of oppression. In the idealizations the women construct about themselves, they conceive CDL as a practical possibility to increase their own autonomy and overcome social divides. Thus, there are good grounds for thinking that they regard CDL as "a choice" and "an opportunity," rather than a lack of alternatives due to extreme destitution, because they cannot imagine that things "should" or "could" be different. The rationale of ideological forms of recognition has a significant impact on coordinating these subjects' action and thus stabilizing relations of domination and exploitation. However, how can subjugated individuals, like the women in our study, contest the promises of ideological recognition that is part of their cultural heritage and imagine alternatives for themselves? Focusing on the women's understanding of harm and their sense of agency, we now go on to examine processes that help cultural and normative interpretative frameworks to rebound.

Vulnerability, agency and ideology-critique

We started this chapter with the premise that moral entrepreneurs can play a critical role in naming injustice, facing collective action problems and seeking to advance specific policy goals – such as measures for eliminating CDL. Our findings show some difficulties in reconciling justice advocates' judgments and the validity of affected persons' sense of harm. Speakers in the media attempted to disclose ideological forms of recognition, which invited oppressed subjects to cognitively understand and affectively accept their own subjugation to others in daily-life routines.

In contrast, the women strove to assert that they are not "those to be pitied" or looked down upon. By seeing themselves as capable of agency as well as forming a life plan, these women assert that they can resist their status as subaltern actors.

To develop our argument on how it is possible to reconcile conflicting evaluative perspectives, when discourses of justice do not resonate with the habitus of subjugated subjects, it is helpful to further inquire into: (i) the women's sense of agency and (ii) the requirements that make the justice advocates' ideology-critique to serve emancipatory purposes.

While it seems correct to say that the interplay of expectations of recognition in different spheres obstructs the women's critical reflection, how one should interpret these women's sense of agency is far less clear. It seems misleading to describe their sense of agency to choose and act to change their life practices in a substantial way as a mere effect of subjugation. They report that since childhood ("as young girls") they worked in the family house, motivated by the desire to widen their horizons, to attain some independence in their lives, and to learn, pursue a career and advance socially. They strive to "follow their own thinking" and persist in dealing with adversity to gain even minimal autonomy and the dignity to live from one's gainful employment. They take on duties at their own home to create or attain resources to care for the needs and well-being of their children even if they themselves have been deprived of care in their own childhood.

> JOANA: "…in the hinterland it is not like here…We struggle there on the farm, fighting, working…Not here, here we can work and earn money."
>
> DEUSA: "…I was 12 when I married; I have never followed the counsel of any man, I have always depended on myself, on my thinking, on my own counsel, that is why I work as a domestic servant; I work there because I have a little girl like this. [I tell her]…look Ranna, I am working, I work a lot as a domestic servant, because what my mother and father could not give me I want to give you. I don't want you to stay on the streets, running around, getting dirty. No, I want to give you what I did not have…."

While the types of struggle described by the women do not cause any change in the existing distribution of material and symbolic resources within society, they do not show feelings of helplessness, fatality, dependency or lack of control, but rather conceive of themselves as agents. It would be premature to think that these women can actually and effectively change adverse situations, and their sense of autonomy is likely to be quite overstated. On the basis of similar concerns, Ruth Gomberg-Muñoz's (2010) ethnographic study with Mexican undocumented immigrants in the US shows that this group's willingness to work with integrity and bravery results, paradoxically, in a vulnerability to exploitation (Gomberg-Muñoz, 2010, p. 302). Gomberg-Munõz's key argument is that undocumented immigrants, in need of recognition, cultivate a social identity as "hard workers," as a means of confronting stigma and converting socially degraded work into a source of self-esteem. While this process has the advantage of sequestering low-wage job opportunities for them and their social networks, it has the negative effect of reproducing exploitation and categorical inequalities.

Tackling the problem, in our case, only from the perspective of agency can gloss too easily over structural factors and social obstacles to emancipation. It can be argued that the women's self-conception as "strong" and able to get ahead despite adversity helps to perpetuate oppression and inequality, by emphasizing their agency at the expense of the context of dominating structural constraints. However, from the theoretical standpoint of recognition, these women's desire to achieve and transform their lives cannot be overlooked. Their effort to constantly "find what is best" when properly articulated with a critique of ideology, is important for them to conceive of themselves as capable of overcoming obstacles in order to pursue a meaningful sense of self-realization.

At this point, we need to clarify how ideology-critique can serve an emancipatory function. Because unraveling this issue requires consideration of sociological models and political normativity, we can only indicate lines of thinking here in a context of a more thorough discussion. In brief, while we understand that ideologies will not disappear until the power structures that uphold them are transformed, we support the argument that a critique of ideology must begin with critical discussion (Bohman, 2000; Rostbøll, 2008). The issue here is not the idealistic assumption that ideology can be overcome merely by critically discussing it. Rather, we contend that social critics have the potential to initiate acts of reflection on obstacles or repressive forces that restrict other people's lives in an arbitrary or unjustifiable way. If we understand the problem of ideological form of recognition as a problem of worldview that makes or implies validity claims (Geuss, 1981; Shelby, 2003), then these claims are open to critical scrutiny.

Second, we do not assume that some groups – intellectuals, the ruling elite, disadvantaged groups or any other group – have special access to truth about the social world or an objective standpoint to evaluate the others' statements or forms of reasoning (Rostbøll, 2008; Shelby, 2003). Thus, even if some claims may be well grounded in human rights and other substantial rights designed to safeguard individual autonomy, we regard ideology critique as a dynamic process of diagnosing oppression, and claim-making and claim-contesting, which takes place irrespective of such normative foundations. Thus, mutual understanding among justice advocates and disadvantaged people's judgment is uncertain; and exactly when counterfactual evidence is met will often be difficult to determine.

Third, we understand that getting people to recognize ideological constructions is not enough to prompt these people to significantly change their social relations. If social advocates really want to subvert the structures of hegemonic power, various measures – including empowerment of disadvantaged subjects; engagement in deliberation in the public sphere; political representation; exercise of pressure on formal collective decisions; and demands of accountability – are necessary, and that will of course depend on a number of factors in each concrete situation.

We assume that the diagnosis of injustice and the struggle for recognition is never quite finished, but open to permanent contestation. Even if specific procedures to deal with injustice are achieved and institutionalized, they are always partial and may even promote new relations of domination. Ideological forms of consciousness can shift in response to changes in social circumstances. Thus, as long as the diagnosis of injustice and just policies require the support of those to whom they are supposed to apply, critique of unquestioned assumptions, norms, principles and forms of power points towards a clear understanding of how social arrangements should be.

Conclusion

Our study exemplifies cases where patterns of recognition are conveyed in legal rules and institutions as well as in actions of certain social agents – notably advocacy agents – before they find expression in practices of a given lifeworld. In our case study, media professionals acted as agents of advocacy, following discourses vocalized by NGOs and local social movements, nationwide, and transnational entities that speak for and act in the name of children and adolescents. Media speakers disseminated ideas about CDL based on a general interpretation of the principles of recognition; their discourses were located on the horizon of human and children's rights, the feminist critique of gender domination and post-colonialism, to challenge domination. Discourses circulating in the media attempted to politicize what is seen as natural, and turn harm into an object of collective reflection. Our findings suggest that while value hierarchies do not go unchallenged in public domains, assessment of justice and injustice is based upon the complex logic of the social agents. Because the legitimacy of discourses (and measures) designed to overcome injustice must be accepted as proper by those to whom they are meant to apply, the definition of injustice is always a tentative, conflict-ridden process.

Our study presents some limitations. A full-scale assessment of the women's perception of CDL, following awareness campaigns conducted by advocacy groups and governmental programs, would require a larger experiment. A broader sample and detailed investigation of the effects of PETID in the long run would be needed.

In addition, this study would have to be complemented by research focusing on structural conditions that affect child and adolescent engagement in CDL and constrain their opportunities. Still, we expect that our study can contribute, if only modestly, in advancing an explanation of ideological relations in work and social bonds in two specific ways.

First, the focus on CDL has proven useful for advancing a fuller and more nuanced understanding of the difficulty that oppressed individuals have in discerning what counts as recognition, under specific conditions. Differently from paradoxes of recognition in post-Fordist work, our study shows the complexities of different logics of recognition in both spheres of love and work at play in CDL; and the alternative ways ideological forms of recognition can establish and stabilize relations of domination. We argued that Honneth's distinction between "ideological" and "morally justified" forms of recognition is productive in analyzing how women in our study define their situation, without assuming a cognitive or a moral incapacitation of the powerless. While we argued that the women's motivation to create and achieve self-realization paradoxically leads to the reproduction of domination, we suggested that their "interest in emancipation" cannot be conceptualized as mere subjugation. We also suggested that such a motivation for transformative agency, when properly incorporated into a critique of ideology, can drive struggles for recognition forward.

The second conclusion that arises from our analysis regards the conflictive assessment of justice and injustice. To outline a way around this difficulty, we argued that multiplying concrete opportunities for dialogue and negotiation among disadvantaged subjects and justice advocates, across formal and informal settings, helps to clarify what is to be taken into account and recognized in each and every situation. This procedure cannot eliminate domination, but it contributes to reducing domination's ideological properties. The more frequently that subordinate actors engage in contestation of injustice and innovative diagnosis, the more likely they are to question "the natural order of things." Similarly, the more frequently social advocates attentively engage with disadvantaged people's claims and contestations, the more likely they are to become aware of limitations in their own claims and of oppressive aspects in their diagnosis and policies. Conceived in this way, critique of ideology can encourage social actors to learn from their mistakes and also to learn from each other in order to define the conditions that have to be met if a justified form of recognition is to be given.

Notes

1. The original meaning of ideology in Marx as a "false consciousness" of class-specific conditions of domination has been modified, corrected and altered by several scholars. The concept of ideology has varied connotations that involve debates in politics and economics, as well as in other sociological traditions, such as the Weberian, Durkheimian and structuralist sociologies. Karl Mannheim's sociology of knowledge, Louis Althusser's concept of the State's ideological apparatus and Antonio Gramsci's concept of hegemony are important developments.
2. A PNAD 2011 (national home sampling) Survey, made public by IBGE (Brazilian Geography and Statistics Institute) in 2012, revealed that 257,691 children and adolescents are domestic workers in Brazil. However, it is quite possible that this number is underestimated, given the survey's nature (by sampling) and the difficulty in defining just what "labour" is.

Part II

Struggle Through Social Network Sites

5
Struggles for Recognition in the Digital Era

Part I of this book analyzes how people use mass media material as "conversational resources" (Gamson, 1992; Maia, 2012d), which establish different interfaces with struggles for recognition. Part II inquires into how interaction through the Internet and Social Network Sites (SNSs) has dramatically altered the shape of everyday life. Today, an interconnected media environment offers venues and occasions for people to interact through synchronous and asynchronous communication, and often through both simultaneously, in different virtual environments. People can not only access a wider-range of issues, discussions and opinions from varied sources, which include media coverage, but also become media producers or co-producers. This ability enables them to find direct routes to mobilization and to influence the civil sphere as well as the formal political-institutional sphere.

The recognition-theoretical approach links an individual's identity constitution and his or her well-being to the social responsiveness of others which accounts for broader social and political conditions that shape the nature of these responses. In a mediated social world, online interactions involve several practices that apply across intimate, social and political relations. Technical devices not only facilitate people's online interactions but also mold features of these interactions. A far-ranging body of research shows that each different platform – with its own logic of functioning, norms, opportunities, and type of public – conditions how people act in a specific environment, and how they connect and interact online.

In this chapter, I revisit approaches that explain how the Internet and related digital technologies such as SNSs have penetrated everyday habits and communicative practices. In light of our effort to further develop the recognition-theoretical approach, I concentrate on surveying networked media as sites for: self-expression and identity-building; everyday discussion and deliberation; political activism and mobilization. It is important to build on recent contributions to these three sub-areas of research to construct a perspective capable of encompassing different dimensions of struggles for recognition in networked media environments. Although in subsequent chapters my collaborators and I elaborate on more specific issues in the theory of recognition, these dimensions of networked media provide the frame for our empirical investigation.

Networked media as sites for self-expression: changing conditions of identity-building

The recent proliferation of Web 2.0 technologies has added new complexities to SNS platforms and forums since participants can use visual representations of themselves – avatars – in their posted messages and present personal information in profiles with real-life photographs. In this section, I focus on how identity-building occurs in multiple levels of communication – linguistic, discursive and visual – in online environments. I assess theoretical contributions of empirical research on the Internet and SNSs to assess changing notions of privacy, speech and community. While acknowledging new online features landscaped for self-expression, I argue that it is important to maintain a healthy skepticism regarding the opportunities and constraints entrenched in networked media environments. Since people's values and interests are constructed within social dynamics, careful analysis is needed to understand radically different types of relations between subjects, and show actors' self-understanding and interpersonal relationships in terms of broader group-level or societal values within more encompassing and enduring processes of social conflict and social integration.

Against earlier views that the Internet would forge a disembodied space, where social hierarchies in the offline world leading to marginalization and discrimination would not really matter – individuals could freely enact multiple identities (Negroponte, 1995; Turkle, 1995) or participants' differences and status could be effaced (Papacharissi, 2002; Suller, 2004) – a great number of scholarly works have shown the complexity of the relationship between online and offline interactions (boyd, 2007, 2011; boyd & Donath, 2004; Chadwick, 2013; Davis, 2012; Ellison & boyd, 2013; Grasmuck, Martin, & Zhao, 2009; Gray, 2009; Kim & Yun, 2008; Papacharissi, 2011).

Different platforms configure specific niches of everyday life, and individuals express themselves differently, according to technological design features as well as social and cultural norms.[1] Unlike anonymous sites where individuals meet new people, sites for dating, and platforms for multiplayer online games, where individuals arguably tend to "play-act" at being someone else or project "a hoped for self" (Grasmuck et al., 2009), researchers share the view that people are inclined to be more "realistic and honest" in their self-presentation in identifiable environments (boyd & Donath, 2004; Ellison & boyd, 2013).

When referring to processes of identity-building in SNSs, scholars highlight changing notions of privacy, intimacy and secrecy.[2] Since utterances informally expressed in previously secluded environments now spread through SNSs, what people say in these platforms can be recorded, archived and replicated on several platforms. Thus, these expressions can have far-reaching and long-lasting effects (Levmore & Nussbaum, 2010; Papacharissi, 2010; van Dijck, 2013, p. 7). Also, people's autonomy to choose with whom they share certain information and experiences, and consent to reveal confidentialities, have become highly ambiguous activities in networked platforms.[3] On Facebook, for example, in spite of referring to a circle of intimates, users also carefully administrate strategies of self-presentation and displays of affection because they know these expressions are likely to be publicized more broadly by other individuals (boyd, 2011; boyd & Donath, 2004; Mendelson & Papacharissi, 2011, p. 266; Papacharissi, 2010, p. 141).[4] Studies show that photos and comments on walls and "profiles of friends," more than one's own profile, affect the manner in which someone is seen in a network of publics (Walther, Van Der Heide, Hamel, & Shulman, 2009).

Activities of self-reflection and self-monitoring are harder to achieve in networked environments. Individuals may face problems in contextualizing their behavior and, thereby, discern what is appropriate, interesting or relevant for shaping one's performance when messages and videos are posted and broadcasted for multiple social audiences. I support the argument that individuals in online environments may emphasize or de-emphasize, exaggerate or even conceal parts of themselves to make certain claims of identity; that users can generate content and select photos intending, consciously or unconsciously, to portray a version of themselves or to produce a certain narrative of identity. Still, the boundary between acceptable and unacceptable online identities is associated not only with norms of different platforms but also with factors in offline contexts (boyd, 2007, 2011; Davis, 2012; Ellison & boyd, 2013; Kapidzic & Herring, 2011).

To build a theoretical-recognition perspective, it is important to note how online interactions are linked to broader processes of socialization and individualization in a given society. Current empirical research on identity-building reveals that self-expression, community-building and conflicts within and between groups occur within and across a range of modes and settings in connective media environments. These studies offer valuable insights for exploring how individuals seek attachments and recognition in online landscapes, which involve bodily aspects, linguistic and non-linguistic expressions.

In their investigation into photo galleries of college students on Facebook, a platform more often used by individuals who already know each other from offline personal connections, Mendelson and Papacharissi (2011) show that visual online autobiography contributes to articulating adolescents' autonomy by signaling both their independence from family and their cohesiveness in terms of closeness of affiliation with a peer group. These scholars argue that the majority of photos display students and paired groups of friends, who explicitly pose for the camera mostly at a playful time, and reveal more friendship connections than romantic ones. This study's basic conclusion is that the display of images – by allowing "college students to speak to each other visually, playing out their college lives for each other" – demonstrates the primacy of relationships in offline social circles (Mendelson & Papacharissi, 2011, p. 267). In some cases, online messages do not reflect social practices but actually depend upon offline group interactions. Danah boyd and Alice Marwick's (2011) study shows that adolescents in SNSs encode public messages – through abbreviation, in song lyrics and the like – to make them understood only to a particular group of friends. People, not familiar with these references, such as parents or a circle of relatives, are likely to infer completely different meanings.

Evidence of how and with what effects power shapes social relations are provided by scholars who examine online interactions across individual and group inequalities based on class, gender, ethnicity, sexual orientation, nationality and so forth. In their study, Sherri Grasmuck, Jason Martin and Shanyang Zhao (2009) show that Harvard University students of African American, Latino, Indian and Vietnamese ancestry intensively invest in presenting their ethno-racial identities in online environments using content analysis of Facebook profiles, as well as in-person interviews of these minorities. Their findings show that these groups use different strategies for projecting a self in ways that racial-ethnic differences are culturally salient and conflict is more or less elaborated. Furthermore, these scholars stress that distinct groups differently engage in political conflict about their own identity that requires explicit negotiation in social relations.[5] While African American, Latino, and Indian students bring up issues of social conflict in their profiles, conveying "a sense of group belonging, color consciousness and identification with groups historically stigmatized by dominant society," white students and Vietnamese students "rarely signaled group identification or ethno-racial themes, reflecting 'strategies of racelessness" (Grasmuck et al., 2009, p. 179). Still, themes related to racial discrimination were discussed by members of these latter groups in face-to-face interactions at the college context.

Dealing with gender differences, Sanja Kapidzic and Suzan C. Herring (2011) inquired into what extent male and female teenagers communicate differently in multimodal online environments and if expressions of gender distinctiveness are becoming less frequent and less traditional than in the 1990s. By examining linguistic features and communication styles in asynchronous messages, in combination with profile pictures on popular English-language teen chats, these scholars found significant differences in speech acts, message tones and signals of gender in pictures related to physical stances and dress – elements that in their view reveal "traditional gender stereotypes."[6] The basic conclusion of this study is that "broader, more stable signals of gender identity across topics" (Kapidzic & Herring, 2011, p. 41) were at play in the chosen online environments. In Kapidzic and Herring's words "despite changes in technology and purported feminist advances in society over the past 20 years, traditional gender patterns in communication style and self-presentation persist in computer-mediated communication (CMC), at least in heterosexual teen chat sites" (Kapidzic & Herring, 2011, p. 41).

To advance a theoretical-recognition approach, the findings of these studies are particularly relevant when showing that claims of identity occur in multiple levels of visual and linguistic communication, and power dimensions that underlie social relations are fairly stable and persistently reproduced in certain online environments. A tentative generalization here should also take into account cases in which online environments offer opportunities for individuals to transcend their cultural contexts of communication in certain communities or localities. More precisely, I am referring to situations in which digital technologies provide the means for online expression and communication that may expand a sense of place and belonging. Online communication can help individuals deal with tensions generated in interpersonal relationships based on broader social norms and thus reframe their sense of self as well as alter expectations of recognition in offline relations.

A good example of how the Internet helps members of marginalized groups construct a new collective identity – or a "shared semantics" to use Honneth's term – is provided by Ananda Mitra's (2001) study on the use of websites by Indians in diaspora. She claims that hyperlinked discourses on the Web opened up the possibility for immigrant Indians to have a voice and produce alliances through cyber communities to renegotiate identities in the host society. Mitra's key argument is that new opportunities to voice themselves in virtual environments helped to challenge naturalized or stereotyped images produced by dominant groups. Focusing attention on the intersubjective nature of identity, Mitra claims that such a process is the initial step for transforming the group identity and their own image.

In a similar vein, the ethnographic study developed by Mary L. Gray (2009) on young people in rural communities shows the potential of digital-media content to enable individuals to weave together broad online communities and local level values of offline communities. Gray argues that digital-media-generated lesbian, gay, bi, trans, queer (LGBTQ) material were crucial for helping rural youth to rework their desires to trigger a LGBTQ identity. She explains that whereas urban and suburban youth might come across an array of both LGBTQ images in public spaces and actions of advocacy organizations, rural youth are unlikely to encounter these images. Since rural communities strongly rely on structures of familiarity and value solidarity, and hegemonic sexual and gender norms are deeply rooted in local cultures, Gray suggests that gay representations in traditional mass media and films lack enough "realness" to enable rural adolescents to explore a personal sense of self and prompt self-disclosure. In such contexts, Gray contends that online coming-out stories and online personal ads were fundamental to rural youth to "rearticulate LGBTQ identities as 'real,' 'natural,' 'unmediated,' and 'authentic'" (Gray, 2009, p. 1182).

Another evocative example of how SNSs help individuals to re-orient and change intersubjective relational patterns in society is offered by Kyung-Hee Kim and Haejin Yun's (2008) study on the South Korean social network site, Cyworld. This SNS employs photos, music and audio-visual resources and offers tools for privacy protection and a selection of conversational partners. According to these scholars, Cyworld enabled Koreans – as members of a collectivist culture, who are not expected to fully express their inner thoughts but rather communicate in indirect ways in any given offline situation – to exchange and elaborate emotional communication. Kim and Yun (2008, p. 313) argue that "relational bonding via SNSs grows as users manage relational conflicts" in disputes with friends and lovers, to explore subtle differences in meanings and take one another's perspective. This study suggests that users can routinely engage in the negotiation of intersubjective tensions that are created within the online world, as transferred from offline to online.

The insights gained from these studies direct our attention to social norms on each platform, the type of engagement with digital media and various socio-political offline relations that contribute to shape self-expression and interaction online. To reiterate, online expression can be observed on different levels – the personal, the interpersonal, the group constitution and so forth.

Since my collaborators and I are interested in surveying struggles for recognition in networked online environments, we focus on conflicts for reframing one's sense of self and the dynamic process through which individuals struggle to be inter-subjectively recognized. In seeking recognition, individuals, by attempting to be seen as having dignity, as being legally responsible agents or as valued contributors to social projects, have to engage in conversation, reasoning and other activities of mutual attunement with others. While online worlds and offline worlds are increasingly interconnected, it is important to ask how people on networking sites express themselves to: exchange opinions and perspectives; negotiate the value and treatment they accord each other; argue about the relevance of whatever happens in light of their allegiances and differences; and, define what they wish for themselves and for others. In the next section, I survey the networked environment as a site for informal discussion and deliberation.

Networked media as site for political talk and deliberation

Since the Internet and SNSs provide multiple venues for communication regarding specific aims – public and private, broadcast and targeted, trivial and more substantive – different types of communicative interaction take place on these platforms. The literature on online informal talk, political discussion and deliberation is growing at a rapid pace. Conscious of this tendency, researchers are now quite cautious about specifying not only features of distinct types of platforms but also different forms of participation as well as individuals' demographic background, group-affiliations, values and behavior. A wide range of research with distinct designs contributes to a fuller understanding of how people and groups interact, talk and discuss in networked environments.

In this section, I argue that, while a great number of studies on online discussions have been developed within deliberative models of democracy and somewhat anchored in Habermasian theory, Honneth's formulations can bring new insights to research in this field. Within online deliberation studies, I pay particular attention to a renewed relevance accorded to everyday talk, emotions, personal storytelling and the so-called pre-political experience.

Most scholars agree that the growth of networked communication offers new opportunities for a variety of groups to have their voices heard in public spheres. Whereas some start with explicitly enthusiastic approaches and others with critical ones, scholars are now more sensitive to real-world opportunities and constraints, and have brought to bear ever more systematic empirical evidence to support their claims. Even when investigators emphasize the potential of the Internet to empower users to express their concerns, interact and "talk back" instantly, they often acknowledge that diverse digital divides create hurdles against participation in virtual environments, and many of the biases that exist in offline forums are reproduced in networked communication (Jenkins, Ford, & Green, 2013; Loader & Mercea, 2012; Norris, 2001; van Dijck, 2013). As I have already discussed, power relations shape participants' role and status and define specific modes of interaction in most online environments.

Deliberative theories, including deliberation online, have provided the most basic concepts that frame the theoretical debate and empirical research alike. Much of the debate has involved scholars contrasting themselves with Habermas's theoretical framework which inquires into several controversies: the significance of principles of deliberation; the role of reason and justification in the theory; the types of communication that could lead to deliberation; different understandings of the common good and legitimacy; the role of consensus and the desirability of agreement as a goal; and whether procedural norms are adequate.[7] In the field of online deliberation, a voluminous body of literature has dealt with these controversies. Empirical research has not only brought new evidence to theoretical debate but has also led to new developments in operational criteria, evaluation methods and instructions for building online designs to make real-world politics more deliberative (Brundidge, 2010; Coleman & Blumler, 2009; Kies, 2010; Stromer-Galley, 2007; Stromer-Galley & Muhlberger, 2009).

While this debate is beyond the scope of this chapter, we should point out that a recognition-theoretical approach helps to analyze power and difference by taking account of meaning-making from the perspective of participants in social conflicts. As already pointed out in Chapter 1, Honneth's approach can be regarded as a continuation of Habermas's effort to provide access to a pre-scientific realm of moral critique (Anderson, 2011; Deranty, 2009, 2011; O'Neill & Smith, 2012; Petherbridge, 2011b).

Distinct research models have been designed to observe discussions in small scale, online forum-based experiments in parliaments or in public consultation as well as on SNSs and sites of civil society organizations, activists and ordinary citizens. These studies have produced mixed findings. Plenty of evidence reveals online debates to be highly antagonistic along with straightforward opinion statements without much interest in further discussion. By the same measure, studies show online discussions following deliberative patterns with varying degrees of justification, respect, mutual consideration for the opponent's arguments, openness to reflectively review preferences (Dahlberg, 2007; Kies, 2010; Steiner, 2012a) and circumstances in which communication is exploitative based on vulgar language, flaming and blaming (Juris, 2005; Zoonen, Vis, & Miheli, 2011).

Despite such a plurality of situations, researchers have been producing a detailed body of knowledge of the technological features, social conditions and circumstances under which argumentative discussions are more likely to occur.[8] A number of scholars have searched ways to build institutional designs and structure incentives for people and groups to deliberate, focusing on mechanisms that can compensate for less than optimal conditions. In this sense, scholars have paid growing attention to informal conversation and different sorts of expressions such as personal narratives, story-telling, humor, and rhetoric that can enhance critical reflection and the conditions under which they favor deliberation (Bächtiger, Niemeyer, Neblo, Steenbergen, & Steiner, 2010; Graham, 2008; Polletta, 2007; Polletta & Lee, 2006; Steiner, 2012a; Wojcieszak & Mutz, 2009).

Our study is based on similar concerns of scholars who attempt to survey how people express themselves in non-political online environments in everyday life. My collaborators and I are also seeking to capture the perspectives of participants, their lived experiences and forms of interaction to show how people articulate their preferences, enhance political knowledge and refine opinions (Brundidge, 2010; Brundidge & Rice, 2009; Kim, 2011; Marques & Maia, 2010; Wojcieszak & Mutz, 2009). In this field of research, our empirical studies presented in the next two chapters help to advance understanding of how power constrains or enables deliberation.

Following the recognition-theoretical approach, my collaborators and I start with the premise that re-orienting (or reframing) one's sense of self and pursuing self-realization are challenging endeavors since individual agency, autonomy, and individual freedom require affirmation and recognition from others. Given the plurality of values and definitions of how subjects want to live their own lives and the lack of resources and goods claimed as necessary for their self-realization, moral disagreements and conflicts of interest inevitably exist within groups as well as among different groups.

The recognition-theoretical approach paves the way for researchers to tap into pre-political experience, as discussed in Chapter 1. It provides conceptual tools to deal with issues that have long been a cornerstone of research on everyday talk and deliberation, such as "discovery of problems," "interpretation of needs" (Habermas, 2006, p. 308), and "acknowledgment of commonalities and differences" (Dhamoon, 2009; Warren, 2001). All these elements are seen as necessary for citizens to more or less freely articulate their aspirations and interests – what Habermas (1996, p. 308) calls "discourses aimed at achieving self-understanding" and Jane Mansbridge (1999, p. 211) elaborates upon in terms of the process through which individuals "come to understand better what they want and need, individually as well as collectively."

Put differently, the recognition-theoretical approach, by articulating a broader notion of inter-subjective dependency, provides a point of departure for researchers to observe how subjects struggle to be seen by others as agents, not to be treated unjustly or as second-class citizens and not to be looked down upon. In our view, Honneth's theory helps to clarify activities of interpretation and struggles on the part of participants as well as their motives to challenge a certain norm while engaging in argumentation on moral conflicts in different spheres.

While supporting the view that deliberation is a rare phenomenon, critics seem not to have fully appreciated motivations of people to engage in discussion and deliberation. Insofar as Honneth's theoretical framework produces insights into various levels of individual negative experiences in intimate, juridical and social spheres, one can find new explanations for why a person feels compelled to make oneself understood, and dispute conflicting values and interests. By re-appraising the link between social conflict in everyday life and political institutions, the recognition-theoretical approach aids in observing the critical potential for discussion and citizens' willingness to deliberate in everyday life as well as in forums where specific measures can be taken up by a representative democratic system.

Honneth attempts to develop a more sociologically-oriented critique of social domination to bring social conflict to the center of his account. Conflict-based interactions and struggles among groups involve strategically-oriented actions – fighting and confrontation. The next section surveys the media networked environment as sites for collective action, which will allow us to bring together many of these themes. Within a recognition-theoretical approach, individual responses to feelings of injustice, which are tied to plexuses of negative experiences and informal discussions in everyday interactions, relate substantively to political praxis and collective action aimed at emancipation.

Networked media as sites for collective action and mobilization

The internet and SNSs are at the heart of contemporary networked action, mobilization and protest. Research on online organization and digital activism is flourishing. Although some scholars are skeptical about the possibility of generalizing forms of association and connective action, due to their diversity and purposes, I argue that it is possible to generalize if we make the right distinctions. In this section, I follow scholars who pay attention to different organizational logic at play in social movement actions and in large-scale networks of contentious actions. I make a further distinction in the "shared semantic" underlying members of social movements and individual and group contentious responses to events and opportunities in large-scale mobilization.

Honneth's program specifically explains the social origins of moral and political discontent but does not survey a wide range of factors described in the literature about social movements – opportunities, resources, incentives, strategic choices, the building of allies, and so forth – when appraising the possible success or failure of a struggle.[9] Certainly, this debate is also beyond the scope of this chapter. My aim is to provide a panoramic view of different "logic" of engagement in collective action in networked media environments since they are more directly linked to our empirical study cases.

A remarkable feature of the recent literature on online activism is to show the sheer diversity of actors as well as multiple connection practices by way of the internet and SNSs. In fact, the terrain of civil society networking is complex and pluralistic but not theoretically indeterminate. Good reasons exist for plurality and differentiation, discerning how collective action is organized and that what sustains them is valuable. In this way, W. Lance Bennett and Alexandra Segerberg's (2012a, 2012b) characterization of two distinct types of engagement – "the familiar logic of collective action associated with high levels of organizational resources and the formation of collective identities, and the less familiar logic of connective action based on personalized content sharing across media networks" (Bennett & Segerberg, 2012b, p. 739) provides a useful starting point. Bennett and Segerberg are cautious enough not to claim that this distinction establishes fixed categorization schemes (Bennett & Segerberg, 2012b, p. 758).[10] They argue that the introduction of digital media does not change the core dynamics of the former, whereas it does in the latter.

Given the low cost of communication, the Internet and various digital platforms have transformed the capacity for social movement communication, enabling them to produce and spread information on various issues of concern. In keeping with Bennett and Segerberg (2012a, 2012b), we can say that each technological innovation tends to be appropriated by social movement organizers for carrying on a variety of tasks in innovative ways but they do not substantially change the organizations' goals (Bimber, Flanagin, & Stohl, 2012; Earl & Kimport 2011).

This is not meant to imply that the co-existence and co-evolution of technologies do not reshape social movement practices; they do. The point here is that long before the Internet, SNSs and micro-blogging appeared, movement organizations were prodigious in autonomously producing and disseminating material with their visions through a number of venues, variously named as alternative media, radical media, independent media and the like (Downing, 2001; Gamson, 2004). Social movements were also effective in coordinating action, engaging publics, running campaigns and promoting mobilizations in different situations in national and transnational contexts.

To understand what happens when social movements use digital technology for a multitude of tasks, one should be sensitive to certain features of these organizations. The literature conventionally points out that social movements need high levels of demand and resources to form collective identities and "collective action frames," understood here as a construction and reconstruction of collective identifications or common awareness of problems (della Porta, 2012; della Porta & Diani, 2006; Gutmann, 2003).

Although social movements, traditionally regarded as protagonists of social change, are to be seen as strategic actors, it is quite misleading to understand them as primarily motivated by instrumental gains. My analysis, based on the recognition-theoretical approach, follows scholars who, moving beyond a rational choice orientation of earlier studies on social movements, argue that mutual identifications, shared awareness of belonging – or what Honneth calls a "shared semantics" – are constructed through dynamic interactions and conflicts among members of the movement and actors outside it (della Porta, 2012, 2013; della Porta & Diani, 2006; Gutmann, 2003; Ryan, Jeffreys, Ellowitz, & Ryczek, 2013).

From an internal perspective, participants, who are part of a social movement, need to construct and reconstruct shared identifications or collective identities as they are always in flux. People have various axes of difference and affiliations as well as complex and distinct experiences, and often differ on how to pursue social change and define goals and strategies. To construct a sense of "we" and elaborate common frames around defining the conflict, members of social movements often need to negotiate their interpretations and forge common actions to seek resolution of contentious issues.

Outside the movement, members need to selectively interact with a set of other actors – potential allies, opponents, bystanders and elected representatives. To be politically effective, movement organizers must be able to strategize and craft communication to fit their organization's adopted goals, resources and opportunities. While social movement organizers intentionally choose certain actions, they often have to engage in highly reflexive processes, as Charlotte Ryan (2013, p. 136) and her colleagues argue, to "position their resources and forces strategically to maximize their chances of increasing their standing/power."[11] Social movements are also typically involved in education and socialization on a long-term basis to transform patterns of recognition and to advance alternative remedies to perceived problems. Thus, they are further concerned with problems of collective action over time.

Therefore, much of the traditional literature on social movements remains valid to make sense of how social movements use digital technology for carrying out different actions with distinct aims – with effects in personal development, public sphere and formal institutions (Rucht, 2004; Warren, 2001).[12] Even if embedded in distinct "cultures of organization," which defines degrees of centralization and hierarchy, leadership lines of control, professionalization of skills and resources, and decision making and participation (Kavada, 2013; see also Warren, 2001), most social movements frequently use traditional mass media and digital technology simultaneously, combining and re-mixing them (Costanza-Chock, 2012; Mattoni, 2013). Still, when and where social movements play a democratic role or produce democratic effects is a much-debated issue (della Porta, 2012, 2013; Gutmann, 2003; Warren, 2001). I return to this question at the end of this chapter.

My concern here is to explore the second type of logic of connective action, that is, digitally-connected contentious actions in large-scale protests that we are less familiar with (Bennett & Segerberg, 2012b). After the Arab Spring mobilizations, the London Riots, the Greek protests, the Spanish *Indignados* and Occupy Wall Street, many other flexible networks were formed through diverse sorts of digital technologies around the globe (Costanza-Chock, 2012; Dahlgren, 2013; Langman, 2013; Tejerina, Perugorria, Benski, & Langman, 2013). These uprisings have attracted the participation and the engagement of a large number of people across socio-economic and demographic divisions.

Although some critics are skeptical about the novelty of such collective actions, since large-scale political protests date back to at least two centuries in modern history, there are several new trends at work now. These connective actions are to be seen as a central organizational structure in large-scale protests; usually they are formed through personally-shaped messages. Thus, the so-called "technology-enabled networking" (Livingston & Asmolov, 2010) or "digitally networked action" (Bennet & Segerberg, 2012a, 2012b) spread without a centralized or a strong organizational control, even if they draw on pre-existent social movement networks or are ignited by a certain group of activists (Dahlgren, 2013; Langman, 2013; Tejerina et al., 2013). Ordinary citizens do not need to be part of a group, nor share an ideological position or values of a given community, to act as protest organizers. People engage in co-production and co-distribution of political material, and personally-shaped messages, posts, twists and videos are replicated then spread out into the networked environment. While mass demonstrations in public squares and streets remain obviously important to these protests, distinct forms of coordination and demonstration occur in and through the media. The co-presence of people in the same space is no longer needed for a contentious performance to emerge.

Different from traditional social movements requiring highly demanding resources to coordinate common goals across different individual and sub-group values, beliefs and interests in large-scale connective action formations, coordinators or activists invite people to engage with each other and take action. Frequently, there is an explicit determination to avoid designating leaders or official spokespeople. Even when there is a stable center of organization employing mechanisms to mobilize concerted widespread actions, including massive street demonstrations and face-to-face interactions, protesters can hardly attempt to induce people into sharing collective identification as in social movements (Bennett & Segerberg, 2012b; Dahlgren, 2013; Langman, 2013; Tejerina et al., 2013). Finding ways to mobilize citizens into diverse paths of action outside protests – supporting causes in online campaigns, petitions and boycotts for example – by no means implies the burden of brokering differences to manage and coordinate goals as in traditional social movements.

Still, it would be misleading to disregard the interactions between contenders and their institutional environment, including rational negotiation and creativity (Dahlgren, 2013, p. 75; Seferiades & Johnson, 2012, pp. 241–44l). The image that we receive from studies on digitally enabled mobilizations is that participants, moved by a constellation of emotions – anxiety, outrage, indignation, humiliation, and hope – attempt to attain or reclaim some valued good. Confronting perceived growing levels of social and economic inequality and degradation, coupled with the alleged neglect of political elites, claimants in various *occupy movements* requested goods such as restoration of dignity, greater opportunities, jobs, social mobility, and the right to live meaningful lives (Dahlgren, 2013, p. 75; Langman, 2013; Tejerina et al., 2013, p. 385). In the face of imposed dictatorship and restrictions on conditions for democratization, claimants in various Arab Spring movements demanded genuine standards and prospects for democratization in addition to the elimination of other obstructions related to gender (Moghadam, 2013) and political socio-economic inequalities (Desrues, 2013).

Most of these studies show that, while a large number of participants are moved by feelings of intolerable burden borne by political and economic institutions and cultural customs, individuals express their personal contentions and demands in various ways across networked environments. It seems correct to say that there is no attempt to create a "united we" that relates to a somewhat particularized community concerned with affirming certain modes of life, interpreting social status or defending specific kinds of rights, as in traditional social movements.

Less certain is how one should understand the "shared semantics" of participants in such cases. Referring to the multi-vocal demands and articulations of all kinds in Occupy Wall Street, Peter Dahlgren (2013, p. 79) claims that participants, in spite of their genuine heterogeneity, managed to provide a "reasonably coherent political identity of the morally enraged, economically victimized, and politically disenfranchised majority." In the same vein, Benjamin Tejerina and his colleagues argue that contending communities in *occupy movements* have been defined and portrayed in the broadest possible ways through terms such as "the 99%," "the people," "the activists," the "militants" (Tejerina et al., 2013, p. 385). Whereas these situations signal deep legitimation crises, one may wonder that claimants demand a foundation or a re-foundation of institutionalized conditions that allow individuals to freely and consistently pursue their different projects of self-realization.

In light of points already made, it comes as no surprise that those broad frames around basic goods that galvanize large-scale protests hardly prompt participants to bridge differences among themselves for constructing an often difficult unified political agenda to intervene constructively in political decision-making.[13] If we understand these struggles as aspiring to secure the fundamental conditions for individual self-determination and self-realization, it is reasonable to argue that a "shared semantics" here is to be seen as including all personal reasons for contestation and demands for innovation. In this situation, the individuals' experience of being subjected by domination is hardly translated back into nature, causes and remedies of particular conflicts. Rather, it transcends particularity to enable a broader public of publics to come to the forefront.

It is not part of the scope of this chapter to inquire into the conditions under which digitally-enabled mobilizations could become stable or successfully achieve political targets, nor how they could affect people on a more permanent basis or even how they could help pre-existing social movements, mobilized around specific struggles, to promote transformative changes. These complex issues pose a challenge to future studies in this field of research.

Conclusion

The three aspects of networked environments I present in this chapter – as a setting for self-expression, political talk and deliberation, and for collective action – are valuable for understanding distinct dimensions of struggles for recognition in contemporary society. The usefulness of the recognition-theoretical approach is that it captures the complexity of these interrelated dynamics which are likely to be treated in separate fields of study.

Nonetheless, conflicts tend to be specific and should be treated as such. Thus, particular problems in the theory of recognition as well as specific relations among social actors within networked media environments will be developed through empirically-based analyses in our two subsequent study cases. Our cases illustrate distinct forms of collective organization, coordination of action and interactions in digital platforms. While Chapter 6 investigates internal conflict that emerges between a traditional social movement of deaf people in Brazil and individual members of that collectivity in a specific online community, Chapter 7, focusing on outrage provoked by a racist comment made by a federal congressman, illustrates the logic of digitally-enabled activism. In both cases, Honneth's theory of recognition offers insights at various levels in understanding the struggle for recognition in everyday life.

Inthe first study, my collaborator and I argue that Honneth's theory of recognition opens up promising avenues for exploring the role of emotion in politics, particularly when issues of injustice are at stake. We show that the construction of "a shared semantics" of identity, both individually and collectively, is related to emotions and conflicting interpretations of needs, rights and social achievements. This study uses storytelling by deaf people gathered in two virtual environments: (a) the website of the main Brazilian organization for deaf persons (FENEIS), and (b) Orkut, an online SNS. While movement organizers mobilize feelings of agency and collective action frames in their efforts to form coalitions and broker differences to support specific policies, deaf people show their moral dissent and different ways of understanding issues and conditions for their personal liberty and autonomy. This chapter investigates how "feelings of injustice" are an important source for the intelligibility of injustice; it suggests that Honneth's approach of subjective reaction to injury as a violation of conditions to practical identity can be articulated with notions of discursive justification in the Habermasian fashion.

In the second study, my collaborator and I analyze how individuals and groups struggling for recognition engage in various types of conflict, and sometimes have to mutually attune themselves with multiple others in a field of experiences of both respect and disrespect. We investigate how an expression of racism and homophobia made by a Brazilian deputy in a TV program provoked people's self-expression, political talk and deliberation, and activism in networked media environments. Focusing on three distinct online platforms – YouTube, Blogs and Facebook, this case offers various pictures of "episodic" struggles for recognition in everyday interactions. It shows different spaces and conditions under which people engage in conflicts to affirm if they are fighting for good causes or not, and if the alleged obstacles in prevailing cultural practices, social institutions and laws are legitimate or not.

Notes

1. For example, while Facebook is mainly used for social relationship maintenance, LinkedIn is used for professional networking; while YouTubers

interact with unknown people as an "imagined mass" (Burgess & Green, 2009, p. 8), bloggers regularly post information and personal opinions and usually see themselves as standing in front of a "public pulpit" (Papacharissi, 2010, p. 145; Tremayne, 2007, Meraz, 2007) before a somewhat known or imagined audience.

2. Saul Levmore and Martha Nussbaum (2010, p. 10) have pointed out that "privacy" can be understood as: (a) seclusion, as the "right to be beyond the gaze of others;" (b) intimacy, as the choice one makes "to share certain information and experiences;" (c) secrecy, referring to protection of "information as seclusion is to the physical person;" (d) autonomy, as the "set of private choices each person makes."

3. Considering the private as a starting point of social connectivity, Zizi Papacharissi (2010, p. 141) argues that "the social utility of the private sphere is magnified in a three-fold way: (a) 'multiplying' the potential audiences of social contacts the individual may communicate with, including family, friends, and acquaintances; b) by allowing the individual to sustain this social contact within a privately public and publicly private space that retains the familiarity of the private and the reach of the public; (c) by affording presentation of the self within a mediated environment that serves the prominent values of autonomy, control and expression for the technologically literate individual."

4. Scholars who work within Goffman's dramaturgy have particularly accentuated different strategies used by individuals to portray a version of themselves in online environments. Admitting that "the sequential arrangement of backstage and front stage is upset," Papacharissi (2010, p. 142) claims that "the backstage no longer signals privacy and the front stage does not guarantee publicity." In a similar vein, Danah boyd (2011, p. 51) argues that "in networked publics, contexts often collide such that a performer is unaware of audiences from different contexts, magnifying the awkwardness and making adjustments impossible."

5. In Grasmuck and colleagues' words: "African Americans, Latinos, and Indian ancestry students...invest more frequently and intensively in displaying a cultural self, marked by specific consumer and popular cultural preferences, and they invest more in the direct "about me" narrations than do Vietnamese or white students" (Grasmuck et al., 2009, p. 179).

6. Sanja Kapidzic and Suzan C. Herring (2011) show different patterns of gender, communication and self-presentation in teen chat sites, in terms of: (a) *linguistic features*, "boys tend to use more self-reference words, social words, articles, and big words in most of the samples. Girls, in contrast, tend to express more negative and positive emotions, although the values for emotion words across the chat samples are quite variable" (Kapidzic & Herring, 2011, p. 46); (b) *acts*, "males use more manipulative acts, while females use more reactive acts and tend to use more acts that contribute to information exchange" (Kapidzic & Herring, 2011, p. 47); (c) *message tone*, "the teenage boys used more aggressive and flirtatious tones, whereas the girls much more often adopted a friendly tone in their messages. Sexual message tone was used slightly more in male than in female messages" (Kapidzic & Herring, 2011, p. 48); (d) *image characteristics*, "photographs revealed that female users were more likely to choose images of themselves at intimate

(male 1 percent, female 11 percent) and close personal (male 30 percent, female 52 percent) distances. In contrast, male users preferred far personal (male 40 percent, female 20 percent) distance by a large margin" (Kapidzic & Herring, 2011, p. 48).

7. A far-reaching body of work has been produced to investigate the central principles underlying deliberative theory. See for example, Benhabib, 1996; Bohman, 1996; Dryzek, 2000, 2010; Gutmann & Thompson, 1996; Maia, 2012a; Mansbridge, 1999; Parkinson & Mansbridge, 2012; Rosenberg, 2007; Steiner, 2012a.

8. Online discussion is significantly and positively associated with individual heterogeneous networks and SNSs, whether or not explicitly selected (Brundidge, 2010; Brundidge & Rice, 2009; Kim, 2011; Stromer-Galley & Muhlberger, 2009). Even when not searching for political difference, individuals can become inadvertently exposed to conflicting political perspectives and challenging information and opinions because of the blurring of boundaries in networked online environments as well as the provision of hyperlinks and interactive communication applications. Corroborating the tendency that I pointed out above, studies on online discussions offer evidence that people tend to be more accountable for what they say, abide by rules of civility and respect, and follow conventional cultural cues on sites where participants are identifiable or compelled to use their real names (boyd & Donath, 2004; boyd & Ellison, 2007; Coleman & Moss, 2012). Moderation practices, regardless of whether they are previous or posterior to posts, are also seen as having a positive impact for maintaining civility (Wright & Street, 2007).

9. See also for example, Cammaerts, Mattoni, & McCurdy, 2013; della Porta & Diani, 2006; della Porta, 2012, 2013; Gamson, 2004; Hobson, 2003; Klandermans, van der Toorn, & van Stekelenburg, 2008; McAdam, 2000.

10. Bennett and Segerberg (2012b) construct a typology of the organizational dynamics of: (i) social movements; (ii) hybrid organizations such as advocacy associations and NGOs; and, (iii) digitally-based large-scale contentious actions. Remarking that "the real world is of course far messier than this three-point model" (Bennett & Segerberg, 2012b, p. 758), Bennett and Segerberg explain that a similar logic of action of social movements is to be found in advocacy associations – including NGOs, international non-governmental organizations, transnational non-governmental associations, etc. – provided we conceive this logic in a looser way. These hybrid associations of distinct groups, with varying levels of organizational resources, also need to construct leadership and to develop common action frames and brokerage of differences in order to bridge coalitions with different viewpoints and constituencies. However, leadership and political hubs are formed in a more decentralized fashion than in social movement organizations and their publics where members or affiliates are invited to participate on the basis of looser ties. Other scholars have shown that NGOs, depending on the context and opportunities, may appear as advocacy groups, policy think tanks and social movements to carry out various types of action (Bimber, Flanagin, & Stohl 2012; Chadwick, 2007).

11. To illustrate such a reflexive process, Charlotte Ryan and her colleagues remark that "movement organizing involves not only action, but constant

thinking, listening and discussion – organizers assess possible alliances and political opportunities, design and execute proactive and defensive strategies, test alternative frames for conveying these strategies to allies and adapt these tactics for future rounds of engagement" (Ryan et al., 2013, p. 136).

12. To illustrate, actions that have: effects on personal developments, referring to advances in individual political and critical skills, empowerment and capacities for participation; effects in the public sphere, referring to development of agendas, provision of voices in public reasoning and participation in collective judgment; and, effects on political formal institutions, referring to political representation, protest, resistance, coordination, or cooperation to exert influence on political decision-making (Rucht, 2004; Warren, 2001).

13. According to Bennett and Segerberg (2012b, p. 744) broad frames require "little in the way of persuasion, reason or reframing to bridge differences with how others may feel about a common problem."

6
Recognition, Feelings of Injustice and Claim Justification: Deaf People's Storytelling on the Internet

Rousiley C. M. Maia and Regiane L. O. Garcêz

In the recent upsurge in research on the role of emotions in politics, ranging from cognitive science to philosophy to the social sciences, several scholars have demonstrated the importance of understanding how emotion affects the cognition and reasoning capacities that underlie political behavior (Marcus, Neuman, & Mackuen, 2000; Thompson & Hoggett, 2012). Emotion helps create group identity and mobilization (Barnes, 2012; Nussbaum, 1995, 2003) as well as engagement in deliberation (Krause, 2008; Mackuen, Wolak, Keele, & Marcus, 2010; Maia, 2012d; Steiner, 2012b). In this chapter we draw on Axel Honneth's work to explore the sensitive dimension of suffering and issues of injustice. We argue that his political philosophy helps to deepen and refine the understanding of subjective reactions to injuries, without assuming that emotions are a kind of individual "property." Despite claims to the contrary, we contend that Honneth's attempt to establish a link between a normative dimension in "feelings of injustice" and collective action opens promising paths through which empirical studies of emotion could be expanded and reconceptualized.

More specifically, this chapter will further the understanding of how "feelings of injustice" enable marginalized and disrespected subjects to articulate an "intersubjective framework of interpretation" in order to generate motivation for social resistance. Following Honneth's lead, we attempt to evince through empirically-based analysis that hurt feelings are an important source of intelligibility for injustice and that disagreement often emerges among members of groups when constructing "a shared semantics." We argue that Honneth's approach is not sufficiently developed to explain either how individuals should deal with dissent in processing moral conflict, or with dissent which emerges when deciding what counts as recognition responses in a given context. As an answer to this problem, we advocate that Honneth's understanding of the role of emotion in struggles for recognition is not incompatible with Habermasian discursive justification; both theoretical frameworks can be jointly applied in empirical research.

Our study focuses on deaf persons, subjects who have been victims of stigmatization and marginalization, who face language barriers, and who generally depend on interpreters to express themselves in spoken debates. Since dominated individuals usually feel the need to tell their own stories to make sense of suffering and to have their experiences of injustice come alive, we chose to focus on storytelling. In supporting Honneth's argument that social suffering should be searched for not only within the context of participation in the public sphere but also in everyday domains, we investigate how claims for recognition are articulated and eventually justified from the perspective of a social movement and also from the point of view of the individual members of that collectivity. As the Internet has become a means for deaf persons to express themselves, we gathered stories in two virtual environments: (a) the website of the main Brazilian organization for deaf persons, the National Federation for the Education and Integration of Deaf Persons or Federação Nacional de Educação e Integração dos Surdos (FENEIS, 2009), and (b) the Orkut, an online social network.

The life histories expressed in these two online environments illustrate a well-known worldwide debate among deaf people who use sign language and those opting to talk – a controversy that can be traced back to the ban on the use of sign language in 1880 that opened the path for oralization until the first half of the 20th century (Dhamoon, 2009; Lane, 1984). According to the World Federation of Deaf (WFD) – representative of the deaf in international agencies such as the UN, UNESCO and the ILO – Brazil is one of the 25 countries in the world that legally recognized sign language. The Brazilian law that promotes sign language was created in 2002 as a result of the struggles of various local associations, led by FENEIS. Historically, the deaf Brazilian movement has been a benchmark reference in the world; it has advocated the use of sign language through protests and continuously brings pressure to bear on elected representatives to participate in the definition and evaluation of public policies regarding sign language (Quadros, 2012). Brazil is the first country to create a national program, supported by government, which offers degree courses in public universities. Between 2010 and 2012, nearly 1000 teachers of sign language and 500 interpreters graduated (Quadros, 2012). In spite of these achievements, the use of sign language is far from consensual among deaf people themselves.

This chapter is organized into two parts. In the first, my collaborator and I present the theoretical debate on Honneth's thesis about the relationship between feelings of injustice and the struggles for recognition, arguing that some critiques have failed to give full justice to Honneth's program. We advocate that his model can be fruitfully operationalized for empirical analysis. Then, we present our methodological choices. In the second part, we examine – in light of the stories gathered from the FENEIS website and Orkut – the tensions underlying the construction of "a shared semantics" and the efforts of deaf persons to justify their demands for recognition in these two virtual environments. We conclude with a summary of empirical results and possible normative implications for further studies on emotion and struggles for recognition.

From feelings of injustice to struggles for recognition

Several studies based on social and cognitive sciences argue that emotion is often intertwined with cognition, and is required to arouse people's attention and to provoke engagement around any issue (Bickford, 2011; Marcus et al., 2000; Nussbaum, 1995; Thompson & Hoggett, 2012). Marcus and colleagues' model of affective intelligence, based on two emotional sub-systems in the brain – "disposition" and "surveillance" – helps to explain how people's emotional states affect political behavior. They argue that citizens' strategies for party identification, vote choice, interest to search for more information, willingness to compromise and so forth are products not of simply prior commitment and attentiveness but also of emotions that manifest situational appraisals (in states of calmness or anxiety, enthusiasm or frustration, aversion, etc.). While this model represents a major advance in explaining how citizens process politics and how emotion structures political behavior, it does not pay much attention to normative dimensions in political judgment.

Sociologists, such as Luc Boltanski (1999, p. 84), emphasize that emotions cannot be taken as a mere private reaction, but rather as a socially constructed and historical variable. From such a perspective, the explanation of the bond between individual actors' interpretative achievements and socio-structural guidelines that stem from the pre-structured normative nature of society become a major theoretical problem.

Martha Nussbaum (2003), drawing on literary description in the Greek Stoics' ideas as well as cognitive psychology, develops a cognitive/evaluative account of emotion for understanding the relationship between different types of emotion, reasoning and morality. Focusing on "social construction" in emotional life, Nussbaum makes clear that emotions involve judgments about important things, through which we can appraise an external object as salient for our own well-being; and thus make practical judgments such as what problems we have or do not have and what picture of ethical change can be adopted as plausible. According to Nussbaum (2003, p. 15), understanding emotion in this way raises a number of normative questions and offers resources for connecting sentiments to the good life. Sharon Krause (2008), by adopting a broad Humean approach, surveys the role of emotion concerning judgment and deliberation and, like Nussbaum, defends the idea that conceptions of the good imply affective modes of consciousness. She offers a powerful analysis that incorporates affective engagement into practical reasoning.

In such a context, Axel Honneth's attempt to articulate feelings of injustice in everyday experience and the normative ideal of self-realization seems highly innovative. Honneth does not mean to call attention to *all* emotions, but rather those related to "feelings of injustice," "the feeling of being unjustly treated and the experience of being disrespected" (Honneth, 1996, p. 168). He does not delve into complex details about the specific content of emotions, but rather begins an analysis of "moral feelings" as "the emotional raw material of social conflict" (Honneth, 1996, p. 168). Based on a pragmatist approach to feelings – derived from Dewey – Honneth defines feelings as "affective reactions generated upon succeeding or failing to realize our intentions" (Honneth, 1996, p. 137). By articulating a theory of psychological development with a broad social theory, incorporating Habermas's lesson of grounding critique in the norms of communication, Honneth argues that subjects expect specific forms of recognition as conditions for their well-being and autonomy. According to Honneth, injustice is first felt as a refusal of intersubjective recognition that violently disrupts one's relationship to oneself: physical abuse (which corresponds to the level of recognition Honneth names "love"); denial of basic moral respect and legal protection ("rights"); denigration of individual or collective ways of life and refusal to acknowledge one's social value ("solidarity" or "achievement").

Honneth's work shares some points with Charles Taylor's (1994) influential *The Politics of recognition*, such as using Hegel's and Mead's writings to build the concept of recognition. As already discussed in Chapter 1, Honneth's endeavor, unlike Taylor's, is not to conceive the rise of new social moments as a distinctive feature of the political landscape of the time, but rather to give critical theory's emancipatory aspiration a more practical and empirical grounding in everyday feelings of disrespect taken as a source for collective transformative praxis. Differently from Taylor, who focuses on Hegel's *Phenomenology*, Honneth surveys Jena manuscripts in order to explain social integration in both antagonist and normative ways, reflecting the influence of Habermas. Honneth draws on Mead also as a means to explain identity as socially constituted and yet open to continuous innovation.

Numerous critics have stated that references to feelings of injustice in people do not adequately explain social struggles. Some scholars argue that feelings are not reliable sources to decide issues of justice. Simon Thompson (2006) argues that feelings of injustice may become distorted and emotional reactions may be unjustified. In Thompson's words, at times persons "may feel that they are being mistreated when in fact they are not" (Thompson, 2006, p. 168). Furthermore, they may use resentment and promote "false comparisons" with other individuals and groups to advance inadequate and unconvincing demands. Likewise, Susan Bickford (2011, p. 1027) stresses that emotion may lead one to mischaracterize a situation; how a person feels seduces that person into misperceiving.

Other scholars are reluctant to tie the content and authority of moral norms to the psychological state of individuals (Alexander & Lara, 1996; Fraser, 2003b; Kalyvas, 1999). Nancy Fraser argues that Honneth, in building an "excessively personalized sense of injury" (Fraser, 2003b, p. 204), does not set down procedures to discern which demands may be justified. Fraser is particularly dissatisfied with Honneth's treatment of recognition as a matter of self-realization because, according to her, any claim that would enhance the claimant's distinctiveness and self-esteem would be justified. Her argument is that in the absence of any principled basis for distinguishing justified from unjustified claims, even racist identities could deserve recognition (Fraser, 2003a, p. 38). In the same vein and considering groups that nurture anger towards others, Alexander and Lara (1996, p. 135) point out that demands for recognition "can easily become demands for domination."

It is true that emotion can be capricious, excessive and may lead one to mischaracterize situations or overemphasize particulars (Bickford, 2011; Thompson, 2006). The objection that hurt feelings may not display an accurate sense of injustice can be relativized if one remembers that perception of injury does not necessarily lead to judgments of injustice or to resistance. Indeed, recognition struggles are always contingent, or even a rare possibility. According to Honneth, a negative experience can only become a motivational basis for collective resistance if: (a) "subjects are able to articulate them [hurt feelings] within an intersubjective framework of interpretation that they can show to be typical for an entire group" (Honneth, 1996, p. 163), and (b) "such inhibition on action is overcome through involvement in collective resistance," such that individuals may "indirectly convince themselves of their moral or social worth" (Honneth, 1996, p. 164).

At the kernel of Honneth's program is not only the expressivist dimension of hurt feelings, but also their cognitive potential to trigger self-reflection about violations of "well-grounded" normative expectations or principles; feelings of injustice thus help disclose unmet demands that can retrospectively be made explicit. Once it is acknowledged that hurt feelings should be understood as a "signal" that expectations of recognition have been violated, it becomes clear that they are not some proof or some kind of justification in themselves. Here we endorse Nikolas Kompridis' argument that subjective experience is "an irreplaceable and absolutely necessary source of intelligibility" (Kompridis, 2007, p. 280) of suffering, but it does not assure any construction of valid demands. We also agree with James Tully that "they [experiences of shame, anger or indignation] do not decide the issue of their moral legitimacy in advance" (Tully, 2004, p. 328).

Honneth's reasoning might well be right for paying attention to what happens in the "underground" of social conflicts (Honneth, 2003a, p. 120). However, argumentation developed to this point does not explain how one can distinguish valid from invalid demands. Honneth clearly acknowledges the problem of certain claims that cannot be accepted: "of course it is obvious that we cannot endorse every political revolt as such – that we cannot consider every demand for recognition as morally legitimate or acceptable" (Honneth, 2003a, p. 171; see also Honneth, 2007c, pp. 77–78, 2012, p. 150).

To check whether "signals" due to feelings of injury constitute an adequate sense of injustice (Honneth, 1996, p. 168), Honneth (2003a, p. 187) proposes the following criteria within the structure of recognition: "for only demands that potentially contribute to the expansion of social relations of recognition can be considered normatively grounded, since they point in the direction of a rise in the moral level of social integration." This statement has two important consequences.

First, reciprocal recognition requires a moral attitude of considering the other; subjects cannot be defined as independent beings seeking to promote their own wishes. Rather than a quest for domination, Honneth in describing the second sphere of recognition, has in view, like Habermas, the equalitarian-universalist normative principle that underlies modern rights, that is, mutual respect and equal treatment for every human being who deserves to see his or her fundamental freedom recognized. Honneth adds two other dependent modes of recognition (based on the principles of love and social esteem), which are seen to have specific duties in preserving the integrity of human subjects.

Second, recognition of social integration depends on the criteria of reciprocity and generality; legitimate demands for recognition in any sphere should result in the inclusion of more people into the "circle of full members of society" (Honneth, 2003a, p. 185). In this sense, the demands for recognition of racist or xenophobic groups, for instance, are asymmetrical and morally inadequate because they imply attitudes such as intolerance, violence, and persecution that cause harm to "outsiders"; and therefore such demands cannot be justified from the perspective of other parties affected by them.

Even though Honneth does not deal systematically with justification, he has made specific propositions concerning this crucial issue (Deranty, 2009, p. 313; Forst, 2002, 2007b). Honneth explicitly admits that each recognition principle provokes a "constant struggle over its appropriate application and interpretation" (Honneth, 2003a, p. 186). He states that what counts as a legitimate or fair demand emerges from the possibility "of understanding the consequences of implementing it as a gain in individuality or inclusion" (Honneth, 2003a, p. 187). He further recommends that if there is moral conflict between demands based on different principles of recognition, the second principle – the claim of all subjects to equally respect their individual autonomy – becomes an absolute priority (Honneth, 2007a, p. 137). Here, Honneth preserves a fundamental Kantian intuition that human beings are equal moral persons able to decide freely and to participate in public debates about collective norms and actions. However, Honneth does not make clear *how* individuals and groups negotiate competing claims for recognition and dispute their conflicting interpretations and/or values within groups or in society at large.

The attempts of a few scholars to translate aspects of mutual recognition into criteria for discursive justification are well suited to helping articulate normative analysis and empirical work further. Tully (2000, p. 445) presents three criteria based on a procedural discursive approach: (a) citizens in whose name a demand (or a proposed identity) is made must support it in the first-person perspective; (b) the demand must respond to and take into account counter-proposals by other members of society; (c) the demand must be made good to others. Rainer Forst, concerned about adopting a procedural approach to establish the legitimacy of demands for recognition, states: "there must be no social and political relations which cannot be reciprocally and generally justified to all those who are part of a political-social context" (Forst, 2007b, p. 295).

From this perspective, we argue that Habermas's discourse ethics is a useful theoretical framework to deal with moral disagreement and conflicting demands for recognition: it provides extensive and theoretically grounded criteria to observe and interpret justification processes. There are a few caveats in our attempt to bring together Habermas and Honneth's formulations on disagreement and moral conflict. To begin with, Habermas assumes a principle of mutual recognition when partners in dialogue reciprocally concede communicative freedom to exchange reasons and justifications. In Habermas's view, recognition implies acknowledgment of individual freedom but not self-realization or self-fulfillment. Second, although Habermas is usually criticized as being rationalist, he has long admitted that emotions play an important role in practical reason (Neblo, 2003; Rehg, 1994): He further argues that the violation of "normative expectation"[1] – supposedly valid not only for a subject but for the entire group – motivates argumentative engagement.[2] In this sense, Habermas admits that certain emotions (for instance, indignation) are important for both moral perception (the ability of an agent to perceive elements in a given situation as morally relevant) and for justification of norms and actions.

In our empirical study, we start with Honneth's premise that subjects' everyday affective reactions to disrespect can be taken as symptoms of violation of some normative expectation. We assume that an ethical integration of persons that suffer injustice is needed to build "a shared semantics"; and we evince that this is a dynamic process of claim-making and claim-receiving rather than a static set of interpretations. Our analysis shows that the display of emotions is differently shaped in distinct online environments; our findings suggest that while representative entities present a more clear-cut interpretative framework of misrecognition and possible solutions, group members refer to a "shared value-horizon" that is often based on dissent, and they raise broader contestations about the true interests of "deaf individuals."

Storytelling and disability

We chose to focus on storytelling because life stories told in the first-person reveal the sensitive dimension of pain or suffering. Telling stories allows people to share their stories and to share affinities with others experiencing common constraints (Dryzek, 2000; Polletta, 2007; Young, 2000). In Iris Young's words, "those who experience the wrong and perhaps some others who sense it, may have no language for expressing the suffering as injustice, but nevertheless they can tell stories that relate a sense of wrong" (Young, 2000, p. 72). Furthermore, telling stories to a wider audience is a way to sensitize people who have different experiences, so that they may understand the harm and oppression that others have gone through (Black, 2008; Polletta & Lee, 2006; Ryfe, 2006).

Narratives, thus, unfold specificities that need to be recognized. There is a vast literature showing that storytelling – particularly when linked to universal principles or general issues – helps to politicize issues and to craft justifications for specific actions (Black, 2008; Dryzek, 2000, p. 69; Ryfe, 2006; Steiner, 2012b). At times, telling stories may become a mechanism to describe, demonstrate, or explain something to others, who may then accept the relevance of certain demands or identify specific orientations as valid. In such circumstances, personal testimonies do not provide clear answers but rather show the moral complexity of some problems. Still, storytelling does not necessarily go unchallenged; and it may also be used in manipulative ways for purely strategic purposes (Dryzek, 2000, p. 71; Steiner, 2012b, p. 85).

Narrative is particularly useful for *disability studies*. Several researchers stress the importance of storytelling because they suggest that disability is not a biological, but rather a social phenomenon that is negotiated and socially constructed (Goodley & Tragaskis, 2006). Furthermore, life stories are important because bodily experience is deeply embedded in narrative. "Narratives are projected from and inscribed into the body. The body is a storyteller, and it is partly through the tales it tells that we may interpret, give meaning to and understand bodies" (Smith & Sparkes, 2008, p. 19). Storytelling can provide different understanding about disability that refutes the tragedy story, which challenges oppression and allows distinct body-self relationships. More specifically, in *deaf studies* a current of thought that focuses not on disability but on deaf cultural and linguistic communities – storytelling is considered a deaf cultural expression that can support social mobilization and linguistic resistance (Burch & Kafer, 2010).

Methodology

To develop our study, we chose to analyze storytelling in two different online sites: (i) one that serves the purpose of a social movement for self-presentation, education and collective claim formulation – the website of the National Federation for the Education and Integration of Deaf Persons (FENEIS); and (ii) one that is meant for internal conversations among one's own group – Orkut. The FENEIS website, being managed by a national front organization that gathers around 120 entities throughout the country, allows us to analyze claims about shared sources of injustice, collective identities and remedies publicly demanded. In contrast, Orkut, being an online social network where deaf people engage in a relatively spontaneous way of talking, exchanging experiences and articulating their preferences, allows us to tap into sources of group internal differentiation.

The FENEIS website seeks to disseminate the Brazilian Sign Language (Libras) and presents information regarding legislation, work, education and news. Storytelling is inserted into several sections. We decided to analyze the 6 first-person life stories among the 25 found on the FENEIS website. Such personal stories were written by deaf people in long and detailed texts.

We chose a very popular forum that had been created in an Orkut community named "Friends among the deaf and the non-deaf" (*Amigos entre surdos e ouvintes*) that at the time had 11,393 members. The forum was named "DEAF Shame (Vergonha SURDO, 2005)" and had 404 postings.[3] For the purposes of our analysis, we highlighted conversations in which storytelling played a central role. We examined the life stories and posts that preceded and that ensued from these conversations, according to the procedures set down by Polletta and Lee (2006) and Black (2008) in their studies of online discussion lists. After eliminating commercial content, divulgation of events, and other posting unrelated to the initial proposition, we ended up with 67 posts.

To duly assess virtual communicative practices, we followed scholars who defend that it is crucial to understand not only the content of online messages but also the context in which people use the web and the broader social practices in which these messages are embedded (Goggin & Newell, 2003; Schrock, Holden, & Reid, 2004). Thus we engaged in an in-depth qualitative reading of the material and adopted more general and long-term analyses of fundamental causes and conditions to draw their consequences, thereby providing the basis for adequate critical research. On both the FENEIS website and the Orkut forum we analyzed:

(a) articulations between the expressive language of storytelling and demands for recognition, and (b) the interlocutors' efforts to eventually justify their claims. We studied how deaf persons stated their commitments and explained what was or was not to be done about the issues in debate.

Feelings of injustice and the construction of a shared semantics

If emotion alone does not suffice to explain moral judgment and struggles that aim at overcoming existing social injustice,[4] we must turn our attention to such emotional/cognitive and normative resources as a collective meaning-making process. In this section, we deal with the problem posed by Honneth's thesis that such a "framework of interpretation" needs to be "typical for an entire group." Our analysis attempts to explore the question of how difference is produced within groups and why it matters for recognition struggles. It shows that identity issues are linked to ethical issues that arise from orientations in a communal world; and imply choices that persons make *for him- or herself,* but *together with others* (Forst, 2002, p. 283).

We assume that conflicts always arise when representatives of groups attempt to frame values, beliefs and preferences in a collective project; it is quite unlikely that any discourse will contemplate the full breadth of the diversity of the aspirations and interests involved (Maia, 2012e). As was discussed in the previous chapter, members of groups frequently engage in conflict among themselves as long as they have different views on how they should live their own lives, including ways to overcome obstacles that restrict them in unjustifiable ways. The issue that we seek to explore in this section is not that identities are constructed within a system of differences, but rather that differences are generally laid out on a hierarchical scale in which some are considered inferior and of lower value than others – an issue which is at the core of Honneth's theory.

Storytelling and demands for recognition on the FENEIS website

The narrators of the storytelling in the FENEIS website not only "bring to the public" the feelings of deaf persons, but they also articulate these feelings in such a way as to construct a positive self-image in different spheres of human interaction. Narratives promote feelings associated with resistance, and shape emotions that motivate people towards being successful, to feel strong and in control of their lives and to achieve self-realization (Schrock et al., 2004, p. 65; Whittier, 2001, p. 241). Our analysis shows that they build an "intersubjective framework of interpretation," which enables them to persuade themselves of their own moral and social value (Honneth, 1996, p. 258).

This is theoretically and politically important because deaf people have been subjected to several sorts of humiliation and disrespect, and multiple negative self-images have been impinged upon them in the past. The history of deaf people shows that they were seen as lacking in relation to the ideal image of God in the early modern era; as "abnormal" or "deviant" as opposed to a "normal" human being within the evolutionary and scientific horizon in the 19th century; and as objects of compassion and medical cure designed to "rehabilitate" their human potential or "recover" their abilities as far as possible within the medical approach in the first half of the 20th century (Arneil, 2009; Lane, 1984; Strobel, 2006).

In the post-war period, policies shaped by the so-called "integrative" model, aimed to bring deaf and disabled people into society. The key effort was to combat the confinement of people with impairment to their home because of their family's shame or were segregated in asylums or hospitals as a form of "banishment of the undesired" (Sacks, 1989; Strobel, 2006). In the 1980s and 1990s, a new inclusive approach – to a large extent the outcome of a series of international conventions favoring people with disabilities, and successful rights campaigns and struggles led chiefly by transnational social movements and scholars with disabilities – guided non-discriminatory norms and policies in several countries to allow equal participation of people with disabilities in systems such as education, work, social security, family life, culture, and leisure (Calder, 2011; Thomas, 2004).

Although non-discriminatory laws are prominent in Brazil and many institutions have re-organized to follow inclusion principles in a great variety of ways, many obstacles remain (Avritzer, 2009). Deaf persons are still often perceived as incapable, as having compromised cognition, and as being unable to advance in professions that require much study (Garcêz & Maia, 2009; Lane, 1984; Strobel, 2006). Against this current social hierarchy of values, the storytelling on the website evinces that deaf persons show a positive self-image.

The six first-person stories that we took from the FENEIS website show very different life histories. There is a deaf priest, teacher, systems analyst, gastronomy student, language and literature teacher, and a deaf and blind person that did not state a profession but who does voluntary work for deaf and blind people. These are varied paths and life histories,

but there are many similarities. All narrators express motivational resistance against shame, alienation, worthlessness and powerlessness; they
construct a politicized interpretation of their capacity for agency; and
show feelings of pride in and solidarity with the larger community.

> FATHER VICENTE (PRIEST): "In 1950, a Holy Year, bishop Dom Justino
> needed to go to Rome and decided to take me so that the Pope
> could get to know me and think of the possibility of ordaining me
> a priest. …When I walked into the Pope's office, I knelt and asked:
> 'may I be ordained a priest?' The Holy Father stood and said: 'wait
> and we shall see.' He then talked to Dom Justino: 'He already speaks
> well, but we need to study this special case and we will answer later'
> [Several days later the Pope allowed Father Vicente to be ordained a
> priest]. I was very happy. And it was on Saint Anthony's September
> when it all started, and here am I with much joy."
>
> SÍLVIA (LANGUAGE AND LITERATURE TEACHER): "During my life as a student
> I found it hard to read. …At school, most of the time, colleagues
> and teachers treated me as if I were a lesser being. I felt completely
> left out. I finished a course in Pedagogy – …My plans and projects
> now are significantly broader. I am preparing myself for entering a
> Master's degree course in Education. I remind everyone that I wish
> to be treated as a deaf person, which I am. That's it. I am deaf. And
> proud of it!"
>
> JULIANA (GASTRONOME): "When I was three years old I went to school
> where I shared the classroom with other deaf children; I learnt
> to read, write, lip reading, and sign language. …I also took ballet
> lessons since I was five years old; when I reached 11 years I started
> horse riding, diving, and tap dancing, and I started to go to evening
> balls at social clubs and meeting places. Currently, I am in the
> fourth term of Gastronomy and Culinary Arts, and I am doing
> very well; I am the first deaf student chef in Brazil. As expected, I
> cook like nobody else does and I travel frequently to participate in
> Gastronomy Conferences and Symposia. Prejudice and bias made it
> very difficult to get the school to hire a sign language interpreter,
> but with effort I overcame this problem."

All narrators express that they enjoyed success after facing hurdles
and overcoming exclusion and social stigma ("to be treated as a lesser
being," "be left completely out," "to have resources and services denied
because of prejudice"). They perceive themselves as persons with self-
confidence that can pursue and be able in many careers, and each of

them can contribute in their own way to fulfill social goals. In a context of denied recognition, the narratives challenge several distorted socio-cultural representations. First, they break down the view that deafness is a personal tragedy and show that deaf people can find joy, fulfillment and happiness through an active and dignified life. Second, they deconstruct the view of deafness as a deficit that limits personal relationships in physical, social and political environments, since narrators show that they can "dance ballet," "ride a horse," "dive," "go to balls and social clubs" as well as earn high degrees and pursue their chosen careers. Third, by reconstructing deafness as one dimension of human diversity, their narratives problematize stigma and discrimination entrenched in existing institutions and in the behavior of hearing people (Arneil, 2009; Calder, 2011; Cole, 2007). João, the systems analyst, says: "Often those who are able to hear do not understand the culture of deaf persons and do not offer respect." The narrators on the FENEIS website demand to be seen as competent and cognitively autonomous subjects, who can make decisions on their own and responsibly take control of their lives.

Let us consider this latter point – the production of difference in the deaf as a means to contest hegemonic hearing norms. Several narrators in the FENEIS website employ the adjective "normal" to characterize self-confidence in their own abilities, a sense of belonging to a collectivity, and freedom to live in valid and dignified ways:

> JOÃO (SYSTEMS ANALYST): "I am able and I live a common life like the rest of humankind. I communicate, by means of Libras and lip reading, with my parents, siblings, friends, and work colleagues, etc., but I have to face hurdles and difficulties in several ways."
>
> JULIANA (GASTRONOME): "My adolescence was very ordinary, I was given attention and orientation, especially by my mother, who also explained sexuality to me and gave me the freedom to ask, so that I could avoid being caught unaware."

Sonia's story is the most surprising among these cases; she is blind and deaf – she lost her hearing at 6 and her eyesight at 19 years of age. Her report underlines the common nature of her daily life:

> SONIA: "My days are ordinary...I do the household chores such as: cooking, washing up, ironing clothes. I am able to do handicraft well, including crochet. And I like to swim. However, I depend on someone to pass me information given on television or on the streets – everywhere, in fact. But I don't think of this situation as a barrier in my life."

In showing their pride at being deaf, using sign language and enjoying "a common life like the rest of humankind," the narrators do not regard deafness as a "problem." Very much in tune with the "social relational model of disability" and the "social model of disability,"[5] they stress that obstacles are born out of relational and social context, since both institutional arrangements and those who hear treat deaf persons in limiting, depreciating and disabling ways. In turn, to use Honneth's term, this is profoundly damaging to their practical self-relation.

On the social movement website, which is meant to influence external institutions and the broader Brazilian public, it seems no coincidence that the emotions displayed by storytellers convey not shame but pride, not fear but strength, not helplessness or submission but transformative agency. By portraying themselves as subjects with the capacity for self-determination, narrators can evoke feelings of potency and efficacy in others. This perception seems particularly conducive to the mobilization of deaf people and to sympathy-winning in society. Furthermore, the stories on the FENEIS website support the argumentation for Libras, since all the narrators attained successful inclusion in society and a positive self-understanding through the use of sign language.

Storytelling and demands for recognition in Orkut

Feelings of injustice assume a different shape in the struggle for recognition in the Orkut forum. Some deaf participants feel that they are not being treated as they believe they deserve, so long as their value, needs or rights are denied by others within the deaf collectivity. Tensions around building a "shared interpretative framework" are particularly acute in this environment, because deaf persons, in order to reaffirm their autonomy and agency to individuate themselves in a discrimination-free environment, need to be recognized by others as moral persons with an inherent value; as citizens with equal and inalienable rights; and as people who have abilities or achievements "valuable for society" (Honneth, 1996, p. 130, 2003a, p. 140).

Conflict emerges in the Orkut forum when one member suggests that deaf persons do not use sign language because of shame: "why is it that the deaf are ashamed to learn Libras? Do oralized deaf persons know little about Libras? This cannot happen." According to Honneth, shame – among other feelings such as guilt, vexation, or humiliation – is "the most open of our feelings" in the sense that it shows a "kind of lowering of one's own feeling of self-worth" (Honneth, 1996, p. 137). In Suzanne Retzinger's words, "in shame the self feels helpless, not in control; the reaction in a shame experience is to hide" (Retzinger, 1991, p. 41).

Two stories in the forum illustrate emotional reactions arising from the attack on individuals' expectations and their conditions for autonomous living. Juan understands deafness as a 'disability,' speech as a rehabilitating device for inclusion in society; he is proud of being able to speak without gestures. Robson regards deafness as a way of living centered on sign language; Libras has enabled him to fully engage in communication with others whereas oral speech made him feel humiliated ("behind" hearing people) and marginalized ("the hearing did not understand him" and had no "patience to listen"):

JUAN: "I find it very strange when someone states with full certainty that those who do not understand Libras do not accept themselves as deaf. I do not understand Libras, but I am aware of my deafness and my difficulties. ... I don't need to live in ghettos; I favor inclusion. Think of the trauma that a deaf person would have by not being able to speak? Going to the market and not knowing how to say what you want, having to depend on interpreters next to you, to depend on your father or mother to work out your things ... Fortunately I have reached a stage in which deafness is a mere detail, rather than a feature of mine."

ROBSON: "I have been deaf since birth. I tried to learn to speak from 1 year and 6 months until 17 years of age, but I gave up, I got tired of trying. I wasted my time ... It is impossible because at times I do not understand and cannot lip read. When I used to speak with my hearing friends they did not understand me. I tried to speak slowly, to repeat myself, until they could understand, but sometimes they had no patience. In a school for hearing kids I was way behind and hardly ever could learn. ... I went crazy when I learnt Libras. My life changed and now I have fun with my deaf and hearing friends who understand Libras."

While both persons reveal that they experienced the pain of exclusion, devaluation, and ostracism in Brazilian society, they express conflicting perceptions about their identity, experiences and means – oralism and sign language – to overcome suffering. A critical analysis of these two modes of structuring differences and identification – deafness as disability or anomaly and deafness as culture (Burch & Kafer, 2010; Dhamoon, 2009) – helps explain how feelings of injustice operate as *clues* of moral violations. When noticing a disruption in their own expectations of "who they are," both participants in Orkut seek to explain their life choices in light of values that are important to them. It is a perception of one's own value, rights or achievements that participants want to confirm by gaining recognition from the other.

In this debate, Juan, who regards deafness as "abnormality" and "physical impairment" ("it is not part of my essence") says that learning oral language is the best way to work towards normalcy. He asserts that "this talk of 'deaf pride' is silly": "Should I tell someone who needs a wheelchair not to use it or a short-sighted person not to use glasses in the name of pride about their handicaps? I am not the type of person that uses deafness as an excuse for everything, or being a victim because a hearing person mistreats me."

In order to refute the allegation that deaf persons who use sign language are accommodated, dependent, and confined to ghettos, Diana fleshes out her identity which is to be seen as a resistance against hearing norms: "Silly???? Dear colleague, I am deaf and I have never used any type of blackmail because of my condition." She reiterates that deafness should be seen as a dimension of human diversity, rather than an abnormality or a deficit: "I just think that you should distinguish what it is like to live without hiding behind something that society imposes as a deficiency and what I call a different way to live."

In the sequence, Elaine, also challenging Juan's view, uses community-driven discourse to demand collective resistance against enduring humiliation: "We should not forget that deaf persons have historically been viewed as inferior to hearing individuals, as handicapped persons that needed to adapt, to walk towards 'normalcy.' For this they needed to oralize." This participant seeks to frame individualized negative social experience ("of being oppressed to 'conform' to the standard of the hearing people") as "typical of the entire group," to use Honneth's term. She calls for collective resistance: "This deeply affected the community of deaf persons, a linguistic minority that has its own non-oral language! Deaf persons who are ashamed to use Libras have been unable to free themselves from a socially imposed view of deafness."

While storytelling on the social movement website reinforces feelings of pride, harmony and strength, and storytellers manage their own feelings, in the chat forum participants express different interpretations of their identities, relations to society and ways to overcome obstacles, and storytellers cannot find validations of their own experiences. Emotional components within the FENEIS website context are modulated according to the norms of the movement, which is aimed at a broader hearing public that had been the reason for all the suffering.

In contrast, participants in the Orkut forum face misrecognition not only from outsiders but also from insiders. In this, "the battleground for signifying difference" to use Rita Dhamoon's words (Dhamoon, 2009, p. 104), what recognition means in a given context is far from clear. What needs to be highlighted here is that when the subjects make demands for recognition, they raise many controversial issues that require constant explanation and justification.

Justification of claim

Despite our emphasis on emotion underpinning the construction of a "shared interpretative framework" by disadvantaged collectivities, we understand that justification mechanisms are important as well. We contend that feelings of injustice not only help persons to take notice of their unmet expectations (Honneth, 1996, p. 137), but also energize struggle over competing interpretations and the validity of different orders of justification. Although Honneth is never sufficiently clear about what should be done about moral disagreement, it is important to acknowledge at this point that emotions also provide the motivational basis for discursive exchange.

Since participants usually use their personal experiences as a basis upon which to reason, affective engagement involves testing presumptions about important things for wellbeing. In this sense, justification is needed for one to engage with others' claims and with other persons who have their own interpretations and life story. As we attempt to demonstrate in this section, what counts as "a legitimate demand" – or in Honneth's terms, "the possibility of understanding the consequences of implementing it as a gain in individuality or inclusion" (Honneth, 1996, p. 187) – often becomes highly controversial. As long as people need to respond in some way to controversial demands, the display of certain emotions contributes to argumentation while others hinder communication altogether. While disrespect frequently reduces the possibilities of an intersubjective negotiation of meanings, moments of discursive engagement help to clarify important differences among people and to search for mutually acceptable solutions.

Claim justification on the FENEIS website

Storytelling on the FENEIS website cannot be contested because this platform is not interactive. Still, the website organizers always assume that there will be indirect interlocution with potential users. For complex issues, ordinary people and indeed political representatives and policy-makers may not have clear answers. Given such limits, narratives may provide relevant information to help others analyze a given situation and appreciate the demands at stake (Black, 2008, p. 109; Polletta & Lee, 2006; Steiner, 2012b, p. 86).

Miriam's personal story on the FENEIS website – she teaches sign language in a public university – helps her to connect the specificities of her personal experiences with more general principles that are morally recognizable (Dryzek, 2000, p. 68; Forst, 2002, p. 283; Habermas, 1996). She exposes institutional and social obstacles to her autonomy to individuate herself and fully participate in society. She claims that a lack of Libras interpreters hinders her education ("it makes following the classes very difficult as well as any participation in forums, meetings, conferences, and current debates in universities"). This lack of interpreters also affects her insertion at work ("I have often paid myself for FENEIS interpreters to help me in my opening classes for the Libras class in undergraduate courses"). What we want to highlight here is that "naming something as injustice," as Douglas Schrock, Daphne Holden and Lori Reid (2004, p. 64) have pointed out, "simultaneously instructs others that anger is appropriate and social change is necessary." Instead of providing clear answers or clear-cut alternatives to solve problems, testimonies about personal stories in this case emphasize the moral complexity of the situation (Steiner, 2012b, p. 72).

While we acknowledge that the stories' openness to interpretation may elicit ambiguous normative conclusions (Polletta & Lee, 2006, p. 718), it seems correct to state that Miriam's story provides elements that fulfill the *generality* requirement for legitimate recognition (Forst, 2007b, p. 295). She defends her demands on the grounds of the equal status of citizens (not so much recognition of identity, as is too often assumed). She claims that sign language is valuable not because it is different but because it is an integral part of deaf culture and is conducive to human development (Cooke, 2009). She also attempts to clarify and give general reasons for Libras to be fully incorporated into social systems.

> MIRIAM: It was only in 2002, after much effort and struggle, that sign language was recognized as the official language of the deaf – in Law of Libras no. 10,436. In spite of this victory, there are still many goals to be met in public schools and universities so that there may be deaf professors with Master's degrees and PhDs; and Libras interpreters, bilingual teachers in classrooms of all subjects, so that deaf persons may feel comfortable to study. The mother tongue of deaf persons is Libras.

Elsewhere, Honneth claims that the political dimension of recognition considers subjects as citizens who have to respect one another as free and equal persons and co-legislators within a political community. This dimension creates expectations that citizens have the right to debate and propose amendments to existing rules, especially those about rights, policies, duties, or powers that in some way affect them. In some cases, claimants also seek to introduce a new principle, a value, or a good that can also be defended and mutually recognized (Tully, 2000, pp. 474–475).

Within the movement website context, it is worth noting that life stories usually "do not tend to antagonize other participants" (Steiner, 2012b, p. 85). Miriam's testimony helps her to present unfamiliar perspectives or unpopular demands in order to request *mutual* recognition (Polletta & Lee, 2006, p. 703; Ryfe, 2006, p. 75). Since the principle of rights implies a moral accountability of all members of the political community, Miriam apparently understands that it is justified to direct a set of demands to formal political representatives. She ends her story challenging the neglect of political representatives and asking for immediate practical measures to ensure conditions for deaf persons achieving self-realization: "How long will Brazilian deaf persons have to wait until gaining the right of having Libras as their natural language and interpreter services for Libras? Is what we ask absurd? We want answers and action." Since FENEIS has a tradition of defending the use of Libras and the culture of deaf people (Perlin, 1998), narratives on the website invite deaf persons to stand up for their rights as well as hearing persons to understand spatial-visual communication as a valuable language with a similar status to, and deserving of respect as, other languages. Leaders of this movement claim that sign language constitutes a concrete good since it enables expressivity and communication and thus fosters self-realization for deaf persons; it is a legally supported right and should therefore be taken into account in public policy decision making.

Claim justification on Orkut

In contrast to the FENEIS website, which is not interactive, participants in the Orkut forum may exchange opinions, endorse or contest recognition demands and problematize the use of life stories to demonstrate the validity of certain claims, all of which contribute directly or indirectly to justification. When facing the issue of "what to do" about decisions that affect them all, the requirement that deaf persons, as situated subjects, should justify their position becomes more evident.

RUBENS: "What is the future of a deaf person that has Libras as L1 and Portuguese as L2 in a society that is predominantly hearing? You should know that every deaf person that I know who has Libras as L1 runs into very serious problems with their vocabulary and writing (as we can see by reading the debates in this community). What about the essays in university entrance tests, what then? And what about the Portuguese tests in public competitions? The fact is: either you try to adapt to society by speaking its language or you become marginalized."

MICHELE: "Rubens, deaf people do not learn oral language the same way that hearing people do; it takes much longer, which could delay language development, what you call abstraction ability...which could be developed if he has acquired sign language."

FERNANDO: "I...argue that deaf persons should have the opportunity to learn Libras at school and to study the subjects in Libras. If a deaf person, because of technical difficulties, learns NO language by the age of four, for instance, they will find it very difficult to learn any language for the rest of their lives."

Dialogic exchanges in Orkut reveal differences among deaf individuals and the formation of shared opinions within sub-groups. Those holding strong positions tend to engage in anger and partisan processing (Mackuen et al., 2010, p. 443). The question that interests us here is the link between subjective emotional reaction to injury and attempts to construct justifications, when expectations of recognition are not confirmed or one's claim fails to be accepted by others (Habermas, 1995, 1996; Neblo, 2003; Rehg, 1994). Rubens, while perceiving deafness as pathological, contests the imposition of an alleged group identity: "My identity is Rubens de Oliveira and I am Brazilian, this is more than my deafness." Regarding himself as a citizen, as the bearer of the right to language self-determination, he appeals to the universal norm of non-domination: "why should I be forced to learn Libras?"

On the other hand, Diana and Elaine contest the notion of identities as individual choices and state that such identities result from historical processes:

ELAINE: "We should not forget that deaf persons have historically been viewed as inferior to hearing individuals. This deeply affected the community of deaf persons, a linguistic minority that has its own non-oral language! Deaf persons who are ashamed to use Libras have been unable to free themselves from a socially imposed view of deafness."

By seeing deafness as the culture of a linguistic minority, a dimension of human diversity (Arneil, 2009), Elaine claims that the use of Libras is not to be universally shared. However, she demands, like narrators on the FENEIS website, recognition not only for the right to speak as they please, but also for the value of sign language as a concrete good.

When Orkut participants' angry responses result in aggression, offense, or mistrust (Alexander & Lara, 1996; Mackuen et al., 2010, p. 454; Thompson, 2006), dialogic and discursive engagement is often blocked:

> DIOZIVAL: "For me this topic is over. After reading 'in their little world,' in their 'ignorance,' I refuse to answer anything"
> RUBENS: "Diozival, if it is for lack of goodbyes, adiós amigo."

Similarly, disrespect may reduce the potential for criticism and the possibilities of questioning and disputing meanings in order to understand the alleged value of beliefs and preferences which one disagrees with:

> ANA: "let us not waste time with this Robson, because it is clear that he does not know how to abstract a text well, as he alters the information. And you know that people with writing problems will never be able to debate with sufficient and well-grounded arguments simply because they understand something different from what we write."

Nevertheless, some participants show respect to others' claims and empathy helps subjects to better understand the perspectives of others, or to place themselves in the other's place (Barnes, 2012, p. 36; Krause, 2008, pp. 162–165; Rehg, 1994, p. 14). Even if opinions remain polarized and forum members continue to disagree, many of them are aware that there are various ways of seeing things; deaf persons have different needs and may choose to live differently:

> FERNANDO: "not everyone finds it easy to become oralized. Insisting on oralization without providing any choice for communication implies delaying or hampering the child's learning both at school and emotionally as a person."
> ANONYMOUS1: "I am not against using Libras, but we also need to speak. I am a speaker. When I was a child, I was ashamed of who I was; today I accept myself much more and am happy with life."

Throughout the ongoing debate, Orkut participants provide justification for many demands that respect the rules of reciprocity and generality and evince that recognition should be provided in many different ways. This has far-reaching consequences for understanding claim justification from a recognition-theoretical approach.

Here we clarify four advantages of discursive engagement in recognition struggles. First, while contestation and disagreement with externally imposed roles and attributes (by society or by community projects) are at the heart of recognition struggles, justification helps increase self-awareness of one's own claims. Second, conflict between different claims within a group reveals the abilities of subjects to articulate their own identity and engage in ways they have chosen to reach self-realization. Justification, in this case, contributes to unravel dominant frames, clarify true differences within groups and why they matter. Third, the give and take of reasons concerning controversial needs, rights and achievements within groups and among all affected people in society contributes to critically examine what counts as "a gain" in individuality or in inclusion in the circle of individuals that recognize each other. Since the legitimacy of claims for recognition should not be conferred *a priori*, justification helps to process the goods envisioned and the judgments entailed in them. Fourth and finally, justification has an educative power to accommodate diversity of values and multiple concepts of good. Moral judgment – even that resulting from wide deliberative exchange – is often mixed in nature (Gutmann & Thompson, 1996, p. 74).

The struggle for legitimate recognition carries with it the promise of a greater opening for the fulfillment of individuality (the *I*) of deaf persons as well as a broader inclusion of this collectivity (the *us*) in society. Policy-makers and whoever makes collective decisions are thus pressed to acknowledge the diversity of dignified ways of life and the variety of legitimate demands; and they should shape institutional arrangements so as to offer a greater range of choices, opportunities and resources in order to enable deaf people to pursue self-realization in multiple ways.

Conclusion

In this chapter, we raised the general claim that Honneth's theory opens promising venues for research on the role of emotion in politics, particularly when issues of injustice are at stake. My collaborator and I analyzed deaf people's expression of feelings of injustice and the construction of "a shared semantics" as an ongoing process of claim-making and claim-receiving, which is often intermeshed with justification. Following Honneth's theoretical concerns, we investigated meaning construction in life stories at two levels – not only from the perspective of those who claim to represent and act on behalf of the group, but also from the point of view of those who perceive themselves as part of that collectivity. Our study points to three main conclusions.

First, focusing on Honneth's account of emotion as a deeply social and intersubjective experience, our study evidences the display of hurt feelings as a source of intelligibility of suffering in different contexts. Our analysis of life stories on the FENEIS website illustrates more agented and empowering emotions: narratives project successful Libras stories and they demonstrate relatively coherent origins of shared injuries and solutions needed for the entire group to gain social recognition. In contrast, when reacting against disrespect – seen as attacks on the conditions of their practical identity – participants in the Orkut forum differ on (i) what causes suffering; (ii) the content of positive recognition; (iii) how to overcome suffering or what solutions are best. Thus our study contributes to showing that the construction of a "collective interpretative framework" by disadvantaged groups is fraught with tensions, and there is often confrontation between conflicting demands for recognition among their members.

Second, while endorsing Honneth's agonistic approach, we contend that it does not offer an adequate explanation of what should be done about moral disagreement. Our study showed that deaf people, within a horizon of concerns that they share in some measure within a given social and political context, appealed to conflicting needs and rights – encompassing both demands for recognizing that some things are valuable for everyone and some things are valuable for just some people or groups.

To deal with this problem, we argued that Honneth's approach can be complemented with theories of discursive justification in the fashion of Habermas. Whereas Habermas appeals to abstract standards for rational justification, as participants want their validity claims to have an impact in discursive responses to, and with, negotiation and conflict, Honneth instructs us to look at feelings of injustice, subjective reactions to damage to practical identity and conditions for self-realization. Therefore, a theoretical-recognition approach seems to clarify why participants attempt to check the general acceptability of their claims. In this sense, our study suggests that Honneth's theory of recognition, when properly articulated with a notion of discursive justification, can well-equip scholars and social observers concerned with practices that aim to overcome injustice.

Third, our study contributes to showing that problems submerged in the context of daily life as well as group tensions may not be fully visible on sites that enjoy notoriety and broad visibility – as in our case study on sites of representative entities. Thus, spaces such as social media sites with far less visibility, where ordinary individuals engage in relatively spontaneous conversation, can be relevant for exposing the full diversity of identity claims, interests and disputes at play, including contestation of representative claims publicly advanced by leaders, advocacy agents and moral entrepreneurs. These sites can thus contribute to broadening and deepening critical analyses of struggles for recognition and social conditions for justice.

Notes

1. In this perspective, scholars such as Rehg (1994) and Neblo (2003) have taken Habermas's discourse ethics in new directions to show the various roles that feelings and emotions have in moral perception and argumentation.
2. Habermas (1995, p. 48) argues that the violation of norms (in particular norms of justice) evokes emotional reactions that arise from a cognitive structure. In particular, he attempts to show that there is a moral dimension in the emotional responses of indignation and resentment "directed to a *specific* other person who has violated our integrity." (Habermas, 1995, p.48) In Habermas's words, "what makes this indignation moral is not the fact that the interaction between the two concrete individuals has been disturbed but rather the violation of an underlying *normative expectation* that is valid not only for the ego and alter but also for all members of a social group" (Habermas, 1995, p. 48).
3. The forum was started on April 4, 2005 and the last post that we studied was dated July 27, 2007.Forum Vergonha SURDO. (2005). [Web log post]. Available at http://www.orkut.com/CommMsgs.aspx?cmm=428446&tid=10024425
4. To be sure, at that normative level, Honneth, as was discussed in Chapter 5, is not concerned with sociological specifications of a wide range of factors – opportunities, resources, incentives, strategic choices, the building of allies – depicted in the literature on social movements. See also for example, Cammaerts, Mattoni, & McCurdy, 2013; della Porta & Diani, 2006; della Porta, 2012, 2013; Gamson, 2004; Hobson, 2003; Klandermans & van der Toorn, 2008; McAdam, 2000.
5. The rise of the "social relational understanding of disability" in the mid 1970s and the "social model" in the 1990s – was promoted by organizations of disabled people and activist scholars of disability studies – with the "explicit commitment to assist disabled people in their fight for full equality and social inclusion" (Thomas, 2004, p. 570; see also Calder, 2011; Goodley & Tragaskis, 2006). Challenging the medical view, some scholars seek to understand disability from a relational perspective to explain social exclusions experienced by disabled people (Thomas, 2004), while others hold, in a more radical fashion, that disability is socially caused and has nothing do with the body (Cole, 2007).

7

Recognition as an Ongoing Struggle: Conflicts Involving Racism and Homophobia in the Networked Media Environment

Rousiley C. M. Maia and Thaiane A. S. Rezende

In his *The Struggle for Recognition*, Axel Honneth traces the dynamics of conflicts that regularly arise in different spheres during the course of individual socialization. The previous chapter examined the construction of "shared semantics" among members of a group. We focused on social movement organizers' attempts at advancing collective causes and speaking for others to define origins of injustice and their remedies. Chapter 6 also evinced the ongoing conflict among members of the group to interpret their needs, rights, and achievements, along with how they build different demands for recognition to attain autonomy, better inclusion in society, and self-realization. In this chapter, my collaborator and I examine conflicts for recognition in everyday interactions, while also establishing how these encounters play out freely with multiple others in a pluralist society.

Theoretically, this chapter advances two major arguments. In a pluralistic world, individuals who seek recognition have to interact and sometimes mutually attune themselves with multiple others, and not only "the other." Threats inherent in non-recognition and misrecognition invite people to engage in practical reasoning, during which they are not completely free to decide what order of justification they will use to solve a certain problem or challenge a particular judgment. Since struggles for recognition occur through various forms of interaction, one cannot fail to appreciate distinct concomitant possibilities for action. While we were inspired by studies about online deliberation to observe and analyze norms of conversation and argumentation, in this chapter we examine how people interact with others more broadly, by also regarding self-expression and mobilization. We do not attempt to "stretch" the concept of deliberation,[1] but rather pay attention to the articulation of deliberative and non-deliberative behavior, regarding the significance of these activities in terms of recognition.

Second, we argue that episodic struggles for recognition, limited to time and subjects, are highly dependent on space and context. We assume that observing episodic practices gives us some picture of the struggles for recognition that take place in everyday interactions that shape and constitute our lives. The majority of empirical studies about online conversation and deliberation focus on one single media or platform and thus, neglect the complete online media spectrum with which people interact. This study aims at examining engagement through different online platforms: YouTube, blogs and Facebook. By extending and deepening trends from existing works, our study corroborates that each online platform has particular technological features and encompasses specific expectations and norms, with particular constraints and affordances for mediated communication. Our work also shows that each platform captures something different and in the absence of these varying pictures, we are bound to misinterpret aspects of the struggle for recognition in everyday life and their potential for social change.

In order to develop our study, we focus on an event that aroused significant indignation and broad mobilization in Brazilian society: a racist comment made by Federal Congressman Jair Bolsonaro who associated having passion for a black woman with promiscuity. He made the statement in response to a question posed by a famous black singer, Preta Gil, daughter of a former Minister of Culture, Gilberto Gil (also a prominent Brazilian singer) on a TV show known as CQC. This is an interesting case because it provoked abundant discussions about racism and homophobia across the digital networked environment, and received broad coverage by the mainstream media and alternative media alike. Brazilian civic and professional entities sued the Congressman for breach of parliamentary decorum, which was also based on the crime of racial intolerance. This episode also triggered a movement known as *"Evento Fora Bolsonaro"* (Event Out With Bolsonaro) on Facebook, which attracted 43,808 participants. Therefore this episode offers the chance to analyze communicative interactions on social networking sites (SNSs), as important venues, where citizens can express themselves, engage in deliberation, and unleash mobilization to exert influence on the civil sphere, as well as on formal institutions.

This chapter is organized as follows. In the first section, we briefly survey controversies regarding subjects' dependencies on the other's response and the complex ways through which rules of recognition are disputed in pluralist societies. Next, we characterize the "Preta Gil and Bolsonaro" event and explain our methodology.[2] In the three sections following that, we examine varieties of communicative interactions provoked by this event in YouTube, blogs and Facebook. We focus on: (i) self-expression; (ii) conversation and deliberation; (iii) political activism and mobilization – different dimensions of struggles for recognition which have already been discussed in Chapter 5.

Recognition and ongoing conflicts in everyday interactions

Axel Honneth's theory assumes that relations of recognition are fundamental to the formation of subjectivity and self-realization. This approach instructs us to conceive the struggle for recognition as an ongoing and endless process. In this chapter, we provide an account of what this type of encounter might look like in everyday interactions. We assume that this conflict does not occur in every case, since denial of recognition does not necessarily lead to a struggle, as Honneth states everywhere. Several critics have discussed a number of such situations in which social strife does not emerge (Celikates, 2012; Ferrarese, 2011; Thompson & Hoggett, 2011).[3] Our basic outlook is that those struggling for recognition need somehow to form a sense of community based on mutuality to affirm self-worth against misrecognition. Our concern here is with the conflictive process through which one is able to gain self-trust, resist social humiliation, and respond in self-assertive ways to the offenses of others as a dynamics that takes place within pluralist horizons of ethical convictions and institutional arrangements.

Several scholars cast doubt on Honneth's definition of the individual's dependency upon social responsiveness. Objections are advanced regarding the alleged effects of subjugation that undermine the sense of us as agents. Nikolas Kompridis argues that Honneth's theory, by exaggerating the degree that we need recognition from others, ends up undermining our identity, our sense of agency, and capacity to speak in a voice of our own. In Kompridis' (2007, p. 283) words, "our power to shape our identity and exercise our agency does not strictly depend on receiving in advance the appropriate form of recognition. We are able to do so, over and over again, despite the denial or absence of such recognition." In a similar vein, Melvin Rogers (2009, p. 185) argues that

Honneth's theory paradoxically "leaves excluded groups open to domination rather than providing resources for understanding how they have resisted it" by placing a major emphasis on the dependence of individuals on recognition from institutions and other people, sources that are precisely the origin of insult and injury.

While admitting that the nature of the responses of others crucially determines the structure of subjectivity, we think it is important to reappraise the link between the historic conditions surrounding claims for recognition that are actually raised by groups and the multifaceted institutional arrangements in a given society. Rather than regarding individuals as helpless in the face of experiences of disrespect, we find it more convincing to see the struggle for recognition as an ongoing activity that occurs in the fields of both experiences of respect and disrespect.

Further explanation is needed in order to understand how experiences of respect and disrespect are embedded in everyday life and how truly diverse is the practical activity of struggling for recognition in pluralist societies. First, one's self-perception and acquisition of a sense of worth in a context of misrecognition can often vary across different realms. Insofar as institutional arrangements in society may be attentive to problems in a particular sphere, but not in others – for example, the fostering of legal rules to assure equal citizenship, but neglecting obstacles to the intimate sphere, as well as in the market's division of labor – individuals face different opportunities for individualization and patterns for inclusion in society. Through a mix of attachments, individuals may thus gain self-confidence and a sense of agency in regards to various types of political struggles, in order to resist enduring experiences of disrespect and even respond to them in self-assertive ways.

Secondly, a range of cultural and social conditions must be fulfilled for individuals and groups to engage in a transformative praxis. Honneth is very cautious to stress that struggles for recognition are related to a political culture that is conducive to resistance. As was discussed in previous chapters, the conditions for forming social movements, enhancing collective actions, and supporting claims for recognition are very unequal among individuals and groups, as well as their chance to question the legitimacy of institutionalized practices and exert influence on collective judgments and decisions. The practical activity of struggling for and against demands for recognition involves critical negotiations, disputes over the recognition rules, and due treatment accorded to each other, in everyday life, as well as in forums where explicit recommendations and measures can be taken up by a representative democratic system.

Third, and finally, according to Honneth, "the relationship between institutions and recognition is not marked by one-sided dependency in either direction, but by 'co-evolution'" (Honneth, 2011, p. 404). If the idea of "co-evolution" is examined in its own terms, Honneth's concept that existing institutions can create strong, shared, expectations of recognition – "mental or social attitudes that have not yet taken the shape of sanctioned institutions" (Honneth, 2011, p. 399), becomes a compelling argument for examining social conflict. The issue here is not only that such expectations are to be seen as underpinning a given group's opinions in the public sphere, the actions of political representation, resistance, coordination of action and cooperation. Discourses and actions motivated by these expectations in a culturally diverse society can also prompt opposition and threats in norms of recognition, even when institutionalized. There is nothing in Honneth's version of recognition theory that precludes institutionalized norms from suffering reversals: "it would be naïve to claim that established norms of recognition cannot ever be revised; ... [under certain circumstances] even the most elementary form of interpersonal recognition can be undermined" (Honneth, 2011, p. 399).

In the context of this chapter, my collaborator and I wish to grasp a picture of the struggle freely enacted in everyday life, in a pluralist society. We assume that in general terms it is difficult to determine how conflicts are shaped and exactly when experiences of disrespect will prompt individuals to engage in practical struggles. Since claims to alter the distribution of resources, status, or respect imbricate with the prevailing organization of the relations of economic, social, and political power (Benhabib, 2002; Celikates, 2012; Fraser, 2003a; Maia, 2012e; Mendonça, 2011; Tully, 2000), we seek to demonstrate how persons striving for recognition engage in "multilogues" – to use James Tully's term (2000, p. 475) – with implicated others in a complex web of relations. For example, some social actors refuse to even listen to the demands of these groups; others contest these demands and defend the *status quo*; others may be willing to cooperate dialogically and negotiate mutually acceptable courses of action or find ways of living together; and still others may make antagonistic demands.

The Preta Gil and Bolsonaro Event: an overview on race and LGBTQ issues in Brazil

On March 28, 2011, the program "CQC" (on Brazil's Band TV network) attracted a large audience[4] with a sketch called "*O povo quer saber*" (The people want to know). Federal Congressman Jair Bolsonaro was asked questions on polemic issues, such as homosexuality and having affection for a black woman. Famous Brazilian singer Preta Gil, pointblank asked Bolsonaro: "If your son fell in love with a black woman, what would you do?" The congressman replied: "Preta, I am not going to discuss promiscuity with anybody. This risk just isn't possible; my children were very well brought up and have never lived in an environment regrettably like yours."

After the TV show, Preta Gil posted indignant messages on her Twitter account: "have already got a lawyer; I am a strong black woman who will go to the end on this issue. Racism is a crime! And he acknowledges being a racist. I'm counting on all of you; let's be grateful to CQC for providing us with great evidence (of what happened)." The congressman's statement on television – an environment with massive visibility – resounded far and wide via the Internet. The morning following his appearance on the program, Jair Bolsonaro spoke publicly. In an interview with *Terra Magazine*[5] he claimed to have misunderstood the question: "I understood that she was asking me what I would do if my son dated someone who was gay ... Had I understood her question correctly, I'd have replied: 'my son can date any woman, as long as she doesn't behave like you do.' Even if I were a racist, I would not be crazy to the point of saying that on television." Aware that racism is a crime in Brazil, Congressman Bolsonaro tried to keep any imputation of racism at bay, while – through a homophobic tone of voice – reaffirmed his position contrary to any affectionate relationship between same-sex persons. The congressman is a chief opponent of homosexual civil union in Brazil. On another TV program, he had already said that children go on to become homosexuals "because the rod is spared on them."

Both groups affected by Bolsonaro's statements – black females and lesbian, gay, bi, trans, queer (LGBTQ) – are subjected to rampant disrespect in Brazil. However, the specificities of these groups must be kept in mind, as regards their histories, forms of collective organization, political agendas, legal norms, as well as public policies. A brief glimpse at social conflicts involving blacks and LGBTQ people in Brazil illustrates different types of recognition in reference to institutional arrangements in respect of these collectivities, as well as distinct types of political struggles carried out by their members.

The racial resistance in Brazil dates back to 16th century colonial days when blacks first arrived from Africa, but an organized movement only took shape in the late 19th century (Domingues, 2007; Pereira & Rodrigues, 2010). Plural in nature from its outset, the Brazilian black movement includes multiple institutions, diversified associative forms, as well as disputes over often-conflicting goals (Gomes, 2007, p. 10). Particularly in 1970, these entities managed to expand their agenda of claims and bring continuous pressure to bear on the state, thus securing for themselves an increasing role of participation in governmental actions.

From a legal standpoint, the 2003 Federal Law 7716 classifies racism as a crime for which no bond can be posted; it stipulates imprisonment for up to five years, plus a monetary penalty. In recent years, Acts of Congress have also approved Law n° 10639/2003 (That "Afro-Brazilian History and Culture" be mandatorily included in teaching curricula nationwide) and the creation of a Statute of Racial Equality (Act 12288/2010). A bill-of-law in the House of Representatives (actually, proposal 116/2011 of a constitutional amendment) seeks to create quotas for black members of Congress, while bill-of-law n° 6738/2013 aims at reserving quotas for blacks in Brazil's public service administration.

The country's current black agenda has strong affirmative and compensatory features. Especially since 2003, when the Workers' Party (PT) reached the nation's Presidency, various racially-oriented policies have been developed in areas such as education, public health, work, and income. Special mention ought to be made of Law n° 12711, passed in 2012, that establishes quotas for students graduating from public schools (among them blacks, mixed-blood, and indigenous) at all federal public universities.

Blacks represent 70.0 percent of the Brazilians in extreme poverty and 68.0 percent of those who are illiterate (Instituto de Pesquisa Econômica Aplicada, 2013, p. 438). The income gap between black and non-blacks, albeit decreasing in the past few years, still remains huge. According to a 2012 survey in the Greater São Paulo Metropolitan Region (the country's largest city), blacks earned 63.2 percent less than non-blacks (Departamento Intersindical de Estatística e Estudos Socioeconômicos, 2013, p. 1). Black females are particularly at a disadvantage. In 2006, The Ministry of Health pointed out that black and mixed-blood women represent 54.0 percent of all rape, sexual harassment, and abuse victims. They are also at the highest economic disadvantage (Neri, 2013, p. 7; Romio, 2013, p. 155).

This brief sketch shows the complexity of distinct forms of oppression affecting blacks in Brazil. Despite the creation of specific offices to help black females – such as the pro-women policy office (*Secretaria de Políticas para as Mulheres – SPM*) and the office for promotion of racial equality policies (*Secretaria de Políticas de Promoção da Igualdade Racial – SEPPIR*), both linked to the President's Office – institutional arrangements are not always aware of, or interested in, tapping into distinct sources of vulnerability and multiple forms of misrecognition effecting these sub-groups.

The LGBTQ movement in Brazil is now one of the strongest and most visible social campaigns in the country, following 30 years of a quite active struggle. Violence is a central theme in this crusade. A 2011 Report on homophobic violence in Brazil reveals that, among the violations reported that year, psychological violence recurred the most (42.5 percent), followed by discrimination (22.3 percent), and physical violence (15.9 percent) (Brasil Secretaria de Direitos Humanos, 2012, p. 40). The "Gay Rights Group in the Northeastern state of Bahia" (Grupo Gay da Bahia), one of the most traditional organizations in this movement, reported the murder of 338 homosexuals in the country in 2012, a 21 percent leap over the previous year, and 177 percent if compared to the past seven years.[6] A study by Fernando S. Teixeira Filho and Carina A. Rondini (2012) among youths aged 12 to 20, in three different cities in the state of São Paulo, concluded that LGBTQs stand a greater likelihood of attempting suicide than heterosexuals.

Only more recently has the Brazilian Executive Branch been receptive to pressure from the LGBTQ movement. Among the main governmental programs for this population are: "*Brasil Sem Homofobia*" *(BSH)* – Brazil Without Homophobia – A 2004 movement to fight off violence and discrimination; a National Conference of Gays, Lesbians, Bisexuals, Transvestites, and Transsexuals (held in 2008), and the creation of an LGBTQ National Council in 2010. In 2011, Brazil's Supreme Court recognized same-sex unions as stable unions, with the same equal rights as the family nuclei of different-sex couples, regardless of their having children or not (Mello, Brito, & Maroja, 2012a, 2012b).

However, the literature shows that even though these initiatives are examples to the world (Reis, 2012), they can be characterized by "institutional fragility and structural deficiencies" (Mello et al., 2012a, pp. 408–418). The Brazilian Association of Lesbians, Gays, Bisexuals, Transvestites, and Transsexuals (ABGLT) claims the chief legal challenge faced by this part of the population resides in the so-called "advance of a religious fundamentalism" (Reis, 2012). A major item in the movement's agenda is bill-of-law 122, an initiative that seeks to criminalize homophobia. After five years, the Brazilian House of Representatives approved the bill in 2006, but so far the Federal Senate has not voted on the proposal. A project known as "School Free of Homophobia," which proposes, among other actions, "an anti-homophobia kit" was approved by the Federal Ministry of Education. Yet, the distribution of this material was vetoed by a 2011 presidential decree, following intensive civil mobilization, including a so-called Evangelical Parliamentary Front (Mello et al., 2012b, p. 307). These conflicts show that advances in norms for recognition can generate harsh disapproval and, depending on situational circumstances, clashes with other groups can lead to a stagnation of such norms and policies, or even to their reversal. The question my collaborator and I wish to addresses is how we should understand the episodic struggle for recognition that freely takes place in pluralist societies.

Methodology

Based on Honneth's research agenda, our analyses focus on three forms of interactions in networked online media, namely: (i) self-expression; (ii) conversation and deliberation; (iii) activism and mobilization. We investigate: (a) YouTube and the page accessing visualization of the aforementioned "CQC"[7] video, with 695 comments; (b) the feminist blog *"Escreva Lola Escreva"*[8] (Write Lola Write), with 49 comments, and the blog *"Papo de Homem"*[9] (Man's Talk or PdH) earmarked for a male audience, Bolsonaro with 164 comments; (c) Facebook; a movement labeled *"Evento Fora Bolsonaro"*[10] (Event Out With Bolsonaro) and the Jair Bolsonaro,[11] Page described as an unofficial community.

To develop this analysis, my collaborator and I draw on studies about informal conversation and cross-cutting political discussion on sites that are not primarily designed to encompass political discussions (Graham, 2008; Kim, 2011; Wojcieszak & Mutz, 2009). Taking into consideration the recent scholarship on online deliberation, we survey the conditions under which the Internet contributes to people's exposure to diverse viewpoints and heterogeneous personal contacts (Brundidge, 2010; Brundidge & Rice, 2009; Mutz, 2006; Sampaio, Maia, & Marques, 2011; Stromer-Galley, 2003, 2007). We also look at the implications of how anonymity, moderation, synchronous, and asynchronous interaction make deliberation more likely to work (Coleman & Moss, 2012; Kies, 2010; Stromer-Galley, 2007).

The unit of analysis is the individual posts. Among the variables used in this chapter,[12] five relate to the *Discourse Quality Index* (DQI), as was developed by Jürg Steiner, André Bächtiger, Markus Spörndli and Marco Steenbergen (2004), and Steiner (2012a). They are: (i) reasoned opinion and justification; (ii) stories; (iii) respect for both the content of a statement and the interaction partners; and (iv) foul language. In addition, we used a revised version of Raphael Kies' (2010) variable adapted to online environments: (v) reciprocity, referring to messages that initiate a debate (threads) and the replies within these threads in digital settings. To tap into the specificities of our case, we created the following variables: (vi) coherence to the topic of discussion through a set of inferences related to the highlighted event; (vii) gender of users and self-identification as black, LGBTQ, or other historically-defined minority; (viii) positioning regarding the congressman's ideas and claims[13]; (ix) expression of experiences of disrespect (discrimination, marginalization, exclusion, offense, domination, oppression, exploitation); (x) reactions against experiences of disrespect.

Since we also sought to establish the dimension of the discussion in terms of political activism and mobilization, we created the following variables: (xi) provision of links to public petitions, bills of law, etc. and quotes to media sources showing the impact of the event; (xii) users' invitations to others to take some kind of action. A summary of our coding procedure can be found at the end of this chapter.

In regards to the aforementioned platforms, all of the available comments were collected, except for those on Facebook,[14] from September 20 to October 20, 2013. Out of 1,496, 600 were analyzed. This corresponds to a simple probabilistic sampling for each of the online environments analyzed, with a 95 percent confidence interval and margin of error of ± 5 percent. An inter-coder reliability test of 10 percent of the 600-posting sample was carried out, using Krippendorff's Alpha. The results obtained ranged from 0.68 to 1.0, with an average of 0.844 and a standard deviation of 0.093 among the variables analyzed. No variable fell short of the minimum recommended reliability level of 0.667 (Krippendorff, 2003).

The conflictive ground in the struggle for recognition

Particular conflicts like the event between Bolsonaro and Preta Gil have many layers of dispute among diverse groups, involving clashes between varying axes of difference defined in terms of ethnicity, religion, sexual orientation, etc. Much of the disputes revolved around issues such as (a) whether the congressman's expression could be reconstructed as involving lack of disrespect and misrecognition; (b) what treatments were due regarding disputed claims for recognition of black people, LGBTQs and other minorities (indigenous population, obese people); (c) what remedies might involve problems of offense, exclusion, and marginalization.

A significant number of codified comments (61.8 percent) in the online environment not only issued a claim, but gave some kind of reason – at

Table 7.1   Justification level (%)

	Lola	PdH	YouTube	Facebook Event	Facebook Page
No justification	27.7	18.0	37.3	70.7	41.8
With justification	72.3	82.0	62.7	29.3	58.2
N	47	100	204	56	169

Source: EME-UFMG Research Group.

Table 7.2   Position (%)

	Lola	PdH	YouTube	Facebook Event	Facebook Page
Posting favorable to Bolsonaro's statements and ideas	2.1	24.0	28.4	8.8	55.3
Posting contrary to Bolsonaro's statements and ideas	80.9	43.0	55.9	66.7	15.3
Posting with no explicit positioning (against or in favor)					
Posting whose contents were	2.1	1.0	10	12.3	7.1
limited to a news link, video etc.	14.9	32.0	14.7	12.3	22.4
Posting related to the polemic (sexual orientation, Bolsonaro, racism, freedom of expression)					
N	47	100	204	56	169

Source: EME-UFMG Research Group.

least a simple one[15] – in regards to what does or does not constitute disrespect and offense; what should or should not be done in relation to those who claim misrecognition (black people, LGBTQs, etc.); and why one should or should not respect and tolerate certain claims.

A map of reasons offered in these environments gives us an image of a pluralist society. People raised a number of justifications for defining why the congressman's statement was morally problematic. The congressman's claims or ideas imply (i) a denial of equal dignity and mutual respect. While some people support their positions with statements grounded in the legal framework of equal and free citizens, others resorted to religious sources of authority for claiming the basic equality of mankind (*the Bible expressly prohibits discrimination of persons based on their social origin, race etc.*); (ii) a violation of rights and legal protections;

and acts of disrespect being equated with pathologies of an undeveloped society (*Homophobia, racism, and xenophobia are the ills of a backwater, not-evolved society*); (iii) an assertion of domination, variously defined as marginalization, offense, exclusion, and oppression, that causes harm, humiliation, and depreciation of people; (iv) a lack of grounds to support the superiority of some groups over groups defined in terms of race or sexual orientation; and (v) a threat to the need to set up, operate, and maintain a legal framework to prove means and opportunities for improving the conditions of the lives of disadvantaged groups, either by securing peace, in the live-and-let-live fashion, resolving conflicts or doing justice and avoiding different types of harm.

Just as there are many reasons for condemning the congressman's values and statements, there are reasons to support his position. They are: (i) affirmation of freedom of conscience and expression "*including whatever may be deemed morally repugnant*"; (ii) appeal to universal rights in a neutral (content-independent) way, in order to re-affirm liberal tenets and reject institutions from establishing special rights, protection measures, and preferential treatment of minorities; (iii) consideration of people's differences and that these cannot be "artificially" effaced (*the wish to dilute or destroy at any cost the cultural identity of others*); (iv) blatant affirmation of superiority or "correctness" that "*tells who a person is and how he or she should be treated.*" In this case, open discrimination was more frequently aimed at LGBTQs rather than racially-defined groups. These arguments were based on the traditionally naturalized view of "normality," a religious world-view, or a supposed medical standpoint that defines homosexuality as a "disease" ("*God Almighty does not approve homosexuality and treats it as an aberration*"); and (v) appeal to non-domination and rejection of institutional measures or pressures exerted by citizens themselves for civic socialization within a project of a multicultural society ("*I don't have to tolerate gays and the damn media … they make everything sound like an anti-gay and anti-negro movement*").

The resulting matrix of arguments gives us a glimpse into the strife of identity-diverse groups for reciprocal and mutual recognition in an ethically pluralist society. Those struggling for recognition must constantly construct and reconstruct their understandings, and sometimes become attuned to others in order to define their identity and the specific concerns they wish to see acknowledged. Even if the majority of the comments made in all settings[16] condemned the congressman's statements and ideas, people are frequently exposed to different beliefs, values, and interests through online environments. Threats inherent in misrecognition often assault the moral standing of the subjects in diverse situational circumstances. In the next section, we examine how people relate to others in different situations and conditions when interacting through the selected online settings.

Self-expression, conversation, and deliberation: YouTube, blogs, and Facebook

We understand that casual conversation is endless. Sometimes it is unstructured and other times focused, sometimes it is playful or foolish, and at others it is reasoned and reflexive (Conover & Searing, 2005; Huckfeldt & Mendez, 2008; Laden, 2012; Maia, 2012b; Steiner, 2012a; Walsh, 2004, 2007). Taking into consideration the specificities of the different online environments, our aim in this study is to examine: (i) self-expression, focusing on identifiability (or non-anonymity) and (ii) conversation and argumentative exchange, observing justification, the use of foul language, agreement/disagreement, and reciprocity or responsive continuation.

The literature on SNSs shows that identifiability is seen as an important factor for the construction of identity in online environments, since anonymous communication tends to favor a lack of civility and disrespect for those holding different points of view (boyd & Ellison, 2007; Coleman & Moss, 2012; Donath & boyd, 2004). Our results partially corroborate this proposition, but also point to some significant nuances. Speakers use foul language in all of the analyzed environments,[17] but under very different circumstances. Online deliberation is significantly and positively associated with heterogeneous settings where participants maintain respect and responsive engagement (Brundidge, 2010; Brundidge & Rice, 2009; Stromer-Galley, 2003), but we found deliberative exchange also in homogeneous settings, along with different types of attunement.

YouTube

YouTube allows a wide range of social actors to become media producers. Different from the mass communication era, this platform radicalizes the idea that citizens with reduced expertise can have their own "do-it-yourself newsroom" (Jenkins, 2009, p. 110) and circulate low-cost amateur videos to a huge audience. In the Bolsonaro and Preta Gil case, mass-media videos and content were reproduced or transformed and retransformed – ranging from different TV programs pertaining to the case; post-event interviews; statements by ordinary people, experts, and personalities; amateur videos featuring fragmented images pasted together, reconnected, and "remixed" from the congressman's or the singer's previous experiences; all the way to protest videos, satire, humor, or just plain nonsense.

Self-expression

YouTube's space for online textual expression is a realm that is sharable and essentially open to the public. The literature shows that people express themselves in this setting mostly in an anonymous way, and are usually aware that they are "interacting and being in touch with other, often unknown, YouTubers," as stressed by Patricia Bou-Franch, Nuria Lorenzo-Dus and Pilar Garcés-Conejo Blitvich (2012, p. 502). Thus, people stand before an "imagined 'mass' of ordinary users" (Burgess & Green, 2009, p. 8), composed of those who participate passively as just observers. In our case study, we found the highest rate of anonymous usernames in this environment, and many participants identified themselves by using bizarre pseudonyms ("Isaywhatlwantandscrewyouifyou don'tlikeit," "Hardrockanchorthat'sme," or "Tellmelies" for example). In this setting, 55.9 percent were men, 14.1 percent were women, and 30 percent of posts could not be identified in terms of gender. Extremely few participants identified themselves as black (1.0 percent) or LGBTQ (0.5 percent). Our data shows that practically no one (0.9 percent) vocalized experiences of disrespect conceived from a first person point of view. Among the postings that referred to disadvantaged groups, the huge majority (95.7 percent) took a third person perspective. This finding suggests that people were neither interested in building a sense of identity and community, nor with being a representative spokesperson of some minority group on YouTube.

Conversation and deliberation

The YouTube textual setting harbored plural and conflicting views (28.4 percent of posts were in favor of Bolsonaro's position and ideas and 55.9 percent were against, and 15.7 percent did not explicit a position). It was the most favorable setting for the use of foul language (54.9 percent) and explicit expressions of racism and homophobia. As participants use extremely vulgar language and expressions of hate, we found an exchange of insults through the "in your face" style. The very offensive words ("idiot," "imbecile," "clown, "fairy," "narrow-minded") immediately stake out inequalities among the participants. People address their objections at alleged offenders with an equal lack of respect. Aggressive speakers see the other as a target for injury, rather than a potential conversation partner, as is illustrated in Table 7.3.

Table 7.3 YouTube Comments

Participant 1-a: "What an idiot! Just how dumb can you be? [...] to say that good upbringing is not to fall in love with negroes and homosexuals (not to mix with them and downgrade yourself), really! If you dig into it, you'll see that he's the one who's married but screws around, like many other married folks."

Participant 2-a: "LOOK HERE, JAIR BOLSONARO, YOU JACKASS FAIRY, UP YOURS! BLACK OR WHITE, WE'RE ALL ALIKE. WHEN GOD MADE US, HE MADE EVERYBODY EQUAL! [...] YOU GAY, IF YOU WERE BLACK, I'D SURE LIKE TO SEE YOU THEN, YOU S.O.B."

Participant 3-a: "Congratulations, hurray to the brave congressman with brains in his head. No one has to accept goons and coons or fairies just because the government says so...."

Participant 4-a: "that slut Preta Gil heard the answer she deserved to hear...the guy was absolutely right: God created man and woman, then the devil decided to stick his nose in and created this third sex, God could go back now to the old testament days and do what he did with Sodom and Gamorrah!!!!! And I think that'd be too little!!! kkkkkkkkkkk"

Participant 5-a: "IN MY CHURCH, BLACKS, POOR FOLKS, GAYS, LESBIANS, HEATHENS, MIDGETS, MENTALLY ILL SHALL NOT INHERIT THE KINGDOM OF HEAVEN. AND, WHILE I AM AT IT, LET ME SAY HOW HAPPY I AM TO BE WHITE, BECAUSE I HAVE ALREADY BEEN CHOSEN BY THE LORD."

Source: YouTube's Textual Space.

In this conflictive and disrespectful forum, racism and intolerance found a fertile ground. Many users not only vehemently reaffirmed Congressman Bolsonaro's ideas, but also celebrated his posture of *"not feeling intimidated"* and of being *"the only one brave enough to speak his mind"* (i.e. *what many think but cannot say because it would be 'politically incorrect'*). This violent treatment and way of dispelling resentment blocks off a participant's engagement into any dialogic cooperation, and it is rather conducive to a "war of interpretations," to quote Jeffrey S. Juris (2005, p. 416). YouTube is also the environment with a higher share of stand-alone opinions (65.5 percent), that is, comments do not allude to the remarks of others or do not receive responses from others. Our findings suggest that most of the time YouTube users were simply speaking *to* others, rather than *with* others. There are good grounds for assuming that participants were indifferent as to whether or not others would respond to them, as well as being completely uninterested in the responses they might receive (Laden, 2012, p. 19).

Blogs

Blogs are usually defined as platforms for regular postings of information and opinions; and interpretation is personal. Unlike other online social networks, where people seek to widen their social circles, make new friends, and search for information, blogs tend to be spaces for interpreting events and exchanging ideas about issues of common interest. Previous studies have shown that when making expressions on blogs – in spite of their distinct structures and despite being used for a variety of purposes – people tend to be self-referential and use a personal and subjective style of writing (Aldé, Chagas & Escobar, 2007; Bailey & Marques, 2012; Papacharissi, 2010; Recuero, Amaral, & Montardo, 2009; Tremayne, 2007). Even when journalistically guided, blogs contrast with more conventional Western standards of journalistic objectivity and impartiality. Whenever bloggers express themselves, they usually have in mind the others as their "audience" (Kaye, 2011, p. 210), and they carefully administrate their performance, as in a "public pulpit" (Papacharizzi, 2010, p. 145).

Self-Expression

The two blogs selected in our study – *"Papo de Homem"* (Man's Talk or PdH) and *"Escreva, Lola, Escreva"* (Write, Lola, Write or Lola Blog) – are organized in a conversational style. In PdH, 73.0 percent of the participants were men, 14.8 percent were women, and 12.2 percent of posts could not be identified in terms of gender. "Lola" is a militant feminist blog, but there is an equitable share of participation between women (41.7 percent) and men (35.4 percent), and 22.9 percent of the posts could not be identified in terms of gender. In both blogs, as with YouTube, extremely few participants provided information about his or her racial identity or sexual orientation – 4.0 percent in PdH and 2.1 percent in Lola Blog. Our results suggest that participants felt a little more comfortable talking about experiences of disrespect from the first person point of view in blogs, rather than on YouTube, with a higher share on Lola Blog (6.1 percent) than PdH (3.5 percent). Still, gender relations, ethnicity issues, and sexual orientation do not seem to have played a prominent role in constructing the identities in both blogs.

Conversation and deliberation

Our study lends credence to online deliberative studies, demonstrating that blogs are forums for jointly cultivating conversation and reasoning (Kaye, 2011; Meraz, 2007; Recuero, Amaral, & Montardo, 2009). While conversation still occurs in a heterogeneous setting in PdH, it takes place among like-minded people in Lola Blog. PdH encompassed comments with opposing views (43.0 percent of comments were against the congressman's positions and ideas, 24.0 percent were for them, and 33.0 percent had no explicit position), Lola Blog's comments reflect similar positions (80.9 percent of posts against, 2.1 percent for, and 17.0 percent with no explicit position). The use of foul language was higher on Lola Blog (51.1 percent) than PdH (33.0 percent). Our study shows that discussion across different viewpoints has important political consequences, but a failure to appreciate alternative forms of reasoning in homogeneous settings and concomitant possibilities for action would impoverish analysis.

The PdH Blog, being a heterogeneous space like YouTube, with a similar share of opposing views, nevertheless presents a picture that more closely resembles a "gentlemen's club" (Dryzek, 2000) or a "public pulpit" (Papacharissi, 2010, p. 145). Participants often respected their potential dialogue partners, and we found there the lowest level of foul language. Even when participants thought they had reason on their side, they showed that they "care" about explaining their propositions by "correcting" partners in their "false" information or visions that were deemed as being "wrong." Thus, participants mutually acknowledge the other's equal status as a source of reasons and claims, which leads to an equalizing of assumptions about one's partners. Reciprocity was high. The majority of the comments (63.5 percent) on PdH showed some connection with previous comments and became part of a conversation, different from YouTube, where most statements stood alone. Rather than just stating a position and providing information, users in this blog engaged activities of mutual attunement – which nevertheless did not mean that they kept emotion, irony, humor, and foul language at bay.

In a respectful and heterogeneous environment, responsive engagement seems conducive to more sophisticated arguments (Brundidge, 2010; Brundidge & Rice, 2009; Risse, 2000; Steiner, 2012a; Stromer-Galley & Muhlberger, 2009). In a previous study, based on qualitative analysis (Maia & Rezende, 2014a, 2014b), my collaborator and I noticed that the string of back-and-forth replies exerted pressure on PdH participants, ultimately forcing them to more fully explain their points and figure out how to be understood by the others. Even when participants were not interested in changing their minds or being convinced by others, they were pressed to issue ever more sophisticated justifications to convince a skeptical, but attentive audience (Risse, 2000). Our results show that some debates on PdH unfolded into refined controversies of moral, ethical, and pragmatic domains.[18] The exposure to political differences showed some benefit listed in the deliberative literature,[19] such as: helping participants to dispute accuracy in their opinions, and facilitating some form of learning regarding differences in values, beliefs, and projects for self-realization; structuring the conflict by clarifying politically distinct diagnoses and remedies for recognition demands; or even showing the moral complexity of some problems.

A different picture of conversation and argumentative exchange is found in Lola Blog, where participants hold widely shared political views and the involved audience knows this information. Participants used foul language, but mostly to indirectly address people or ideas from "the other side" (Mutz, 2006) – who were individuals typically absent from these forums[20] – such as the congressman (38.3 percent) and conservatives or people generally standing up for Christian family values (12.8 percent). In this aspect, our study endorses the proposition that people's exposure to similar points of view may reinforce their belief that this is the proper way to proceed. Still, there are important distinctions.

Participants in Lola Blog not only showed reciprocal respect (and refrained completely from attacking other participants on a personal level), but also displayed a high level of responsive engagement (44.7 percent) and careful construction of arguments. Even if they were not exposed to cross-cutting political views, Lola Blog participants showed a willingness to engage in various forms of reasoning. Thus, our results challenge studies proposing that environments with like-minded people would preclude the debate.

To begin with, in spite of sharing similar views, Lola Blog participants did not endorse the exact same points, as studies about social movements and activists make clear.[21] Being aware that they favor similar values and ideas, Lola Blog participants could state more plentiful nuances in their positions and the reasons constituting each justification, discover more differences among themselves than was initially thought, and negotiate what counts as an appropriate response to their divergences. Secondly, participants frequently tried to bridge differences in order to construct and reconstruct contents of a shared "we." Our qualitative analysis showed that participants often took pains to figure out how they could speak for others, and negotiate divergences to bring partners of conversation close to shared goals. Third and finally, even if participants were not exposed to a direct, one-on-one basis with those with whom they sharply disagreed, they engaged with the claims and reasons identified as being from the "other side." This was needed to imagine ways for combating discrimination, transforming patterns of recognition, and advancing alternative remedies for perceived problems.

To sum up, our analysis suggests that blogs were environments appropriate to both conversation and reasoning. While participants in PdH take some responsibility for maintaining the dialogue across deep divides, they frequently become interested in scrutinizing and considering each other's arguments. Thus they attempt to persuade others to revise unjust or intolerable recognition norms, negotiating grounds for problem-solving across differences and so forth. In Lola Blog, while participants engaged in attentive listening, reflection, and responsive engagement, they often showed concern for enhancing attitude strengths, generating reasons for their political position, as well as mobilizing citizens for political activities to advance a certain recognition cause.

Facebook

Facebook has been characterized as a social network focused on – but not only – maintaining previously-established social relationships (Ellison, Lampe, Steinfield, & Vitak, 2011; Papacharizzi, 2010). Several studies have shown that users mostly employ Facebook to interact with persons with whom they have an off-line connection, be it a circle of friends, family, school, work, etc. Facebook also facilitates, albeit to a lesser degree, relations with people unknown to the user, but who share some connection within a network of mutual friends (boyd & Ellison, 2007; Grasmuck, Martin, & Zhao, 2009). The literature shows that individuals on Facebook tend to adopt a private behavior, in a personal-intimate sense. Publicly-shared comments on Facebook signal an individual's bond with his/her private group; and public demonstration of affection indicates a set of private choices made by each individual (Mendelson & Papacharissi, 2011; Walther et al., 2009). Such a characteristic has led Patrick O'Sullivan (2005) to label the posts in this platform "mass personal communications." Zizi Papacharissi (2010, p. 143) remarks that Facebookers "delineate private space in public domain." Previous studies on Facebook found that people tend to be more "realistic and honest" in their self-presentation, and that minorities intensively invest in presenting their ethno-racial identities (Ellison, Lampe, Steinfield, & Vitak, 2011; Grasmuck, Martin, & Zhao, 2009). Still, Facebook is a quite complex SNS. Since the users can block the access of other specific users to some parts of their accounts, people can portray themselves differently to distinct audiences.

Self-expression

In our study, we selected two Facebook environments that are essentially public, open, and sharable – a pro-Bolsonaro Page (Jair Bolsonaro's unofficial community) and the "*Evento Fora Bolsonaro!*" (Out with Bolsonaro!). The Bolsonaro page attracted 1,746 participants and the emphasis is on family values and what users see as wholesome life habits, in tune with the congressman's speeches. By contrast, "Out with Bolsonaro!" attracted 43,808 participants. The emphasis is on the condemnation of racism and homophobia, and highlights aims at raising awareness in the circle of known individuals, as well as large participants of SNSs. Taking into consideration those who identified themselves in terms of gender, we found that the participation of men was larger in both settings – 41.2 percent on the Facebook Event and 68.5 percent on Bolsonaro Facebook Page. Like in other settings of our study, participants here neither expressed their racial identity nor their sexual orientation.

Typically, people did not provide information about their belonging to any sort of social group in Facebook's public setting. Still, many participants took a first person stance when referring to groups who suffer from injustice – the highest share on both spaces (23.7 percent on Facebook Event and 27.3 percent on the Bolsonaro Facebook Page) in comparison with other forums. This finding suggests that people resorted to personal experiences of disrespect and supported them in the first person, when discussing problems about identity and social inclusion on Facebook. Identification with certain values and world visions in each space of this environment allowed participants to build a sense of community and distinguish themselves from those conceived as being different. Common awareness of being on a "side" of a particular conflict can also be interpreted as a source of solidarity for fostering collective action.

Conversation and deliberation

Since people self-selected themselves to cultivate political activism in both Facebook settings, it is not surprising that each page was comprised of like-minded persons – on Facebook Event 66.7 percent of comments were against the congressman's claims and 8.8 percent were for (24.6 percent of posts had not explicit positioning); on Bolsonaro Facebook Page 55.3 percent were for and 15.3 percent were against (29.5 percent of posts expressed no explicit position). These spaces are best understood through the logic of "technology-enabled networking," for large-scale political activism (Bennett & Segerberg, 2012a, 2012b; Dahlgren, 2013; Langman, 2013; Tejerina et al., 2013) – since they attracted 43,808 and 1,746 participants, respectively. Different from Lola Blog, we can assume that participants' engagement in these forums occurred across large socio-economic and demographic divisions.

In both Facebook settings, participants used foul language, intolerance, and leveled personal attacks at those who expressed divergent values and political positions. When "inadvertently" exposed to conflicting views

(Brundidge, 2010; Brundidge & Rice, 2009), participants simply tend to expel the "intruders," who then become a target of disrespect and offense. On the Bolsonaro Facebook Page, a participant regretted the absence of mediation for obstructing access to those who hold different opinions (*"only those who support Bolsonaro should be interacting in these postings – that was the intended idea"*). Likewise, on the Facebook Event page, a person who expressed support to the congressman was called a "fake" and invited to leave the forum. In the sequence, a participant indicated to this individual the link of the group favoring Bolsonaro (*"Some people think like you. Go join them and support whomever you see fit"*). Examples of intolerance can be found in Table 7.4.

Inter-group solidarity in a large scale network and hostility towards those who think differently seem to mutually reinforce collective confidence that one need not negotiate his or her preferences and identities with those who think otherwise. Still, it is worth noting that we found a high level of comments that allude to others and received responses on Facebook Event (56.8 percent), as well as Bolsonaro Facebook Page (66.2 percent). Our qualitative analysis shows that while Facebook Event participants exhibited reciprocity, mutual attunement was typically meant for concerting strategies for action, thus executing proactive or defensive tactics to amplify mobilization across society (Bennett & Segerberg, 2012a, 2012b; Mattoni, 2013; Ryan et al., 2013). Participants were not inviting others to reason together, interpret situations, judge claims, or check alternative choices for their goals, as in PdH Blog. As opposed to the reaction from the feminist Lola Blog, participants did not attempt to create a "united we" related to a particular group, which would have bridged eventual differences in their values, beliefs, and interests, in this large-scale connective environment (Bennett & Segerberg, 2012b). Even if participants wanted to advance mobilization against discrimination, they felt no need to build a shared awareness of problems experienced

Table 7.4 Expressions of intolerance on facebook

Participant 1-d: "YOU DON'T LIKE IT? BUZZ OFF!"

Participant 2-d: "Look, Mara, why don't you just get out of here? We're all in favor of Bolsonaro here. You're butting in! Go to the 'opposition' and leave us alone."

Participant 3-d: "Janete, it's so regrettable to read these things. Leave here; you're not welcome... This is his page; here we're all with him! Except, of course, some imbecilic morons like yourself."

Source: Pro-Jair Bolsonaro Facebook Page.

by specific disrespected groups or find a common ground for remedies, like in traditional social movements, as was discussed in Chapter 5. Indeed, participants invited users to engage with others to take action; and were enthusiastically commanding and ordering others to act (*"MAKE THIS EVENT KNOWN FAR AND WIDE! E-MAIL NEWSPAPERS AND MAGAZINES AND WRITE THEM LETTERS!"*).

A caveat is in order here. Since our date was extracted from the public and sharable spaces of Facebook, we may not assume absence of reflexive reasoning among Facebook users in other settings of their accounts. Based on previous studies about this social networking site (Kim, 2011), we may well accept that participants could discuss controversial issues related to this event, search for reasons underpinning their positions, or even dispute different understandings within a Facebook setting restricted to a circle of relatives, friends, and an extended net of relations.

Our study shows different pictures of self-expression, conversation, and deliberation on racism and homophobia via YouTube, Blogs, and Facebook. The struggle for recognition is not only a matter of where each one stands, or what position one holds, but also how subjects relate to one another. Conversely, we can inquire into how certain interactions and the mediation of the space in question construct more or less favorable conditions for political activism and mobilization in these settings.

The networked media as sites for political activism and mobilization

Much of our findings on self-expression and conversation in different online platforms clear the path for understanding specific configurations of political action in the networked media environment. We see mobilization in the broad sense as the process of motivating sympathizers of a cause to participate in collective action to advance that effort.[22] Assuming that conflict-based interactions and struggles among groups involve strategically oriented actions – fighting and confrontation – we attempt to unpack the distinctive element in each online space.

We found very similar patterns around activism in heterogeneous settings. On YouTube – the environment with the highest rate of conflicting views and use of extremely vulgar language and explicit expressions of direct disrespect and offense – it comes as no surprise that these conditions are likely to obstruct attempts to coordinate actions around some shared goal. A similar image is found on PdH Blog, where participants were attuned in a civilized way for the purpose of exchanging views and reasoning across deep differences and political views. As was already noted, almost all participants on both YouTube's (95.7 percent) and PdH's (81.0 percent) textural space spoke about racism and homophobia using a third person point of view. Participants showed no interest in inviting others to engage in any sort of offline conversation (1.5 percent) on YouTube or (1.0 percent) PdH alike. The provision of links to other online settings (videos, media locations, and online campaigns) was equally low (17.2 percent on YouTube and 11.0 percent on PdH).

In contrast, we found highly politically active citizens in the homogeneous settings of our study. It is reasonable to expect that interactions among like-minded people reinforce group solidarity and cohesion. This favors the co-production and co-distribution of political material that is replicated and then spread out into the networked environment (Bennett & Segerberg, 2012a, 2012b; Mattoni, 2013). Self-selected activists in the homogeneous settings of our study demonstrated a clear intention to disseminate discourses and take actions in an orchestrated way to mobilize society. Amidst the total number of comments, there were high shares of links to other settings on Lola Blog (53.2 percent), Facebook Event (53.4 percent), and Bolsonaro Facebook Page (31.8 percent). Invitations to offline engagements and enthusiastic commands to encourage the advancement of their cause were also present within the three settings (10.6 percent on Lola; 10.3 percent Facebook Event; 6.5 percent Bolsonaro Facebook Page).

Participants protesting against discrimination, on Lola Blog as well as on Facebook Event, offered links for contextualizing the polemic.[23] Users were directed to TV program portals of mainstream media, as well as the alternative media discussing the case, texts written by OAB (Brazilian Lawyers Association), and dictionary entries defining homophobia.[24] Links were also provided to identify individuals and social groups for and against Bolsonaro,[25] including members of the Federal Congress and State Assemblies.[26] We also found links with invitations to join an online campaign to pass anti-homophobia legislation[27] and take Bolsonaro to court,[28] as well as standard emails for users to demand that public authorities take legal action.

As several scholars have argued (Brundidge, 2010; Brundidge & Rice, 2009; Mutz, 2006), being surrounded by people with similar orientations is important for ensuring that citizens join certain causes and facilitate collective action. As was discussed in Chapter 5, solidarity among people can be used in actions that can either benefit or harm democracy. While participants in Facebook Event and Lola Blog were engaged to combat prejudice and discrimination, the Bolsonaro Facebook Page participants expressed hostility towards minority groups, and protested against norms designed to check discrimination, as well as to protect and grant special rights to vulnerable groups.

Regarding larger recognition goals, it is very hard to say under which conditions specific struggles promote transformative democratic changes. The broad adhesion to Facebook Event (43,808 participants *versus* 1,746 joining the Pro-Bolsonaro page) shows the ability of ordinary citizens to express their preferences and document them. Rather than mere "slacktivism," we argue that this act can best be understood as a public gesture against discrimination. Even if the use of SNSs obviously depends on demographic variables, cultural backgrounds, and personality traits, the broad online mobilization around Facebook Event shows that public protest was not only performed by those who were victims of the injury (blacks and gays), but by all who condemn discrimination and the lack of respect in society. Since public settings on Facebook can also be seen by one's network of friends, broad adhesion to Facebook Event suggests that participants wished to be acknowledged as someone who condemns discrimination. Still, just how such a "public persona" on Facebook – one that projects a socially-desirable self that is discontent with discrimination – takes a position in relation to others in the face of countless controversial issues in each and every specific struggle for recognition is an entirely different story.

Conclusion

In this chapter we examined the struggle for recognition as an ongoing conflict that takes place in an antagonistic field of experiences of both respect and disrespect. Since sociality that is mediated by online environments has become a fabric of society, our study presents a mosaic of distinct pictures that usefully reminds us of highly diverse political environments that people inhabit.

The controversies unleashed by the Bolsonaro and Preta Gil Events were useful to show how people choose different frames and strategies to vocalize claims, engage in debates, and deploy protest mechanisms in networked media environments. Whereas threats to disrespect are more likely to happen in some settings than in others, people are neither completely free to choose with whom to interact nor to decide what order of justification they will use in their attempts to solve disagreements and conflicts. There are at least three suggestions that arise from the analysis of this case.

The first recommendation is that good reasons exist for the differentiation of self-expression, political talk, and activism within distinct online platforms. Our study demonstrated that each environment has different norms and types of public; and episodic struggles for recognition are highly dependent on interaction situations and contexts. On YouTube – an environment open to the public, largely anonymous, and wherein one speaks to an "imagined mass of ordinary users" (Burgess & Green, 2009, p. 8) – individuals and groups spontaneously set forth their visions with vehemence, obviously sacrificing political tolerance; offenses flew back and forth unabashedly. Reasons were offered merely to register positions, rather than in an attempt to establish some kind of attunement. In blogs – an environment wherein interpretations are usually personal, as if speaking from a "public pulpit" (Papacharissi, 2010, p. 145), participants attempted to forge a shared space of reasoning or to enlist affirmation on beliefs or opinions. While PdH Blog participants engaged discursively across deep differences; participants in Lola Blog discussed how to construct and reconstruct shared identifications or shared goals that are always in flux with like-minded people. In both settings, participants showed that they cared to justify their concern of recognition and frequently engaged with other's disagreements. On Facebook, a community environment with frequent "mass personal communications" (O'Sullivan, 2005), participants, who were concerned with large-scale digitally-enabled mobilizations, tended to reaffirm their preferences over rules of recognition and avoided engaging in discussions with people "from the other side."

The second suggestion that can be made from this chapter is that observing online interaction via different settings expands our interpretation and explanation of the struggle for recognition as an on-going practice in everyday life. While conventional analysis usually explains online interactions by focusing primarily on one single environment or separate institution, our work contributes to these studies by enabling the crossing of data. Our study showed that episodic struggles for recognition take a different shape in each platform, and without such a variety of pictures we are bound to overlook different forms of engagement and their potential for social change. For instance, in observing the verbal offenses and mutual hostility of YouTubers, we can visualize a divided society, in which racial and sexual orientation differences drastically minimize personal communication. On the other hand, observing how blog users are willing to regard their conversation partners as being on an equal-status footing, when justifying their preferences across disagreements or attempting to find common ground, we can construct an image of "social citizens." This picture proposes that citizens are concerned with mutually educating each other regarding rules for living in civility with different people. In observing interaction through the open spaces of Facebook, we find a picture of citizens enthusiastically engaged in mobilization to promote desired changes in society. Our study not only shows that there are hybrid online settings, where attunement for discussion and digital activism can co-exist, but also advances a view that a person can engage in different types of interactions within these platforms. To illustrate this concept, a person can enter into a playful or aggressive interaction on YouTube, in which the audience can easily be a mass of opponents (Juris, 2005); engage in conversation and argumentative exchanges in blogs; and unleash activism on Facebook, through personalized content sharing.

The third proposal arising from the analysis of this case is that those seeking recognition reshape their self-understanding and dispute their position in the social "grammar of recognition" during everyday interactions, as messy as they are, in a terrain of respect and disrespect. This chapter contends that the grounds of everyday interaction in an open democracy, allow individuals to freely question and challenge claims of recognition. The characterization of the space mediating individuals' interactions, situations, and contexts was just a sketch meant for observing the interplay of processes of identity criticism and the negotiation of conflict in episodic struggles for recognition. The ongoing attempt to recognize rights, freedoms, and duties will continue through processes of discussion and contestation, as well as activism and mobilization.

The understanding of whether conversation, deliberative exchange, and activism contribute to advancing mutual recognition processes represents a challenging task for further research in this field. Considerably more theory-building would be needed to assess this issue in the context of a deeper discussion and we can only indicate lines of thinking in this analysis. By bridging normative political theory and social theory, Honneth's theory allowed us to delve into contributions of different fields of study that tend to be treated separately. By looking at the intersections between self-expression, conversation, and deliberation, as well as activism, our study showed the permeability of the borders of these practices in everyday life. Insofar as our research points towards the need to consider, in conjunction, the value or disvalue of these practices in normative and empirical studies, the real difficulty posed by the theory of recognition remains: how to make society more democratic and advance relations of recognition?

The approach adopted in both of the empirically-based case studies in Part II of this book shows a mosaic of conflicts – what my collaborators and I have called "episodic struggles" for recognition – enacted in everyday life. As Honneth states in all of his analyses, his theorization of recognition is to be seen as a "permanent struggle for recognition" (Honneth, 2002, p. 502). Such a "permanence" is obviously also being understood through historical development. Part III of this book deals with struggles for recognition from a historical standpoint. This perspective provides different lenses for observing the dynamics of social conflict and makes alternative scenarios plausible in order to assess transformations in patterns of recognition.

Appendix

Variables and summary of coding procedures

We present here the variables and coding procedures the analyses of Chapter 7. In our study we adapted the "Levels of Justification for demands" (Steiner, Bächtiger, Spörndli, & Steenbergen, 2004) (0 = without justification, 1 = with justification). Given the importance of life stories and the narrative of experiences to underpin and strengthen arguments, we have adopted the variable "Stories" proposed by Steiner (2012a, p. 271), so that we might consider the following categories: 1 = no story, 2 = story unrelated to argument, and 3 = story related to argument.

We measured respect for the content of statements and the interaction partners based on DQI's most recent version (Steiner, 2012a). Likewise, we developed an adaptation of the variable "Respect (foul language)." In addition to attacks on arguments and conversation participants, we also took into account the use of gutter language, cuss words, and four-letter words not aimed at anyone specifically, as well as those directed at social actors involved in the polemic event. These actors include: Federal Congressman Jair Bolsonaro; minority members; people ideologically on the left extreme of the ideological spectrum defending political correctness in general; and persons from the right – conservatives and those generally standing up for Christian family values. "Respect (respectful language)" was used, as proposed by Steiner (2012a, p. 269), and indicates language use expressing inter-participant appreciation and agreement.

In order to capture reciprocity throughout the analyzed discussions, we made an adaptation of the variable "Reciprocity" inspired by Kies (2010). We measured the messages that initiate a debate (threads) and the replies within these threads.

Through a variable questioning the existence of an explicit relation to some themes (race, gender, sexual orientation, freedom of expression, political correctness, family values under discussion, political formality, quotas, Federal Representative Jair Bolsonaro) we filtered those comments that would be codified under the other categories in our analysis. Comments with no explicit reference to any of these themes were codified only under the variable "Posting author's gender."

We measured each comment's positioning (1 = postings favorable to Bolsonaro's statements and ideas, 2 = postings contrary to Bolsonaro's statements and ideas, 3 = postings with no explicit positioning – against or in favor, 3B = postings whose contents were limited to links, 3C = postings related to the polemic topic (sexual orientation, Bolsonaro, racism, freedom of expression).

In two other variables built for the purpose of our study, we attempted to capture whether or not there was any explicit opinion on: (1) idea of freedom (0 = no, 1 = freedom as an absolute value: freedom tops and trumps all other values and must be respected with no restrictions whatsoever, 2 = freedom as a relative value: freedom is not an unrestricted value; freedom of expression differs from freedom to discriminate); (2) affirmative action policies to repair injustices versus the idea of formal equality (1 = affirmative action defense rests on historical discriminations and injustices; inequality exists; diversity among social actors, 2 = against affirmative action, formal equality (we are all equal), no intergroup differentiation, universality argument, 3 = no explicit relation to any of the previous choices).

To analyze how members of groups that suffer from injustice interpret assaults they receive from others, we created the variable "Is there exposure to interpretations of experiences with disrespect?" This factor is meant to pinpoint disrespect imputed to a historically marginalized group or an individual belonging to a certain group. The possible answers to this variable were: 0 = no; 1 = there is an experience of disrespect exposed/made explicit, but no elements in the comment indicating a process of struggle for recognition; 2 = there is an experience of disrespect exposed/made explicit, and the disrespect is deemed a motivational impulse in a struggle for recognition.

Comments coded as 1 had perceptions of disrespect for minorities, but did not make any explicit link to the struggle for recognition (example: *I am an atheistically bisexual female – often threatened, mistreated, disrespected, humiliated on account of being these three things. Many people close to me lived through the same things because of their being black, transsexual, homosexual, atheist, indigenous, or from the Brazilian Northeast. However, although I know many white men who've been beaten, they were never beaten for being men or white, even less so for being a combination of both. ...).*

In code 2 comments, disrespect was deemed as a motivational impulse in a struggle for recognition, and some action, such as condemnation or being combative, was made explicit (example: *I guess there is not much left for us minorities, like me, a black, poor, feminist female. The road ahead is long and the work is hard, fighting against this type of speech, asking folks to be conscious and aware, even if just a tiny little bit conscious and aware*).

Comments coded as 1 and 2 in the variable "Is there exposure to interpretations of disrespectful experiences?" were also coded based on the question "Who was disrespected?" which resulted in the possible answers 1 = first person, when the comment's author was part of the disrespected group; 2 = impersonal, third person; when it was not explicit whether the comment's author was part of the disrespected group, then the individuals disrespected were labeled third person.

In relation to the dimension of self-expression and identity-building, we measured: "Identification of the posting's author," "His/her gender," and "How he/she identifies himself/herself" (1 = black male, 2 = black female, 3 = LGBTQ, 4 = none of the above, 5 = not possible to identify), in order to identify accessibility and the characterization of participants interacting in online environments. The variable that refers to users' provision of links related to the event was coded as follows: 1 = presence of links to public petitions, bills of law and media sources; 2 = absence of link. In relation to users' willingness to engage in actions, we measured: 1 = user explicitly takes some kind of action or invites others to do so; 2 = absence of explicit action.

Notes

1. Some caveats must be observed here to avoid the concept of deliberation from being stretched to the point of rendering it useless (Steiner, 2008) and to avoid the failure to differentiate between deliberation and other kinds of discussion.
2. A special acknowledgment is due to Alicianne G. Oliveira for providing relevant information used in the historical contextualization of this case study; we also thank Anne Júlia Rocha for working on the coding procedures of the data presented in this study.
3. For example, Estelle Ferrarese (2011) argues that political representatives may grant rights and institutionalize policies aimed at combating certain injustices without any clashes taking place.
4. "CQC"'s average audience is five IBOP points (a Nielsen-type TV rating).
5. http://terramagazine.terra.com.br/interna/0,OI5034595-EI6578,00-Bolsonaro+Meu+filho+nao+namoraria+Preta+Gil+por+causa+do+comportamento+de

la.html http://terramagazine.terra.com.br/interna/0,,OI5034595-EI6578,00-Bolsonaro+Meu+filho+nao+namoraria+Preta+Gil+por+causa+do+comportamento+dela.html. Accessed on July 10, 2013.

6. *Uol Notícias.* Available at: http://noticias.uol.com.br/cotidiano/ultimas-noticias/2013/01/10/brasil-e-pais-com-maior-numero-de-assassinatos-de-ho-mossexuais-uma-morte-a-cada-26-horas-diz-estudo.htm Accessed on October 20, 2013.

7. http://www.youtube.com/watch?v=y8imZAGzO_c Accessed on January 3, 2012.

8. http://escrevalolaescreva.blogspot.com/2011/03/bolsonaro-e-seu-nicho-de-mercadoreaca.html http://escrevalolaescreva.blogspot.com.br/2011/03/bolsonaro-e-seu-nicho-de-mercado-reaca.html Accessed on January 3, 2012.

9. http://papodehomem.com.br/bolsonaro-meu-bom/ Accessed on January 03, 2012.

10. https://www.facebook.com/events/103062809777752/ Accessed on January 03, 2012.

11. https://www.facebook.com/pages/Jair-Bolsonaro/145284638861357comuni dade https://www.facebook.com/pages/Jair-Bolsonaro/145284638861357?fr ef=ts Accessed on January 03, 2012.

12. The code book is not available in this text. However, it can be directly obtained from any of the authors.

13. We also used variables to measure comment's positioning in relation to (vii. 1) restriction on freedom of expression in cases of discriminating discourses; (vii. 2) affirmative action. However, our results related to this date will not be discussed in the context of this chapter.

14. Due to the great number of postings on the Jair Bolsonaro Page, we chose to collect only those comments posted on March 31, 2011 (totalling 635 comments). It was not possible to collect all comments on the "*Evento Fora Bolsonaro,*" because of a technical problem in this platform, which obstructed the visualization of postings after April 8, 2011 (totalling 159 postings).

15. We believe that justification is relatively high because we coded only the first level of justification, referring to at least one single explanation regarding proposal, deduction, command, judgment, etc.

16. The only exception to this was the Bolsonaro Facebook Page, which was created with the explicit aim of providing support to the congressman.

17. The percentage of speaker's use of foul language is: YouTube (54.9 percent), Lola Blog (51.1 percent), PdH (34.0 percent), Facebook Event (44.8 percent), Bolsonaro Facebook Page (35.3 percent).

18. My collaborator and I analyzed in particular (i) the debates on freedom of expression, legitimate limits on offensive discourses, and the paradox of tolerance. We investigated discussions on clashes between different demo-cratic principles and values; what should be tolerated and what the law should prohibit and for what reason, as well as difficulties in defining what offence is and how society could reach a definition; (ii) the debates on virtues and perils of affirmative action, exclusion and humiliation due to structural oppression. We analyzed issues of systematic insult and disrespect, as well as the difficulties of protective policies, redistribution of resources, and oppor-tunities for improving the conditions of the lives of disadvantaged groups and avoiding different types of harm.

19. See for example, Dryzek, 2000; Gutmann & Thompson, 1996; Habermas, 1996; Steiner, 2012a.
20. PdH Blog illustrates how the target of foul language was more varied (12.0 percent the congressman; 4.0 percent people identified with the congressman's ideas and positions; 5.0 percent minorities; 9.0 percent without a clear addressee).
21. See for example, della Porta, 2012, 2013; della Porta & Diani, 2006; Ryan, Jeffreys, Ellowitz, & Ryczek, 2013.
22. See for example, Cammaerts, McCurdy, & Mattoni, 2013; della Porta & Diani, 2006.
23. http://extra.globo.com/noticias/rio/mais-dedez-mil-pessoas-apoiam-protesto-contra-bolsonaro-1454918.html Accessed on October 10, 2013 http://www1.folha.uol.com.br/cotidiano/896500-mobilizacoes-contra-bolsonaro-crescem-na-internet.shtml Accessed on October 12, 2013.
24. http://www.youtube.com/watch?v=HyaqwdYOzQk Accessed on September 27, 2013.
25. "*Quem protege Bolsonaro?*," available at: http://colunas.epoca.globo.com/paulomoreiraleite /2011/03/31/quem-protege-bolsonaro/ Accessed on September 22, 2013.
26. "*Deputados Assinam Representações contra Bolsonaro*," available at: http://www.tijolaco.com/a-representacao-contra-bolsonaro/ Accessed on September 26, 2013.
27. Definition of "Homophobia," available at: http://michaelis.uol.com.br/moderno/portugues/index.php?lingua=portugues-portugues&palavra=homofobia http://michaelis.uol.com.br/moderno/portugues/index.php?lingua=portugues-portugues&palavra=homofobia Accessed on September 27, 2013.
28. http://ultimainstancia.uol.com.br/conteudo/noticia/OAB+PEDIRA+CASSACAO+DE+JAIR+BOLSONARO+POR+DECLARACOES+HOMOFOBICAS_73725.shtml http://ultimainstancia.uol.com.br/conteudo/noticias/50892/oab+pedira+cassacao+de+jair+bolsonaro+por+declaracoes+homofobicas.shtml Accessed on September 27, 2013

Part III

Struggle, Media and the Dynamics of Political Cultural Change

8
Media, Social Change, and the Dynamics of Recognition

While social conflicts undergo changes, new contradictions and forms of domination are also created. By further examining the development of recognition patterns, referring to a configuration of evaluative properties of individuals and respect for rights in the media arena, it is possible to view the dynamics of social conflicts over time. In this part of our book, my collaborators and I inquire into how the media participates in the historical process of political cultural transformation from a recognition-theoretical approach.

In Part I, I argued that mass media imagery and discourse participate in the larger field of cultural and political processes. My collaborators and I also surveyed theoretical and empirical studies that showed the manner through which the mainstream media contribute, under certain conditions, to misrepresenting people and groups and yet raising consciousness regarding injustice and rights. We attempted to show how members of disadvantaged groups emotionally and critically engage with mass media material through interpersonal conversation to make sense of their position in the social structure and in the "moral grammar of social conflicts" (Honneth, 1996).

In Part II, my collaborators and I expanded our analysis to the use of the Internet and digital technologies to show interactive processes of individual self-expression, discussion and mobilization related to struggles for recognition in online environments. In this Part, we inquire into the possibility of progressive change in the media environment as a process of reflexivity of those struggles structured in the fabric of everyday life.

My basic argument is that real struggles for recognition generate certain moral perspectives, concerning the dignity, needs, rights and social worth of people or groups, that become somewhat incorporated in film, TV programs, news coverage, etc. If we regard the mass media environment as a place where struggles for recognition are played out, we need to be sensitive to the possibility that changes might be, at least in part, a result of recognitional responses. I do not question that the mass media produce trivializing, ridiculing and denigrating representations. I understand that negative media stereotypes can reinforce cultural patterns, which become naturalized and influence how people feel, perceive, think and behave towards each other. In addition, I admit that media content strengthens social hierarchy and exclusion, and legitimizes policies favoring privileged groups. Still, our evaluative judgments need to be sensitive to conditions, and progressive historical change regarded as a "provisional end-state" (Honneth, 1996, p. 171) of current struggles for recognition in society. For this reason, it is important to investigate recognition struggles from a long-term perspective in the mass media environment.

This chapter is structured into three sections. First, I explain why attitudes of recognition are harder to perceive than operations of power in the media environment. Second, I explore, in media fields, different forms of accountability that focus on public and social responsibility mechanisms. I then seek to reappraise the link between mobilized publics and activism intended to change mass media content and performance from three perspectives: (i) within mass media organizations; (ii) outside media industries; and, (iii) alternative media. In the fourth section, I discuss conditions for understanding progressive changes in a mass media environment, and defend the argument that these changes should be seen as a reflexivity of struggles for recognition embedded in everyday life.

Can we expect expressions of recognition in the mass media?

I have argued in previous chapters that to investigate power relations in the mass media, it is important to pay attention to the conditions under which media professionals construct meaningful representations and discourses, on the one hand, and the interplay of these constructs, on the other, with given ideas that circulate in society about disadvantaged groups or other types of injuries. For several decades, media researchers have shown that stereotyping, denigration and exclusion abound in fiction and non-fiction media material. I contend that recognition attitudes are also present in a mass media environment. Searching for ways in which recognition responses can be accommodated and balanced differently with misrecognition processes can open new prospects for understanding social conflicts and the media environment.

Arguments that show domination in mass communications are easier to accept than arguments that seek to show recognition attitudes. While the debate on media representation has been fuelled by a deep concern with showing how power relations operate in the mass media environment, evidence for recognition attitudes are arguably more difficult to demonstrate.

First, presenting certain circumstances of marginalization, oppression or denigration can expose practices of domination. In contrast, to show recognition attitudes, one has to put forward an abstraction from the present or suggest a context-transcendence in a particular situation. Even if a certain study on recognition has a sound premise, it needs to entail a historical perspective to show that rights, public respect and inclusive conditions have been achieved "at least" to some degree. The starting point must be an acknowledgment that social institutions and people have taken certain measures against disrespect and exclusion. Without such an acknowledgment, the entire argument of recognition makes no sense in a given social context.

A second complementary reason is that recognition responses can easily be dismissed as a gain. While admitting that current evaluative patterns and respect towards members of disadvantaged groups have improved in relation to the past, most scholars look to prevailing or new forms of exclusion, offensive practices, lack of due consideration of relevant issues and so forth. This concern, while understandable and necessary for challenging injustice, can prevent us from acknowledging the full measure of progressive change.

Third and finally, recognition attitudes are often suspiciously regarded for being inconsistent. While evidence of domination, without question, reveals that damage is caused to one's self-confidence, self-respect and self-esteem, recognition attitudes are always open to doubt. This suspicion is, in part, a product of the criticism put forward by affected or concerned individuals that public commitments and people's treatment are precarious or limited, as previously mentioned. However and in most cases, this doubt also exists because the precise definition of what can be accepted as "recognition" is uncertain.

This dilemma is at the heart of Honneth's theory. According to Honneth, "the provisional end-state" of social struggles in the context of social interactions always projects certain expectations of recognition, which are not substantiated in existing institutions and current social relations. Socially institutionalized forms of recognition never exhaust their normative potential. Indeed, each form of recognition, Honneth argues, has a "surplus of validity" that carries with it the promise of further expansion (Honneth, 2003a, p. 186). Any recognition achieved by norms, public policies, social relations or media representations is more precarious than recognitive claims made by people struggling for recognition. These claims nevertheless have the potential to exert pressure on ongoing learning processes (Honneth, 2003b, p. 264). I will return to this topic in the last section of this chapter.

Recognition and accountability mechanisms in the media environment

State policies and market mechanisms are important for transforming structures and practices in the mainstream media, for example, media law, ownership, financing, media employment, and media content. Still, as I have argued, citizens have increasingly regarded the media as a sphere of political action. To see media representations as a part of cultural dynamics, rather than focusing on abstract "media power," compels us to observe a variety of initiatives that take place both within and outside media industries to influence media performances and strategies. My concern here is with relations between media professionals and the public, including activists who seek to change mass media representational constructs to promote awareness of certain issues and exert pressure on media professionals to be socially responsible. In other words, I seek to reappraise the link between distinct efforts of citizens and civic organizations to change media practices and promote media accountability.

Several scholars have developed important theories on diverse forms of media accountability. Claude-Jean Bertrand (2001) speaks in terms of "media accountability systems" and José Luiz Braga (2006) uses the term "system of social responses" to show that efforts to create or influence mass media organizations should not be regarded as discrete interventions but rather as a set of differentiated initiatives that are to some extent interrelated, and form a complex whole. Braga (2006) examines practices that play different roles in controlling the media, such as: entities monitoring media content; media self-regulatory bodies and internal mechanisms, for example, through contact with the ombudsman reader recommendations and letters to the editor; sites concerned with ethics in the media; news about media performance; criticism of TV and cinema; and books written by academics and media professionals assessing media performance. Instead of viewing the parts independently, this systemic approach is useful for grasping the interrelations of distinct forms of media criticism and contestation.

Because of their varying locations, capacities and purposes that cannot be found in any singular initiative, the systemic approach enhances our ability to grasp the greater potential these initiatives have in the aggregate to transform media content and performance. Still, it is necessary to avoid using the term "accountability" as an "elusive notion" (Bovens, 2006, p. 9) or as "an umbrella term" (Steffek, 2010, p. 46), and thus glossing too easily over distinct phenomena such as the responsibility to improve media services, the responsiveness to listen to consumer's opinions and the effectiveness of supervisory bodies.

Here, I follow scholars who use a narrower concept of accountability defined as "the obligation to explain and justify conduct" (Pollitt, 2003, p. 89). Accountability presupposes a relationship in which "some actors have the right to hold other actors to a set of standards, to judge whether they have fulfilled their responsibilities in light of these standards and to impose sanctions if they determine that these responsibilities have not been met" (Grant & Keohane, 2005, p. 29). Grant and Keohane (2005) have identified seven accountability mechanisms, some of which, for example, hierarchical, supervisory, fiscal and legal accountability, rely mostly on delegation and operate when standards of legitimacy are encoded in law, while other mechanisms, for example, market, peer, and reputational accountability, involve forms of participation and enforce less formal norms. Accordingly, different power-wielders in the media field, entitled to hold the media accountable, have differing types of authority, such as: distinct ways of posing questions about media behavior and varying degrees of constraints to pressure media agents to explain or justify their conduct; and finally, distinct ways to pass judgment, with distinct consequences or costs for media agents (Maia, 2012c; McQuail, 2003; Porto, 2012).

Dennis McQuail (2003) has differentiated between four types of media accountability related to the political-juridical, the market and the civil spheres. *Legal/regulatory accountability* is based on specific responsibilities assigned to media industries wherein control implies a legal scrutiny of abuse of power regarding formal or legal standards prescribed by civil, penal or administrative statutes. *Financial/market accountability* is related to investors and consumers whose influence is exercised through market mechanisms such as audience ratings and commercial investments wherein control is based on refusal to consume or to invest in media products they dislike. *Professional accountability* arises as a result of self-regulatory mechanisms within media companies themselves, involving mutual evaluation by peers and counterpart organizations wherein control is exercised through mechanisms to assess performance and by rating the quality of media information and products. *Public and social responsibility accountability* is based on the reputations of media organizations wherein control is exercised by external public pressure through criticism, debate and the collective actions of citizens.

In the context of this study, I am particularly interested in exploring *public and social responsibility accountability.* It should be noted that this mechanism should not be regarded in isolation from other forms of accountability but as operating in conjunction with them. Despite being based on a type of "soft power" (Grant & Keohane, 2005, p. 37), public and social accountability is pervasive because reputation is involved in all other forms of accountability. Since the reputation of media agents is considered by courts, markets, supervisory bodies, peers, monitoring agencies, etc., public responsiveness and social responsibility can provide a mechanism for accountability in combination with other apparatuses or their absence.

My initial claim, here, is that the terrain of civil society is highly pluralistic (Chambers & Kopstein, 2001, 2008; Edwards, 2004; Warren, 2001), and "progressive social change" in the mass media environment should be regarded as a problem of civic and public participation, among other factors. For this reason, it might be useful to clarify how different civic actors have specific roles and resources in such a process.

William K. Carroll and Robert A. Hackett (2006) propose a typology of "media activism" organized around three concentric circles: (i) in the center, there are groups within and around the media institutions, such as media workers, journalists, independent producers, and communication researchers, "whose working life or professional specialization may stimulate awareness of the alienation, exploitation and/or constraints on creativity and public information rights" (Carroll & Hackett, 2006, p. 85); (ii) in the second circle, there are disadvantaged groups and social movements who seek to gain access to public communication to promote their causes and to pursue their political projects; and (iii) in the outermost circle, there are more diffuse sectors "for whom communication policy and practices are not a central concern but may mobilize occasionally" around certain sporadic indignation or perceived threat (Carroll & Hackett, 2006, p. 85). With these remarks, I want to highlight that, in contrast to approaches that criticize media power in the abstract, one should constantly inquire into the viability of citizens and mobilized publics to exerted influence in the mass media environment.

My second claim is that insofar as civil society is ethically pluralist and composed of highly heterogeneous associations, mass media accountability for matters of public interest is intrinsically related to citizens' ability to specify those things that are necessary for the general welfare and conducive to citizenship. Civic mobilizations, through media-related practices frequently touch on diverse interests in varying ways without establishing any unified common interest or clear priority of one value over another. Thus, to understand media's *public and social responsibility accountability*, that is, an account "performed with a view to the judgment to be passed by the citizens" (Bovens, 2006, p. 12), requires a critical assessment of the complex articulations between media activism, media organizations and the broader political system.

To explore the dynamics of the *public and social responsibility accountability* in the next section, I will draw on studies that help to illuminate citizens' attempts to influence mass media performance from three perspectives: (i) *within* the mainstream media; (ii) *outside* the mainstream media; and, (iii) from an alternative media standpoint. Next, I will address some difficulties involved in defining democratic and emancipatory social change through media-related practices.

Practices to change the mass media

Attempts to influence media content and practices from within mainstream media

In pluralistic and complex societies, transcultural flows pervade many areas of social interaction. A multiplicity of institutions that are based on different value patterns coordinate social interactions. If we conceive of media organizations as a heterogeneous field, permeable to the influence of other fields, then it must be acknowledged that some media workers do seek to stimulate awareness of specific forms of oppression, marginalization and exploitation, or even advance certain causes.

In the nineties, Herman Gray's study showed how black producers and writers participating in mainstream American television had helped to open creative spaces, introducing black viewpoints and perspectives that transformed conventional television's treatment of blackness during the 1980s and 1990s, even if racial equality was not achieved (Gray, 1995, p. 73). Similarly, Karen Ross's (2010) investigation on women working in news companies in England, from the 1990s to 2010, suggests that the presence of women in these organizations provoked significant gains in including an alternative voice in news production. She argues that, even if newsrooms remain a "male-order environment which is often hostile to women" (Ross, 2010, p. 90), "slow and piecemeal" changes have opened a space for new frames in journalistic coverage and broader attentiveness to previously neglected issues (Ross, 2010, p. 115; see also Ross & Carter, 2011). However, in his study on the role of the liberal and popular press in reproducing racism in Europe, the US and most countries of Central and South America, Teun van Dijk (2012, p. 21) finds that "minority journalists are virtually absent from most newsrooms, especially in Europe." He contends that "this not only means that news production in general will be biased by a white perspective but also that fundamental knowledge and expertise on ethnic communities and experiences are usually lacking in reporting" (van Dijk, 2012, p. 21).

The point that I want to make here is that since media organizations are not fixed and uncontested status hierarchy organizations, media professionals, who are also moral entrepreneurs of certain causes, take initiatives to change their working environment. In addition, certain programs produced by small independent companies, that exist by selling formats to large broadcasting institutions and networks, can contribute to expand issues, voices and perspectives in mainstream media – refer to Chapter 3, wherein my collaborators and I investigated a TV series called *Cidade dos Homens* which was produced by an NGO that aimed to empower socially-excluded populations to make video and perform in films in partnership with TV Globo.

Attempts to influence media content and practices from outside mainstream media

By seeking to give visibility to their causes and pursue policy reform and cultural transformation, social movements, NGOs and advocacy group activists develop a set of initiatives to exert influence on mainstream media. Research on social movements has constantly noted the limited capacity of social movements to influence news-making routines and journalistic news values, if they do not systematically develop tactics and long-term strategies to interact with media agents (della Porta, 2013; Gamson, 2004; Ryan, 1991; Sobieraj, 2011). Most often, scholars describe the relationship between mainstream media and social movements as asymmetrical insofar as activists need the mass media to gain visibility and journalists do not need to rely on social movements to build their stories. While the former wish to disseminate information, which usually does not have fundamental newsworthy value, the latter seek stories that fit journalistic parameters and resonate with audiences (Waisbord, 2009). To produce newsworthy events, social movements and activists usually have to mobilize costly resources and adapt to media logic, which implies a risk of sensationalizing contentious events as well as placing too much emphasis on distant audiences at the expense of activities focused on relevant audiences (Rucht, 2004; Sobieraj, 2011). Furthermore, scholars have observed that when activists assess the effectiveness of their actions through the amount of media attention gained, they tend to modify the character of their social movements (Gitlin, 1980).

In this context, it is worth noting the reflexive attitude that activists develop towards mass media environments. Patrick McCurdy (2013) calls attention to the fact that social movement actors build an understanding of media communication opportunities and constraints, and they are also producers of media material such as activist videos. Thus, they interact with the process of news making in various ways, for example, "through letters addressed to editors, issuing press releases, giving interviews to the media and being active players in a news media event" (McCurdy, 2013, p. 70). In the same vein, Alice Mattoni (2013) argues that activists usually conceive a set of media practices that could potentially be used in latent and visible stages of mobilization; hence they construct semantic maps of the overall media environment, including "sets of assumptions, predispositions and attitudes towards different types of media outlets, technologies and even professionals" (Mattoni, 2013, p. 48). The lesson we take from these studies is that activists cultivate a significant knowledge about the broad media system, which is crucial for them to effectively interact with mainstream media journalists and alternative media practitioners. Such an understanding is also important for social movements and activists to produce their own media outlets and strategies for public communication.

Particularly important in challenging symbolic media representations and improving news coverage of social problems are the so-called Civic Advocacy Journalism (CAJ)[1] (Correia, Morais & Sousa, 2011; Dorfman, 2003; Waisbord, 2009) and Media Accountability Movements (Porto, 2012, pp. 156–162).[2] These organizations include press observatories, media watch groups, etc., that are highly selective about the issue they choose to champion, for example, public health, children's issues, and domestic violence. In the context of this book, an NGO created in 1992 by a group of journalists, ANDI – News Agency for Children's Rights – was particularly important in promoting media accountability on issues related to domestic child labor as well as disability, which are discussed in Chapter 4 and Chapter 10, respectively.

While confirming the prevalence of "mass media logic," many of these entities mobilize their constituents and other institutions, including state agencies, to make media professionals sensitive to civic demands. They use strategies such as: (a) *learning capacity-building*: offering training to media professionals for familiarizing them with relevant aspects of the issue at hand and bringing them into close contact with experts; becoming regular and credible sources among other key stakeholders; elaborating a set of principles to guide reporting; and giving awards to acknowledge quality reporting (Dorfman, 2003; Waisbord, 2009); (b) *systematic media monitoring*: maintaining regular forms of surveillance over the volume and quality of media content; developing or sponsoring studies on the media content of problematic issues; and publicizing and sharing study data with media organizations to identify media achievements, shortcomings and actions for improvements; and (c) *media criticism*: divulging rankings of media programs with greater levels of complaints; and creating discussion forums of media content to enhance the context of regular reporting and pinpointing news making areas.

Media Accountability Movements (MAM) initiate mobilizations when certain media programs, whether professional or commercial, are seen as disrespectful or as causing embarrassment to people or to particular political projects. Mauro Porto's (2012) study on MAM in Brazil has shown that by coordinating actions with other entities, MAM try to build public demonstrations, boycotts, petitions and the like. When media performance is deemed unlawful, legal action is taken to demand investigation and reparation for failure of responsibility. The literature shows that activists are firmly oriented on making these conflicts widely and publicly known; media organizations neglecting or marginalizing social perspectives are likely to jeopardize their public reputation (Porto, 2012, pp. 160–161; Waisbord, 2009).

Since *public and social responsibility accountability* is mostly based on informal mechanisms, it is not often clear how such constraints relate to state policies and market dynamics. The above-mentioned initiatives, that is, *learning capacity-building* of media professionals, *media monitoring*, and *media criticism*, including protests and legal action, contribute reflexively to constrain biased news coverage, media stereotyping and marginalization, and change frame-building and issue-relevance. These actions help to increase not only media agents' attentiveness to specific problems, or social conflicts, but also intensify citizens' awareness of media performance. Insofar as legal accountability has become increasingly important with the expansion of minorities and human rights, media corporations are increasingly pressured to pay attention to the expansion of issues and diversification of perspectives. Media corporations also tend to avoid content that adversely affects members of disadvantaged groups, causes harm or violates public interests.

Alternative media

As already mentioned, civic groups usually engage in different media practices and frequently create independent media outlets. Civic organizations with broader resources and networks of experienced media activists not only interact with professionals working with mainstream media but also develop channels in print and audio-visual media, at radio stations, on the Internet and Social Network Sites (SNSs) (Costanza-Chock, 2011, 2013; Mattoni, 2013). The so-called alternative media[3] –defined as autonomous, independent, radical, and tactical,[4] to mention just a few modalities – are usually small-scale organizations which express group-related perspectives and interests. These establishments have a wide range of organizational forms with distinct degrees of formality, centralization and professionalization involving journalists as well as non-media people (Downing, 2001; Kavada, 2013). In spite of such diversity, scholars stress that a defining characteristic of alternative media outlets is their attempt to produce critical and counter-hegemonic content, spread outside the commercial media distribution system (Atkinson, 2010, p. 22; Carpentier, 2011; Downing, 2001, p. v). This does not mean, however, that alternative media do not generate profit or they do not create niches of publics for advertisers.

It should be noted that alternative media, whether affiliated with social movements or not, offer opportunities for activists to communicate their own issues of concern and develop agendas that are not met by mainstream mass media (Atkinson, 2010; Downing, 2001, 2003). By making public assertions on how a problem should be understood or by taking critical public positions, insofar as they try to frame contentious issues, alternative media form a communicative infrastructure of what we might call *subaltern publics*, to use Nancy Fraser's Gramscian term (Fraser, 1992, pp. 123–124), that is, publics that attempt to formulate and sustain counter-hegemonic discourses to change minds and solidify support.

The alternative media, which is scattered and reaches a small audience, mostly an internal, like-minded audience, usually has a reduced capacity to exert influence through public communication. Still, scholars have long stressed that alternative outlets, even if they do not contribute directly to forming public opinions and developing broader agendas, help to increase plurality in the media environment (Atkinson, 2010; Downing, 2001; Sreberny, 2000). A hybrid, multi-leveled and interconnected media system, as discussed in Chapter 5, makes room for opinions, issues and perspectives generated at the periphery of the political system or outside the mainstream media to reach central arenas of debate. When their flows of communication spread out across multiple publics, subaltern publics can leverage their influences in ways that change the parameters of collective debate. They can thus bring previously neglected voices or issues into discussion and provoke new forms of reasoning and justification.

This brings us back to where we started; referring to a plurality of public interest and dissonant political projects of civil society groups. In addition to a set of initiatives from within and outside mainstream media challenging symbolic representations and mass media performance, multiple kinds of media, modes and levels of media-related practices, create a network supporting more or less spontaneous and uncoerced talk across several settings. However, this level of analysis of the plurality of practices seeking to challenge power structures and transform social roles does not solve the problem of progressive social change. The real difficulty posed by the recognition-theoretical approach is to develop an account of social change consistent with the notion of emancipatory personal development and democratic social inclusion.

Recognition and progressive social change

As argued in previous chapters, demands for recognition are usually open to question whether they are claims for equal legal treatment, for redistributing opportunities and resources needed for the well-being of individuals and groups, for protecting cultural integrity, etc.,. Since these demands often affect other individuals and groups in society in various ways, they are usually tested, contested and worked out collectively.

It is difficult to generalize about factors that lead to emancipatory struggles and substantial goals that transform individual behavior or society at large. Even liberal and "well-meaning" groups and associations, apart from extremist and clearly anti-democratic groups, may generate anti-democratic effects in certain contexts. In this sense, social change should be viewed as a product of a contingent set of social forces and, as such, may emerge and dissipate, and move in the direction of new forms of domination.

According to Honneth, the key issue here is in differentiating between "progressive" or "reactionary forms" of social struggle in the present day (Honneth, 2003a, pp. 182–183) and "normatively determining what should count as an indicator of emancipatory progress at a particular time" (Honneth, 2003b, p. 264). In recognition-theoretical terms, a struggle for recognition can be seen as having democratic and emancipatory effects when it contributes to increasing individual and political autonomy, or to institutional conditions that expand social inclusion. Since subject formation and individualization, seen as expansion of identity features, and social inclusion are intrinsically linked, both conditions are important, that is, "the more social integration is institutionalized ... the more it includes all individuals into relations of recognition and helps them to articulate their personalities" (Honneth, 2003b, p. 262).

According to Honneth, the transformation in social acts of recognition in different spheres is not to be seen as "an ahistorical *given*" but as the result of a "directional *process*" (Honneth, 2002, p. 511). Honneth interprets the use of the principle of universal equality of all individuals as a historical normative progression. As was discussed in Chapter 1, as a consequence of modernity, the articulation of a legal-social order that grants the extension of rights to an ever-greater number of individuals has institutionalized the conditions that safeguard individual autonomy and self-realization. To justify individual civil liberties and equal opportunities for political participation in a democratic order, Honneth shares a basic premise with many democratic thinkers, including Habermas, that the legal sphere of recognition allows people to be recognized as having 'equal status,' not a 'different identity' as assumed by some commentators, and to understand themselves as morally responsible and autonomous subjects equal to all others in the context of legal relations. In the public sphere, this development creates ever-greater argumentatively mediated claims to "difference." However, Honneth adds to this formulation two other forms of intersubjective recognition, the principles of love and achievement that have an individualized basis and enable or impede self-realization.

The idea of moral progress as a "directional process" in Honneth's program is a much-debated issue (Düttmann, 2000; Fraser, 2003a; Markell, 2003). In Chapter 10, I address criticisms of Honneth's account of moral progress in more detail. Let us provide a caveat at once since it would be inaccurate to describe Honneth's notion of moral progress as positive improvement, as a universal history of human progress, or as a perfection of society by eliminating value pluralism. During the 18th and 19th centuries, value pluralism was a key notion in various traditions of thought. Honneth is fully aware that in post-traditional societies, with the demise of religious and metaphysical references, group specific values are now fragmented and pluralized. Social order is open to conflict and continuous social questioning, and thus social integration results from undetermined compromises between social forces and groups. Social struggles emerge when the dominated, that is, all oppressed and marginalized groups, in addition to the proletarian movement, challenge the values and the justifications legitimizing the present social order and contest domination. Therefore, the very notion of struggle for recognition can be interpreted as a competition of multiple claims regarding valuable human qualities, achievements and ways to achieve self-realization.

According to Honneth (2002, p. 511), the three principles of recognition, while historically developed, create normative expectations, seen as "normative surplus," without ever being completely or clearly determined (Honneth, 2003b, p. 264). The knowledge underpinning recognition principles is seen as embedded in the *lifeworld*, and this means a pre-reflexive knowledge not completely articulated that influences processes of socialization. In Honneth's account, social learning is better approached as a negative process, and is particularly observable when there is a disruption in expectations for recognition. In previous chapters, our empirical studies show how individuals, by facing experiences of disrespect and denigration, articulate their expectations of recognition via value-based interpretations under various conditions, in culturally-specific contexts. According to Honneth, such dynamics help to produce innovative knowledge to overcome narrow horizons of interpretations and challenge existing institutions, social relations and practices. Real struggles for recognition are thus seen as important for exerting pressure through experience-based arguments, to enrich and expand the principles of recognition.

This line of thinking suggests that moral forms of justification, which are constituted by generally accepted reasons through public processes of justification, are to be thought of in conjunction with ideas that account for conditions for subjects' healthy self-relations and integral inclusion in society. As my collaborators and I have already explored in Chapters 6 and 7, innovative interpretations concerning needs, rights and achievements may or may not be validated by others. It is thus an empirical matter to observe the extent to which demands for recognition, actually raised by individuals and groups, are considered justifiable by other social actors in a given context.

From the perspective of observers and empirical researchers, my collaborators and I understand that appraising the meaning of political cultural transformation is not something that can be deduced from outside by merely applying some "external," normative criteria for social change. Put another way, this task involves an attempt to capture how affected individuals make sense of a set of events, and then interpret and evaluate the world around them. This approach is somewhat different from the one adopted in Parts I and II of this book in that the priority, here, is to analyze changes from a historical perspective. Hence, we try to assess and reconstruct the dynamics of interpretative schemes and the available data around a sequence of events over time. Honneth's model provides us with a valuable criterion to observe changing aspects of social life over patterns of recognition.

Conclusion

In this chapter, I contended that struggles for recognition generate certain perspectives concerning a subjects' dignity, needs and rights, that may become somewhat incorporated into a mass media environment. First, I suggested that acknowledging the ways through which citizens change media content and performance requires abandoning the belief of "media power" as an abstract entity, as impermeable organizations. To support this argument, I explored attempts by mobilized publics to change media performances and patterns of representation as a set of practices that come from different sources, both within and outside media industries.

In defending this approach, I do not expect that misrecognition and operations of power in the mainstream media will end. I instead suggest that media is an important sphere of political action. Not all publics are equally interested, capable, and organized in exerting pressure on media organizations. In addition, not all civic groups advance values and interests that create equitable conditions for negotiation with media interests, including interests in the political and market spheres, to gain equal visibility or to successfully change media practices. Attending to the conditions under which *public and social responsibility accountability* work can open up new prospects for understanding how claims for recognition can be differently accommodated and balanced with operations of power in specific contexts.

Second, I claimed that plural conceptions of the good life and dissonant political projects pervade civil society, and conflicts of interest and moral disagreements are constant and inevitable in democratic politics. Therefore, individual and group efforts to change power structure in society and social roles through media-related practices require close examination. Without normative criteria to instruct us on how transformative practices should be assessed, we cannot say in more precise terms what is good and bad in media activism for democratic politics and for social justice.

In the following chapters, my collaborators and I investigate changes in public interpretation of certain issues related to socially-excluded groups, specifically, people with Hansen's disease and people with impairment. We inquire into the nature of the changes in news media coverage regarding patterns of representation of affected people and public policies implemented to remedy perceived problems in Brazil from a long-term perspective. It must be clear that we have no intention of developing a normative-theoretical argument to assess Honneth's thesis on moral progress. Our aim is much more modest. My collaborators and I seek to show that Honneth's ideas can be fruitfully applied to empirical research, and we argue that his theory can sharpen our thinking on a number of points to critically examine claims of injustice that have historically been raised, including the normative presupposition within them, as well as real efforts to change the social order on those grounds.

The analysis developed in this part of the book may be disconcerting for at least two reasons. First, moral progress is one of social philosophy's most unsettled and problematic issues. As already mentioned, we do not make any claim to explore the issue of moral progress as professional philosophers, but rather take the perspective of empirical researchers. We attempt to investigate historical transformations of discourse regarding people with Hansen's disease and people with disabilities. We do this through the concept of frames in the media arena. Also, we explore justifications for changing social arrangements in Brazilian society. Since our studies are located in a particular society, we acknowledge that we will inevitably measure certain proposed policies on deals with the issues at hand in a specific historical context.

The second difficulty we face is that problems of moral and social philosophy are not always easily connected to sociological and political empirical investigation, as we have argued in Chapter 1. However, in agreement with Honneth, we understand that "social reality must be described in a way that shows how norms and principles considered justified could already have become socially valid" (Honneth, 2003b, p. 257). We understand that evaluative perceptions of a given social phenomenon cannot be based only on empirical data, but must instead mobilize normative standards and values. Thus, we contend that Honneth's normative theory can offer not only guidance for empirical observation but also tell us something about how we can evaluate our findings according to certain standards.

In Chapter 9, my collaborator and I investigate if political conflicts regarding Hansen's patients are portrayed in two leading Brazilian newspapers between 1998 and 2007. We ask what issues are more extensively covered, what kind of treatment these issues receive and whether or not opportunities exist for civic expression and the presence of civic voices in the mainstream media. We explore a specific form of misrecognition, namely the obliteration of the conflictive aspect of social struggles and the invisibility of activists' voices as well as their agency in the mainstream media sphere.

In Chapter 10, my collaborators and I investigate, through frame analysis, transformations in the portrayal of people with impairment as well as in public discourse on the issue of disability in the major Brazilian news media from 1960 to 2008. This chapter addresses three controversies: (a) the notion of progress as a directional process; (b) the problem of moral disagreement and conflict of interest in struggles for recognition; and (c) the processes of social learning. By articulating empirically-based arguments and Honneth's normative discussions, we conclude that one can talk about moral progress without losing sight of value pluralism and conflict of interest.

Notes

1. Investigating Civic Advocacy Journalism in Latin America, Silvio Waisbord (2009) cites examples of associations that "promote reporting of children's issues, (e.g., Brazil-based *Agência Notícias de Direitos da Infancia*), women's issues (e.g., Argentina's PAR network, Mexico's *Comunicación e Información de la Mujer*), HIV/AIDS (e.g., Brazil's *Agência AIDS*), environment (e.g., *Red de Comunicación Ambiental de América Latina y el Caribe*) and social issues in general (Argentina's *Red de Periodismo Social*, Ecuador's *Agencia Latinoamericana de Información)*" (Waisbord, 2009, p. 107).
2. Mauro Porto (2012, p. 149) uses the term "media accountability movements" referring to "the broader set of actions and strategies developed by civic groups…to monitor the media and eventually establish stronger levels of control over them." In addition to the NGO ANDI, a number of other organizations focus on Brazil – Porto cites: "Patrícia Galvão Institute," – an NGO launched in 2001 by activists in the feminist moment to promote women's rights by focusing on mass media related practices; "Geledés" – the Institute of Black Women, a political organization created in 1988 to represent the interests of black women; "GGB" – the Gay Group of the State of Bahia, the oldest gay organization in Brazil, founded in 1980.
3. John Downing (2001, p. v) has defined alternative media as diverse, small-scale outlets that "express an alternative vision to hegemonic policies, priorities, and perspectives." Downing (2003) lists an array of media outlets, including those used to mobilize the specific concerns of social movements,

groups and individual activists, for example, migrant workers, political refu-
gees, indigenous people, lesbians and gays, labor organizations, local issue
groups, minority-ethnic communities, religious groups, and hobby groups.
4. According to Jeffrey S. Juris (2005, p. 202), "Rather than creating alternative
counter publics, tactical media aim to creatively intervene along dominant
media terrains...This can involve either the juxtaposition of incommensu-
rate elements to generate subversive meanings, as in 'guerrilla communication'...or the playful parodying of corporate advertisements and logos to
produce critical messages, which activists call 'culture jamming.'"

9
Recognition Without Struggles: The Reporting of Leprosy in Brazilian Daily Newspapers

Ricardo F. Mendonça and Rousiley C. M. Maia

Struggle is an idea built into the very definition of recognition. Through conflicts, oppressed subjects seek to displace social practices and inter-pretations, which render unfeasible for many persons the possibility of self-realization. Axel Honneth always treated the reconfiguration of moral grammars as an agonistic process, wherein social transformation is rooted in struggle.

Nevertheless, the notion of recognition has often been reduced to some sort of group cultural appraisal or to a visibility of traditionally-oppressed subjects. We have dealt with such an erroneous reduction of the concept in Chapter 1 and other texts (Mendonça, 2009, 2011, 2014). Our interest here lies in discussing how such reductions of recognition may become practices of misrecognition, feeding processes of injustice and disrespect. Towards this end, we have investigated the visibility accorded by two Brazilian national daily papers to an illness around which much struggling for recognition has been organized, namely, Hansen's Disease.

As opposed to previous chapters, we inquire here into recognition patterns in the mass media arena from a long-term perspective. The initial idea was to understand whether – and how – political conflicts of and around leprosy patients were portrayed by the mass media. However, the analysis revealed an obliteration of recognition's conflictive dimen-sion, as the link between problem diagnosis and the production of solu-tions is either simply lost or seen as government-provided. Thus, it is possible to note the manifestation of a specific form of misrecognition wiping out the agency of critical actors.

This chapter is organized in four sections. We firstly seek to briefly conceptually discuss the notion of misrecognition. Next, we justify our choice of the case analyzed and bring up two issues at the core of leprosy struggles in Brazil – namely, the future of the former colonies and the access to financial funds. In the third section, we lay out our methodological procedures and some general remarks on leprosy-related matters, published by two leading Brazilian dailies: *Folha de S. Paulo* and *O Globo*, between 1998 and 2007. Lastly, we analyze the two aforementioned issues, from the lenses of Honneth's spheres of recognition.

Non-recognition and misrecognition through recognition

The concepts of Non-recognition and Misrecognition remain under-explored in political theory (Thompson & Yar, 2011, p. 1). In Honneth (2003c), they are used for the comprehension of obstructions to self-realization, and thus involve the three types of disrespect linked to the spheres of recognition. To Nancy Fraser (2000, 2003a), non-recognition and misrecognition are made manifest through institutionalized cultural patterns of devaluation that undermine the intersubjective condition of parity of participation. Patchen Markell (2003) claims that the struggles for recognition breed non-recognition, to the extent that they freeze identities in a quest for sovereignty.

Simon Thompson and Majid Yar (2011, p. 169) synthetically point out that the diverse approaches to non-recognition and to misrecognition have dealt with these concepts as the absence of recognition or as synonymous to injustice, without going any deeper. This likewise seems to be Veit Bader's vision (2007); for him, Honneth's wide-ranging definition, contemplating all forms of disrespect (discrimination, exclusion, exploitation, marginalization), would jeopardize a sharper analysis. Bader (2007) thus proposes a more restrictive and theoretically plural vision, claiming that it is more important to conceptualize misrecognition precisely than to build a positive definition of recognition, as the former allows us to perceive oppression.

An attempt to go deeper into conceptualizing non-recognition appears in Yar's work (2011), which distinguishes between non-recognition and misrecognition. Yar claims that the former emerges from denying the other's human condition, while the latter involves some form of distorted or incomplete recognition. Ana Ogando (2012) also operates with this distinction, realizing that while non-recognition would be a more evident disrespect, misrecognition points to an alleged emancipation, albeit not questioning the basis for oppression.

Even if this distinction is didactic, we nevertheless argue that separating non-recognition and misrecognition may undermine the comprehension of the complexities of disrespect. Misrecognition risks suggesting that there would be a true and final recognition. To the extent that one acknowledges that recognition is not heading towards a pre-established end, but is a permanent *becoming* (Mendonça, 2009, 2014), it seems evident that both misrecognition and non-recognition are concepts whose meanings can only be set contextually. Today's misrecognition might become the basis for tomorrow's non-recognition. After all, what is seen as an incomplete form of recognition may generate forms of oppression which end up denying the human condition of some individuals or groups – and this keeps the struggle for recognition in permanent motion.

The endless nature of struggles is due to the complexity of the oppression that precludes the self-realization of subjects. At this point, we must highlight the existence of a specific type of misrecognition: the wiping off, not of the oppressed subjects, but of their struggles and the controversies they are immersed in. This could lead to the comprehension that there is a ready end, which may hinder the perception of new forms of oppression that emerge throughout a struggle. As already warned by Markell (2003), non-recognition can emerge from alleged forms of recognition that put a stop to the struggle and strips it of its political dimension.

In this sense, it is important to go back to the idea of ideological recognition discussed by Honneth (2007b). According to him, Louis Althusser would have made clear how some forms of recognition can work as effective means of domination, generating a feeling of self-worthiness that reinforces subordination. The author recalls that effective recognition involves perceiving in another "a value quality that motivates us intrinsically to no longer behave egocentrically, but rather in accordance with the intentions, desires, and needs of that person" (Honneth, 2007b, p. 337). There are ways of "recognizing" the other that Honneth deems neither effective nor ideological, because they see no value in the other. Xenophobia and racism are examples of this. Ideological recognition is more subtle, inasmuch as it seems to positively value another person, ensuring his/her integration. As was discussed also in Chapter 4, ideological recognition uses present-day evaluation vocabulary, to be credible and able to interpelate (Honneth, 2007b, p. 338). Admitting a major difficulty in distinguishing between ideological and justified forms of interpelation and considering that one can lead to the other, Honneth argues that the greatest flaw in ideological recognition is its "structural inability to ensure the material prerequisites for realizing new evaluative qualities" (Honneth, 2007b, p. 346).

Driven by these ideas, we now come to analyzing the visibility accorded to leprosy by the two aforementioned Brazilian daily newspapers. We seek to show that the way former patients become visible seems to contain ideological-recognition elements, as they omit the existence of conflicts and suggest that there are no moral issues to be debated. The politically correct acknowledgement of former patients has (and here lies the other side of the coin) the non-recognition of the collective actor who struggles and fosters claims. Ideological recognition both makes it natural and crystallizes the status of second-class citizenship to which these former patients are relegated. Prior to coming to this, however, we must set the context and justify our choice of the case herein.

Leprosy: from disrespect to struggles for recognition

Choosing to study the struggles of leprosy patients involves the depth and historical length of the sheer disrespect they have long been subjected to. Systematically segregated and excluded for centuries, they have been treated with a mix of terror, disgust and disdain.[1] Their non-recognition has led to segregation and a plethora of other practices, including castration, tortures and execution. Various forms of non-recognition discussed herein include: physical violence, denial of rights and humiliation overlap in the maintenance of a deep disrespect.

These disrespectful practices have significant implications in the building of healthy self-relations, as discussed by Honneth (2003c). However, these same practices have also fostered struggles seeking to promote conditions for self-realization. Given the amount of disrespectful practices towards leprosy patients, their struggles ended up dealing with a wide-ranging set of issues. In this paper, we will focus on two of them.

The first such issue in regard to the *future of the former leprosy colonies*. This takes us back to the end of compulsory segregation. As the cure for leprosy was discovered and out-patient therapy regimes were implemented, the institutions built to house patients soon became obsolete. The transformation of such units often neglected the needs and desires of those who lived in them (Edmond, 2006; Gould, 2005; Shen, Liu, & Zhou, 2007). In Brazil, this process started with Federal Decree 968 (May 7, 1962), that sought to downplay the importance of *leprosários* (literally, *"leper institutional homes"* in Portuguese) and to strengthen sanitary-education policies. Ever since then, many former colonies have been deactivated, followed by a series of irregular occupations. This process brought about problems, which those who lived in them were not used to, such as violence, drug traffic, pollution, and destruction of historical buildings. Many former colonies no longer have schools or public transportation (Grupo de Trabalho Interministerial de Ex-Colônias de Hanseníase, 2007, p. 4).

Against such a backdrop, some voices emerged in the wilderness. One of them was *Movimento pela Reintegração das Pessoas Atingidas pela Hanseníase*/Movement to Reintegrate People Affected by Hansen's Disease (MORHAN). *Morhan* mobilizes those who dwell in these former colonies, organizes and carries out debates and cultural projects aimed at bringing new life into these institutions. Government actions addressing this problem include the formation of a committee at the Brazilian Health Ministry in the late 1980s, a diagnosis carried out in 2004, and the creation of an Inter-Ministry Work Group (*Grupo de Trabalho Interministerial* – GTI) in 2006.

This issue is complex and filled with nuances. There are, for instance, land-ownership claims, but how this could be happen remains notoriously unclear. Lands in different units have diverse modes of ownership and management, belonging to the Federal or State governments or even to Catholic dioceses. The future of these former colonies is one of issues discussed in this chapter. We are interested in understanding how their restructuring was dealt with by major newspapers.

The second issue deals with funding, that is, *seeking of financial resources*. As with the former issue (the colonies), this struggle too is very old, involving discussions on retirement, pensions, work therapy, benefits and payments to former patients and their children, who at one time were sent to children's homes. These demands included a claim that persons compulsorily segregated be compensated by the state.

MORHAN was quite vocal about this demand in the 1980s and 1990s. In 2006, it proposed, through Federal Senator Tião Viana (Workers' Party/State of Acre), a bill of law to financially compensate those whom society had isolated. This bill sparked high interest and considerable motion in the colonies. Very soon a wide-ranging campaign sought to speed this bill through the Brazilian Congress. The campaign involved the signing of petitions, lobbying with congressmen, political rallies and other forms of public manifestations. This process peaked on April 18, 2007, when the residents of several colonies held a public act was in Brasília. They were received by then President Lula. In May 2007, the President changed the bill into a decree, later approved by Congress. Since December 2007, nearly seven thousand claims have been approved.[2] Several protests were also aimed at speeding the slow-moving approval process.

There was controversy around this legislation – and not just because hurdles and obstacles stood in its approval path. The entire discussion and elaboration process was riddled with tensions regarding its objectives, beneficiaries, rationale and justifications supporting it.[3] Some former patients claimed that the new law did not ensure the dignity of those in dire need of resources just to survive.

Both these issues should not be understood as entirely distinct from each other. Indeed, the future of colonies and the quest for financial resources are related in many dimensions. We separated them for didactic purposes and to guide the presentation of our analysis herein.

Methodological procedures

Our empirical corpus has 440 news stories published in two leading Brazilian dailies, *Folha de S. Paulo* and *O Globo* between 1998 and 2007. Data-collecting came from the electronic archives of both publications, based on the word *hanseníase* (the official term for leprosy in Brazil). Once the pieces were located, we moved on to a two-step analytical stage. Firstly, we described the entire corpus, mapping out the themes in the texts as well as the mobilized sources. We then coded the texts, based on the spheres of recognition discussed by Honneth.

Stage 1: Descriptive mapping

Our mapping started with the distinction between *tangent and focused stories*. The former mentioned the word *hanseníase* but without it being the text's focus. A total of 282 (64.09 percent) of the 440 materials in our corpus fitted this category.[4] The focused stories, on the other hand, had their attention centered on *hanseníase*. We found 158 (35.91 percent of the total) of them in the corpus.

Once this distinction was made, we classified the focused stories according to their main themes:

1. *Eradication and Action effort in the health area* – health action and strategies; indexes, statistics and evaluation of goals.
2. *Science World* – scientific discoveries, activities of researchers and institutes.
3. *Social Mobilization* – articulation of civic actions for the sake of leprosy issues.
4. *Colonies* – focus on the situation of colonies and their residents; re-structuring actions.
5. *Stigma* – stories denouncing and questioning stigma.
6. *Compensation/Pension* – core concern with accessing financial funds and resources.

Obviously, some stories touch on more than one theme, but the first classification sought to capture the predominant line in each text.

The data point to a great prevalence of texts focused on efforts to eliminate the disease. Over 42 percent of all *focused stories* center on the presentation of disease indexes, actions and goals. The *Science World* category is likewise quite significant (15.19 percent of *focused stories*) and it is often linked to the elimination effort. Although both dailies widely deal with the *disease-eradication effort, Folha de S. Paulo* shows far more of a science bent. *O Globo*, on the other hand, extensively covers government actions and strategies.

Table 9.1   Theme related to focused stories in *FSP* and *O Globo* 1998–2007

THEME	Number of stories	Percent /Focused (n = 158)	Percent/Total (n = 440)
Eradication efforts and health actions	67	42.41%	15.23%
Science World	24	15.19%	5.45%
Social Mobilization	12	7.59%	2.73%
Colonies	34	21.52%	7.73%
Stigma	8	5.06%	1.82%
Compensation/Pension	7	4.43%	1.59%
Others	6	3.80%	1.36%
TOTAL	158	100.00%	35.91%

Source: Mendonça research (2009).

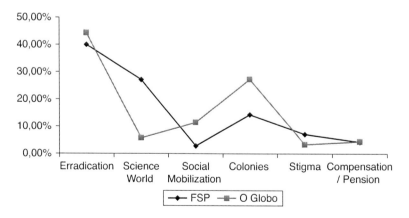

Figure 9.1   Distribution of focused stories per theme in the Press 1998–2007
Source: Mendonça research (2009).

Two points are also interesting for our analysis of the struggles around leprosy: an expressive number of texts dealing with former colonies (21.52 percent of the *focused coverage*), especially in *O Globo*, and a restricted visibility of the struggle for compensations and pensions (seven texts, amounting to 4.43 percent of the *focused coverage*).

Following this initial content mapping, we sought to map out the sources cited by the two newspapers (Table 9.2). The number of utterances from government agencies (28.11 percent) and from experts (21.35 percent) far outpaces other categories. This corroborates the usual findings in newsmaking studies about the strength of official sources (Schudson, 2003; Traquina, 2001; Waisbord, 2009). Also significant is the number of utterances by leprosy patients (16.73 percent of the total), who are generally mobilized to illustrate how contemporary Brazil still remains plagued by this disease. The relatively low number of activists' utterances (8.18 percent) suggests that the tone of the news coverage is not marked by political confrontation.

Stage 2: Recognition analysis

Once the initial mapping was done, all discursive fragments in the corpus dealing with the themes studied (namely the future of colonies and the

Table 9.2 Distribution of utterances per type of actor in *FSP* and *O Globo* 1998–2007

Actor	Number of Utterances*	Percent
Specialists	60	21.35
World Health Organization	6	2.13
Hansen's patients and relatives	47	16.73
Other citizens	10	3.56
Activists	23	8.18
Celebrities	8	2.85
Representatives of the Executive (persons & institutions)	79	28.11
Legislative Representative	12	4.27
Judiciary Representative	1	0.36
Colony-Hospital Management	22	7.83
Others	13	4.63
TOTAL	281	100.00

Source: Mendonça research (2009).
*An utterance was counted whenever a source is cited. Hence, one piece may contain several utterances from one source or from many sources. Space for each type of source has not been measured.

access to financial resources) were selected. Next, the fragments were coded on the basis of the dimensions related to the spheres of recognition. We sought to see how *love, rights and social esteem* cut through the themes in the newspaper texts on leprosy.

The data also underwent a second classification, now based on three axes: (1) injustices; (2) claims and actions; (3) celebration of enhancements and victories. This second classification allowed us to understand if texts were centered on denouncing injustices, on fighting for something, or on celebrating changes. These categories proved quite revealing on the comprehension of the news coverage.

It should be pointed out that this coding had no quantitative aspirations. It was just an initial step to explain our data. Therefore, the heart of our analysis was not classification but, rather, a *qualitative analysis of discursive content*. The results of this analysis are presented next, based on the two highlighted themes.

Analysis

Whenever discussing both the colonies' future and former patients' access to financial resources, the newspapers tended to neglect conflicts and tensions. A coverage, focused on *problems and solutions*, tended to downplay, if not downright obliterate, political strife. Such an operation pre-empts the link which allows passing from problematic situations to their remedies, thus deleting the existence of demands.

In developing our analysis, we do not intend to hold exclusively media professionals responsible for producing such an interpretation and reporting. Attending to the conditions under which news is built reveals how complex journalistic output is (Blumler & Gurevitch, 2000; Maia, 2006, 2012a; Waisbord, 2009). Leprosy is a quite invisible subject and, whenever it gains visibility in the media it is strongly guided by a focus on health. In a previous study (Mendonça, 2009; Mendonça & Maia, 2012), we showed that Morhan's leaders, during the period under analysis, have adopted a strategy of approximation with governmental agencies rather than focusing on attempts to foster public debate in the media arena. Having said that, let us now refine our own analysis, through the three spheres of recognition proposed by Honneth.

Suffering subjects: lack of affection, family separation and the impact of violence

The sphere of love emerges in several news media reports that mention that the former leprosy colonies are institutions that house persons who have lost their affective bonds. This type of focus is detected, for instance, in texts emphasizing that the vast majority of former patients have been simply "forgotten." A secretary at the Brazilian Health Ministry states that the hospitals are full of "people abandoned by their families."[5] Another newspaper piece claims that in the colonies "sick persons and former patients abandoned by their families still live in precarious conditions."[6] Many living in these hospitals, points another article, are there "because patient-family bonds no longer exist. No one has anywhere to go back to."[7]

The affective dimension of recognition also emerges when the violence to which colony residents are subjected is mentioned. This form of disrespect, seen by Honneth (2003c) as undermining any possibility of self-confidence, emerges constantly in news coverage. In September 2005, a series of texts published by *Folha* made that evident. One such text tells of a patient who had his house burned down and who was separated from his parents.[8] And violence is not restricted to the time of compulsory institutionalization:

> Prejudice and ignorance often lead to violence, especially against youngsters. … The disease cost her long periods of study, so that at age 18, she was in the sixth grade, in a school outside the colony. But they discovered that I lived here and they sent me a threatening note. Days later, *this huge guy entered the school yard and hit me so hard that I just passed out and had to be taken to a hospital.*[9]

Living in a colony was reason enough for a person to be beaten until fainting. How can self-realization be imagined when the possibilities of building basic trust in oneself and in the world are so deeply restricted?

It is interesting to note, nevertheless, that the journalistic coverage also contains some expressions of joy in the face of social changes. Such expressions mainly emerge due to the possibility of living with one's family, after these institutions were opened. One woman who was interviewed said how happy she was to receive her parents: "Sometimes she and my sister come and visit me. I have no greater joy than this."[10] Some texts show the achievement of such joys to be hitherto impossible: joys associated with the possibility of raising their children, visiting one's family or having kids in the colonies. However, there is no discussion on how such joys became possible.

As regards the issue of accessing funds, the affective dimension is made manifest only in the image of the "suffering individual." In general, stories seek to trace the history of violence marking these people's lives, in order to explain why there should be some form of financial compensation. For instance, in Japan, compensation is justified because the State subjected individuals to violent inhuman conditions. "The ill, children included, were taken from their homes and sent to these centers. ... *Several never saw their families again, and indeed some were sterilized.*"[11]

Separated from their families and sterilized in order not to multiply the "evil" they carried, these patients have had all their affection bonds cut. This included past affection bonds, but also the future one, since the possibility of raising kids they might have was removed from them. This violence is deemed unjust in news stories, as it tramples on basic conditions for self-realization.

In Brazil, compensation is also justified on the basis of violence one has suffered: "Most colony-hospital inmates were captured while still in their youth. *They were violently yanked from their families* to be institutionalized against their will' as says a document signed by seven ministers. Colony discipline was harsh and cruel. *Babies were separated from their parents at birth.*"[12]

"All *patients were removed from their families and taken away, regardless of their age.* Those born in the colonies, fruit of inter-inmate relationships, were immediately separated from their parents."[13]

Seen as an injustice, the sudden rupture of affective ties justifies compensation. Several excerpts are biographic narratives illustrating the general idea of suffering. The chief focus of news stories reproduces the core argument of the compensation legislation, namely, that these persons have suffered, that this suffering was unfair, and, lastly, that the State has acknowledged its social debt towards them.

Rights denied and rights granted

There is a dual approach to the rights issue when the future of former leprosy colonies is at stake: (1) showing how rights are denied to colonies' residents; and (2) discoursing on actions carried out to ensure some rights. In the newspapers, former patients are the target of the denial of rights and of attempts to remedy such situation. They are not, however, active citizens struggling for their rights.

The most common way colonies find their way into newspaper pages is through their flaws and shortcomings. Frequently their problems are seen from the standpoint of rights being denied, curtailing the possibility of a life worth living, relegating thousands of people down to a second-class citizenship status. These hospitals' problems are portrayed, for instance, in texts bemoaning the existence of child pornography,[14] murders,[15] and violent gangs[16] in some former hospitals. Some colonies seem to be in a situation of "total misery."[17] An *O Globo* reader is "furious at how abandoned the colony is."[18] Buildings are dirty and poorly maintained.[19] "Damaged pavement is terrible for those using wheelchairs and crutches, obviously restraining patients' right to come and go.[20] The then Health Secretary of Rio de Janeiro acknowledges the situation: "It is total neglect with people's dignity and life: buildings filled with infiltrations and moth, broken equipment, and wings wherein patients live together with animals and have to lie down on the floor because there are no beds."[21]

The focus is not just on the abandonment of these institutions, but also on the overall framing that this is unjust. In these public institutions, patients lack the bare-minimum living conditions. The focus on dignity reveals the centrality of the rights dimension.

A diagnosis published by Brazil's Ministry of Health, on the situation of the 33 still-existing former colonies, synthesizes living conditions in them:

> *The diagnosis detected problems in the colonies' infrastructure, buildings in risk of crashing down, lack of medical assistance, employees not honoring their work schedule and duties....* "In some places, at night, employees padlock the infirmary from the outside, locking the patients inside, in bed, unable to come out..." says Magda Levantezi, a Ministry technician who coordinated a survey. Other problems include *lack of medication, no basic sanitation or garbage collection, access difficulties, restrictions to visiting, insufficient number of employees.*[22]

There is hence considerable journalistic coverage pointing to disrespect for life in the colonies. There is also, however, the other side of the coin: coverage also shows some actions which are aimed at ensuring a better life. For instance, the Health Office of Rio de Janeiro has conducted a census in the Curupaiti colony prior to "drawing up service-improvement strategies."[23] The same hospital has renovated some wings and pavilions.[24] Brazil's Ministry of Health not only diagnosed the serious condition of the 33 former colonies in the country, but also "decided to approve eight million *reais* to restore 12 units."[25] The government of Rio de Janeiro was "renovating the building's façade, installing an elevator and putting up ramps" as well as "building 50 houses" in a hospital complex, in addition to making improvements in the "rehab center" and in the "electricity and water grids" in another hospital.[26] President Lula created a housing project in a former colony in the Amazonian city of Manaus. This was a 1.2 million reais project, which is part of his effort to "take good care of Brazil."[27]

All such works were proposed by state authorities and carried out by them. Leprosy patients are targets seen as persons that should be cared for; they are not subjects who make claims and speak up. Such an approach ends up emptying out the agonistic dimension of struggles over rights as well as the controversies on the achievement of these changes. Colonies are not seen here as a political issue. They are regular buildings that should be renovated.

It is also important to point out how, in some newspaper stories, charity is presented as a solution for these hospitals' problems. Donation campaigns, beneficent events and volunteer actions help with placing leprosy into a charity framework. In *O Globo*, a significant number of short texts (six, in all) announce that donations are being collected for state colonies.[28] Such charity framework helps keep leprosy at arm's length from politics and perpetuates the image of the "wandering-beggar leper."

However, it must be noted that the erasure of political conflict regarding rights is not complete. There are loopholes (so to speak) or *flashes of visibility* (Mendonça & Vaz, 2006), when it is possible to glimpse the role of the subjects challenging disrespect. These few texts illustrate the fact that rights are not a foregone conclusion. A case in point here might be a text published by *O Globo*, which discusses violence in a colony. In this text, a resident raises several problems regarding the opening of the colony and proposes specific actions.[29] The text points to the existence of a problem (*violence*), attributes a cause to it (*colony gates being open*), illustrates its existence (*two pubs have been held up at gun point*) and lays out a claim (*installation of a police unit*). This resident is not just a target to receive a benefit.

Political struggle also appears in a two-piece article.[30] The main text criticizes the delay of necessary funds to restore two colonies in Rio de Janeiro. The other piece, titled "Reform divides residents' opinions," makes it obvious there is a controversy around these hospitals. The text is not very clear on this issue, though it contains some statements that suggest it is contentious. A resident is skeptical about reforms proposed for the hospital and criticizes its abandonment. She questions the renovation process and ponders whether it could imply a loss of rights. Even if the material does not explore this controversy, it still makes its existence evident.

The second issue in our study, the financial topic, acquires visibility in the newspapers through the law-mandated compensation to former patients that had been compulsorily institutionalized. If rights are understood as moral guarantees allowing subjects to mutually see themselves as equals, then it must be shown that those inhumanly treated are worthy of everyone's respect. Such generalization of equality renders damnable those acts which diminished it.

Unlike the colonies' coverage, the texts that deal with access to funds and financial resources through the lenses of rights are not so much centered on the suffering of former patients; the way that the lack of funds can render unfeasible the experience of dignity never becomes a problem. The same applies to the impossibility to work or to the issue of retirement pensions. However, as with the texts on colonies, the focus remains firmly fixed on benefit grants.

Altogether, eight texts explore the compensation issue, and a sense of *conceding or granting* a benefit becomes clear. The texts portray compensation as a government creation to "rescue" a "social debt." The State is seen simply as a neutral justice-promoting entity; something criticized by Leonard Feldman (2002, p. 418).

Just days prior to the signing of the Executive Decree, one of the newspapers informed as follows:

> The government is going to pay compensation to some four thousand victims of leprosy who had to live isolated from society as leper colony inmates ... *President Luiz Inácio Lula da Silva will sign a temporary executive measure* in the next few days *conceding* a lifetime monthly compensation of R$760 to each of the beneficiaries.[31]

Then Federal Health Minister José Gomes Temporão remarked that the President "was moved by this cause" after meeting a group of former patients. Even if we can see these persons being mobilized, the focus is on the President's action. The same text mentions that MORHAN would see the President's act as the State asking for forgiveness for a segregationist practice it once endorsed.

On May 24, 2007, when the decree was signed, a text highlighted the humanitarian nature of the President's gesture. After all, Brazil had, until 1976, filled up its "leper colonies" ("deposits of those doomed to unhappiness").[32] The day after the decree signing, another text tells of "how President Lula was so moved yesterday at the ceremony in which he authorized a R$ 750 monthly pension pay to Hansen's victims."[33] Let it be noticed that this "lifetime pension, granted by an executive decree, is personal and non-transferable."

The decree sparks no debate. There seems to have been no discussions about the fairness of this compensation, about whom it should benefit, or about the possibility of bequeathing it to heirs. It is as if this benefit was born ready-made. All of a sudden the government decided to express "the acknowledgement of the rights of those once confined," as put by the then head of the Federal Human Rights Office.[34] All the texts see the action as centered on government agencies. The president himself spoke about the compensation as part of his deep concern to "take good care of the poor."[35]

Such a focus on the State's – and the President's – actions hinders the outlining of a struggle for recognition. Not just because the focus erases the agency of these subjects, but also because it assumes that they operate in accordance with the State's own operational logic. According to Markell (2003, p. 30), as the state generally wields more power, "it will often be able to set the terms of exchanges of recognition, creating incentives for people to frame their claims about justice in ways that abet…the project of state sovereignty."

In saying this, we are not contesting the state's role. We agree with Iris Young (2000, pp. 181–183) that its role should not be minimized. We do say, however, that there are dimensions of recognition not understandable from the standpoint of government policy logic. In seeing access to funds simply as a benefit grant, the media coverage hollows out the deep political complexity of this theme, while reinforcing the state-action logic.

Among the exceptions to this frame, one text reveals the specificity of compensation in Japan.[36] Compensation there is presented as the fruits of litigation, with activists struggling against Japan's government. Likewise, two texts on Brazilian compensation also suggest the existence of conflict. In one of these texts, a former patient emphasizes his struggle:

> "*Hansen's Disease did not take away my right to live nor to defend my rights* and my companions." I am not to be blamed for contracting leprosy. All that is left of my dream today are sequels, due to a lack of health policy in those days,' says Costa.

This former patient's struggle seems to be for survival, despite all "those sequels." Another text worth mentioning cites MORHAN, thus pointing to the existence of a social movement.[37] However, this brief mention does not take the focus away from government action. Compensation is not shown as a victory after a struggle, but, rather, as the state asking for "forgiveness."

Social esteem: ambivalences and disconnections

As regards the social esteem dimension in the issue of the future of former colonies, news media's tendency to downplay struggles and political conflicts should again be emphasized. First of all, it is important to note that the stories are ambivalent. On the one hand, they can help challenge stigmas but, on the other, they crystallize certain derogatory images, such as that of colonies being "dirty places" and of "lepers as targets for charity."

Yet, there are alternative approaches. One text, which mentions the aforementioned MORHAN, claims that the movement seeks to "rescue patients' self-esteem regarding his/her bodily image," which would be essential for former patients' reintegration.[38] This text insinuates that the colony issue cannot be reduced to a hospital reform. It is a wideranging social problem, dependent on the configuration of new values conducive to social insertion.

Other stories question colony stigmatization. For instance, some texts narrate scenes from a colony's daily life. A case in point is a piece titled "A Sunday in the Village," that seeks to portray the countryside-town easy-going atmosphere of a former colony:

> As soon as the car crosses Pira's entry gate, *one's first sensation is of peace*. Having left a city like São Paulo, you now feel that you just entered the most peaceful soil in the hinterlands. A quick initial tour and presto – the atmosphere is so bucolic all around! *Wide shady streets* not (yet) invaded by cars, *couples dating* in a religious center's stairway, *children playing* with dogs at a Christian church's doorway, over there *a bike rider cheerfully saying "good morning" to folks unknown*. It is Sunday and many buses bring caravans and haul in donations. A sign hanging from a gate announces the services of a "furniture assembler." A banner in a street corner reads "We Serve Lunch."[39]

The text goes on, portraying everyday scenes: a woman cooks; there is a group of people lazily shooting the breeze; boy and girl dating on a plaza bench; a young lady sprucing herself up because today is a feast day. Such scenes challenge the strong images of a decadent leper colony, so prevalent in the social imagination. If it is hard to imagine that one can esteem a *biblical leper*, it is far easier to imagine esteeming people as they are shown in these laid-back images of everyday life.

These texts show that colonies have become communities that are important for their residents. An article by the then-director of a colony argues that the hospital has become a "solidarity-marked" environment.[40] Gradually, a reduction of prejudice and bias is ushering in social integration.

> *It is easier to bring someone healthy into a neighborhood* with all the infrastructure *than attempting to fully integrate those here in a city outside*, admits the hospital's general director, Márcio da Cruz Leite. "That would be a fantasy."[41]

The argument here is to restructure the colonies as neighborhoods. However, no emphasis is given to problems generated by the arrival of new people, something that many residents resent as a "loss of rights." Sometimes, the newspapers suggest that enhancements (including those related to self-esteem) could come from the outside.

> Optimism took over the Curupaiti State Hospital, in Jacarepaguá. This colony of former leprosy patients has faced down serious problems of violence and drug use, but now offers computer classes, painting and sculpture to its inmates. The project, coordinated by therapist Jô Lisboa, contemplates 16 patients and their relatives.... The building... has been fully restored with funds from the Catholic Church. Now equipped with TV and VCR, the unit has become a living room for the patients.
>
> "They lacked motivation and were very vulnerable. This project intends to change all this" says the therapist.[42]

The project would target 'patients' in order to make them less vulnerable. The importance of self-esteem is signaled, but it is not seen as an outcome of struggles or outrage. It is as if social esteem could be built from the outside.

We find a somewhat different picture on the issue of leprosy patients' access to funds. The social esteem dimension remains quite invisible in journalistic texts. Honneth's discussion (2003b, 2003c) on the centrality of work for recognition and for individual self-realization cannot be illustrated by the content found in news media. Neither is the impact of humiliation on the capability of former patients to live a worthy life dealt with.

The sole exception appears in a text about a football player allegedly removed from the team after contracting leprosy.[43] The player says he did not receive the expected support. In another text, the club's president claims to have extended his contract and doubled his salary – which the athlete denies.[44]

Save for this exception, no other text indicates how the depreciating interpretive frameworks associated with the disease can take away from individuals their sources of self-realization and of income. We should also highlight how, in our empirical corpus, the compensation discourse is mainly rooted on the dimension of rights. More than a way to acknowledge and value these subjects' lives, it is a rescuing of citizenship.

Discussion and conclusion

The analysis of the 1998–2007 material in *Folha de S. Paulo* and *O Globo* made evident the social grounding of the media discourse. This becomes very clear when one notices how ambivalent this discursive arena is. On the one hand, there is an attempt to build a politically correct discourse, showing the ills and woes in former leprosy patients' lives and stressing the need to fight against both this disease and its stigma. On the other hand, however, it is also possible to see some deep-seated prejudice and bias, and the illness being linked to poverty, dirt and incapacity.

To the extent that the two analyzed newspapers reproduce a socially-strong discourse, they tend to keep leprosy within the health framework, but without delving into other political issues related to it. Conflicts, claims and protests linked to the lives of those marked by this illness gain no visibility. Granted, there is some talk about injustice and about changes, the latter are seen as an outcome of government concessions or private donations. Laying out the problem and some triumphs, without articulating the conflict itself, ends up de-politicizing the issue and, indeed, can stand in the way of social struggle – something that Honneth (2003c) sees as vital to society's moral evolution.

If there is little room for protest and if transforming actions are always hailed and praised, there is no place for discussions, for tensions and for questioning. Tensions run deep in the discussion of the future of colonies. The same happens with debates on the limits of the compensation. Yet neither of these issues really finds their way into the newspapers' pages. The certainties presented by the media are socially rooted; they are easily accessible, understandable and acceptable, because they resonate shared interpretive frameworks, such as defending public health or the need to renovate a hospital. However, none of these discourses promote a broad clash of discourses, which we deem important for future development of struggles for recognition.

In the long run, the kind of recognition promoted by the newspapers' politically correct discourse can rein in the conflictive potential inherent to these issues. Media visibility, albeit important to the social development of certain struggles, instead of displacing moral grammars, reproduced already-accepted modes of interpretation. To perceive former leprosy patients as victims and as beneficiaries of handout concessions advances forms of *misrecognition*, to the extent that it dehumanizes and strips these individuals from agency capability. As long as they are acknowledged as victims or as targets for public policies, their citizenship is not fully recognized. Such recognition is of major importance for a wide transformation of the oppressive moral grammars that steer many of their interactions. In this sense, we argue that the type of visibility reached by former leprosy patients in Brazilian daily newspapers can feed a non-recognition process.

This research corroborates studies that emphasize that social movements usually have little access to mainstream media and they face many hindrances in influencing ordinary news-making routines and newsworthiness criteria (Cottle, 2008; Ferree, Gamson, Gerhards, & Rucht, 2002; McAdam, 2000; Ryan, 1991; Sobieraj, 2011; Waisbord, 2009). Because of this frequent invisibility, some social movements may have to frame their claims in ways that could attract the attention of media professionals, at the risk of taming their more conflictive dimensions. This seems to have been the case with Morhan, who has made efforts to acquire visibility in the media by presenting itself as a relevant social actor in the struggle of humanity against the disease (Mendonça, 2011). The more conflictive agenda, however, remains out of the picture.

Notes

1. On this, vide Gould (2005), Gussow (1989), and Mendonça (2007).
2. Data updated on June 29, 2011.
3. Some controversial points kept former patients at bay from each other: (1) would compensation be paid only to former colony residents or to everyone? (2) would the payment be monthly or in one lump-sum payment? how much would it amount to? (3) would descendants be entitled to this benefit? (4) could this compensation come with other pensions too?
4. Many of them (36.53 percent) explored health issues, citing the existence of Hansen's disease in Brazil.
5. *Fraud turns TB patient into terminally ill*, in *FSP*'s *Cotidiano* (daily life), on 01/28/1998, p. 3.
6. *Technical opinion criticizes Hansen hospital*, in *FSP*'s *Cotidiano*, 03/31/2005, p. C1.

7. *Hansen patients find their voice in a film*, in *FSP*'s *Ilustrada*, 09/02/2005, p. E12.
8. *Brazil still has leper institutions and disease*, in *FSP*'s *Cotidiano*, 09/18/2005, p. C6.
9. *Leper houses and disease resist in Brazil*, in *FSP*'s *Cotidiano*, 09/18/2005, p. C6.
10. *A Sunday in the Village*, in *FSP*'s *Revista*, 09/18/2005, pp. 8–9.
11. *Court orders Japan to compensate confined Hansen patients*, in *FSP*'s *Mundo*, 05/12/2001, p. A18.
12. *Government to pay pension to Hansen victims*, in *FSP*'s *Cotidiano*, 09/02/2007.
13. *Hansen victims about to receive their pension*, in *FSP*'s *Cotidiano*, 12/30/2007.
14. *A Hospital is held up*, in *O Globo*, 09/16/2003, p. 13.
15. *Drug traffickers terrorize hospital*, in *FSP*'s *Cotidiano*, 03/10/2000, p. 1.
16. *Two persons charged with terrorizing colony are arrested*, in *O Globo*, 03/11/2000, p. 17.
17. Ricardo Boechat's *O Globo* column, in *O Globo*, 06/19/1999, pp. 16–7.
18. *Nobody Cares*, in *O Globo*'s Letters from Readers, 02/09/1999, p. 2.
19. *Curupaiti*, in *O Globo*, 03/10/03/2000, p. 2; *Curupaiti in sorry precarious conditions*, in *O Globo*, 07/20/2003, p. 2.
20. *Previous administration under fire*, in *O Globo*, 03/15/2007, p. 10.
21. *Signs of abandonment*, in *O Globo*, 03/15/2007, pp. 8–9.
22. *Technical opinion criticizes Hansen hospital*, in *FSP*'s *Cotidiano*, 03/31/2005, p. C1.
23. *Hospital Census*, in *O Globo*, 03/11/2000, p. 16.
24. *Curupaiti still waiting for works*, in *O Globo*, 07/12/2007.
25. *Technical opinion criticizes Hansen hospital*, in *FSP*'s *Cotidiano*, 03/31/2005, p. C1.
26. *R$30 million injected into health*, in *O Globo*, 11/19/2007, p. 8.
27. *I am not governing. I am taking care of the country*, in *O Globo*, 04/23/2004, p. 5; *President makes four speeches in one day and says he is taking care of the country*, in *FSP*, p. A4.
28. *Solidarity*, in *O Globo*, 07/11/1999, p. 6; *Volunteer Work*, in *O Globo*, 09/13/2001, p. 31; (*No Title*) in *O Globo*, 01/03/2003, p. 16; *Saint Michael the Archangel Charity House*, in *O Globo*, 01/16/2000, p. 2; *Tavares de Macedo*, in *O Globo*, 03/12/2000; *Itaboraí*, in *O Globo*, 10/08/2000, p. 2.
29. *Optimism Takes Over at Curupaiti*, in *O Globo*, 08/03/2000, p. 6.
30. *Curupaiti still waiting for reforms/Reform divides residents' opinions*, in *O Globo*, 07/12/2007, p. 3.
31. *Hansen victims to receive R$760 monthly pay*, in *O Globo*, 05/12/2007, p. 11. This R$760 *Reais* amount was incorrect.
32. *Old Debt, Ugly Wound*, in *O Globo*, 05/24/2007, p. 2. In addition to being too short, this text contains three errors, namely: (1) it says the pension would be one minimum wage; (2) it would be for persons confined between 1959 and 1976; and (3) it estimates the total number of beneficiaries to be 35,000.
33. *Hansen patients to be compensated*, in *O Globo*, 05/25/2007, p. 13.
34. *Government to pay pension to Hansen patients*, in *FSP*'s *Cotidiano*, 09/02/2007.
35. *Public Money goes down the Drain*, in *O Globo*, 05/25/2007, p. 3.
36. *Court orders Japan to compensate formerly-confined Hansen patients*, in *FSP*'s *Mundo*, 05/12/2001, p. A18.

37. *Hansen victims to receive R$760 monthly pay*, in *O Globo*, May 12, 2007, p. 11. This published amount of R$760 *Reais* was incorrect.
38. *One's own experience against prejudice*, in *O Globo*, 05/23/2004, p. 2.
39. *A Sunday in the Village*, in *FSP's Revista*, 09/18/2005, pp. 8–9.
40. *Paying back a debt*, in *O Globo*, 08/14/2007, p. 7.
41. *Leper colonies and disease still resist in this country*, in *FSP's Cotidiano*, 09/18/2005, p. C6.
42. *Optimism takes over at Curupaiti*, in *O Globo*, 08/03/2000, p. 6.
43. *Former Hansen-plagued soccer football player says the Flu club never came to his aid*, in *O Globo*, 08/31/2003, p. 51.
44. *(Coach) Joel promises Flu will be in the offensive playing in Minas*, in *O Globo*, 09/02/2003, p. 32.

10
Recognition and Moral Progress: Discourses on Disability in the Media

Rousiley C. M. Maia and Ana Carolina Vimieiro

Axel Honneth's work supports the idea that an increase in both individuality and autonomy should be regarded as a "normative progress." As Chapter 1 discusses, the three relations of recognition in different spheres are to be seen as normative expectations that safeguard conditions to individual autonomy and self-realization, and such expectations have emerged in the historical passage to modernity. To discuss the notion of moral progress in the theory of recognition, this chapter investigates, through frame analysis, transformations in the portrayal of people with impairment as well as in public discourses on the issue of disability in major Brazilian news media from 1960 to 2008. It addresses three controversies: the notion of progress as a directional process; the problem of moral disagreement and conflict of interest in struggles for recognition; and the processes of social learning.

Claims that cultural change progresses in a particular direction are highly controversial. Some theorists argue that Honneth's program is problematic because it seeks to build an evaluative framework without taking cultural relativism and value pluralism seriously (Düttmann, 2000; Fraser, 2003b; Markell, 2003; van den Brink, 2011). Others are skeptical about the possibility of securing normative criteria to provide a critical yardstick for the social conditions of the good life (Cooke, 2006; Kalyvas, 1999; van den Brink, 2011; Zurn, 2000) while some argue that Honneth's recognitive norms do not provide coherent moral guidance for citizens challenging the social order (Fraser, 2003b, pp. 222–233). In such a debate, Honneth (2002, p. 518) is fully aware that he is "confronted...with problems that are difficult to solve."

This chapter argues that some critics do not do full justice to Honneth's ideas. We address Honneth's discussions of moral progress under conditions of value pluralism as well as his discussions of processes of social learning. Our findings show moral progress on the issue of disability in the media arena, in that institutional innovations have been justified through reference to the ideas of individuality and social inclusiveness. Supporting Honneth's argument, we conclude that although certain Brazilian institutions have attempted to reorganize themselves to follow the inclusion principles in varied ways, there remains disagreement and moral conflict across several policy fields and a wide range of criticism on the oppressive nature of some social arrangements. The "ideal of inclusion" provided by international entities and by disabled people movements is far more demanding than the achievements made by local institutions. Viewed in this way, political critique advanced by these actors helps uncover potentialities for recognition improvement.

The chapter is structured as follows. In the first section, we survey the major problems surrounding the notion of moral progress in Honneth's program. In the second section, we provide an overview of the legal norms aiming to assure rights and promote inclusion of people with impairment in order to contextualize our case study in Brazilian society. We describe our methodology, coding procedures and results in the third section. In the fourth section, we discuss our results in light of some normative controversies such as: (a) the notion of progress as a directional process; (b) the problem of value pluralism and conflicts of interest; and (c) the processes of social learning. In the conclusion, we point out some implications of our empirical findings for the debate on moral progress and transformation of recognitional attitudes.

Controversies regarding the notion of moral progress

Honneth regards the three spheres of recognition as a historical normative progression accomplished by modernity. He shares a premise with many moral and political thinkers that the implementation of modern rights based on the principle of the universal equality of individuals, paved the way for modern societies to become structured around basic norms of value pluralism and individual freedom. Like Jürgen Habermas, he asserts that a legal-social order has institutionalized the conditions that safeguard individual autonomy, self-realization, and equal opportunities for political participation in a democratic order. Individual autonomy and self-respect are seen as being fundamental for persons to articulate their aims. Also of note, according to Honneth, the principles of love and esteem, which have an individualized basis, allow persons to be recognized for their particular qualities and achievements.

As a result of historical evolution, Honneth indicates that the three relations of recognition in a post-traditional society create normative expectations that enable individuals to demand ever-greater individualization and full inclusion in society. This comprises demands for deepening general rights, as well as special rights related to group-specific values and forms of life; and demands the consideration of individual needs and alternative interpretations of valuable qualities and performances in the system of the social division of labor. The point to be stressed here is that Honneth (Honneth, 2002, p. 511, emphasis in original) sees such expectations not as "an ahistorical *given*" but as the result of a "directional *process*."

The idea of moral progress as a "directional process" in Honneth's research program has opened a number of theoretical controversies (Düttmann, 2000; Fraser, 2003b; Markell, 2003; van den Brink, 2011). Several scholars have argued that principles of recognition would have normative value only to a single culture (Düttmann, 2000; Fraser, 2003b; Kalyvas, 1999). We acknowledge the complexity of the issue here, but it would be misleading to equate the notion of progress with culturally specific commitments. Honneth stresses that he speaks of "autonomy" and "self-realization" "in the most neutral sense possible" (Honneth, 2002, p. 515). Elsewhere, Honneth (1996, p. 144, 2003b, pp. 256–265, 2011, p. 408) claims that he attempts to build a "formal conception of ethical life" – an articulation of Kant's and Hegel's moral philosophy – to avoid privileging any specific concept of the good. In his reading of Hegel, Honneth argues that the struggle for recognition is the dynamic historical force moving the normative development of society. Higher stages of social organization were the enabling conditions for the institutionalization of recognition relations which allowed the development of subjective liberty and autonomy. In accordance with neo-Kantianism, Honneth attempts to explicate normative standards of evaluation that are neither culturally nor socially contingent, but that make it possible for members of various forms of life to express freely their differences and pursue cultural ways of self-realization. According to Jean-Philippe Deranty (2009, p. 294) such a "Kantian moment" in Honneth's thinking allows this philosopher to develop, like Habermas, an "interpretation of the modern rule of law, as an order ideally conceived by a community of equal co-legislators." In the same vein, Christopher Zurn (2010, p. 5) has remarked that the recognition theory "gives a distinctive twist" to the neo-Kantian analysis of the institutions of constitutional democracy that safeguard individual autonomy by understanding them neither as a result of a hypothetical social contract nor as a consequence of an abstract cognitive rationality, but as the outcome of historical struggles that can be rationally reconstructed. In Honneth's (2002, pp. 515–516) words, "a formal concept of 'autonomy' or 'self-realization' should rather let differences come to the fore regarding the various cultural ways of realizing, within history, the 'telos' of a relation-to-self that is free from domination or compulsion."

A number of objections can be raised here. For example, Alexander Düttmann (2000, p. 151) and Patchen Markell (2003, p. 23) are particularly dissatisfied with the notion of moral progress and the perfection of moral action based on the telos of full recognition because it arguably eliminates tensions and creates a mirage of general agreement. In Düttmann's words, such an ideal projects a "complete" and "successful" stage "freed of all tensions and contradictions" (Düttmann, 2000, p. 151). This seems also to be the source of Bert van den Brink's (2011) skepticism. To be sure, Honneth understands that throughout modernity the social order has been reshaped towards more equality – that is, greater numbers of areas of subjective life have become protected by rights, and an ever greater number of individuals benefit from autonomy and liberty. Because subject formation and social integration are intimately linked, this means both an expansion of subjective identity features and an expansion of recognition at the social level (Deranty, 2009, p. 277). However, Honneth neither eliminates conflict or social struggle from social life nor does he endorse the view that moral progress is conducive to a harmonious condition of perfect understanding.

A fuller and more nuanced understanding of progress at stake here requires us to take into consideration the following aspects of Honneth's theory: (a) the characterization of recognition norms by a "normative surplus"; (b) the differentiation between the process of internal evolution in the lives of institutions and the process of external contestation; and (c) the account of the effort to overcome discrepancies between the ideal and the practice as a social learning process.

First, differently from positivist thinkers who hold that advances converge on principles that are already fully substantiated, Honneth (2002, p. 517, 2003a, p. 186) claims that norms of recognition are characterized by a "normative surplus." This means that recognition principles have a validity potential that goes beyond the existing social order. In Honneth's (2003a, p. 143) words, "Love … the equality principle … and the achievement principle … represent normative perspectives with reference to which subjects can reasonably argue that existing forms of

recognition are inadequate or insufficient and need to be expanded."
Following the desideratum of critical theory, emancipatory impulses are
seen to be located immanently in the actual world of social relations. As
Deranty has observed, the normative surplus enables "one ... [to] say that
the principles already exist. But they exist as grounds for the rejection of
injustice, not as realisations of a potential for full rationality" (Deranty,
2009, p. 398; see also Zurn, 2010, p. 11). Under favorable circumstances,
social agents can reflexively employ principles of recognition to identify pathologies in social arrangements and rely on them to make their
claims that institutions and social relations are one-sided or restricted
and then need to be expanded and further developed. Viewed from this
perspective, one can talk about moral progress while preserving the view
of perpetuity of social struggle as constitutive of social life.

Second, the ideal of full recognition – that is, all people both fully
individuated and perfectly included – is best understood as a regulative
ideal. This ideal, although never accomplished in the real world, orients
practices of contestation. It can be read as "imaginative projection," as
Maeve Cooke (2006, 2009) has argued, that "gradually opens up ways of
innovative interpretation without ever being completely or finally determinate" (Cooke, 2006, p. 65). The tensions between the confrontation
of demands aimed at the internal life of institutions and the experiences
of injustice and expectations that point beyond the existing order imply
that full, mutual recognition is never realized in any particular reality
(Honneth, 2002, p. 516, 2003b, pp. 262–263). Struggles for recognition
never end and practices of recognition are dynamic relations – even
when social relations of recognition are achieved and institutionalized,
they are always subject to new contestation.

Third, Honneth argues that the ethical knowledge through which we
value potential qualities in others and develop appropriately rational
patterns of recognition should be understood as a learning process that
is part of the historical process itself.[1] These patterns of recognition –
acquired through socialization – while forming "ethical certitudes" in
the background of our lifeworld, need constantly to be actualized in acts
of recognition. While Honneth (2002, p. 512) agrees that the "space of
reasons" in a given society changes dynamically, he adds that "what we
then do, in such acts of recognition, involves publicly making explicit
the knowledge that we have acquired in the process of socialization."
On these grounds he defends the idea that within the relations of recognition there is a continuous demand to perfect further our moral action.
As a consequence, the historical attempt to overcome *de facto* practices
and the ideal norms – the claims of injustice that have been historically

raised and the real attempt to change social arrangements on that basis – sets in motion a "permanent pressure to learn" (Honneth, 2002, p. 516; see also Honneth, 2012, p. 115).

We understand that Honneth's endeavor to provide conceptual tools for cross-cultural and transhistorical criticism is hard to achieve. We agree with Zurn's (2000, p. 119) argument that "there is the perennial difficulty of drawing an 'ought' from an 'is.'" We accept that Honneth's remarks on the "validity surplus" do not put an end to the problem of validity of the three normative expectations of recognition in a context-transcending sense, and that his theory of collective learning is under-developed (Cooke, 2006, pp. 66–67). Still, we advocate that Honneth's program can be fruitfully applied to empirical research; it allows us to ask both empirical and normative questions about historical transfor-mations in recognitional attitudes towards marginalized people, and emancipatory achievements of disadvantaged groups in contemporary politics. To carry out our study, we do not need to assume that Honneth's theory exhausts the terrain of all possible normative criteria to provide a critical yardstick for the social conditions of the good life, or that his idea of good society is ethically superior to the ideas evoked by other contemporary critical social theorists.

Legislation and disability

The theme of disability – although often neglected within studies of recognition (Calder, 2011, p. 107; Danermark & Gellerstedt, 2004) – seems very suitable for exploring the issue of recognition and moral progress. Despite the existence of people with impairment in all socie-ties and in all times, a systematic political and social theorization about these groups of people has emerged only in the last four decades, led chiefly by scholars with disabilities (Thomas, 2004, p. 570; see also Smith, 2005, p. 554; Terzi, 2004, p. 141). Furthermore, disabled people's activism and rights movements have been successful in shaping inter-national conventions and legislation in several countries in a rela-tively short period of time (Oliver, 1996; Oliver & Barnes, 1998; Santos, 2001; Smith, 2005, p. 555; Swain, French & Barnes, 2004). Following the Universal Declaration of Human Rights, several treaties and inter-national conventions have emphasized the dignity, inherent value, and equal and inalienable rights of persons with disabilities. The UN Declaration for the International Year of Disabled Persons (1981); UN Decade of Disabled Persons (1983); ILO Convention no. 159 (1983) and UN Rules on Equalization of Opportunities for Persons with Disabilities

(1994) stand out as being important initiatives for establishing principles and actions to guide national policies. The latter elaborates the requirements, rules and measures for implementing the equal participation of persons with disabilities in systems such as education, work, social security, family life, culture, and leisure. The recent UN Convention on the Rights of Persons with Disabilities (2007) clearly defines the duties of the state and the rights of persons with disabilities, seeking thereby to overcome the social divides and marginalization that affect such persons.

Brazil has been internationally acknowledged as a country with one of the most advanced laws in this area. The 1988 Constitution is considered quite inclusive and the Federal Law no. 7853 (1989) is the first nationwide law establishing that prejudice against persons with disabilities is a crime. The OAS Guatemala Convention (1999) for the Elimination of All Forms of Discrimination against Persons with Disabilities, held to be a key point in this process, has been law in Brazil since 2001. The resolution no. 2 (2001), by the National Education Council (Conselho Nacional de Educação) adopted a clear inclusive perspective to shape national education policies. Since then, several other resolutions have been published on specific topics, such as priority service, social support, professional rehabilitation, quotas, transport, accessibility, and recognition of the Libras language as a legal form of communication. In Brazil, as in many other countries, juridical regulations favoring people with disabilities are to a large degree the result of struggles and successful campaigns for rights promoted by many civil society groups, NGOs and academics (Figueira, 2008; Sassaki, 1997).

Methodology: an indirect analysis of media frames

To investigate discourses in the media on the issue of disability, we adopted the concept of frame and the accompanying methods from the field of frame analysis. In their famous work analyzing news content on nuclear power, William Gamson and Andre Modigliani (1989, p. 3) have stated that frames are "central organizing ideas" for making sense of and interpreting issues, by showing certain associations of elements in social reality. A frame is an abstract construct – meaningful, collectively shared patterns or structures which, in Erving Goffman's terms, help us to "locate, perceive, identify and label a seemingly infinite number of concrete occurrences defined in its limits" (Goffman, 1974, p. 21). These organizing principles are usually implicit within the messages, and are expressed in the form of attributions of specific causes and solutions

Table 10.1   Framing elements/signature matrix

Symbolic devices	Reasoning devices
– metaphors	– specific definition of the issue
– examples	(actors, sub-topics, and headings)
– slogans	– causes
– representations	– moral judgments
– visual images	– solutions
– words	

Source: EME-UFMG Research Group.

to given issues, slogans and metaphors, among other modes (Entman, 1993, 2004; Matthes & Kohring, 2008).

One of the inherent difficulties of frame analysis – taken as abstract constructs – is how to operationalize them for empirical research (Matthes, 2009; Matthes & Kohring, 2008; Reese, 2007). Scholars in this area have used data reduction techniques (dividing frames into representative categories) in order to produce more reliable studies (Matthes & Kohring, 2008; Vimieiro & Maia, 2011). In our case, we have adopted similar procedures to those of Jörg Matthes and Mathias Kohring (2008). We have also followed the indications provided by Gamson and Modigliani (1989) and Robert Entman (1993, 2004) to define analytical categories that, taken together, are able to evince frames in the text. Our study is then based on indirect frame analysis, as the frames are generated from interpretative packages or sets of devices that express frames in the messages. Table 10.1 presents our set of elements used in an empirical analysis of news.[2]

Sample and unit of analysis

Our empirical sample consists of news stories published in major Brazilian newspapers – *Folha de S.Paulo* and *O Globo* – as well as in a news weekly, *Veja*. The analysis period encompasses 1960 to 2008,[3] which is compatible with the moment when the idea of disability started to be thematized publicly in Brazil (Figueira, 2008; Sassaki, 1997). It would be impossible, however, to investigate all the news about disability published across 38 years, particularly because most of this material has not been digitized. Thus, we divided the corpus into eight-year intervals and gathered news from two months in each of these years from both newspapers, as follows: 1960, 1968, 1976, 1984, 1992, 2000 and 2008. We searched the entire twelve months in the news weekly, as its content was digitized. After the non-digitized material had been manually clipped and the digitized material searched,[4] we ended up with 364 news texts.

Coding

Our unit of analysis was the news story and the coding procedure was done in three stages. To begin, we created codes referring to the frame elements and to possible variables found in a first detailed reading of the material as well as in other sources on disability. Next, the codebook was reduced by clustering similar variables into broader variables to improve the classification method. Finally, we analyzed the data cross-sectionally and discarded the variables with less than at least a 5 percent recurrence rate, as Matthes and Kohring (2008) have recommended. A reliability test[5] of the sample was conducted in 10 percent of texts, and we reached a 0.704 agreement rate in the coding made by two coders.

Data processing

Following the coding procedures, data were processed using the RapidMiner program. We applied data-clustering techniques, bringing together news with similar elements and generating sets of those with greater internal similarity. The purpose of clustering was to form sets that differed as much as possible from each other. Thus we could identify, at each moment of history, news with similar patterns or groups with common recurring elements over time.

We analyzed the social and historical context to label the frames in each set based on the most evident features of each group. A few frames – such as the medical frame – occurred in several years; thus, the interpretative analysis enabled us to discern important differences in the construction of meaning in these frames over time.

Empirical results

Figure 10.1 presents the frame chart per year along the period under research, including the percentage of news in each frame in the corresponding year. In summary, we may divide public discourses on the topic of disability in the media into two phases: (a) one that extends from the 1960s to the 1970s, when the integrative model is the central approach through frames of a charitable behavior towards people with disabilities and a medical perspective on impairment; at this point, disability is viewed as a problem of the individual; (b) a second period from the 1980s to nowadays, when the perspective of human rights gains

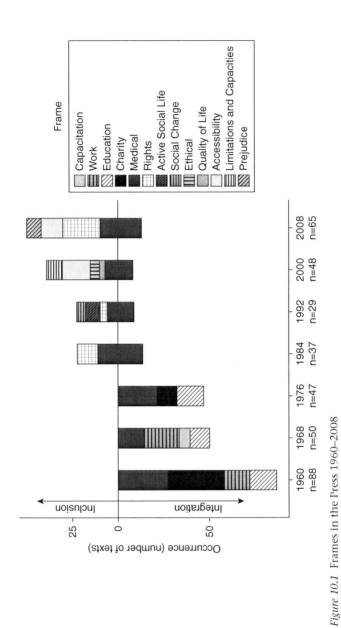

Figure 10.1 Frames in the Press 1960–2008

Source: EME-UFMG Research Group.

strength and the notion of inclusiveness becomes central through frames of accessibility, quality of life, limitations and abilities, and denouncements of prejudice, among others; in this phase, people with disability are regarded as persons who do not yet enjoy equal rights and society is responsible for overcoming barriers that obstruct their autonomous living. The interpretation of the results was intended to answer the following questions: can eventual changes in the view of impairment and in policies on disability be justified through reference to the ideas of social inclusiveness and individuality? Is it possible to identify in the mass media arena an agonistic confrontation of demands for recognition aimed at the national institutions? Can we speak in terms of collective learning regarding the issue of disability?

Can eventual changes in the view of impairment and in policies on disability be justified through reference to the ideas of social inclusiveness and individuality?

The prominence of "medical frames," "work frames" and "education frames" in the first phase shows a concern for integration of people with disability in society as a means to combat "segregation." Traditional segregation of people with impairment had infused feelings of ignorance and fear, and thus integrative policies aimed to abolish barriers to acceptance and bring people into society. Regarding the sphere of intimate relations, we find several appeals in the news to treat the "retarded child and the mental deficient" with love, kindness and patience. For instance, a news article announces an awareness campaign – entitled "The Retarded Child Can be Helped," launched by the Governor of Rio de Janeiro in 1960 – aiming to "draw the general public's and the official authorities' attention to several problems experienced by these children and their need for treatment and education."[6] In another article, a specialist mentioned that "treatment of the retarded people requires patience, perseverance and love as well as tranquil discipline and energy." He recommended that "one should not regard them with pity and complaint, but instead make a real effort to obtain benefit from what remains unaffected by their defect and recover what is possible."[7] While regarding disability as a personal tragedy, several speakers in the news media are concerned that disabled people grow up in an environment marked by "indifference, fear and hostility" that severely damages their possibilities of "recovery."

> The chances of recovery are zero: they [the exceptional children] are not ready for life in society and do not learn a useful job at the

right time. "People should understand that the exceptional need care and sympathy," says the president of the Association of Parents and Friends of the Exceptional, Ignês Félix Pacheco de Britto, who coordinates the three APAE units in Rio de Janeiro among the 300 units this entity has throughout the country. (*The Opportunity to Treat the Mentally Deficient at APAE schools*, *O Globo*, November 21, 1976)[8]

The integration perspective tends to view impairment as a physical defect – that is, a restriction or a lack of ability to perform an activity in a normal manner (Terzi, 2004, p. 141). Therefore, any policy is likely to focus on reducing or eliminating physical segregation alone – and providing adequate health care, education and training for "recovering" or "resettling" disabled people to live in society. In the news surveyed in this period, the notion of education is related to training, in addition "to surgery, medical treatment and correction of defects" – a view expressed by a specialist in the following article:

> Depending on the case of each retarded child – adds professor Elso Arruda – one has to think of education to cultivate the intellectual, social and moral potentialities of these children, to correct antisocial and abnormal tendencies by teaching and discipline, and to provide them with all possible knowledge within the possibilities of each case. Training at home, school, or at specialized institutions aims to introduce useful automatisms [sic], hygiene and feeding habits, and to correct their gait, language, and sense organs. The three Rs program (repetition, relaxation and routine) should be followed strictly. (*The Treatment of Retarded Children Requires Patience, Discipline and Love*, *Folha de S. Paulo*, August 16, 1960)

The concept of work is related to occupational therapy or to the performance of simple and programmed activities, such as handcrafts and the assemblage of products, carried out in protected environments that are not regulated by the labor market.

> Rehabilitating the incapable requires a dedicated facility equipped with the indispensable means to apply surgical and clinical techniques, as well as occupation therapy, trained and able people to deal with the incapable to process their adaptation or reeducation, rehabilitating and restoring them for useful activities in society. (*A Modern Facility for Rehabilitating the Incapable*, *O Globo*, July 25, 1960)

The integration approach has been severely criticized from the mid-1970s onwards. Although the integrative model claims to offer disabled people the opportunity to take part in society, critics contest that its promises are not fulfilled; this model is seen to promote further forms of oppression and exclusion. First, critics have claimed that social integration is based on the concept of "normalization" which requires people with disability to "conform" to the standards of non-disabled people, by "assimilating" the terms and conditions that currently exist within a given society (Northway, 1997, p. 159; Oliver, 1996). Second, some scholars argue that this model ascribes a very passive role to people with disabilities – viewed as an object of solutions posed in terms of medical cure or charitable assistance. As Ruth Northway has put it, "If the 'problem' resides in the individual rather than in society then the 'solution' is for the individual to work towards normality in so far as this is possible" (Northway, 1997, p. 163; see also Cole, 2007). Third, critics hold that the integrative model restricts the choices of disabled people – by assuming that people with impairment should achieve happiness and self-realization only in the normal community, and thus overlooking their eventual frustration with integration and the blocking of their opportunities for self-determination. Fourth, this model is regarded as being prone to perpetuate exclusion because integration policies give technical responses to impairment and do not challenge the status quo; it rather sustains values and social norms that lead primarily to the devaluation of people with disabilities.

In the second phase in our case study, we note that speakers in the news media from 1984 onwards start using frames of rights, of accessibility, of active social life and of quality of life, when discussing issues related to people with disability. This change can be explained by the rise of the "social relational understanding of disability" in the mid-1970s and the "social model" in the 1990s – promoted by organizations of disabled people and activist scholars of disability studies – with the "explicit commitment to assist disabled people in their fight for full equality and social inclusion" (Thomas, 2004, p. 570; see also Smith, 2005, p. 554; Terzi, 2004, p. 141). Such a perspective, despite encompassing different chains of thought,[9] has significantly influenced educational and social policies on inclusion in several countries.

Our findings show that people with disability also became sources of news stories from the 1980s onwards. This is theoretically and politically important because it enables the public also to understand disability from a perspective informed by disabled people's reflections on their own experience. In several articles, people with impairment address the issue of oppression and discrimination embedded in institutions and in socio-cultural practices. In the extract below from the 1980s, a speaker clearly expresses that discrimination and oppression undermined her psycho-emotional well-being. She had become disabled nine years before "because of one of these accidents [that frequently happen]"; and she mentions that only "after a tremendous struggle with herself" was possible to achieve "the goal to start living again in spite of being disabled." The current view of impairment as a tragic, personal loss and the way non-disabled people see persons with impairments are condemned as profoundly disabling:

> I feel that people see something strange in us, the disabled, a unique difference as if part of the reasoning mechanism to attain a precise judgment of things and events is missing. And this part is the disability (which may happen to anyone, and which nobody wants) in the sense that society traditionally is set relative to us: we only receive alms but no rights. (Mrs Cintia de Souza Clausell, *The Disabled, Something Strange*, *Folha de S. Paulo*, January 12, 1984)

This speaker in the news media also uses the language of rights to vocalize what should be done to alleviate barriers that restrict disabled people's chances to enjoy life and achieve self-realization:

> I have written to the media to support our struggle to attain rights. The most important battle is to achieve – for all of us – better rehabilitation, public transport, work, elimination of barriers, leisure, etc. In other words, improvements for this huge minority consisting of 13 million disabled persons. I am fighting and experiencing the struggle. How? By claiming our rights relative to cars parked on sidewalks, on pedestrian crossings, and for public transport to take us to rehabilitation centers, work, and leisure. (Mrs Cintia de Souza Clausell, *The Disabled, Something Strange*, *Folha de S. Paulo*, January 12, 1984)

On the same wavelength as the "social model" perspective, speakers in the news begin to shift the "problem" of disability from the individual towards the structure of society, that is, institutional forms of exclusion and cultural marginalization. Leaders of social movements, people with impairments, some specialists and moral entrepreneurs claim that people with disabilities cannot be treated as second-class citizens; they have the right to the same opportunities as other citizens to participate in social activities – in labor markets, educational institutions, transport, communication, and other public and private services, including participation in collective decision making.

Special attention should be given to the "frame of rights" in the news media in this phase because claims based on rights imply the conviction that society owes respect to people with disability as morally or politically autonomous and potentially capable of co-determining how they want to live among other citizens. In 2008, one news story entitled "Respect and Inclusion" announced that the Brazilian National Congress had ratified the UN's "Convention on the Rights of People with Disability." This was celebrated as a means to "empower disabled people's banner and cause":

> This important, promising and unheard of decision (over three fifths voted Yes) raises the terms of the treaty to a dimension of constitutional equivalence. It means that the State and society are compelled – and under even more healthy pressure – to enforce the Higher Law. This assures rights to 15.4% of our population, people who daily face huge difficulties in the harsh and complex search for quality of life and social inclusion. (*Respect and Inclusion*, O Globo, July 11, 2008)

In the legal sphere, the institutionalization of rights enables disabled people and those who speak on their behalf to advance their demands – based on reasons that can be articulated through reference to mutual recognition. The representatives and policy-makers are then made accountable to change the physical environment that previously fitted the needs of non-disabled people as well as to incentivize deconstructing social value hierarchies that underscore social exclusion practices. In the following news story, the journalist uses the issue of "accessibility" to explain the political question at stake:

> If it is right and legitimate that persons with impairment be offered tools for better personal mobility, then the states should implement concrete measures to overcome hurdles of all kinds. This novel approach is not limited to individual success in overcoming the limitations of his or her physical setting. The focus broadens, and the social setting itself is now responsible for bringing down these hurdles. As a consequence, public powers will be compelled to set aside resources in the budget for this end. (*Respect and Inclusion*, O Globo, July 11, 2008)

Based on Honneth's theory, claims of rights can be best understood as a reflection of expectation in the legal sphere, anticipating that political commitments should ensure both increased equality and inclusion. When disabled people regard themselves as rights holders they expect to be recognized as capable of making their own decisions, and thus as morally responsible to demand from their political representatives what they need both to develop their particularized identity and to become full participants in collective life. This explains the emergence of frames of accessibility, of active social life and of quality of life in this period.

Regarding health care, it should be noted that the medical frame is prominent during all years under analysis. However, while in the first phase there is a concern with "surgery," "rehabilitation" and "training" to seek cure, as already mentioned, in the second phase there is a concern with prevention, early diagnosis and assistance following the logic: "For each patient, a different treatment."[10] We find reports on clinics for people with disabilities that have been reshaped to provide assistance and services beyond physical care: "the patients count also on the support of psychologists and occupational therapists to help them to live better with their families, overcoming the stigma of disability" (*O Globo*, August 14, 2000).

In the work domain, we have frequently observed pieces of news expressing a common concern with policies to "overcome barriers" and "prejudices" for people with disability finding real opportunities "to ascend normally in their self-chosen careers"[11] in sectors organized by the labor market. Furthermore, there have been news stories from the 2000s onwards informing the public about changes in social arrangements to provide appropriate access for disabled people, such as bars and restaurants providing their menu in Braille,[12] dealers offering "discounts on cars adapted to fit the needs of people with impairments,"[13] as well as news highlighting a "new market sector" for people with disability and thereby forming a promising group of consumers.[14]

In this second phase, our data show that people with disability are not simply brought to society as it used to be organized, but a set of rules has been modified to promote expanded forms of inclusion. Thus there are good grounds for thinking that these changes have increased the variety of ways through which disabled people can achieve self-realization, and that they have increased the possibilities for them to cooperate in social arrangements and to contribute to society.

To sum up, our findings show that broader cultural transformations of valuable human qualities of people with disabilities and changes in policies – examined across four decades in the Brazilian news – can be justified through reference to the ideas of social inclusiveness and individuality. In the next section, we will discuss the agonistic dimension in the struggle for recognition of disabled people, focusing on problems of value pluralism, moral dissent and conflicts of interest.

Is it possible to identify in the mass media arena an agonistic confrontation of demands for recognition aimed at the national institutions?

Although the Brazilian legal framework has endorsed the ideal of democratic inclusion and many institutions have been reorganizing themselves to follow the inclusion principles in a great variety of ways (Santos, 2001; Avritzer, 2009), people with disabilities claim that they are currently excluded from many aspects of society. Two complementary reasons explain this. First, the move from the "integration" to the "inclusion" perspective in disability politics cannot be regarded as a linear process – the goals of some reforms remain attached to the "normalization" logic; some policies and provisions are still seen as a means to stigmatize and further exclude disabled people; and there remain societal attitudes that devalue people with disability. Second, the interpretation and application of principles of recognition, as Honneth (2003a, p. 186) claims elsewhere, is not self-evident or conflict free, but it frequently raises controversies in each particular situation. Accordingly, the formulation and implementation of inclusive policies usually unleashes contestation and dispute within and between specific groups of people with disability and other groups in society who claim that they are adversely affected. Moreover, new scientific discoveries related to certain kinds of disability constantly trigger off discussion of different types of technical response, their possible impact on affected people, and their social implications. Therefore, it is not surprising that, although we have noticed that there is a direction towards moral progress on the issue of disability in the Brazilian news media, public interpretations are pervaded with multiple conflicts throughout the four decades under analysis.

The first source of conflict we noticed in the news media arena is related to fragmentation of perspectives and controversies among policy-makers and specialists, as well as among people with disabilities, who hold group-specific values and interests. For example, we observed an intensified dispute from the 1980s onwards about what "inclusion" means in each and every situation. Because people with impairment regard their own experience of disability (and their relation with society) in distinct ways, they express different needs arising from these differences. Even if disabled people share a critical rejection of marginalization and social exclusion, they hold different positions about medical responses and recommendations, and ways of providing personal assistance or independent living. Good examples are the Association of Parents and Friends of the Exceptional (APAE) which does not endorse the view that all children with disabilities – with different degrees of learning difficulties and mental illness – should be included in regular schools rather than in special educational establishments. Also the National Federation for the Education and Integration of Deaf People (FENEIS) defends the implementation of special programs in organizations properly fitted for the education of deaf children, as discussed in Chapter 6 (Maia & Garcêz, 2013). In the second phase of our research particularly, we find a wide range of demands of people with impairment to accommodate new aspirations or interests that also may be defended through appeals to principles, values and goods.

Second, we observe a clash of agonistic interpretations of key societal norms in the media arena. Claims for recognition, as Honneth says, challenge the way that society is currently organized and the hierarchy of values is structured. The demands to alter the distribution of resources, respect or prestige are imbricated, in a complex way, with the prevailing organization of the relations of economic, social and political power. For example, the project of implementing inclusive education also implied demands for alterations in relations linked to economic power (such as incentives to grant access to public and private education, employment, promotions, etc.), to legal organization (such as implementation of a quota system) or to political power (such as redefinitions of who is entitled to new policies of redistribution of resources and opportunities). Michael Oliver has acutely observed that both the "new" integration and the "new" inclusion of people with disabilities must always "be struggled for" (Oliver, 1996). In this sense, my collaborator and I noticed that struggles for recognition provoked moral disagreement and conflict of interest among several groups in Brazilian society over the entire period under analysis.

A third source of conflict observed in the news media is related to public contestation of flaws and shortcomings in the already institutionalized norms and policies addressed to people with disabilities. The current criticism of the quota system of employment for persons with impairments, legally regulated in Brazil since 1991, is a typical example of struggles of the "third sphere of recognition," according to Honneth. In spite of regarding themselves as right holders, disabled people are permanently struggling to renegotiate social valuation of their individual abilities and achievements in the system of economic exchange. In several pieces of news, different speakers – particularly social workers, people with impairment and leaders of movements – claim that although people with disability have been employed via the quota system, they "perform less valued activities," the work environment is not properly adapted to their special needs, the recruiting team is frequently insensitive to their particular demands and they are often fired for not "corresponding to the expectations" of the companies.[15] In one news story, a journalist mentions that public officers have been monitoring the policy of quota for people with disabilities more intensively, but "the lack of opportunity and prejudices are the main barriers faced by people with disability...[and] even those who hold high degrees face these difficulties."[16] In keeping with Honneth, we can say that struggles for recognition, as dynamic relations, never reach a final point – even when principles of recognition are institutionalized, they are open to new contestations that rights, policies, duties and powers are somehow restrictive or fail to acknowledge certain needs, claims and abilities.

Our findings show that the idea of moral progress, as defended by Honneth, is compatible with value pluralism and conflict of interest in complex societies. Here we recall Honneth's (2003a) and Cooke's (2006, 2009) argument that the ideal of full recognition, although it will never be completely fulfilled or determined in a final way, opens up modes of innovative interpretation of ways of perfecting forms of recognition.

Can we speak in terms of collective learning regarding the issue of disability?

In the previous sections, we have attempted to show that it is possible to observe moral progress towards patterns of social inclusiveness and individuality of people with disability in Brazilian society. We have also attempted to evince an ongoing agonistic competition of multiple claims for recognition of people with impairment in the media arena, and to show that moral conflict and social strife cannot be avoided throughout the four decades under examination. Now, taking into consideration that social integration results from undetermined compromises between many groups and social forces, we ask what it means exactly to speak in terms of social learning in the case of people with disability in the Brazilian context.

Honneth (2002, p. 512) says that ethical knowledge through which we value potential qualities in others and develop appropriately rational patterns of recognition is acquired through socialization, and this should be understood as a learning process that is part of the historical process itself. Although Honneth's theory of collective learning is under-developed, his proposition that patterns of recognition form "ethical certitudes" in the background of our lifeworld seems to provide a cogent explanation of why many moral achievements seem "invisible" or go unnoticed when one looks at current relations of (mis)recognition at a given moment in time.

To develop this point, it is worth recalling a number of objections that have been raised by recent studies about representation of disability in the mass media. Research carried out in Brazil by ANDI – the Brazilian News Agency for Children's Rights – and the Brazilian Bank Foundation examined 1,992 pieces of news on the issue of disability published in 53 major Brazilian newspapers in 2002. This study concluded that Brazilian journalists were not acquainted with the principles, values, and policies of inclusion; they often used the term "inclusion" interchangeably with "integration" and they could not critically assess problems and flaws in practices that contradicted the inclusive ideals (Vivarta, 2003). Furthermore, the study argued that journalists, while giving prominent attention to issues of accessibility and work for people with disability, tended to focus on physical barriers and technological innovations alone, thereby neglecting the nuances of conditions across cognitive, physical and sensory impairments. The media agents – so the authors contend – paid attention neither to the complexities of different groups of people with disability nor to important questions such as enablement practices for enhancing their family life and sexual life. In addition, this study showed that the explicit portrayal of people with impairment as rights holders appeared only in a minority of news stories (16 percent) – this representation could not be identified in the majority of pieces of news (74 percent) and the stigmatized view of disabled people as wanting, pitiable victims or outcasts was rare (3.1 percent). This study basically concluded that journalists mostly assumed a "common sense" approach to disability in all its manifestations .

The discrepancies between ANDI's conclusions and our own findings can be explained by some obvious and not so obvious reasons. First, our research surveyed four decades of media coverage on disability issues and could detect a cultural change in the portrayal of people with impairment and in the patterns of justifications underscoring disability policies, while the ANDI study examined pieces of news disseminated in one single year. The objections raised by the ANDI study take the form of understandable worries about the deficits of the media coverage from the standpoint of inclusive ideals and the human rights perspective. If we recall the historical transformation from 1960 to 2008 in the understandings of impairment, the vocabularies used to refer to people with disability, and the legal norms and concrete policies implemented with the aim to enable people with impairment to take part in society, much of the pessimism expressed by the above-mentioned study can be challenged.

Second, the conclusion reached by the ANDI study that Brazilian journalists adopted "a common sense" perspective to deal with disability issues can be more revealing than one might think. If we conceive of the notion of "social learning" – following the theoretical framework of Honneth (2002) and Habermas (1987, p. 125) – as a generalization of values and accumulated knowledge that is pre-given to the individual subject (as a pre-interpreted domain of what is culturally taken for granted), then the stock of knowledge about disability supplying the journalists' interpretation reveals some important degrees of recognitional attitudes in the present moment. The media agents – despite their alleged short-sighted view, their misunderstandings or their negligence of supposedly important questions – expressed a view of people with impairment as individuals with needs, and as subjects who deserve to be treated with respect.

Such a view, far from stemming from a "simplistic" or "naïve" perspective, can be best assessed as the result of a historical complex learning process that understands disability as a "moral issue" – that is, an issue, in Northway's words, including "a set of principles which ensure that disabled people are seen as valued and needed" (Northway, 1997, p. 164; see also Calder, 2011; Terzi, 2004, p. 156). What is appealing here is that such a "common sense" attitude – a knowledge that has an unproblematic nature, in the sense of being commonly accepted and internalized – forms a background intersubjectively shared in society. The norms and principles considered justified, and now immersed in the complexity of stored-up cultural content, have already become socially valid and thus implicit in the ways in which people respond to one another.[17]

Third, it may not be surprising that media coverage falls far behind the patterns of interpretation and valuation of disabled people's movements and advocacy groups, if we assume, along with Honneth, that forms of recognition already achieved in a given society always "call for greater degrees of morally appropriate behavior, than is ever practiced in that particular reality" (Honneth, 2002, p. 517). The multiple claims that have been raised on behalf of particular needs, specific rights and possible contributions of people with impairment are far from consensual in Brazilian society. As already discussed, some demands for recognition need clarification, as some present limits to the achievement of the group's own aims of inclusion and some can be harmful to others. In this sense, we align ourselves to scholars who argue that demands for recognition call for open-ended debates in the public sphere as well as in the formal instances of the political system (Cooke, 2009, p. 91; Deranty, 2009, p. 313; Forst, 2007b; Maia, 2012a, 2012e). Individuals and groups seeking recognition will attempt to convince others of the value of their conceptions, practices and beliefs through reciprocal justification.

The transformation of "historical reasons" and "moral recognition responses" as "ethical certitudes" which underscore "the evaluative human qualities to which we can respond rationally in recognizing others," as Honneth (2002, p. 512) says, seems to be grasped best in a long-term perspective. When disabled people, activist scholars and leaders of social movements invite non-disabled people to see impairment in a new way, when they challenge other people's simplistic views of the experience of disability and try to open their eyes to the oppressive character of some social arrangements, these critical actors ask for revision of antecedent interpretative knowledge. Individuals and groups seeking recognition may express highly demanding requests or may hold unfair demands; such claims may not be the right ones and frequently they do not go unchallenged. Yet these critical actors play, in the spirit of Honneth, an important role in the process of contestation of actual social practices and institutionalized policies, while putting in motion a "permanent pressure" to learn.

Conclusion

In our study, we can observe cultural transformations of valuable human qualities of people with disabilities in the media arena across the four decades under investigation. While protected by rights and regarded as individuals with needs, people with disabilities have been expressing an ever-greater range of differences in their identity features and in their ways of pursuing self-realization. Greater degrees of recognition of people with impairment in Brazilian society have not been conducive to the removal of tensions and conflicts from social life, as Düttmann and Markell feared. The increased variety of voices of disabled people (from their own perspective) in the public arena and their involvement in taking the initiative to control their lives (collectively and individually) have also expanded contestation of different forms of marginalization, discrimination and disrespect embedded in society. As we can clearly see in the news media, moral disagreement and conflict of interest come to the fore across the ever-expanding domains of social life from the 1980s onwards. Honneth's work enables us to pay attention to the important transformative role played by groups seeking recognition in their effort to challenge unquestioned norms, assumptions, practices and social arrangements currently existing in a given society. Therefore, this theoretical framework can sharpen our perception about the centrality of public contestation and the perpetuity of struggles as constitutive of social life. It makes us even more aware of the different types of injustice and claims for recognition that have actually been raised. It also prompts us to broaden our notion of what should count as collective learning processes in how recognition responses might be further improved.

Notes

1. In Honneth's words, "The institutionalized normative structures...or the correctly understood polities, have not developed by accident; they have emerged from practical experiences in which certain norms of recognition have proven over time to be sensible or appropriate when it comes to managing central problems of coordination" (Honneth, 2012, p. 115).
2. The methodological procedures that were used in the survey are discussed in detail in Vimieiro and Maia (2011).
3. The *Veja* news weekly enters our study in 1968 when it was launched.
4. Our survey found 158 search items for commonly used words and expressions to denote persons with disabilities or specific types of disability, or popularly recognized acronyms and names of entities involved with this topic.
5. In this test, which is aimed to measure the inter-coder reliability, we used a
6. *O Globo*, August 20, 1960.
7. *Folha de S.Paulo*, August 16, 1960.
8. All translations are the work of the authors.
9. Scholars who adopt this approach regard disability from a relational perspective to explain social exclusions experienced by disabled people (Thomas, 1999, 2004; Finkelstein, 2004). They argue that people are disabled both by social arrangements and by their impairments. A more radical argument is advanced by others who claim that disability is socially caused and it has nothing do with the body (Cole, 2007; Oliver, 1996). The key idea is that there is not a clear distinction between the body and the social, political and cultural meaning, since an aspect of the body only is seen as an impairment under specific socio-cultural conditions.
10. *O Globo*, May 14, 2000.
11. *O Globo*, March 29, 1992.
12. *Folha de S.Paulo*, May 20, 2000.
13. *Folha de S.Paulo*, Jun 11, 2000.
14. *O Globo*, July 27, 2008.
15. *Folha de S.Paulo*, August 17, 2008.
16. *Folha de S.Paulo*, August 17, 2008.
17. In Honneth's words, the 'space of reasons' is also a historically changing domain; the evaluative human qualities to which we can respond rationally in recognizing others form ethical certitudes whose character changes unnoticeably with the cultural transformations of our lifeworld (Honneth, 2002, p. 512).

Conclusion

In the Introduction, I stated that a recognition-theoretical approach provides sound social and political guidelines for empirical research. In this book, my collaborators and I have endeavored to show that identity-building and the expansion of relations of recognition or misrecognition in contemporary, complex, multicultural societies are played out to a large degree through processes of technological mediation. I argued that the media plays an important role in conflicts that emerge from individuals and groups' claims for needs, rights or achievements, and the nature of social response. In addition, the media is crucial for the constitution of debates in the public sphere, as well as for dynamics of mobilization and social learning as a social-wide process. In this section I summarize major findings of our study, considering the interplay between insights of the theory of recognition and our empirical research.

It goes without saying that philosophical debates and normative theory sometimes address questions that are not meant to be subjected to direct empirical investigation. As empirical researchers, my collaborators and I sketched specific controversies in Honneth's theory of recognition – the morality of recognition, ideological forms of recognition, the role of "feelings of injustice," the building of a "shared interpretative framework of injustice" and problems of claim justification, the notions of non-recognition and misrecognition, and the concept of moral progress – and took up these points to specify our research questions. It is worth noting that a recognition-theoretical approach offered us tools for both describing and evaluating our findings.

To attempt to clarify the relationship between struggles for recognition and technological mediation, one of the major objectives of this book was to align the literature on the theory of recognition with that of political communication and media studies. My collaborators and I started by using a model of an interconnected and hybrid media system, where older and newer media logics are seen as interlocked, and individuals constantly interact with various fields of media in everyday life. We focused on three interfaces between struggles for recognition and processes of technological mediation: (i) mass media representations that examine how disadvantaged individuals interpret media-related materials to make sense of their own identity, their place in societal hierarchies, and in the dynamics of social conflicts; (ii) interactions via the networked media environment that focus on individuals' reactions against experiences of disrespect; their discursive engagement to advance values and interests at the intergroup level, as well as between groups, and online activism; and finally (iii) long-term progressive changes in the patterns of recognition in the media arena.

The first and second-generation scholars of the Frankfurt School have long been interested in media power and media-based communication's impact on the dependence and interdependency of individuals in modern society. In this book, we adopted the critical theory outlook, in addition to other current approaches on political communication, in order to conceive of media practices located in broader structures of society. We argued that this perspective is important for making us attentive to the conditions of social interactions and the power structure embedded in institutional organizations, as well as in cultural norms of society. Congruent with the aspiration of Honneth's critical theory, we believe that such a "groundwork" enabled my collaborators and I to be in touch with the "reality" of individuals who suffer from domination, severe poverty, marginalization, exploitation, and undervaluation – such as slum-dwelling adolescents, women who were domestic laborers as children, deaf individuals, leprosy patients, people with disabilities, black women, and lesbian, gay, bisexual, transgender, queer (LGBTQs) individuals. In the context of our research, we attempted to explore the differentiated role played by the media in these individuals' struggles for recognition.

Mass media representation, identity-building and social conflicts

I argued that mass communication is an important site of struggle, given the huge visibility of mass media press, film, radio, and television, aimed at reaching large audiences. The key expectation that mass communication outlets exert major political and social power – due to their wide appeal, high status, and high level of attention received – has driven research in the field for decades. I contended, following current mainstream communication theory and research, that purposes, forms, and applications of the media's "power to influence" vary greatly. While the mass media paradigm has been declining and it has been "demassificated" because of the expansion of plural online-communication, I endorse the view that changes in the relationship between the mass media and society must be approached across an interconnected media system. As was argued in Chapter 2, the logics of the traditional media need to be redefined, as it becomes intermeshed with a number of features of networked communication. However, the traditional media logic has not been eliminated.

Mass communication organizations prioritize ties to political elites and large market interests. Their professionals usually follow norms favoring hegemonic patterns that sustain privilege and subordination in contemporary societies. Operating as active agents, they manage a wide range of resources to shape mediated communication and everyday culture – by creating and selecting images, controlling the prominence of certain claims, and steering information flows and certain interpretations that favor or obstruct, enable or disable the agency of others. By exploring a number of examples of representations of disadvantaged individuals in the mass media environment, Chapter 2 showed operations of invisibility, stereotyping, denigration, exclusion, and so forth. I argued that meaning-making is a relational process; media representations are shaped by societal relations, including inequalities and oppression, that are historically constituted. While endorsing the view that media professionals tend to produce an elite discourse, and the structure of opportunities for accessing media channels tends to reproduce societal power asymmetries, I contended that these organizations are, nevertheless, permeable fields. Media professionals' actions are shaped by an interactive exchange with other agents and they face very different situations when producing symbolic and discursive materials.

The empirical studies discussed in this book help to draw attention to the contradictory and often tense relationships between media professionals and other participants involved in the dynamics of social conflicts. Chapter 3 illustrates a situation in which mainstream media agents are aware of their dominant position and arguably sought to counteract prevalent stereotyping practices within mass communication settings. The production team of the largest television broadcasting company in Brazil, *Rede Globo*, joined efforts with an NGO, *Nós do Cinema*, to produce a TV series that was filmed in a slum and the cast, including the protagonist, consisted mostly of slum-dwellers. Chapter 4 shows media professionals' attempts to stimulate awareness of children and adolescent rights. Our study demonstrates that local media journalists developed a reflexive attitude towards Child Domestic Labor (CDL), through interactions with civic associations and social movements that fight against this type of work. To build news stories, journalists systematically chose sources from these organizations and adopted their framework to challenge a set of assumptions, predispositions, and attitudes that feed exploitation and domination in CDL. Our case studies, even if they constitute exceptions within mass communication organizations, show that media-based representations and discourses are not simply a selective meaning-making practice in one direction, but this process is also made up of and transformed by agents of contending groups.

My collaborator and I attempted to examine processes of interpretation and definition related to problems of recognition from the perspective of affected subjects. We organized focus groups and stimulated participants to engage in discussions about media-based material addressing questions related to their identity, needs, rights, and achievements. Our findings largely corroborate the view that individuals use media material to make sense of themselves, their aspirations, interests, and experienced problems, and build shared understandings of how these issues matter to them. In both case studies, adolescent slum-dwellers, as well as women who worked as housemaids in their childhood, showed that they are not passive spectators, but purposeful and often reasoning agents who selectively examine media material. Study participants engaged with meanings displayed in the mass media either to corroborate or defy demands for recognition, to articulate their own inferential associations, and to develop argumentation in new directions, based on a different set of assumptions that were not present in the media environment.

Our results show that slum-dwellers, being participants of civic associations, displayed a common awareness of a vast number of problems that feed misrecognition. This case discusses the morality of recognition and demonstrates several levels of tension in the attitudes of recognizing and being recognized. Study participants showed high levels of conflict with the TV series' representation of inhabitants of slums and their daily lives, and complained about stereotypes, along with a neglect of their important qualities and achievements. Still, they did not openly address the unfair redistribution that prevails in Brazilian society and this issue remained largely invisible during group discussion. While contending that the series remained attached to conventional distorted forms of representations, they vocalized what they considered relevant about themselves and their communities. It was this knowledge – so they defended – that would need to be correctly perceived in order to grant them recognition. A new level of tension in granting recognition was revealed in this case, as study participants tended to use socially-dominant presumptions that nourish misrecognition when they referred to inhabitants of other slums.

The case on CDL shows that women who were housemaids in their childhood also critically engaged with media-material. Study participants contested media advocacy discourses denouncing CDL as oppression and a violation of children's rights, and reaffirmed that this type of work constitutes a good or useful chance to gain autonomy and integrate more positively into society. Attached to their modes of living, and valuing what they regarded as opportunities for self-development offered by the employing family, they rationally and reflexively rejected the definition of CDL as domination. Our findings suggest that study participants mobilized hegemonic cultural background knowledge of their life to challenge premises in the public reasoning that sought to grant recognition. Inasmuch as study participants were not struggling against a particular form of disrespect or undervaluation, Honneth's definition of the "ideological form of recognition" provided useful insights for investigating this case. This study showed the interweaving of logics across the spheres of love and work, along with the complexities of class- and gender-based oppressions, to shape the self-conceptions of disadvantaged subjects. My collaborator and I argued that cultural knowledge in this situation blocked criticism and stabilized relations of domination. Yet, we attempted to explore the link between these women's sense of transformative agency and moral entrepreneurs' critiques of ideology, as a means to overcome the subjecting effects of ideological forms of recognition.

The mass media remains an important site of struggle and its logic continues to shape practices. To develop a scenario of the interconnected and hybrid media system, Part II of this book was dedicated to investigating conditions for expression and engagement in multiple practices related to struggles for recognition in the digital environment.

Interactions through the networked media environment

In Part II of this book, my collaborators and I explored how people engage in different types of interactions for self-expression and identity-building, by also involving conflicts within and between groups using different online platforms. I argued that the struggle for recognition in the digital environment should be understood through specificities of the mediating platform. These precise settings display particular resources, logics of functioning, norms, and types of public, as well as social processes of dependencies and interdependencies between individuals and groups within institutional arrangements of society, broader ethical horizons, and historical contexts.

In developing our empirical studies, my collaborators and I paid particular attention to everyday talk, emotions, and meaning-making from the perspective of the participants engaging in social conflicts. We started from the premise that seeking recognition and pursuing self-realization are challenging endeavors, and individuals engage in everyday conflicts in order to re-affirm that they make valuable choices. They display a belief they should not be treated unjustly or as second-class citizens to be looked down upon. Honneth does not say in sufficient detail how people engage in discussions aimed at solving moral disagreements or conflicts of interest that emerge in disputes for recognition. We argued that deliberative scholars have made invaluable contributions for understanding the norms of democratic deliberation and the significance of reasoning together in everyday life, within larger goals of democracy. In this respect, we advocated that Honneth's account of intersubjective dependency for self-realization helps to explain individuals' motivations to engage in argumentation in order to both check the acceptability of their claims and to link specificities of personal experiences with more general principles that are morally recognizable.

In surveying the online environment, my collaborators and I attempted to look at practices of conversation, deliberation, and mobilization. While these practices tend to stand apart in specific fields of study, their boundaries are quite permeable in struggles for recognition in everyday life, articulation and contestation of demands, and collective action aimed at transformative social change. As was argued in Chapter 5, social movement scholars have offered major contributions towards understanding the ability of citizens to mobilize and fight against distinct forms of power in society. In this respect, Honneth's account of the "moral grammar of social conflicts" helps us to delve deeply into the participant actors' self-understanding in this dynamic. While in Chapter 6 we tapped into intra-group conflict, in Chapter 7 we explored disputes for recognition between different groups in the pluralist context of Brazilian society.

By examining the website FENEIS (the National Federation for the Education and Integration of Deaf Persons), as well as an online community of deaf people (in Orkut), Chapter 6 showed conflicts that emerge at the intra-group level, when seeking to build a "shared interpretative framework of injustice." While representatives mobilized feelings of injustice based on empowering emotions, a capacity for agency and pride, and presented relative coherent origins of shared injuries and proposed solutions, ordinary deaf individuals and concerned people contested what causes harm and the proposed remedies to overcome suffering, along with what solutions are best for tackling specific issues. Representatives of FENEIS attempted to speak and act in the name of others, foster solidarity, and bridge differences among themselves for constructing an often difficult unified political agenda to intervene positively in political decision making, whereas, ordinary citizens contested biases in the public reasoning carried out by the group representatives, different goals to promote and achieve, and defended the right to freely define identification within the community. In this chapter, my collaborator and I explored the problem of claims justification. We argued that contested claims for recognition are constantly subjected to deliberation among those who identify with a certain group, and are within a horizon of concerns that they share to some measure. This study usefully shows that conflict between different claims within a group contributes to expanding the meaning of valuable choices and rights, and renders what seemed a consensual topic to be in fact a matter of dispute and concern for legitimate political representation.

Chapter 7 was devoted to examining how certain events – in this case, a federal congressman's expression of racism and homophobia on a TV show – can irrigate engagements for and against recognition in the lives of ordinary citizens in a pluralist society in which different cultural, ethnic, and religious groups coexist. Our analysis showed that struggles for recognition are played out freely with multiple others. People interact in radically distinctive ways to "express themselves," engage in "public discussion," and deploy mobilization mechanism in different online platforms. Relatively spontaneous encounters within YouTube showed intense hostility between individuals and groups, the breakout of aggression, and limited spaces for dialogue across differences. In contrast, blogs showed a picture of a setting where civility, listening, and mutual respect among participants permitted them to contest claims and continue interaction through responsive engagement. Facebook, in its turn, figured as a proper place for collective action. Our findings, in spite of revealing a set of nuances in each platform, suggested that engagement between groups finds more adequate conditions for the negotiation of identity and the acknowledgment of demands in deliberative settings. We suggested that encounters in civil society can be beneficial for processing intra- and inter-communal tensions to generate "civil" and mutually agreeable outcomes in terms of recognition. These spontaneous encounters can also be threatening and disturbing, insofar as they provoke heated confrontations and apparently irreconcilable separations.

Interestingly enough, looking at episodic struggles for recognition in a given moment in time – as illustrated by the case studies presented in Parts I and II of this book – suggests that struggles for recognition are marked by indeterminacy and contingency. Contestation and disagreement are at the heart of recognition struggles; a clash between diverse claims within and between groups, while pointing towards the ability of subjects to articulate their own identity and pursue self-realization, does not assure that a shared comprehensive view may be achieved; and controversies in what counts as "a gain" in individuality or in inclusion in society often unravel new forms of domination. While some struggles seem to lead to the acknowledgement of a multiplicity of legitimate concerns and rights for an individual's positive self-development, others appear to lead to irreconcilable demands and a refusal to accept pluralism. Our findings largely corroborate the thesis that struggles for recognition are fraught with difficulties, and these complications are rooted not only in civil society, but also in official arenas of debates and formal political institutions within society.

The dynamics of recognition and political cultural change

Part III is dedicated to investigating eventual changes in patterns of recognition in the media arena, utilizing a long-term perspective. Our results suggest that changes in patterns of recognition are easier to detect in long-term analyses than in short-term studies. While acknowledging that preferences are constantly being altered throughout political processes and that change can be caused by many factors, I argued that the struggle for recognition and discourse contestation can produce reciprocal influences; and these influences can cause unexpected outcomes. Still, I advocated that mutual understanding and social learning can open new possibilities for cultural, legal, and political transformation towards the expansion of recognition.

In Chapter 8, I argued that the possibility of progressive change in patterns of recognition in the media environment should be understood as a process of the reflexivity of struggles structured in the fabric of everyday life. My key argument was that such conflicts generate certain moral perspectives concerning the dignity, needs, rights, and social worth of people or groups, and these perspectives feed demands for media professionals to change their interpretations and behavior. Still, such a change is not to be seen as an automatic process, but one that needs to be fought for. Chapter 8 explored different forms of accountability in media fields, focusing on public and social responsibility mechanisms. I examined the link between mobilized publics and activism intended to change mass media performance from three perspectives: (i) within mass media organizations; (ii) outside media industries; and (iii) alternative media perspectives.

I have argued that activists, by seeking to challenge symbolic representations and improve news coverage of social problems, frequently cultivate a significant knowledge about the broad media system. This knowledge is crucial for them to successfully interact with mainstream media journalists and alternative media practitioners, as well as develop their own media outlets and strategies for public communication. Media Accountability Movements (MAM) and Civic Advocacy Journalism (CAJ) are particularly adept at effectively connecting with the mainstream media to develop a series of actions (such as educational practices, monitoring, and media criticism) to transform the pattern of interpretation and advance alternative solutions to perceived problems. In addition, they perform disruptive actions (such as demonstrations, boycotts, and petitions) and take legal initiatives when the media's performance causes harm or violates public interests. Nevertheless, it is important to keep in mind that not all publics are equally organized and capable of exerting pressure on media organizations; not all civic group interests are equally positioned in relation to media concerns, including interests in the political and market spheres, to gain public visibility or to successfully change media practices.

Empirical research in Part III shows that the characteristics of news coverage and the media's symbolic representation are constituted through political processes, within broader struggles and collective action. Both of our case studies provide evidence of how claims for recognition can be differently accommodated and balanced with operations of power in the mainstream media, under specific conditions. Chapter 9 investigates news media coverage of issues involved in conflicts of leprosy patients (the future of the former colonies and the access to financial funds) by corroborating the hypothesis that journalists do not need to rely on social movements to build their stories. Scholars in this field frequently address this problem and argue that social movements usually have a limited capacity for influencing news-making routines and journalistic news values, if they do not systematically develop tactics and long-term strategies for interacting with media professionals. In our case, the leaders of the Movement to Reintegrate People Affected by Hansen's Disease (MORHAN), while developing venues that approximate to governmental agents, did not create strategies to foster public debate in the media arena. Our analysis showed that news media coverage focused on *problems* faced by leprosy patients and *solutions* offered by governmental agents, and thus it obliterated political strife carried out by the movement activists. MORHAN's role as an active agent for promoting social change was not only downplayed, but its voice was also not present in mainstream news.

The case study presented in Chapter 10 indicates a different picture. The activism and rights movements of disabled people have been successful in shaping international conventions and legislation. Activists in Brazil have promoted a major reshuffling of institutional arrangements and social relations over the last 40 years; and they also developed strategies to interact with media professionals. Despite shortcomings in Brazilian norms and policies that address people with disabilities, these changes brought an opportunity for content diversification in the media arena, including a broader coverage of issues and the pluralization of civic voices.

By surveying four decades of media coverage, our study showed a clear re-signification in the understanding of impairment, including a readjustment of vocabularies and the portrayal of disabled people, as well as in the patterns of justifications underscoring disability policies. We argued that notions of individualization and social inclusion – related to frames of accessibility, quality of life, and denouncements of prejudice, among others – become central in news media coverage. We have shown that activists and Media Accountability Movements, such as ANDI (News Agency for Children's Rights), have criticized media coverage that focuses on disabilities for not being acquainted with relevant issues in the social movement agenda and for neglecting complexities of different groups of people with impairments. Examining news media coverage by using a long term-perspective, our study showed a significant change in the patterns of recognition throughout time. We contended that the valorization of disabled people as self-interpreting agents, as well as explicit political concern with the inclusion of this group, enabled people with impairments to bring an ever-greater range of differences to the public sphere and to demand that society is responsible for overcoming barriers that obstruct their autonomous living. Our analysis showed that this condition (and the normative structure of recognition implicit in it) is radically different from the one captured in the 1960s.

Struggles for the re-signification of cultural meanings and the production and reproduction of public reasons for rearranging institutions in terms of recognition are fraught with difficulties. Oppressed individuals may not have the means to develop self-reflection; several obstacles may block contestation and collective action; opportunities for public communication do not merely occur, but they must to some extent be created; engagement with other affected individuals and contesting groups requires creativity, innovation, and planning; ultimately, political representatives may ignore demands for recognition or may not be interested in institutionalizing legitimated policies. Our findings are fully consistent with the view that progressive change based on recognition principles does not rule out ongoing conflict and value-pluralism. Even when institutionalized, norms, rights, and policies are open to permanent contestation in order to disclose flaws, limitations, and inadequate interpretations. Ultimately, norms of recognition can suffer threats and reversals.

Conclusion

One of the goals for this book is to contribute to the advancement of empirical research on the dynamics of recognition. Having presented our research in earlier chapters, I now hope to have a set of theoretical issues, arguments, and evidence of recognition struggles that take place in the real world. My collaborators and I presented studies on historical forms of domination. Our reflections are based on Brazil, and thus our research reveals the workings of particular institutions and cultural tensions shaping conflicts in our country. We believe, nevertheless, that problems of class, race/ethnicity, disability, sexual orientation, and undervalued work are comparative and transnational. Our purpose of problematizing different aspects of Honneth's theory of recognition was nurtured by the belief that our study could provide elements for continuing a research dialogue on recognition in other parts of the world.

A second hope for this book is that it contributes to increasing awareness among scholars of the important role played by the media in the struggles for recognition. The hybrid media environment is very complex; the role of mass media agents in managing images and discourses is highly diversified; and interactions through the Internet and SNSs are continuously altering the shape of everyday life. This book was an attempt at shedding some light on certain interfaces between struggles for recognition and processes of mediation, which are highlighted in three parts of the book.

Finally, this book aimed at promoting a combined diagnosis of different cases of the struggle for recognition. Whereas each specific conflict was approached in a nuanced way, we end this book by reassuring our belief that the recognition-theoretical approach has relevance for political praxis. Having surveyed criticisms on Honneth's program from several standpoints – and having benefited from his critics' discussions on shortcomings, skepticisms, puzzles, and merits in the theory of recognition – we found a valuable lens through which to observe a wide range of social suffering in empirical situations. Most importantly, we believe that studies on recognition, while searching for existing structures of domination, as well as social resources for their practical overcoming, have the potential to provide suggestions to adequately respond to social problems. This intends to make explicit what is needed to achieve justice in particular situations and what the institutional requirements are for deepening or expanding forms of recognition in democratic societies.

References

Agência de Notícias dos Direitos da Infância. (2003). *Crianças invisíveis: O enfoque da imprensa sobre o trabalho infantil doméstico e outras formas de exploração* [Invisible children: Press coverage on child domestic labor and other forms of exploitation]. São Paulo, SP: Cortez.

Albuquerque, A. (2012). On models and margins: Comparative media models viewed from a Brazilian perspective. In D. C. Hallin & P. Mancini (Eds), *Comparing media systems beyond the western world* (pp. 72–95). Cambridge, MA: Cambridge University Press.

Alcoff, L. M. (1991). The problem of speaking for others. *Cultural Critique, 20,* 5–32.

Aldé, A., Chagas, V., & Escobar, J. (2007). A febre dos blogs de política [The trend of political blogs]. *Revista FAMECOS, 33,* 34.

Alexander, J. C. & Jacobs, R. N. (1998). Mass communication, ritual and civil society. In T. Liebes & J. Curran (Eds), *Media, ritual, identity* (pp. 23–41). London: Routledge.

Alexander, J. C. & Lara, M. P. (1996). Honneth's new critical theory of recognition. *New Left Review, I*(220), 126–136.

Allen, A. (2010). Recognizing domination: Recognition and power in Honneth's critical theory. *Journal of Power, 3*(r), 21–32.

Alsultany, E. (2012). *Arabs and Muslims in the media: Race and representation after 9/11.* New York, NY: New York University Press.

Anderson, J. (2011). Situating Axel Honneth in the Frankfurt School Tradition. *Social and Critical Theory, 12,* 31–57.

Anderson, J. & Honneth, A. (2005). Autonomy, vulnerability, recognition, and justice. In J. Christman & J. Anderson (Eds), *Autonomy and the challenges to liberalism: New essays* (pp. 127–149). New York, NY: Cambridge University Press.

Aranda, K. & Jones, A. (2010). Dignity in health-care: A critical exploration using feminism and theories of recognition. *Nursing Inquiry, 17*(3), 248–256.

Arneil, B. (2009). Disability, self image and modern political theory. *Political Theory, 37*(2), 218–242.

Atkinson, J. D. (2010). *Alternative media and politics of resistance.* New York, NY: Peter Lang.

Avila-Saavedra, G. (2009). Nothing queer about queer television: Televised construction of gay masculinities. *Media Culture Society, 31*(1), 5–21.

Avritzer, L. (2009). *Participatory institutions in Democratic Brazil. Baltimore*: The Johns Hopkins University Press.

Bächtiger, A., Niemeyer, S., Neblo, M., Steenbergen, M. R., & Steiner, J. (2010). Disentangling diversity in deliberative democracy: Competing theories, their blind spots and complementarities. *Journal of Political Philosophy, 18*(1), 32–63.

Bader, V. (2007). Misrecognition, power and democracy. In B. van den Brink & D. Owen (Eds), *Recognition and power: Axel Honneth and the tradition of critical social theory* (pp. 238–269). New York, NY: Cambridge University Press.

Bailey, O. G. & Marques, F. P. J. (2012). Brazilian news blogs and mainstream news organizations: Tensions, symbiosis, or independency? In E. Siapera &

A. Veglis (Eds), *The handbook of global online journalism* (pp. 393–411). West Sussex: Wiley-Blackwell.

Barbour, R. & Kitzinger, J. (2001). *Developing focus group research: Politics, theory and practice*. London: SAGE.

Barker, C. (1999). *Television, globalization and cultural identities*. Buckingham: Open University Press.

Barnes, M. (2012). Passionate participation: Emotional experiences and expression in deliberative forums. In S. Thompson & P. Hoggett (Eds), *Politics and the emotions: The affective turn in contemporary political studies* (pp. 23–40). New York, NY: Continuum.

Barnhurst, K. G. (2003, February). Queer political news: Election-year coverage of the lesbian, gay, bisexual, and transgendered communities on national public radio, 1992–2000. *Journalism 4*, 5–28.

Barnhurst, K. G. (2007). Visibility as paradox: Representation and simultaneous contrast. In K. G. Barnhurst (Ed.), *Media Q: media/queered: Visibility and its discontents* (pp. 1–22). New York, NY: Peter Lang Publishing.

Benhabib, S. (Ed.). (1996). *Democracy and difference*. Princeton, NJ: Princeton University Press.

Benhabib, S. (2002). Deliberative democracy and multicultural dilemmas. In S. Benhabib (Ed.), *Claims of culture: Equality and diversity in the global era* (pp. 82–146). Princeton, NJ: Princeton University Press.

Bennett, W. L. & Segerberg, A. (2012a). Digital media and the personalization of collective action. In B. D. Loader & D. M. Mercea (Eds), *Social media and democracy: Innovations in participatory politics* (pp. 13–38). New York, NY: Routledge.

Bennett, W. L. & Segerberg, A. (2012b). The logic of connective action: Digital media and the personalization of contentious politics. *Information, Communication & Society, 15*(5), 739–768.

Bennett, W. L., Pickard, V. W., Iozzi, D. P., Schroeder, C. L., & Caswell, T. C. E. (2004). Managing the public sphere: Journalistic construction of the great globalization debate. *Journal of Communication, 54*(3), 437–454.

Bentes, I. (2007). Sertões e favelas no cinema brasileiro contemporâneo: Estética e cosmética da fome [Badlands and slums in contemporary Brazilian movies: The aesthetics and cosmetics of hunger]. *ALCEU, 8*(15), 242–255.

Bertrand, C. J. (Ed.). (2001). *An arsenal for democracy: Media accountability systems*. Cresskill: Hampton Press.

Bickford, S. (2011). Emotion talk and political judgment. *The Journal of Politics, 73*(4), 1025–1037.

Bimber, B., Flanagin, A. J., & Stohl, C. (2012). *Collective action in organizations: Interaction and engagement in an era of technological change*. New York, NY: Cambridge University Press.

Black, L. W. (2008). Deliberation, storytelling and dialogic moments. *Communication Theory, 18*, 93–116.

Black, M. (2002). *A handbook on advocacy: Child domestic workers finding a voice*. Horsham: Printed Word/Anti-Slavery International.

Blagbrough, J. (2008). Child domestic labor: A modern form of slavery. *Children & Society, 22*, 179–190.

Blumler, J. & Gurevitch, M. (2000). Rethinking the study of political communication. In J. Curran & M. Gurevitch (Eds), *Mass media and society* (pp. 155–172). London: Arnold.

Bohman, J. (1996). *Public deliberation: Pluralism, complexity and democracy.* Cambridge, MA: MIT Press.

Bohman, J. (2000). "When the water chokes": Ideology, communication, and practical rationality. *Constellations, 7*(3), 382–392.

Bohman, J. (2007). Beyond distributive justice and struggles for recognition: Freedom, democracy, and critical theory. *European Journal of Political Theory, 6*(3), 267–276.

Boltanski, L. (1999). *Distant suffering: Morality, media and politics.* Cambridge, MA: Cambridge University Press.

Bou-Franch, P., Lorenzo-Dus, N., & Blitvich, P. G.-C. (2012). Social interaction in YouTube text-based polylogues: A study of coherence. *Journal of Computer-Mediated Communication, 17,* 501–521.

Bourdieu, P. (1977). *Outline of a theory of practice.* Cambridge, MA: Cambridge University Press.

Bourdieu, P. (1984). *Distinction: A social critique of the judgment of taste.* London: Routledge and Kegan Paul.

Bovens, M. (2006). Analyzing and assessing accountability: A conceptual framework. *European Governance Papers (EUROGOV),* C-06–01. Available at: http://www.connex-network.org/eurogov/pdf/egp-connex-C-06-01.pdf

boyd, D. (2007). Social network sites: Public, private, or what? *Knowledge Tree, 13,* 1–7.

boyd, D. (2011). Social network sites as networked publics: Affordances, dynamics, and implications. In Z. Papacharissi (Ed.), *Networked self: Identity, community, and culture on social network sites* (pp. 39–58). New York, NY: Routledge.

boyd, D. & Donath, J. (2004). Public displays of connection. *BT Technology Journal, 22*(4), 71–82.

boyd, D. & Ellison, N. (2007). Social network sites: Definition, history, and scholarship. *Journal of Computer-Mediated Communication, 13*(1), 210–230.

Boyden, J. (1997). Childhood and the policy makers: A comparative perspective on the globalization of childhood. In A. James & A. Prout (Eds), *Constructing and reconstructing childhood* (pp. 187–226). London: UK Falmer Press.

Braga, J. L. (2006). *A sociedade enfrenta sua mídia: Dispositivos sociais de crítica midiática* [Society faces its media: Social tools in media critique]. São Paulo, SP: Paulus.

Brasil Secretaria de Direitos Humanos. (2012). *Relatório sobre violência homofóbica no Brasil: Ano de 2011* [Report on Homophobic violence in Brazil: Year 2011]. P. P. Calaf, G. C. Bernardes, & G. S. Rocha (Org.), Brasília, DF: Secretaria de Direitos Humanos.

Brundidge, J. (2010). Encountering "difference" in the contemporary public sphere: The contribution of the Internet to the heterogeneity of political discussion networks. *Journal of Communication, 60*(4), 680–700.

Brundidge, J. & Rice, R. E. (2009). Political engagement and exposure to heterogeneous political discussion: Do the (information) rich get richer and the similar get more similar? In A. Chadwick & P. N. Howard (Eds), *The handbook of internet politics* (pp. 144–156). New York, NY: Routledge.

Bryman, A. (2001). Focus groups. In A. Bryman (Ed.), *Social research methods* (pp. 335–351). Oxford: Oxford University Press.

Burch, S. & Kafer, A. (2010). *Deaf and disability studies: Interdisciplinary perspectives.* Washington, DC: Gallaudet University Press.

Burgess, J. E. & Green, J. B. (2009). *YouTube: Online video and participatory culture*. Malden, MA: Polity Press.

Burgos, M. B. (2005). Cidade, territórios e cidadania [City, territories and citizenship]. *Dados, 48*(1), 189–222.

Schmidt am Busch, H.(2010). Can the goals of Frankfurt School be achieved by a theory of recognition? In H. C. Schmidt am Busch & C. F. Zurn (Eds), *The philosophy of recognition: Historical and contemporary perspectives* (pp. 257–285). Lanham, MA: Lexington Books.

Schmidt am Busch, H. & Zurn, C. F. (Eds). (2010). *The philosophy of recognition: Historical and contemporary perspectives*. Lanham, MA: Lexington Books.

Butsch, R. (Ed.). (2007). *Media and public spheres*. New York, NY: Palgrave.

Cal, D. (2007). *Entre o privado e o público: Contextos comunicativos, deliberação e trabalho infantil doméstico* [Between the private and the public: Communicative contexts, deliberation and child domestic labor]. (Master's thesis). Faculdade de Filosofia e Ciências Humanas da UFMG, Belo Horizonte, MG.

Cal, D. & Maia, R. C. M. (2012). Making sense about child domestic labor: Between diplomatic or agonistic deliberation. In R. C. M. Maia (Ed.), *Media, deliberation and political talk* (pp. 255–286). New York, NY: Hampton Press.

Calder, G. (2011). Disability and misrecognition. In S. Thompson & M. Yar (Eds), *The politics of misrecognition* (pp. 105–125). Aldershot: Ashgate.

Cammaerts, B., Mattoni, A., & McCurdy, P. (Eds). (2013). *Mediation and protest movements*. Chicago, IL: Intellect Books.

Campbell, C. (1995). *Race, myth and the news*. Thousand Oaks, CA: SAGE Publications.

Canclini, N. G. (2009). *Culturas híbridas: Estratégias para entrar e sair da modernidade* [Hybrid cultures: Strategies for accessing and exiting modernity]. São Paulo, SP: Universidade de São Paulo.

Carneiro, M. T. & Rocha, E. (2009). Do fundo do buraco: O drama social das empregadas domésticas [From the bottom of the hole: The social drama of domestic workers]. In J. Souza (Ed.), *A ralé brasileira: Quem é e como vive?* [Brazil's lowest people on the totem pole: Who are they and how do they live?]. (pp. 125–142). Belo Horizonte, MG: UFMG.

Carpentier, N. (2011). *Media and participation: A site of ideological-democratic struggle*. Bristol: Intellect Publishers.

Carroll, W. K. & Hackett, R. A. (2006). Democratic media activism through the lens of social movement theory. *Media, Culture & Society, 28*(1), 83–104.

Celikates, R. (2012) Recognition, system justification and reconstructive critique. In C. Lazzeri & S. Nou (Eds), *Reconnaissance, identité et intégration sociale* (pp. 85–99). Paris: Presses Universitaires de Paris Ouest.

Chadwick, A. (2007). Digital network repertoires and organizational hybridity. *Political Communication, 24*(3), 283–301.

Chadwick, A. (2013). *The hybrid media system: Politics and power*. Oxford: Oxford University Press.

Chambers, S. & Kopstein, J. (2001). Bad civil society. *Political Theory*, 837–865.

Chambers, S. & Kopstein, J. (2008). Civil society and the state. In J. Dryzek, B. Hong, & A. Phillips (Eds), *The Oxford handbook of political theory* (pp. 363–381). Oxford: Oxford University Press.

Chouliaraki, L. & Fairclough, N. (1999). *Discourse in late modernity: Rethinking critical discourse analysis*. Edinburgh: Edinburgh University Press.

Cole, P. (2007). The body politic: Theorizing disability and impairment. *Journal of Applied Philosophy, 24*(2), 169–176.

Coleman, S. & Blumler, J. (2009). *The internet and democratic citizenship.* New York, NY: Cambridge University Press.

Coleman, S. & Moss, G. (2012). Under construction: The field of online deliberation research. *Journal of Information Technology & Politics, 9*(1), 1–15.

Connolly, J., Leach, M., & Walsh, L. (2007). *Recognition in politics: Theory, policy and practice.* Newcastle: Cambridge Scholars Press.

Conover, P. J. & Searing, D. D. (2005). Studying everyday political talk in the deliberative system. *Acta Politica, 40*(3), 269–283.

Cooke, M. (2006). *Re-presenting the good society.* Cambridge, MA: The MIT Press.

Cooke, M. (2009). Beyond dignity and difference revisiting the politics of recognition. *European Journal of Political Theory, 8*(1), 76–95.

Correia, J. C. (2002) Jornalismo e espaço público [Journalism and public space]. Covilhã: Imprensa da Universidade da Beira Interior.

Correia, J. C., Morais, R., & Sousa, J. C. (2011). Agenda dos cidadãos: Práticas cívicas na imprensa regional portuguesa [Citizens' agenda: Civic practices in Portuguese regional press]. *Revista Estudos de Comunicação*, 1646–4974. Available at: http://www.labcom.ubi.pt/sub/investigador/60a8d8673e5d679e9 63c2dcff3d36e00#sthash.3Ua2HTYW.dpuf

Costanza-Chock, S. (2011). Digital popular communication: Lessons on information and communication technologies for social change from the immigrant rights movement. *National Civic Review, 100*(3), 29–35.

Costanza-Chock, S. (2012). Mic check! Media cultures and the Occupy Movement. *Social Movement Studies, 11*(3–4), 375–385.

Costanza-Chock, S. (2013). Transmedia mobilization in the popular association of the Oaxacan Peoples, Los Angeles Sasha. In B. Cammaerts, P. McCurdy, & A. Mattoni (Eds), *Mediation and protest movements* (pp. 95–144). London: Intellect Ltd.

Cottle, S. (2008). Reporting demonstrations: The changing media politics of dissent. *Media, Culture & Society, 30*(6), 853–872.

Couch, M., Pitts, M., Croy, S., Mulcare, H., & Mitchell, A. (2008). Transgender people and the amendment of formal documentation: Matters of recognition and citizenship. *Health Sociology Review, 17*(3), 280–289.

Couldry, N. (2000). *The place of media power: Pilgrims and witnesses of the media age.* London: Routledge.

Couldry, N. (2013). *Media, society, world: Social theory and digital media practice.* Hoboken, NJ: Wiley.

Cox, R. (2012). Recognition and immigration. In S. O'Neill & N. H. Smith (Eds), *Recognition theory as social research: Investigating the dynamics of social conflict* (pp. 192–212). New York, NY: Palgrave Macmillan.

Cruz, M. M. (2007).Vozes da favela: Representação, identidade e disputas discursivas no ciberespaço [Slum voices: Representation, identity and discursive disputes in cyberspace]. *Review of Latin American Studies, 2*, 77–91.

Dahlberg, L. (2007). Rethinking the fragmentation of the cyberpublic: From consensus to contestation. *New Media & Society, 9*(5), 827–847.

Dahlgren, P. (1988). What's the meaning of this? Viewers' plural sense-making of TV news. *Media, Culture and Society, 10*, 285–301.

Dahlgren, P. (1995). *Television and the public sphere.* London: SAGE.

Dahlgren, P. (2009). *Media and political engagement: Citizens, communication and democracy*. Cambridge, MA: Cambridge University Press.

Dahlgren, P. (2013). Occupy Wall Street: Discursive strategies and fields. In P. Dahlgren, *The political Web: Media, participation and alternative democracy* (pp. 67–87). New York, NY: Palgrave McMillan.

Dahlgren, P. & Sparks, C. (1993). *Communication and citizenship: Journalism and the public sphere in the new media age*. London: Routledge.

Dan Meraz ah, boyd & Marwick, A. (2011). *Social privacy in networked publics: Teens' attitudes, practices, and strategies*. Paper presented at Oxford Institute's Decade in Time Symposium, September 22.

Danermark, B. & Gellerstedt, L. C. (2004). Social justice: Redistribution and recognition – a non-reductionist perspective on disability. *Disability and Society, 19*(4), 339–353.

Davis, K. (2012). Tensions of identity in a networked era: Young people's perspectives on the risks and rewards of online self-expression. *New Media & Society, 14*, 634–651.

Dayan, D. (1998). Particularistic media and diasporic communication. In T. Liebes & J. Curran (Eds), *Media, ritual, identity* (pp. 103–113). London: Routledge.

della Porta, D. (2012). Communication in movement: Social movements as agents of participatory democracy. In B. D. Loader & D. M. Mercea (Eds), *Social media and democracy: Innovations in participatory politics* (pp. 39–54). New York, NY: Routledge.

della Porta, D. (2013). Bridging research on democracy, social movements and communication. In B. Cammaerts, A. Mattoni, & P. McCurdy (Eds), *Mediation and protest movements* (pp. 21–38). Chicago, IL: Intellect Books.

della Porta, D. & Diani, M. (2006). *Social movements: An introduction*. Padstow: Wiley-Blackwell.

Demo, P. (2002). *Charme da exclusão social* [The charm of social exclusion]. Campinas: Autores Associados.

Dennis, J. P. (2009). Gazing at the black teen: Con artists, cyborgs and sycophants. *Media Culture & Society, 31*, 179–195.

Departamento Intersindical de Estatística e Estudos Socioeconômicos. (2003). Pesquisa de emprego e desemprego. Os negros no mercado de trabalho da região metropolitana de São Paulo [Employment and unemployment survey: Blacks in the labor market in the Sao Paulo Greater Metropolitan Region]. Available at: http://www.dieese.org.br/analiseped/2013/2013pednegrossao.pdf

Deranty, J. P. (2009). *Beyond communication: A critical study of Axel Honneth's social philosophy* (Vol. 7). Leiden: Brill.

Deranty, J. P. (2010). Critique of political economy and contemporary critical theory: A defense of Honneth's theory of recognition. In H. Schmidt am Busch & C. F. Zurn (Eds), *The philosophy of recognition: Historical and contemporary perspectives* (pp. 285–319). Lanham, MA: Lexington Books.

Deranty, J. P. (2011). Reflective critical theory: A systematic reconstruction of Axel Honneth's social philosophy. In D. Petherbridge (Ed.), *The critical theory of Axel Honneth* (pp. 59–88). Leiden, BO: Brill.

Deranty, J. P. (2012). Expression and cooperation as norms of contemporary work. In N. H. Smith & J. P. Deranty (Eds), *New philosophies of labor: Work and the social bond* (pp. 151–180). Leiden, HO: Brill.

Deranty, J. P. & Renault, E. (2007). Politicizing Honneth's ethics of recognition. *Thesis Eleven, 88*, 92–111.

Desrues, T. (2013). Mobilizations in a hybrid regime: The 20th February Movement and the Moroccan regime. *Current Sociology, 61*(4), 409–423.

Dhamoon, R. (2009). *Identity/difference politics: How difference is produced, and why it matters*. Vancouver: UBC Press.

Dhoest, A. (2009). Establishing a multi-ethnic imagined community? Ethnic minority audiences watching Flemish soaps. *European Journal of Communication, 24*(3), 305–323.

Domingues, P. (2007). Movimento negro brasileiro: Alguns apontamentos históricos [Brazil's black movement: Some historical issues]. *Revista Tempo, 12*(23), 100–122.

Donath, J. & boyd, D. (2004). Public displays of connection. *BT Technology Journal, 22*(4), 71–82.

Dorfman, L. (2003). Studying the news on public health: How content analysis supports media advocacy. *American Journal of Health Behavior, 27*(3), S217–S226.

Downing, J. (2001). *Radical media: Rebellious communication and social movements*. Thousand Oaks, CA: SAGE.

Downing, J. (2003). The independent media center movement and the anarchist socialist tradition. In N. Couldry & J. Curran (Eds), *Contesting media power: Alternative media in a networked world* (pp. 243–257). Lanham, MA: Rowman & Littlefield Publisher.

Dryzek, J. S. (2000). *Deliberative democracy and beyond: Liberals, critics, contestations*. Oxford: Oxford University Press.

Dryzek, J. S. (2010). *Foundations and frontiers of deliberative governance*. New York, NY: Oxford University Press.

Duchesne, S. & Haegel, F. (2010). What political discussion means and how do the French and (French-speaking) Belgians deal with it? In K. Ikeda, M. R. Wolf, & L. Morales (Eds), *Political discussion in modern democracies: A comparative perspective* (pp. 44–61). New York, NY: Routledge.

Duits, L. (2010). The importance of popular media in everyday girl culture. *European Journal of Communication, 25*(3), 243–257.

Düttmann, A. G. (2000). Between cultures: Tensions in the struggle for recognition. In A. G. Düttmann (Ed.), *The culture of criticism: Recognition as presupposition and result* (pp. 140–166). London: Verso.

Earl, J. & Kimport, K. (2011). *Digitally enabled social change: Activism in the internet age*. Cambridge, MA: The MIT Press.

Earls, F. (Ed.). (2011). The child as citizen. *The Annals of the American Academy of Political and Social Science, 633*, 6–16.

Edgerly, L., Toft, A., & Veden, M. L. (2011). Social movements, political goals, and the May 1 marches: Communicating protest in polysemous media environments. *The International Journal of Press/Politics, 16*(3), 314–334.

Edmond, R. (2006). *Leprosy and empire: A medical and cultural history*. New York, NY: Cambridge University Press.

Edwards, M. (2004). *Civil society*. Cambridge, MA: Polity Press.

Ellison, N., Lampe, C., Steinfield, C., & Vitak, J. (2011). With a little help from my friends: How social network sites affect social capital processes. In Z.

Papacharissi (Ed.), *A networked self: Identity, community and culture on social network sites* (pp. 124–145). New York, NY: Routledge.

Ellison, N. B. & boyd, D. (2013). Sociality through social network sites. In W. H. Dutton (Ed.), *The Oxford handbook of internet studies* (pp. 151–172). Oxford: Oxford University Press.

Entman, R. M. (1993). Framing: Toward clarification of a fractured paradigm. *Journal of Communication, 43*(4), 51–58.

Entman, R. M. (2004). *Projections of power: Framing news, public opinion, and US foreign policy.* Chicago IL: University of Chicago Press.

Entman, R. M. & Rojecki, A. (2000). *The black image in the white mind: Media and race in America.* Chicago, IL: University of Chicago Press.

Ettema, J. (2007). Journalism as reason-giving: Deliberation, democracy, institutional accountability, and the news media's mission. *Political Communication, 24*, 143–160.

Fairclough, N. (1995a). *Media discourse.* Trowbridge, UK: Redwood Books.

Fairclough, N. (1995b). *Critical discourse analysis. The critical study of language. Language in social life series.* London: Longman.

Fairclough, N. (1998). Political discourse in the media: An analytical framework. In A. Bell & P. Garrett (Eds), *Approaches to media discourse* (pp. 142–162). Oxford: Blackwell.

Federação Nacional de Educação e Integração dos Surdos (FENEIS). (2009). *Storytelling of deaf persons.* Available at: http://www.feneis.org.br

Feldman, L. C. (2002). Redistribution, recognition, and the state: The irreducibly political dimension of injustice. *Political Theory, 30*(3), 410–440.

Ferrarese, E. (2009). "Gabba-gabba, we accept you, one of us": Vulnerability and power in the relationship of recognition. *Constellations, 16*(4), 604–614.

Ferrarese, E. (2011). Axel Honneth's antagonism: What changes when the mode of acquiring recognition changes. In S. Thompson & M. Yar (Eds), *The politics of misrecognition* (pp. 33–45). Farnham: Ashgate Publishing.

Ferree, M. M., Gamson, W. A., Gerhards, J., & Rucht, D. (2002). *Shaping abortion discourse: Democracy and the public sphere in Germany and the United States.* Cambridge, MA: Cambridge University Press.

Figueira, E. (2008). *Caminhando em silêncio: Uma introdução à trajetória das pessoas com deficiência na história do Brasil* [Walking in silence: Introduction to the life of disabled people in Brazil]. São Paulo, SP: Giz Editora.

Finkelstein, V. (2004). Representing disability. In J. Swain, S. French, & C. Barnes (Eds), *Disabling barriers: Enabling environments* (pp. 13–20). London: SAGE.

Forst, R. (2002). *Contexts of justice: Political philosophy beyond liberalism and communitarianism.* Berkeley, LA: University of California Press.

Forst, R. (2007a). "To tolerate means to insult": Toleration, recognition and emancipation. In B. van den Brink & D. Owen (Eds), *Recognition and power: Axel Honneth and the tradition of critical social theory* (pp. 215–237). New York, NY: Cambridge University Press.

Forst, R. (2007b). First things first: Redistribution, recognition and justification. *European Journal of Political Theory, 6*(3), 291–304.

Forum Vergonha SURDO. (2005). [Web log post]. Available at: http://www.orkut.com/CommMsgs.aspx?cmm=428446&tid=10024425

França, V. R. V. & Corrêa, L. G. (Eds). (2012). *Mídia, instituições e valores* [Media, institutions and values]. Belo Horizonte, MG: Autêntica.

França, V. R. V. & Guimarães, C. G. (Eds) (2006). *Na mídia, na rua: Narrativas do cotidiano* [On the media, on the streets: Narratives of everyday life]. Belo Horizonte, MG: Autêntica.

Fraser, N. (1992). Rethinking the public sphere: A contribution to the critique of actually existing democracy. In C. Calhoun (Ed.), *Habermas and the public sphere* (pp. 109–142). Cambridge, MA: MIT Press.

Fraser, N. (2000). Rethinking recognition. *New Left Review, 3*(7), 107–120.

Fraser, N. (2001). Recognition without ethics? *Theory, Culture & Society, 18*(2–3), 21–42.

Fraser, N. (2003a). Social justice in the age of identity politics: Redistribution, recognition, and participation. In N. Fraser & A. Honneth (Eds), *Redistribution or recognition? A political-philosophical exchange* (pp. 07–109). New York, NY: Verso.

Fraser, N. (2003b). Distorted beyond all recognition: A rejoinder to Axel Honneth. In N. Fraser & A. Honneth (Eds), *Redistribution or recognition?: A political-philosophical exchange* (pp. 198–236). New York, NY: Verso.

Fraser, N. (2004). Recognition, redistribution and representation in capitalist global society. *Acta Sociológica, 47*(4), 374–382.

Fraser, N. (2005). Mapping the feminist imagination: From redistribution to recognition to representation. *Constellations, 12*(3), 295–307.

Fraser, N. (2010). Rethinking recognition. In H. Schmidt am Busch & C. F. Zurn (Eds), *The philosophy of recognition: Historical and contemporary perspectives* (pp. 211–223). Lanham, MA: Lexington Books.

Fraser, N. & Honneth, A. (2003). *Redistribution or recognition? A political-philosophical exchange*. London: Verso.

Freire-Medeiros, B. (2007). A favela que se vê e que se vende: Reflexões e polêmicas em torno de um destino turístico [Slums as they are seen and as they are sold: Reflections and polemics around a sightseeing destination]. *Revista Brasileira de Ciências Sociais, 22*(65), 62–72.

Fürsich, E. (2010). Media and the representation of others. *International Social Science Journal, 61*(199), 113–130.

Gaines, J. (2001). *Fire & desire: Mixed-race movies in the silent era*. Chicago, IL: University of Chicago Press.

Gamson, J. (1999). Taking the talk show challenge: Television, emotion, and public spheres. *Constellations, 6*(2), 190–205.

Gamson, W. A. (1992). *Talking politics*. New York, NY: Cambridge University Press.

Gamson, W. A. (2004). Bystanders, public opinion, and the media. In D. Snow, S. A. Soule, & H. Kriesi (Eds), *The Blackwell companion to social movements* (pp. 242–261). New Jersey: Wiley-Blackwell.

Gamson, W. A. & Modigliani, A. (1989). Media discourse and public opinion on nuclear power: A constructionist approach. *American Journal of Sociology, 95*(1), 1–37.

Garcêz, R. L. & Maia, R. C. M. (2009). The struggle for recognition of the deaf on the internet: The political function of storytelling. *Communication, Politics & Culture, 42*(2), 45–64.

Gastil, J. (2008). *Political communication and deliberation*. London: SAGE.

Geuss, R. (1981). *The idea of a critical theory: Habermas and the Frankfurt School*. Cambridge, MA: Cambridge University Press.

Gitlin, T. (1980). *The whole world is watching: Mass media in the making & unmaking of the new left*. Los Angeles, CA: University of California Press.

Goffman, E. (1974). *Frame analysis: An essay on the organization of experience*. Cambridge, MA: Harvard University Press.

Goggin, G. & Newell, C. (2003). *Digital disability: The social construction of disability in new media*. Lanham, MA: Rowman & Littlefield.

Gomberg-Muñoz, R. (2010). Willing to work: Agency and vulnerability in an undocumented immigrant network. *American Anthropologist, 112*(2), 295–307.

Gomes, A. C. (2007). Prefácio [Foreword]. In V. Alberti & A. Pereira (Eds), *Histórias do movimento negro no Brasil: Depoimentos ao CPDOC* [Brazil's black movement: History and stories at CPDOC]. (pp. 9–12). Rio de Janeiro, RJ: Pallas.

Gomes, W. (2004). *Transformações da política na era da comunicação de massa* [Transformations in politics in the mass communication era]. São Paulo, SP: Paulus.

Gomes, W. & Maia, R. C. M. (2008). *Comunicação e democracia: Problemas e perspectivas* [Communication and democracy: Problems and perspectives]. São Paulo, SP: Paulus.

Goodin, R. E. (1985). *Protecting the vulnerable*. Chicago, IL: University of Chicago Press.

Goodley, D. & Tragaskis, C. (2006). Storying disability and impairment: Retrospective accounts of disabled family life. *Qualitative Health Research, 16*, 630–646.

Gould, T. (2005). *A disease apart: Leprosy in the modern world*. New York, NY: St. Martin's Press.

Graham, T. (2008). Needles in a haystack: A new approach for identifying and assessing political talk in non-political discussion forums. *Javnost – The Public, 15*(2), 17–36.

Grant, R. W. & Keohane, R. O. (2005). Accountability and abuses of power in world politics. *American Political Science Review, 99*(01), 29–43.

Grasmuck, S., Martin, J., & Zhao, S. (2009). Ethno racial identity displays on Facebook. *Journal of Computer Mediated Communication, 15*(1), 158–188.

Gray, H. (1995). *Watching race: Television and the struggle for "blackness"*. Minneapolis, MN: University of Minnesota Press.

Gray, M. L. (2009). Negotiating identities/queering desires: Coming out online and the remediation of the coming-out story. *Journal of Computer-Mediated Communication, 14*(4), 1162–1189.

Grijó, W. P. & Sousa, A. H. F. (2012). O negro na telenovela brasileira: A atualidade das representações [Blacks in Brazilian TV soap operas: Current status]. *Estudos em Comunicação/Communication Studies, 11*, 185–204.

Grupo de Trabalho Interministerial de Ex-Colônias de Hanseníase. (2007). *Resgate da cidadania das pessoas atingidas pela hanseníase*: Relatório [Rescuing the citizenship of Hansen patients: Report]. Brasília, DF: Secretaria Especial de Direitos Humanos da Presidência da República.

Gussow, Z. (1989). *Leprosy, racism and public health*. Boulder: Westview Press.

Gutmann, A. (2003). *Identity in democracy*. Princeton, NJ: Princeton University Press.

Gutmann, A. & Thompson, D. (1996). *Democracy and disagreement*. Cambridge, MA: Harvard University Press.

Habermas, J. (1987). *The theory of communicative action* (Vol. 2: Lifeworld and system: A critique of functionalist reason). Boston, MA: Beacon Press.

Habermas, J. (1991). *The structural transformation of the public sphere: An inquiry into a category of bourgeois society*. Cambridge, MA: MIT Press.

Habermas, J. (1992). Further reflections on the public sphere. In C. J. Calhoun (Ed.), *Habermas and the public sphere* (pp. 421–461). Cambridge, MA: The MIT Press.

Habermas, J. (1993). *Justification and application*. Cambridge, UK: Polity Press.

Habermas, J. (1995). *Moral consciousness and communicative action*. Cambridge, MA: The MIT Press.

Habermas, J. (1996). *Between facts and norms: Contributions to a discourse theory of law and democracy*. Cambridge, UK: Polity Press.

Habermas, J. (2005). Concluding comments on empirical approaches to deliberative politics. *Acta Politica, 40*(3), 384–392.

Habermas, J. (2006). Political communication in media society: Does democracy still enjoy an epistemic dimension? The impact of normative theory on empirical research. *Communication Theory, 16*(4), 411–426.

Habermas, J. (2009). *Europe: The faltering project*. Cambridge, UK: Polity Press.

Hall, S. (1980). Encoding/decoding. In S. Hall, D. Hobson, A. Lowe, & P. Willis (Eds), *Culture, media, language* (pp. 128–138). London: Routledge.

Hall, S. (1997a). The work of representation. In S. Hall (Ed.). *Representation: Cultural representation and signifying practices* (pp. 13–74). Thousand Oaks, CA: SAGE Publications.

Hall, S. (1997b). The spectacle of the other. In S. Hall (Ed.). *Representation: Cultural representation and signifying practices* (pp. 223–290). Thousand Oaks, CA: SAGE Publications.

Hamburger, E. (2007). Violência e pobreza no cinema brasileiro recente: Reflexões sobre a idéia de espetáculo [Violence and poverty in recent Brazilian movies: Reflecting on the notion of a spectacle]. *Novos Estudos-CEBRAP, 78*, 113–128.

Hamburger, E. (2011). Telenovelas e interpretações do Brasil [TV soap operas and interpretations in Brazil]. *Lua Nova, 82*(82), 61–86.

Hartmann, M. & Honneth, A. (2006). Paradoxes of capitalism. *Constellations, 13*(1), 41–58.

Haugaard, M. (2010). Power: A "family resemblance" concept. *European Journal of Cultural Studies, 13*(4), 419–438.

Hobson, B. (Ed.). (2003). *Recognition struggles and social movements: Contested identities, agency and power*. New York, NY: Cambridge University Press.

Honneth, A. (1991). *The Critique of power*. Cambridge, MA: The MIT Press.

Honneth, A. (1995). Decentered autonomy. The subject after the fall. In C. C. Wright (Ed.), *The fragmented world of the social. Essays in social and political philosophy* (pp. 261–272). New York, NY: Sunny Press.

Honneth, A. (1996). *The struggle for recognition: The moral grammar of social conflicts*. Cambridge, MA: The MIT Press.

Honneth, A. (1997d) Pathologies of the social. In A. Honneth (Ed.), *Disrespect. The normative foundations of critical theory* (pp. 3–48). Cambridge: Polity Press.

Honneth, A. (2001). Invisibility: On the epistemology of "recognition". *The Aristotelian Society, 75*, 111–126.

Honneth, A. (2002). Grounding recognition: A rejoinder to critical questions. Inquiry: An interdisciplinary. *Journal of Philosophy, 45*(4), 499–520.

Honneth, A. (2003a). Redistribution as recognition: A response to Nancy Fraser. In N. Fraser & A. Honneth, *Redistribution or recognition? A political-philosophical exchange* (pp. 110–197). London/New York, NY: Verso.

Honneth, A. (2003b). The point of recognition: A rejoinder to the rejoinder. In N. Fraser & A. Honneth (Eds), *Redistribution or recognition: A political-philosophical exchange* (pp. 237–268). New York, NY: Verso.

Honneth, A. (2003c). *Luta por reconhecimento: A gramática moral dos conflitos sociais* [Struggling for recognition: The moral grammar of social conflicts]. São Paulo, SP: Ed. 34.

Honneth, A. (2004). Organized self-realization. Some paradoxes of individualization. *European Journal of Social Theory, 7*, 463–478.

Honneth, A. (2007a). Between Aristotle and Kant: Recognition and moral obligation. In A. Honneth (Ed.), *Disrespect: The normative foundation of critical theory* (pp. 129–143). Cambridge, UK: Polity Press.

Honneth, A. (2007b). Recognition. In B. van den Brink & D. Owen (Eds), *Recognition and power: Axel Honneth and the tradition of critical theory* (pp. 323–347). Cambridge, MA: Cambridge University Press.

Honneth, A. (2007c). Rejoinder. In B. van den Brink & D. Owen (Eds), *Recognition and power: Axel Honneth and the tradition of critical social theory* (pp. 348–370). New York, NY: Cambridge University Press.

Honneth, A. (2010). Work and recognition: A redefinition. In H. Schmidt am Busch & C. F. Zurn (Eds), *The philosophy of recognition: Historical and contemporary perspectives* (pp. 223–239). Lanham, MD: Lexington Books.

Honneth, A. (2011). Rejoinder. In D. Petherbridge (Ed.), *Axel Honneth: Critical essays. With a reply by Axel Honneth* (pp. 391–426). Leiden, BO: Brill.

Honneth, A. (2012). Dissolution of the social: The social theory of Luc Boltanski and Laurent Thévenot. In A. Honneth (Ed.), *The I in We: Studies in the Theory of Recognition* (pp. 98–118). Cambridge, MA: Polity Press.

Hoyos, S. (2000). Y quién la mandó a ser niña? El trabajo infantil doméstico desde una perspectiva de género [Who asked her to be a girl? Child domestic labor from a gender perspective]. In G. A. Vargas, E. García-Méndez, & S. Hoyos (Eds), *Trabajo infantil doméstico: Quién la mandó a ser niña.* [Child domestic labor: Who asked her to be a girl?]. (pp. 109–135). Bogotá: TM Editores/UNICEF.

Huckfeldt, R. & Mendez, J. M. (2008). Moths, flames, and political engagement: Managing disagreement within communication networks. *The Journal of Politics, 70*(01), 83–96.

Ikäheimo, H. (2009). A vital human need: Recognition as inclusion in personhood. *European Journal of Political Theory, 8*(1), 31–42.

Ikäheimo, H. (2010). Making the best of what we are – recognition as an ontological and ethical concept. In H. Schmidt am Busch & C. F. Zurn (Eds), *The philosophy of recognition: Historical and contemporary perspectives* (pp. 343–369). Lanham, MA: Lexington Books.

Ikäheimo, H. & Laitinen, A. (2007). Analyzing recognition: Identification, acknowledgement and recognitive attitudes towards persons. In B. van den Brink & D. Owen (Eds), *Recognition and power: Axel Honneth and the tradition of critical social theory* (pp. 33–56). New York, NY: Cambridge University Press.

Instituto de Pesquisa Econômica Aplicada. (2013). *Políticas sociais: Acompanhamento e análise* [Social policies: Follow-up and analysis]. (vol. 21). Available at:

http://www.ipea.gov.br/portal/images/stories/PDFs/politicas_sociais/bps_21_completo.pdf

International Labor Organization. (2013). *Ending child labor in domestic work and protecting young workers from abusive working conditions.* Geneva: ILO.

Jenkins, H. (2009). What happened before YouTube? In J. Burgess, & J. Green (Eds), *YouTube: Online video and participatory culture* (pp. 109–125). Cambridge, MA: Polity Press.

Jenkins, H., Ford, S. & Green, J., (2013). *Spreadable media: Creating value and meaning in a networked culture.* New York, NY: New York University Press.

Juris, J. S. (2005). The new digital media and activist networking within anti–corporate globalization movements. *The Annals of the American Academy of Political and Social Science, 597*(1), 189–208.

Kalyvas, A. (1999). Critical theory at the crossroads: Comments on Axel Honneth's theory of recognition. *European Journal of Social Theory, 2*(1), 99–108.

Kapidzic, S. & Herring, S. C. (2011). Gender, communication, and self-presentation in teen chatrooms revisited: Have patterns changed? *Journal of Computer-Mediated Communication, 17*(1), 39–59.

Kavada, A. (2013). Internet cultures and protest movements: The cultural links between strategy, organizing and online communication. In B. Cammaerts, P. McCurdy, & A. Mattoni (Eds), *Mediation and social movements* (pp. 75–94). London: Intellect.

Kaye, B. (2011). Between Barack and a net place: Users and uses of social network sites and blogs for political information. In Z. Papacharissi (Ed.), *A networked self: Identity, community and culture on social network sites* (pp. 208–231). New York, NY: Routledge.

Kies, R. (2010). *Promises and limits of web-deliberation.* London: Palgrave Macmillan.

Kim, K. H. & Yun, H. (2008). Cying for me, Cying for us: Relational dialectics in a Korean social network site. *Journal of Computer-Mediated Communication, 13*(1), 298–318.

Kim, Y. (2011). The contribution of social network sites to exposure to political difference: The relationships among SNSs, online political messaging, and exposure to cross-cutting perspectives. *Computers in Human Behavior, 27*, 971–977.

Klandermans, B., van der Toorn, J., & van Stekelenburg, J. (2008). Embeddedness and identity: How immigrants turn grievances into action. *American Sociological Review, 73*, 992–1012.

Kleist, N. (2008). In the name of diaspora: Between struggles for recognition and political aspirations. *Journal of Ethnic and Migration Studies, 34*(7), 1127–1143.

Kompridis, N. (2004). From reason to self-realization? Axel Honneth and the "ethical turn" in critical theory. *Critical Horizons, 5*(1), 323–360.

Kompridis, N. (2007). Struggling over the meaning of recognition: A matter of identity, justice, or freedom? *European Journal of Political Theory, 6*(3), 277–288.

Krause, S. R. (2008). *Civil passions: Moral sentiment and democratic deliberation.* Princeton, NJ: Princeton University Press.

Krippendorff, K. (2003). *Content analysis: An introduction to its methodology.* Thousand Oaks, CA: SAGE.

Kulick, D. & Klein, C. H. (2003). Scandalous acts: The politics of shame among Brazilian travesti prostitutes. In B. Hobson (Ed.), *Recognition struggles and social movements: Contested identities, agency and power* (pp. 215–238). New York, NY: Cambridge University Press.

Laden, A. S. (2012). *Reasoning: A social picture.* Oxford: Oxford University Press.

Laitinen, A. (2002). Interpersonal recognition: A response to value or a precondition of personhood? Symposium on Axel Honneth and recognition. *Inquiry, 45*, 463–476.

Laitinen, A. (2009). Recognition, needs and wrongness: Two approaches. *European Journal of Political Theory, 8*(1), 13–28.

Laitinen, A. (2010). On the scope of "recognition": The role of adequate regard and mutuality. In H. Schmidt am Busch & C. F. Zurn (Eds), *The philosophy of recognition: Historical and contemporary perspectives* (pp. 319–343). Lanham, MA: Lexington Books.

Lamarão, M. L. N. (2008). *A constituição das relações sociais de poder no trabalho infanto-juvenil doméstico: Estudo sobre estigma e subalternidade* [The constitution of social power relations in child domestic labor: A study on stigma and subordination]. (Master's thesis). Universidade Federal do Pará, Belém.

Lamarão, M. L. N., Menezes, S. M. L., & Ferreira, W. B. (2000). *O trabalho doméstico de meninas em Belém* [The domestic labor of girls in Belem]. Belém, PA: Cedeca-Emaús.

Lane, H. (1984). *When the mind hears: A history of the deaf.* New York, NY: Random House.

Langman, L. (2013). Occupy: A new social movement. *Current Sociology, 61*(4), 510–524.

Larson, S. G. (2006). *Media & minorities: The politics of race in news and entertainment.* Lanham, MA: Rowman & Littlefield.

Leal, B. S. & Carvalho, C. A. (2012). *Jornalismo e homofobia no Brasil: Mapeamentos e reflexões* [Journalism and homophobia in Brazil: Mapping out and reflecting]. São Paulo, SP: Multimeios.

Leite, M. P. (2003). Novas relações entre identidade religiosa e participação política no Rio de Janeiro hoje: O caso do Movimento Popular de Favelas [New relations between religious identity and political participation in Rio de Janeiro today: Popular movements in slums – a case]. In P. Birman, (Ed.), *Religião e espaço público* [Religion and public space]. (pp. 63–95). São Paulo, SP: Attar.

Levmore, S. & Nussbaum, M. C. (Eds). (2010). *The offensive internet: Speech, privacy, and reputation.* London: Harvard University Press.

Liebes, T. (1997). *Reporting the Israeli–Arab conflict: How hegemony works.* London: Routledge.

Liebes, T. & Kampf, Z. (2009). Black and white and shades of gray: Palestinians in the Israeli media during the 2nd Intifada. *The International Journal of Press/Politics, 14*(4), 434–453.

Livingston, S. & Asmolov, G. (2010). Networks and the future of foreign affairs reporting. *Journalism Studies, 11*(5), 745–760.

Livingstone, S. & Lund, P. (1994). *Talk on television: Audience participation and public debate.* London: Routledge.

Loader, B. D. & Mercea, D. M. (2012). *Social media and democracy: Innovations in participatory politics.* New York, NY: Routledge.

Lukes, S. (2005). *Power: A radical view.* New York, NY: Palgrave Macmillan.

Machado da Silva, L. A. & Leite, M. P. (2004). Favelas e democracia: Temas e problemas da ação coletiva nas favelas cariocas [Slums and democracy: Themes and problems of collective action in Rio's slums]. In L. A. Machado da Silva et al. (Eds), *Rio: A democracia vista de baixo* [Rio de Janeiro: A bottom-up view of democracy]. (pp. 61–78). Rio de Janeiro, RJ: Ibase.

Mackuen, M., Wolak, J., Keele, L. & Marcus, G. E. (2010). Civic engagements: Resolute partisanship or reflective deliberation? *American Journal of Political Science*, *54*(2), 440–458.

Maia, R. C. M. (2006). Mídia e vida pública: Modos de abordagem [Media and public life: Ways to approach them]. In R. C. M. Maia & M. C. P. S. Castro (Eds), Mídia, esfera pública e identidades coletivas [Media, public sphere and collective identities]. (pp. 11–46). Belo Horizonte, MG: UFMG.

Maia, R. C. M. (Ed.). (2008). *Mídia e deliberação* [The media and deliberation]. Rio de Janeiro: FGV.

Maia, R. C. M. (2012a). *Deliberation, the media and political talk.* New York, NY: Hampton Press.

Maia, R. C. M. (2012b). From public sphere to deliberative system: Locating the place of the media. In R. C. M. Maia (Ed.), *Deliberation, the media and political talk* (pp. 59–76). New York, NY: Hampton Press.

Maia, R. C. M. (2012c). Demands for accountability: The media debate over the Bus 174 hijacking. In R. C. M. Maia (Ed.), *Deliberation, the media and political talk* (pp. 153–182). New York, NY: Hampton Press.

Maia, R. C. M. (2012d). Political talk and democratic deliberation. In R. C. M. Maia (Ed.), *Deliberation, the media and political talk* (pp. 211–226). New York, NY: Hampton Press.

Maia, R. C. M. (2012e). Non-electoral political representation: Expanding discursive domains. *Representation, 48*, 429–443.

Maia, R. C. M. & Garcêz, R. L. O. (2013). Recognition, feelings of injustice and claim justification: A case study of deaf people's storytelling on the internet. *European Political Science Review*, 1–24. doi: http://dx.doi.org/10.1017/S1755773913000143

Maia, R. C. M. & Cal, D. (2014). Recognition and ideology: assessing justice and injustice in the case of child domestic labor. *Journal of Political Power*, *7*, 63–85.

Maia, R. C. M. & Rezende, T. A. S. (2014a, forthcoming). Democracia e a ecologia complexa das redes sociais online: Um estudo de caso de conversações sobre o racismo e a homofobia em diferentes ambientes virtuais [Democracy and online social networks' complex ecology: A case study of conversations on racism and homophobia in different virtual environments]. In W. Gomes, R. Sampaio, & G. Rosseto (Eds), *Democracia digital no Brasil* [Digital democracy in Brazil]. Salvador, BA: UFBA.

Maia, R. C. M. & Rezende, T. A. S. (2014b). Deliberative system and discussions on racism and homophobia in networked media environment. Paper presented at the International Communication Association Conference 22–26 May 2014, Seattle.

Maia, R. C. M. & Vimieiro, A. C. (2013). Recognition and moral progress: A case study about discourses on disability in the media. *Political Studies*. doi: http://dx.doi.org/10.1111/1467-9248.12083

Mansbridge, J. (1999). Everyday talk in the deliberative system. In S. Macedo (Ed.), *Deliberative politics: Essays on democracy and disagreement* (pp. 211–239). New York, NY: Oxford University Press.

Marcus, G. E., Neuman, W. R., & Mackuen, M. (2000). *Affective intelligence and political judgment*. Chicago, IL: University of Chicago Press.

Markell, P. (2003). *Bound by recognition*. Princeton, NJ: Princeton University Press.

Marques, A. C. M. & Rocha, S. M. (2006). A produção de sentidos nos contextos de recepção: Em foco o grupo focal [Meaning-making in reception contexts: Assessing the focus group]. *Revista Fronteiras – Estudos Midiáticos, 8*(1), 38–53.

Marques, A. C. S. & Maia, R. C. M. (2010). Everyday conversation in the deliberative process: An analysis of communicative exchanges in discussion groups and their contributions to civic and political socialization. *Journal of Communication, 60*, 611–635.

Martín-Barbero, J. (2009). *Dos meios às mediações: Comunicação, cultura e hegemonia* [From means to mediation: Communication, culture and hegemony]. Rio de Janeiro, RJ: Universidade Federal do Rio de Janeiro.

Matthes, J. (2009). What's in a frame? A content analysis of media framing studies in the world's leading communication journals, 1990–2005. *Journalism and Mass Communication Quarterly, 86*(2), 349–367.

Matthes, J. & Kohring, M. (2008). The content analysis of media frames: Toward improving reliability and validity. *Journal of Communication, 58*(2), 258–279.

Mattoni, A. (2013). Repertoires of communication in social movement processes. In B. Cammaerts, A. Mattoni, & P. McCurdy, *Mediation and protest movements* (pp. 39–56). Chicago, IL: Intellect Ltd.

McAdam, D. (2000). Movement strategy and dramaturgic framing in democratic states: The case of the American civil rights movement. In S. Chambers & A. Costain (Eds), *Deliberation, democracy and the media* (pp. 117–134). New York, NY: Rowman & Littlefield Publishers.

McBride, C. (2009). Demanding recognition: Equality, respect, and esteem. *European Journal of Political Theory, 8*(1), 96–107.

McCurdy, P. (2013). Mediation, practice and lay theories of news media. In B. Cammaerts, A. Mattoni, & P. McCurdy (Eds), *Mediation and protest movements* (pp. 57–74). Chicago, IL: Intellect Ltd.

McQuail, D. (2003). *Media accountability and freedom of publication*. Oxford: Oxford University Press.

McRobbie, A. & Garber, J. (1976). Girls and subcultures: An exploration. In S. Hall & T. Jefferson (Eds), *Resistance through rituals* (pp. 209–222). London: Routledge.

Mead, G. H. (1934). *Mind, self and society: From the standpoint of a social behaviourist* (Vol. 1). Chicago/London: The University of Chicago Press.

Mello, L., Brito, W., & Maroja, D. (2012a). Políticas públicas para a população LGBT no Brasil: Notas sobre alcances e possibilidades [Public policies for LGBTs in Brazil: How far they can go and their possibilities]. *Cadernos Pagu, 39*, 403–429.

Mello, L., Brito, W., & Maroja, D. (2012b). Por onde andam as políticas públicas para a população LGBT no Brasil [Where are the public policies for the LGBT population in Brazil?]. *Sociedade e Estado, 27*(2), 289–312.

Mendelson, A. L. & Papacharissi, Z. (2011). Look at us: Collective narcissism in college student Facebook photo galleries. In Z. Papacharissi (Ed.), *The networked self: Identity, community and culture on social network sites* (pp. 251–273). New York, NY: Routledge.

Mendonça, R. F. (2007). Hanseníase e mundo da vida: As diferentes facetas de um estigma milenar [Hansen's disease and life in the world: Different facets of an ancient stigma]. *Eco-Pós, 10*(1), 120–147.

Mendonça, R. F. (2009). *Reconhecimento e deliberação: As lutas das pessoas atingidas pela hanseníase em diferentes âmbitos interacionais* [Recognition and deliberation: The struggles of Hansen patients in different international spheres]. (Doctoral dissertation). Communication Science Program, FAFICH, Federal University of Minas Gerais, Belo Horizonte, MG.

Mendonça, R. F. (2011). Recognition and social esteem: A case study of the struggles of people affected by leprosy. *Political Studies, 59*(4), 940–958.

Mendonça, R. F. (2014, forthcoming). Contradictions of recognition: The struggles of people affected by leprosy in Brazil. *Constellations.*

Mendonça, R. F. & Maia, R. C. M. (2012). Deliberation across arenas? Assessing the constitution of general claims about the future of leprosy colonies. In R. C. M. Maia (Ed.), *Deliberation, the media and political talk* (pp. 287–316). New York, NY: Hampton Press.

Mendonça, R. F. & Vaz, P. B. (2006). Só preto sem preconceito? [Just black but no prejudice?]. *Intexto, 14*, 1–15.

Meraz, S. (2007). Analyzing Political Conversation on the Howard Dean Candidate Blog. In M. Tremayne (Ed.), *Blogging, citizenship and the future of media* (pp. 59–81). New York, NY: Routledge.

Miège, B. (2010). *L'espace public contemporain* [L'espace public contemporain]. Grenoble: PUG.

Miguel, L. F. & Biroli, F. (2009). Mídia e representação política feminina [Media and female political representation]. *Opinião Pública, 15*, 55–81.

Mitra, A. (2001). Marginal voices in cyberspace. *New Media & Society, 3*(1), 29–48.

Mittell, J. (2010). *Television and American culture.* New York, NY: Oxford University Press.

Moghadam, V. M. (2013). What is democracy? Promises and perils of the Arab Spring. *Current Sociology, 61*(4), 393–408.

Molinier, P. (2012). Care as work: Mutual vulnerabilities and discrete knowledge. In N. H. Smith & J. P. Deranty (Eds), *New philosophies of labor: Work and the social bond* (pp. 251–270). Leiden, HO: Brill.

Morgan, D. L. (1997). *Focus groups as qualitative research* (Vol. 16). Thousand Oaks, CA: SAGE.

Morley, D. (1980). *The "nationwide" audience: Structure and decoding.* London: British Film Institute.

Morley, D. (1986). *Family television: Culture power and domestic leisure.* New York, NY: Routledge.

Morley, D. & Chen, K. (1996). *Stuart Hall: Critical dialogues in cultural studies.* London: Routledge.

Mutz, D. (2006). *Hearing the other side: Deliberative versus participatory democracy.* Cambridge, MA: Cambridge University Press.

Neblo, M. A. (2003). *Impassioned democracy: The role of emotion in deliberative theory.* Paper presented at the Democracy Collaborative Affiliates conference, Washington, DC.

Negroponte, N. (1995). *Being digital.* New York, NY: Alfred Knopf.

Neri, M. C. (2013). Apresentação IPEA. In M. M. Marcondes, L. Pinheiro, C. Queiroz, A. C. Querino, & D. Valverde (Eds), *Dossiê mulheres negras: Retrato das condições de vida das mulheres negras no Brasil* [A brief on black females: Life status of black females in Brazil]. (pp. 7–8). Brasília, DF: IPEA.

Neuman, W. R. & Guggenheim, L. (2011). The evolution of media effects theory: A six-stage model of cumulative research. *Communication Theory, 21,* 169–196.

Noble, G. (2009). "Countless acts of recognition": Young men, ethnicity and the messiness of identities in everyday life. *Social & Cultural Geography, 10*(8), 875–891.

Norris, L. (2012). Rights, recognition and judgment: Reflections on the case of welfare and asylum. *The British Journal of Politics and International Relations, 14*(1), 39–56.

Norris, P. (2000). *A virtuous circle: Political communications in postindustrial societies.* Cambridge, MA: Cambridge University Press.

Norris, P. (2001). Digital divide: Civic engagement, information poverty and the Internet in democratic societies. *Prometheus: Critical Studies in Innovation, 21*(3), 365–378.

Northway, R. (1997). Integration and inclusion: Illusion or progress in services for disabled people? *Social Policy and Administration, 31*(2), 157–172.

Nussbaum, M. C. (1995). Emotions and women's capabilities. In M. C. Nussbaum & J. Glover (Eds), *Women, culture, and development* (pp. 360–395). Oxford: Oxford University Press.

Nussbaum, M. C. (2003). *Upheavals of thought: The intelligence of emotions.* Cambridge, MA: Cambridge University Press.

Ogando, A. C. (2012). *Da república sem mulheres à modernização patriarcal: Origens e metamorfoses das relações de gênero no Brasil* [From a republic with no women to patriarchal modernization: Origins and metamorphoses of gender relations in Brazil]. (Doctoral dissertation). Political Science Program, FAFICH, Federal University of Minas Gerais, Belo Horizonte, MG.

Oliveira, L. (1997). Os excluídos existem? Notas sobre a elaboração de um novo conceito [Do those excluded even exist? Notes on elaborating a new concept]. *Revista Brasileira de Ciências Sociais, 12*(33), 49–60.

Oliver, M. (1996). *Understanding disability: From theory to practice.* Basingstoke: Macmillan.

Oliver, M. & Barnes, C. (1998). *Disabled people and social exclusion: From exclusion to inclusion.* London: Longman.

O'Neill, S. (2012). The politics of ethno-national conflict transformation: A recognition-theoretical reading of the peace process in Northern Ireland. In S. O'Neill & N. H. Smith (Eds), *Recognition theory as social research: Investigating the dynamics of social conflict* (pp. 149–172). New York, NY: Palgrave Macmillan.

O'Neill, S. & Smith, N. H. (Eds). (2012). *Recognition theory as social research: Investigating the dynamics of social conflict.* New York, NY: Palgrave Macmillan.

Ong, J. C. (2009). Watching the nation, singing the nation: London-based Filipino migrants' identity constructions in news and karaoke practices. *Communication, Culture & Critique, 2,* 160–181.

Orozco, G. (Ed.). (2002). *Recepción y mediaciones. Casos de investgación en América Latina.* Buenos Aires: Norma.

O'Sullivan, P. (2005, May). *Masspersonal communication: Rethinking the mass interpersonal divide.* Paper presented at The Annual Meeting Of The International Communication Association, New York, NY. Available at: http://www.academia.edu/468715/Masspersona l_communication_Rethinking_the_mass_interpersonal_divide

Owen, D. (2007). Self-government and democracy as reflections on Honneth's social and political ideal. In B. van den Brink & D. Owen (Eds), *Recognition and power: Axel Honneth and the tradition of critical social theory* (pp. 290–320). New York, NY: Cambridge University Press.

Owen, D. (2008). Recognition, reification and value. *Constellations, 15*(4), 576–586.

Owen, D. (2012). Recognition as statecraft? Contexts of recognition and transformations of state membership regimes. In S. O'Neill & N. H. Smith (Eds), *Recognition theory as social research: Investigating the dynamics of social conflict* (pp. 173–191). New York, NY: Palgrave Macmillan.

Page, B. I. (1996). *Who deliberates? Mass media in modern democracy.* London: University of Chicago Press.

Papacharissi, Z. (2002). The virtual sphere: The net as a public sphere. *New Media & Society, 4*(1), 5–23.

Papacharissi, Z. (2010). *A private sphere: Democracy in a digital age.* Cambridge, MA: Polity Press.

Papacharissi, Z. (Ed.). (2011). *A networked self: Identity, community, and culture on social network sites.* New York, NY: Routledge.

Parkinson, J. & Mansbridge, J. (Eds). (2012). *Deliberative systems.* Cambridge, MA: Cambridge University Press.

Pereira, E. & Rodrigues, V. (2010). Amor não tem cor?! Gênero e raça/cor na seletividade afetiva de homens e mulheres negros(as) na Bahia e no Rio Grande do Sul [Is love color blind? Gender and race/color in affectionate selectivity of black males and females in the Brazilian states of Bahia and Rio Grande do Sul]. *Revista da ABPN, 1*(2), 157–181.

Perlin, G. (1998). Identidades surdas [Deaf identities]. In C. B. Skliar (Ed.), *A surdez: Um olhar sobre as diferenças* [Deafness: Casting a gaze upon the differences]. (pp. 51–73). Porto Alegre, RS: Mediação.

Peters, B. (2008). On public deliberation and public culture. In H. Wessler (Ed.), *Public deliberation and public culture: The writings of Bernhard Peters, 1993–2005* (pp. 68–118). New York, NY: Palgrave Macmillan.

Petherbridge, D. (Ed.). (2011a). *Axel Honneth: Critical essays. With a reply by Axel Honneth* (Vol. 12). Leiden, BO: Brill.

Petherbridge, D. (2011b). Introduction: Axel Honneth's project of critical theory. In D. Petherbridge (Ed.), *Axel Honneth: Critical essays. With a reply by Axel Honneth* (Vol. 12, pp. 1–30). Leiden, BO: Brill.

Pitkin, H. F. (1967). *The concept of representation.* Berkeley, CA: University of California Press.

Polletta, F. (2007). Just talk: Public deliberation after 9/11. *Journal of Public Deliberation, 4*(1), 2.

Polletta, F. & Lee, J. (2006). Is telling stories good for democracy? Rhetoric in public deliberation after 9/11. *American Sociological Review, 71*(5), 699–721.

Pollitt, C. (2003). *The essential public manager.* London: Open University Press/McGraw-Hill.

Porto, M. (2012). *Media power and democratization in Brazil: TV Globo and the dilemmas of political accountability* (Vol. 8). New York, NY: Routledge.

Potter, W. J. (2011) Conceptualizing mass media effect. *Journal of Communication, 61*(5), 896–915.

Prout, A. & James, A. (1997). A new paradigm for the sociology of childhood? Provenance, promise and problems. In A. James & A. Prout (Eds), *Constructing and reconstructing childhood* (pp. 7–32). London: UK Falmer Press.

Quadros, R. M. (2012). Linguistic policies, linguistic planning, and Brazilian sign language in Brazil. *Sign Language Studies, 12*, 543–564.

Recuero, R., Amaral, A., & Montardo, S. (2009). Blogs: Mapeando um objeto [Blogs: Mapping an object]. In A. Amaral, R. Recuero, & S. Montardo (Eds), *Blogs.com: Estudos sobre blogs e comunicação* [Blogs.com: Studies on blogs and communication]. (Vol. 1). São Paulo, SP: Momento.

Reese, S. D. (2007). The framing project: A bridging model for media research revisited. *Journal of Communication, 57*(1), 148–154.

Rehg, W. (1994). *Insight and solidarity: The discourse ethics of Jürgen Habermas.* Los Angeles, CA: University of California Press.

Reis, T. (2012). *Argentina lidera o Mercosul* [Argentina leads Mercosur]. 14th Mercosur Social Summit, on November 27, 2012. Paula Daibert interview. Available at: http://socialmercosul.org/argentina-lidera-o-mercosul-nos-direitos-dos-homossexuais/

Renault, E. (2010). Taking on the inheritance of critical theory: Saving Marx by recognition? In H. Schmidt am Busch & C. F. Zurn (Eds), *The philosophy of recognition: Historical and contemporary perspectives* (pp. 241–256). Lanham, MA: Lexington Books.

Retzinger, S. (1991). *Violent emotions: Shame and rage in marital quarrels.* Newbury Park, CA: SAGE.

Risse, T. (2000). "Let's Argue!" Communicative action in international relations. *International Organization, 54*(1), 1–39.

Roberts, N. (2009). Recognition, power, and agency: The recent contributions of Axel Honneth to critical theory. *Political Theory, 37*(2), 296–309.

Rocha, S. M. (2005). Favela, soma de exclusões e assimetrias: Em busca de uma mobilidade simbólica na cena midiática [Slum, a sum total of exclusions and asymmetries: Searching for a symbolic mobility in the media scene]. *Contemporânea, 3*(1), 185–217.

Rocha, S. M. (2006). Debate Público e Identidades Coletivas: A representação de moradores de favela na produção cultural da televisão brasileira [Public debate and collective identities: Slum dwellers represented in Brazilian TV's cultural output]. *Intexto, 14*, 1–21.

Rogers, M. L. (2009). Rereading Honneth: Exodus politics and the paradox of recognition. *European Journal of Political Theory, 8*(2), 183–206.

Romio, J. A. F. (2013). A vitimização de mulheres por agressão física, segundo raça/ cor no Brasil [Female physical aggression victimization, by race/color in Brazil]. In M. M. Marcondes, L. Pinheiro, C. Queiroz, A. C. Querino, & D. Valverde (Eds), *Dossiê mulheres negras: Retrato das condições de vida das mulheres negras no Brasil* [Black female brief: Life status of black females in Brazil]. (pp. 133–158). Brasília, DF: IPEA.

Rosenberg, S. (Ed.) (2007). *Can the people govern? Deliberation, participation and democracy.* New York, NY: Palgrave Macmillan.

Ross, K. (2010). *Gendered media: Women, men, and identity politics.* Lanham, MD: Rowman & Littlefield.

Ross, K. & Carter, C. (2011). Women and news: A long and winding road. *Media, Culture & Society, 33*(8), 1148–1165.

Rössler, B. (2007). Work, recognition, emancipation. In B. van den Brink & D. Owen (Eds), *Recognition and power: Axel Honneth and the tradition of critical social theory* (pp. 135–164). New York, NY: Cambridge University Press.

Rostbøll, C. F. (2008). *Deliberative freedom: Deliberative democracy as critical theory.* Albany, NY: State University of New York Press.

Rubenstein, J. (2007). Accountability in an unequal world. *The Journal of Politics, 69*(3), 616–632.

Rucht, D. (2004). The quadruple "A": Media strategies of protest movements since the 1960s. In W. van de Donk, B. D. Loader, P. G. Nixon, & D. Rucht (Eds), *Cyberprotest: New media, citizens and social movements* (pp. 25–48). New York, NY: Routledge.

Ryan, C. (1991). *Prime time activism: Media strategies for grass roots organizing.* Boston, MA: South End Press.

Ryan, C., Jeffreys, K., Ellowitz, T., & Ryczek, J. (2013). Walk, talk, fax or tweet: Reconstructing media-movement interactions through group history telling. In B. Cammaerts, A. Mattoni, & P. McCurdy, *Mediation and protest movements* (pp. 133–158). Chicago, IL: Intellect Ltd.

Ryfe, D. M. (2006). Narrative and deliberation in small group forums. *Journal of Applied Communication Research, 34*(1), 72–93.

Sacks, O. (1989). *Seeing voices: A journey into the world of the deaf.* Berkeley, CA: University of California Press.

Sampaio, R. C., Maia, R. C. M., & Marques, F. P. J. A. (2011). Participation and deliberation on the Internet: A case study on digital participatory budgeting in Belo Horizonte. *Journal of Community Informatics, 7*(1), 1–22.

Santos, M. P. (2001). Inclusion and/or integration: The debate is still on in Brazil. *Disability and Society, 16*(6), 893–897.

Sassaki, R. (1997). *Inclusão: Construindo uma sociedade para todos* [Inclusion: Building a society for everyone]. Rio de Janeiro, RJ: WVA.

Schrock, D., Holden, D., & Reid, L. (2004). Creating emotional resonance: Interpersonal emotion work and motivational framing in a transgender community. *Journal of Social Problems, 51*(1), 61–81.

Schudson, M. (2003). *The sociology of news.* London: W. W. Norton.

Seferiades, S. & Johnston, H. (Eds). (2012). *Violent protest, contentious politics, and the neoliberal state.* London: Ashgate Publishing.

Seglow, J. (2009). Rights, contribution, achievement and the world: Some thoughts on Honneth's recognitive ideal. *European Journal of Political Theory, 8*(1), 61–73.

Seglow, J. (2012). Recognition and religious diversity: The case of legal exemptions. In S. O'Neill & N. H. Smith (Eds), *Recognition theory as social research: Investigating the dynamics of social conflict* (pp. 127–147). New York, NY: Palgrave Macmillan.

Sen, A. (1999). *Development as freedom.* New York, NY: Knopf.

Seymour, M. (Ed.). (2010). *The plural states of recognition.* New York, NY: Palgrave Macmillan.

Shelby, T. (2003). Ideology, racism and critical social theory. *The Philosophical Forum, 34*(2), 153–188.

Shen, J., Liu, M., & Zhou, M. (2007). Current situation of leprosy colonies/leprosaria and their future in P.R. China. *Leprosy Review, 78*(3), 281–289.

Shoemaker, P. J. & Vos, T. P. (2009). *Gatekeeping theory.* New York, NY: Routledge.

Shohat, E. & Stam, R. (1994). *Unthinking eurocentrism: Multiculturalism and the media.* London: Routledge.

Silverstone, R. (1994). *Televisión y vida cotidiana.* Buenos Aires: Amorrutu.

Simon, A. & Xenos, M. (2000). Media framing and effective public deliberation. *Political Communication, 17,* 363–376.

Sinnerbrink, R. (2011). Power, recognition, and care: Honneth's critique of post-structuralist social philosophy. In D. Petherbridge (Ed.), *Axel Honneth: Critical essays. With a reply by Axel Honneth* (Vol. 12, pp. 177–206). Leiden, BO: Brill.

Skillington, T. (2009). Demythologising a neo-liberal model of healthcare reform: A politics of rights, recognition, and human suffering. *Irish Journal of Sociology, 17*(2), 90–111.

Smith, B. & Sparkes, A. C. (2008). Narrative and its potential contribution to disability studies. *Disability & Society, 23*(1), 17–28.

Smith, N. H. (2009). Work and the struggle for recognition. *European Journal of Political Theory, 8*(1), 46–60.

Smith, N. H. (2012). Work as a sphere of norms, paradoxes, and ideologies of recognition. In S. O'Neill & N. H. Smith (Eds), *Recognition theory as social research: Investigating the dynamics of social conflict* (pp. 87–108). New York, NY: Palgrave Macmillan.

Smith, N. H. & Deranty, J. P. (2012). *New philosophies of labour: Work and social bond.* Leiden, HO: Brill.

Smith, S. R. (2005). Equality, identity and the disability rights movement: From policy to practice and from Kant to Nietzsche in more than one uneasy move. *Critical Social Policy, 25*(4), 554–576.

Sobieraj, S. (2011). *Soundbitten: The perils of media-centered political activism.* New York, NY: New York University Press.

Sodré, M. (1999). *Claros e escuros. Identidade, povo e mídia no Brasil* [Light- and dark-skinned: Identity, people and media in Brazil]. Petrópolis, RJ: Vozes.

Souza, J. (Ed.). (2006). *A invisibilidade da desigualdade brasileira* [The invisibility of Brazilian inequality]. Belo Horizonte, MG: UFMG.

Souza, J. (Ed.). (2009). *A ralé brasileira: Quem é e como vive?* [Brazil's lowest people on the totem pole: Who are they and how do they live?]. Belo Horizonte, MG: UFMG.

Souza, J. (2011). Para compreender a desigualdade brasileira [To understand Brazil's inequality]. *Teoria e Cultura, 1*(2), 83–100.

Souza, J. D. (2004). Modernização periférica e naturalização da desigualdade: O caso brasileiro [Outskirts modernization and naturalization of inequality: The Brazilian case]. In M. C. Scalon (Ed.), *Imagens da desigualdade* [Images of inequality]. (pp. 75–114). Belo Horizonte, MG: UFMG.

Sreberny, A. (2000). Media and diasporic consciousness: An exploration among Iranians in London. In S. Cottle (Ed.), *Ethnic minorities and the media* (pp. 179–196). Buckingham, UK: Open University Press.

Staiger, J. (2005). *Media reception studies.* New York, NY: New York University Press.

Steffek, J. (2010). Public accountability and the public sphere of international governance. *Ethics & International Affairs, 24*(1), 45–68.

Steiner, J. (2008). Concept stretching: The case of deliberation. *European Political Science, 7*, 186–190.

Steiner, J. (2012a). *The foundations of deliberative democracy: Empirical research and normative implications.* Cambridge, MA: Cambridge University Press.

Steiner, J. (2012b). Rationality and stories in deliberative justification. In J. Steiner, *The foundations of deliberative democracy: Empirical research and normative implications* (pp. 57–87). Cambridge, MA: Cambridge University Press.

Steiner, J., Bächtiger, A., Spörndli, M., & Steenbergen, M. (2004). *Deliberative politics in action: Cross-national study of parliamentary debates.* Cambridge, MA: Cambridge University Press.

Strobel, K. L. (2006). Visão histórica sobre a in(ex)clusão dos surdos [A historic vision of inclusion/exclusion of the deaf]. *ETD – Educação Temática Digital, 7*(2), 244–252.

Stromer-Galley, J. (2003). Diversity of political conversation on the Internet: Users' perspectives. *Journal of Computer-Mediated Communication, 8*(3). doi: 10.1111/j.1083–6101.2003.tb00215.x.

Stromer-Galley, J. (2007). Measuring deliberation's content: A coding scheme. *Journal of Public Deliberation, 3*(1), 12.

Stromer-Galley, J. & Muhlberger, P. (2009). Agreement and disagreement in group deliberation: Effects on deliberation satisfaction, future engagement, and decision legitimacy. *Political Communication, 26*, 173–192.

Suller, J. (2004). The online disinhibition effect. *Cyberpsychology & Behavior, 7*(3), 321–326.

Swain, S., French, S., & Barnes, C. (2004). *Disabling barriers: Enabling environments.* London: SAGE.

Taschner, P. S. (2003). O Brasil e suas favelas [Brazil and its slums]. In P. Abramo (Ed.), *A cidade da informalidade. O desafio das cidades latino-americanas* [The city of informality: The challenge for Latin American cities]. (pp. 13–42). Rio de Janeiro, RJ: Sette Letras/FAPERJ.

Taylor, C. (1994). The politics of recognition. In A. Gutmann (Ed.), *Multiculturalism: Examining the politics of recognition* (pp. 25–73). Princeton, NJ: Princeton University Press.

Teixeira-Filho, F. S. & Rondini, C. A. (2012). Ideações e tentativas de suicídio em adolescentes com práticas sexuais hetero e homoeróticas [Ideation and suicide attempts among adolescents with heterossexual and homoerotic practices]. *Saúde e Sociedade, 21*(3), 651–667.

Tejerina, B., Perugorría, I., Benski, T., & Langman, L. (2013). From indignation to occupation: A new wave of global mobilization. *Current Sociology, 61*(4), 377–392.

Terzi, L. (2004). The social model of disability: A philosophical critique. *Journal of Applied Philosophy, 21*(2), 141–157.

Thomas, C. (1999). *Female forms: Experiencing and understanding disability.* Buckingham: Open University Press.

Thomas, C. (2004). How is disability understood? An examination of sociological approaches. *Disability & Society, 19*(6), 569–583.

Thompson, E. P. (1989). *A formação da classe operária inglesa: A força dos trabalhadores* [The formation of the British working class: The force of workers]. Rio de Janeiro, RJ: Paz e Terra.

Thompson, S. (2006). *The political theory of recognition: A critical introduction.* Cambridge, UK: Polity Press.

Thompson, S. & Hoggett, P. (2011). Misrecognition and ambivalence. In S. Thompson & M. Yar (Eds), *The politics of misrecognition* (pp. 17–32). Farnham: Ashgate.

Thompson, S. & Hoggett, P. (Eds). (2012). *Politics and the emotions: The affective turn in contemporary political studies.* New York, NY: Continuum.

Thompson, S. & Yar, M. (Eds). (2011). *The politics of misrecognition.* Farnham: Ashgate Publishing.

Traquina, N. (2001). *O estudo do jornalismo no século XX* [Study of 20th century journalism]. São Leopoldo, RS: Unisinos.

Tremayne, M. (2007). Harnessing the active audience: Synthesizing blog research and lessons for the future of media. In M. Tremayne (Ed.), *Blogging, citizenship and the future of media* (pp. 261–272). New York, NY: Routledge.

Tully, J. (2000). Struggles over recognition and distribution. *Constellations, 7*(4), 469–482.

Tully, J. (2004). Recognition and dialogue: The emergence of a new field. *Critical Review of International Social and Political Philosophy, 7*(3), 84–106.

Turkle, S. (1995). *Life on the screen: Identity in the age of the internet.* New York, NY: Simon & Schuster.

Valladares, L. D. P. (2005). *A invenção da favela: Do mito de origem a favela.com* [Slum invention: From the myth of its origin to favela.com]. Rio de Janeiro, RJ: FGV.

van den Brink, B. (2011). Recognition, pluralism, and the expectation of harmony: Against the ideal of an ethical life "free from pain". In D. Petherbridge (Ed.), *Axel Honneth: Critical essays. With a reply by Axel Honneth* (Vol. 12, pp. 155–176). Leiden, BO: Brill.

van den Brink, B. & Owen, D. (Eds). (2007). *Recognition and power: Axel Honneth and the tradition of critical social theory.* New York, NY: Cambridge University Press.

van Dijck, J. (2013). *The culture of connectivity: A critical history of social media.* New York, NY: Oxford University Press.

van Dijk, T. A. (1991). *Racism and the press.* London: Routledge.

van Dijk, T. A. (1993). *Elite discourse and racism.* London: SAGE Publications.

van Dijk, T. A. (2012). The role of the press in the reproduction of racism. In M. Messer, R. Schroeder, & R. Wodak (Eds), *Migrations: Interdisciplinary perspectives* (pp. 15– 29). New York, NY: Springer-Verlag Wien.

Vimieiro, A. C. & Maia, R. C. M. (2011). Análise indireta de enquadramentos da mídia: Uma alternativa metodológica para a identificação de frames culturais [Indirect analysis of media framing: A methodological alternative to identify cultural frames]. *Revista FAMECOS, 18*(1), 235–252.

Vivarta, V. (2003). *Mídia e deficiência* [Media and disability]. Brasília, DF: Andi e Fundação Banco do Brasil.

Waisbord, S. (2009). Bridging the divide between the press and civic society: Civic media advocacy as "media movement" in Latin America. *Nordicon Review, 30*, 105–116.

Walsh, K. C. (2004). *Talking about politics: Informal groups and social identity in American life.* Chicago, IL: University of Chicago Press.

Walsh, K. C. (2007). The democratic potential of civic dialogue. In S. Rosenberg (Ed.), *Can the people govern? Deliberation, participation and democracy* (pp. 45–63). New York, NY: Palgrave Macmillan.

Walther, J. B., Van Der Heide, B., Hamel, L. M., & Shulman, H. C. (2009). Self-generated versus other-generated statements and impressions in computer-mediated communication: A test of warranting theory using Facebook. *Communication Research, 36*(2), 229–253.

Warr, D. (2005). It was fun ... but we don't usually talk about these things: Analyzing sociable interactions in focus groups. *Qualitative Inquiry, 11,* 200–225.

Warren, M. (2001). *Democracy and association.* Princeton, NJ: Princeton University Press.

Weber, M. H. (2011). Estratégias da comunicação de Estado e a disputa por visibilidade e opinião [The strategies of communication of the State and dispute for visibility and opinion]. In M. Kunsch (Ed.), *Comunicação pública, sociedade e cidadania* [Public communication, society and citizenship] (pp. 101–120). São Caetano do Sul, RS: Difusão.

Weiss, G. & Wodak, R. (2003.) Introduction: Theory, interdisciplinarity and Critical Discourse Analysis (pp. 1–32). In G. Weiss & R. Wodak (Eds). *Critical discourse analysis: Theory and interdisciplinarity.* New York: Palgrave Macmillan.

Weldon, L. (2011). Perspectives against interests: Sketch of a feminist political theory of "women". *Politics & Gender, 7*(03), 441–446.

Wessler, H. (Ed.). (2008). *Public deliberation and public culture: The writings of Bernard Peters, 1993–2005.* New York, NY: Palgrave Macmillan.

Wessler, H. & Schultz, T. (2007). Can the mass media deliberate? Insights from print media and political talk shows. In R. Butsch (Ed.), *Media and public spheres* (pp. 15–27). New York, NY: Palgrave Macmillan.

Wessler, H., Peters, B., Brüggemann, M., Königslöw, K. K., & Sifft, S. (Eds). (2008). *Transnationalization of public spheres.* New York, NY: Palgrave Macmillan.

Whittier, N. (2001). Emotional strategies: The collective reconstruction and display of oppositional emotions in the movement against child sexual abuse. In J. Goodwin, J. M. Jasper, & F. Polletta (Eds), *Passionate politics: Emotions and social movements* (pp. 233–250). Chicago, IL: The University of Chicago Press.

Wojcieszak, M. E. & Mutz, D. C. (2009). Online groups and political discourse: Do online discussion spaces facilitate exposure to political disagreement? *Journal of Communication, 59*(1), 40–56.

Wright, S. & Street, J. (2007). Democracy, deliberation and design: The case of online discussion forums. *New Media & Society, 9*(5), 849–869.

Yar, M. (2003). Honneth and the communitarians: Towards a recognitive critical theory of community. *Res Publica, 9,* 101–125.

Yar, M. (2011). And every cruelty will cloud it: On love, damaged selfhood and criminal harm. In S. Thompson & M. Yar (Eds), *The politics of misrecognition* (pp. 125–144). Farnham: Ashgate Publishing.

Yar, M. (2012). Recognition as the grounds of a general theory of crime as social harm? In S. O'Neill & N. H. Smith (Eds), *Recognition theory as social research: Investigating the dynamics of social conflict* (pp. 109–126). New York, NY: Palgrave Macmillan.

Young, I. M. (2000). *Inclusion and democracy.* Oxford: Oxford University Press.

Young, I. M. (2007). Recognition of love's labor: Considering Axel Honneth's feminism. In B. van den Brink & D. Owen (Eds), *Recognition and power: Axel Honneth and the tradition of critical social theory* (pp. 189–212). New York, NY: Cambridge University Press.

Zaluar, A. (1997). Exclusão e políticas públicas: Dilemas teóricos e alternativas políticas [Exclusion and public policies: Theoretical dilemmas and political alternatives]. *Revista Brasileira de Ciências Sociais, 12*(35), 29–47.

Zaluar, A. (2004). *Integração perversa: Pobreza e tráfico de drogas* [Perverse integration: Poverty and drug-trafficking]. Rio de Janeiro, RJ: FGV.

Zaluar, A. & Alvito, M. (2003). *Um século de favela* [One hundred years of slums]. Rio de Janeiro, RJ: FGV.

Zoonen, L. V., Vis, F., & Mihelj, S. (2011). YouTube interactions between agonism, antagonism and dialogue: Video responses to the anti-Islam film Fitna. *New Media & Society, 13*(8), 1283–1300.

Zurn, C. F. (2000). Anthropology and normativity: A critique of Axel Honneth's "formal conception of ethical life". *Philosophy & Social Criticism, 26*(1), 115–124.

Zurn, C. F. (2003). Identity or status? Struggles over "recognition" in Fraser, Honneth, & Taylor, *Constellations, 10*(4), 519–537.

Zurn, C. F. (2005). Recognition, redistribution, and democracy: Dilemmas of Honneth's critical social theory. *European Journal of Philosophy, 13*(1), 89–126.

Zurn, C. F. (2010). Introduction. In H. Schmidt am Busch & C. F. Zurn (Eds), *The philosophy of recognition: Historical and contemporary perspectives* (pp. 1–21). Lanham, MA: Lexington Books.

Zurn, C. F. (2012). Misrecognition, marriage, and derecognition. In S. O'Neill & N. H. Smith (Eds), *Recognition theory as social research: Investigating the dynamics of social conflict* (pp. 63–86). New York, NY: Palgrave Macmillan.

Author Index

Subject Index

Printed and bound by CPI Group (UK) Ltd, Croydon, CR0 4YY